Recent Advances in Environmental Economics

NEW HORIZONS IN ENVIRONMENTAL ECONOMICS

Series Editors: Wallace E. Oates, *Professor of Economics, University of Maryland, USA* and Henk Folmer, *Professor of General Economics, Wageningen University and Professor of Environmental Economics, Tilburg University, The Netherlands*

This important series is designed to make a significant contribution to the development of the principles and practices of environmental economics. It includes both theoretical and empirical work. International in scope, it addresses issues of current and future concern in both East and West and in developed and developing countries.

The main purpose of the series is to create a forum for the publication of high quality work and to show how economic analysis can make a contribution to understanding and resolving the environmental problems confronting the world in the twenty-first century.

Recent titles in the series include:

Recent Advances in Environmental Economics

Edited by

John A. List

Professor, Department of Agricultural and Resource Economics, University of Maryland, US

Aart de Zeeuw

Professor of Environmental Economics, Department of Economics and CentER, Tilburg University, The Netherlands

NEW HORIZONS IN ENVIRONMENTAL ECONOMICS

Edward Elgar
Cheltenham, UK • Northampton, MA, USA

Published by
Edward Elgar Publishing Limited
Glensanda House
Montpellier Parade
Cheltenham
Glos GL50 1UA
UK

Edward Elgar Publishing, Inc.
136 West Street
Suite 202
Northampton
Massachusetts 01060
USA

A catalogue record for this book
is available from the British Library

Library of Congress Cataloguing in Publication Data

Recent advances in environmental economics / edited by John A. List, Aart de Zeeuw.
    p. cm.—(New horizons in environmental economics)
Papers from a workshop held in Orlando, Florida, 30 November–2 December 2000.
Includes index.
  1. Environmental economics—Congresses. 2. Environmental policy—
Congresses. 3. International cooperation—Congresses. 4. Greenhouse gas
mitigation—Congresses. I. List, John A., 1968– II. Zeeuw, Aart de, 1952–
III. Series.

  HD75.6.R426 2002
  333.7—dc21   2002021391

ISBN 1 84376 002 9

Printed and bound in Great Britain by MPG Books Ltd, Bodmin, Cornwall

Contents

Contributors

Mark Agee, Penn State University, USA

Ian Bateman, University of East Anglia, UK

David Bjornstad, Oak Ridge National Laboratory, USA

Paul Brewer, Hong Kong University of Science and Technology, Hong Kong

Todd Cherry, Appalachian State University, USA

Thomas Crocker, University of Wyoming, USA

Ronald Cummings, Georgia State University, USA

Na Li Dawson, University of Connecticut, USA

Chris Elbers, Free University Amsterdam, The Netherlands

Peter Frykblom, Swedish University of Agricultural Sciences, Uppsala

Shelby Gerking, University of Central Florida, USA

Jacob Goeree, University of Virginia, USA

Michael Hoel, University of Oslo, Norway

Charles Holt, University of Virginia, USA

Surjinder Johal, University of Southampton, UK

Susan Kask, Western Carolina University, USA

Mitch Kunce, University of Wyoming, USA

Susan Laury, Georgia State University, USA

Arik Levinson, Georgetown University, USA

Carol Mansfield, Research Triangle Institute, USA

Michael McKee, University of New Mexico, USA

J. Walter Milon, University of Central Florida, USA

William Morgan, University of Wyoming, USA

Wallace E. Oates, University of Maryland, USA

Gregory Poe, Cornell University, USA and University of East Anglia, UK

Michael Rauscher, University of Rostock, Germany

Daniel Rondeau, University of Victoria, Canada

William Schulze, Cornell University and University of Washington, USA

David Scrogin, University of Central Florida, USA

Kathleen Segerson, University of Connecticut, USA

Jason Shogren, University of Wyoming, USA

V. Kerry Smith, North Carolina State University, USA

Alistair Ulph, University of Southampton, UK

Cees Withagen, Free University Amsterdam and Tilburg University, The Netherlands

Anastasios Xepapadeas, University of Crete, Greece

ʿ

Introduction

A few years ago, the Department of Economics at the University of Central Florida decided to commit a considerable amount of resources in the area of environmental and resource economics. The Galloway Professorship in Environmental and Resource Economics was established and preference was given to this research area in the recruitment of junior faculty. In line with this policy of 'selected excellence', the *Center for Environmental Policy Analysis*, which has a mission to improve the quality of Florida's public and private decisions that have environmental, economic, and resource-use implications, was created and the idea was born to inaugurate this institute with a premier conference in Orlando.

A few years earlier, the CentER for Economic Research at Tilburg University in the Netherlands had developed a successful niche in environmental and resource economics. The optimal strategy was to combine forces and to organize the conference jointly. A major notion driving this cooperation was to bring together different strands of research in environmental and resource economics that could be considered frontier developments in both Europe and North America. In Europe, the dominant direction in the area seems to be a strong use of theoretical applications to solve policy problems, whereas in North America one distinct trend seems to be toward a more empirically oriented approach. The interaction between the two strands has traditionally been somewhat weak, as scholars tend to meet in large conferences with separate (often parallel) sessions or organise distinct workshops. The UCF/CentER conference aimed to produce a forum for a small group of leading researchers from these distinct directions. The workshop came to fruition in Orlando, 30 November–2 December 2000.

Our invitation policy was simple: a theme was not compulsory, rather our main focus was on research quality. While the size of the workshop only permitted us to invite a handful of scholars, we were pleasantly surprised that several top-notch scholars in this area of research were open to the idea of attending the conference. During the workshop the quality of research presented led many to believe that a refereed volume based on the papers should be pursued. It was clear that the participants were willing to contribute manuscripts toward a volume that could become a landmark of recent advances in environmental and resource economics.

Although *ex ante* no central theme was chosen, *ex post* it can be concluded that the volume has two larger clusters: environmental policymaking within a federalist context and valuation issues, including experimental design. This outcome reflects the larger interests in environmental economics today, but is also somewhat biased by the interests of scholars at UCF and CentER. Besides these broader themes, the volume also contains a few papers that stand alone, simply because these areas do not get as much attention in general. Running the risk of short-changing the authors, we now turn to certain highlights of each chapter, but we welcome you to become engulfed in the research herein; we did, and found it well worth our time. Enjoy!

In Chapter 1, Wallace Oates provides a thoughtful review on the debate over environmental federalism – the issue of the roles of the various levels of government in environmental management. While the chapter provides an in-depth overview of the theoretical literature, including the presentation of three benchmark cases that provide a framework for thinking about the issue, we believe Oates's provocative empirical literature survey on the race to the bottom may attract many readers' attention. The literature review is even-handed and provides the reader with the current state of the art. The chapter should represent an excellent introduction for any researcher interested in understanding the important theoretical and empirical work in environmental federalism. It concludes that there remains an important role for local governments in the setting of environmental standards and the design of regulatory programmes under certain circumstances.

Concerns that countries may set relatively lax environmental standards in case of transboundary pollution, or in order to gain a strategic trade advantage, usually get the response that environmental policies should be coordinated at a supranational level. However, it is not clear *ex ante* that this procedure is always desirable because of certain potential deficiencies in the political process. In Chapter 2, Surjinder Johal and Alistair Ulph address two such deficiencies: supranational bodies may not be as well informed as local governments and may be more accessible for some lobby groups than for others ('democratic deficit' problem). In a previous study, they focus on the issue of strategic trade incentives and show that regardless of the asymmetrical structure in political influence, all parties are *always* better off when policy is set at the supranational level. In this chapter, they extend that analysis to allow for transboundary pollution. They find that in general the result – that supranational coordination of environmental policies is still desirable – is strengthened. We do not expect that these results will depress all anti-globalization protests, but they should become important in the debate.

Much of the literature in environmental economics assumes that transboundary pollution depends on natural parameters only, such as the direction of winds or patterns of precipitation. When meeting tighter environmental standards, however, polluters often have a choice: to prevent pollution or to distribute pollutants over a wider area ('to build high smokestacks'). The last option effectively means that transboundary pollution is endogenous, and the result of important economic trade-offs. In Chapter 3, Michael Rauscher develops a very interesting analytical framework to address this issue. Within this framework, Rauscher is able to derive some surprising results. At first glance, one may think that from a supra-jurisdictional point of view building smokestacks is just a waste of resources. Pollution and, therefore, environmental problems are shifted and not solved. However, Rauscher shows that it may be possible that more concern for damage abroad leads to higher smokestacks, due to a shift from production capital to smokestack capital. We believe that his framework will prove quite important in altering the mechanic treatment of transboundary pollution.

In the case of global pollution, such as greenhouse gas emissions, even if countries decide to enter into an international agreement, conflicts of interest remain. Countries may differ on how much emissions in total should be reduced, but definitely disagree on how the emission reduction should be allocated amongst countries – it is considered common wisdom that each country strives for the lowest share in emission reduction (or the highest share in emission quotas) possible. However, Michael Hoel shows in his chapter that this is not generally true. A critical assumption concerns population mobility. In the case of a perfectly homogeneous and mobile population, the conflict of interest vanishes: all countries will agree on a particular allocation of emission quotas. If population is heterogeneous, the conflict of interest remains but it is not true that each country is better off the larger its share of emission quotas. Perfect mobility is a strong assumption, but no mobility is a strong assumption as well. We think that the challenge put to common wisdom in this chapter is an important new point of view, and should be a piece that influences future modelling efforts.

Another popular view is that countries should impose environmental taxes below the Pigouvian level on exporting firms in order to enhance the competitiveness of home firms on the world market ('ecological dumping'). This view is supported by partial equilibrium analyses, but in a general equilibrium context it may not be true. As the extant literature suggests, countries may want to increase environmental taxes in order to improve the terms of trade. Chris Elbers and Cees Withagen revisit the issue and arrive at more precise results. It is shown that the sheltered, non-exporting, sector should be taxed according to marginal damage and examples are given where higher emission taxes should be levied on the exporting sector. In general, no support is found for a lax treatment of the export sector, at least from a social welfare perspective. We think that the analysis is important for a balanced view on an important policy issue.

Recently, much attention has been given to modelling the relationship between economic growth and the environment. The typical shape of the income–pollution relationship reported in most empirical studies has been an inverted-U. Although this finding is appealing, within this literature little rigorous attention has been given to the econometric and theoretical properties of the relationship. In his thoughtful and provocative chapter, Arik Levinson takes this chore to task by arguing that the fundamental insight of the empirical literature is merely that pollution does not necessarily increase with economic growth. From a theoretical standpoint, Levinson argues that the observed inverted-U relationship is neither necessary nor sufficient for Pareto-efficient environmental policies. Levinson concludes that all of the lessons learned from the literature can be had without most of the econometric or theoretical constructs that are published. We view this contribution as fundamental, and the main message should be quite important to scholars interested in growth and the environment, especially at a time when estimation of the environmental Kuznets curve seems to have become an industry (in and of itself).

Textbooks in environmental economics usually focus on standards, taxes and permits as instruments of environmental policy. Because in practice one increasingly observes voluntary agreements between government and industry, recently some important theoretical papers on the issue have appeared. The basic notion is that the threat of regulation may induce firms to meet an environmental target voluntarily, in order to avoid costs of regulation. In this context, Na Li Dawson and Kathleen Segerson address the issue of free riding in the industry. If a certain number of firms have an incentive to meet the target, the remaining firms should free ride on that effort. In a previous paper, they show that an equilibrium of this type always exists, but the question is whether the profit differential between participating firms and free riders can sustain in the long run when firms have free entry and exit. An interesting insight gained from the model is that for zero entry costs, the long-run equilibrium involves full participation. With positive entry costs, free riding may remain, but the long-run participation rate is always at least as high as the short-run rate. We view this particular piece as a novel line of research on environmental policy, and one that should gain increased recognition as regulators rely more heavily on voluntary compliance.

A very different topic concerns the irreversible development of an exhaustible resource with uncertainty on both the profits in the developed state and the environmental value in the undeveloped state. By using new advanced techniques for stochastic control problems, Anastasios Xepapadeas is able to derive results that go beyond the existing literature. It is well-known that when uncertainty only exists with respect to profits, the pace of development is slower under social optimization than under profit maximization (by the private developer). However, in this seminal chapter it is shown that when uncertainty exists for use and non-use values, the pace of development can be reversed. Furthermore, it is shown that in this case no fixed tax exists that induces the regulated developer to follow the socially optimal path. We believe the finding that it may be socially optimal to develop the resource faster than a private developer would is interesting and counter to what one usually believes.

Thomas Crocker and Mark Agee's novel theoretical study investigates the linkage between neighbourhood circumstances and a child's home environment. The underlying contribution is to point out that extant empirical work examining the effects of neighbourhood circumstances on individual well-being without considerations of family (for example, air pollution and human health) may be biased. Intuitively, this finding is based on the endogeneity of mothers' behaviour: a mother who recognizes that her choices of home environment influence her earnings will be inclined to invest more in this environment and subsequently be at home more than will a mother who fails to account for this linkage. Crocker and Agee also show that in a majority of cases, this behaviour will be accentuated when the mother's payoffs to home investment are less delayed and less uncertain. Within the growing area of the environment and family, this piece should be a building block for scholars interested in specifying empirical relationships concerning local characteristics and the home environment.

The total costs associated with environmental regulations have been the subject of widespread debate, at least since the beginning of the environmental movement in the early 1970s. While some recent studies suggest that regions with stringent pollution control regimes attract less manufacturing capital than regions with lax environmental regulations, the study due to Mitch Kunce, Shelby Gerking and William Morgan examines the effects of environmental regulations from a much different perspective. Using a unique panel data set that covers more than 319000 on-shore oil and gas wells drilled in the US over the period 1987–98, Kunce et al. carefully examine the role that environmental regulations play on the timing and intensity of activities of firms in the oil and gas industry. A first key result derived from their rigorous empirical analysis is that drilling costs on federal land, which has more stringent application of environmental regulations, is more expensive than drilling on other types of land. This extra cost burden results in substantially lower drilling rates in earlier periods as well as lower cumulative production. Given that strict exogeneity of the treatment variable is very difficult to find in field data, the reader should find this particular piece quite appealing, as it combines the control of a laboratory study with the realism of the field.

Although policymakers have a decent understanding on measuring the costs associated with increased environmental protection, at present, several disparate approaches are used to measure economic values of environmental goods. One contentious approach is the contingent valuation method, which allows the researcher to determine the total value of the commodity in question. Susan Kask, Todd Cherry, Jason Shogren and Peter Frykblom recognize that estimating benefits for complex goods, such as lowering health risks associated with the long-term, low-dosage exposure to hazardous chemicals, may be difficult. They propose an alternative approach to estimating benefits from complex environmental goods that allows endogenous scenario definition – flexible scenarios. This 'flex-scenario' approach attempts to mitigate problems of embedding and scope by providing more clarity on the sensitivity of willingness to pay estimates to the various components of an environmental good or service. They apply their novel approach using data on the benefits of risk reduction from long-term exposure to the hazard posed by the pulp and paper industry.

The Kask et al. chapter highlights the fact that proper recognition of the beneficial results of environmental programmes remains invaluable. Carol Mansfield and V. Kerry Smith recognize that many economists approach this issue by measuring avoided damages, while policymakers typically focus on more tangible items, such as whether the costs of the programmes, such as output and employment losses for the affected industries, are held within certain limits. The novel synthesis that the authors propose is to treat the problem as giving rise to general equilibrium (GE) effects on a regional economy. More specifically, the authors propose an alternative to efforts to compute GE benefit–cost analysis. In the process, Mansfield and Smith uncover a very important and surprising result: households appear to have strong preferences for policy elements intended to respond to GE income effects. Thus, even if the analytical machinery were available to reliably compute GE welfare measures, other important issues need to be addressed. We view this finding as a key step toward a better recognition of the overall effects of environmental programmes, and the overall research approach as seminal, as it extends well beyond the partial equilibrium framework that seems to be the rule, rather than the exception, in the current literature.

The Florida Everglades restoration project is the most costly restoration project undertaken in the world. It provides a classic example of the need to provide information on economic benefits to guide plan selection and cost-sharing decisions. Research to support environmental policy decisions often makes the simplifying assumptions that consumers have homogeneous preferences and that the environmental public good is one-dimensional. In their well-thought out chapter, J. Walter Milon and David Scrogin consider heterogeneous preferences and multi-attribute complex environmental goods and test several models with a large survey in South and Central Florida. They show that information can differ significantly. For example, the heterogeneous preference model yields significantly lower total benefits of restoration. We view this piece as a relevant first step in advancing the literature on restoration projects, and more broadly the modelling concept of handling heterogeneous agents.

Recent experimental evidence strongly suggests that free-riding incentives induce underprovision of public goods. Jacob Goeree, Charles Holt and Susan Laury further this line of inquiry via several unique experimental treatments designed to evaluate the effects of externalities by altering the benefit/cost ratio of an investment that corresponds to pollution abatement. In this novel experimental setting, a subject can make an investment with a private (internal) return that fails to cover the investment cost, but with a public (external) return that makes the investment socially optimal. They find that even in the absence of repeated interactions, investments are *increasing* in both internal and external returns. Moreover, investments are essentially identical for two treatments with the same 'price', where price is defined to be the ratio of the external benefit to the internal loss from making an investment. Combining these findings with the authors' insightful discussion about dealing with pollution abatement externalities, the reader will quickly appreciate the value of laboratory research in the area of environmental and resource economics.

In another thoughtful laboratory study, David Bjornstad, Paul Brewer, Ronald Cummings and Michael McKee address the relevance of options value to stated preference elicitation. Their lab exercise is important in this respect, because unlike field data, they can separate behaviour associated with non-symmetrical responses to expected gains and losses. They find sharp evidence that suggests individuals systematically evaluate positive and negative returns differently – subjects tend to focus on the downside risk when making their investment choice while ignoring potential upside gains. This result is intuitively appealing, and is a principal result of the option model that is called the 'bad news principle'. Given that responses in contingent markets may also contain an option premium, the authors conclude that such responses may not pass scope tests and other tests for internal consistency, even though they are seemingly logical. We believe that this line of work is seminal to the area of valuation, and may set forth an entire research agenda.

Other-regarding behaviour has been found to be quite prevalent amongst economic actors – from its role in the private provision of public goods to various bargaining settings. William Schulze, Gregory Poe, Ian Bateman and Daniel Rondeau explicitly link this burgeoning literature to the important work on scope testing in contingent valuation. Their review of the experimental literature yields significant evidence that suggests warm glow and altruistic values are not only present in hypothetical scenarios, but also influence contributions for real public goods. They develop a theoretical model that integrates these key insights to show that the scope test may be inadequate since contingent values are potentially comprised of private values, warm glow, and paternalistic as well as non-paternalistic altruism. Since the second and fourth of these (warm glow and non-paternalistic altruism) are invalid sources of value, a scope test alone may not demonstrate validity. Given that commentators have argued for years that certain tests serve to invalidate responses from stated preference methods, Schulze et al. provide an intuitively pleasing and even-handed approach to the key issues.

Finally, we would like to thank all of the anonymous referees who have been an enormous help in shaping this volume and the people at Edward Elgar Publishing Ltd for the very pleasant cooperation in producing this volume; their time and patience is very much appreciated. Last but not least, support from our families is gratefully acknowledged.

John A. List   Aart de Zeeuw
University of Central Florida   CentER
University of Maryland   Tilburg University

To: Tara, Annika, Elijah, Noah and Dakota

1. A reconsideration of environmental federalism

Wallace E. Oates*

Environmental policymaking typically takes place in the context of a system with several levels of government. And this raises the important issue of the appropriate role of the various governments in the setting of environmental standards, the design of regulatory measures to attain the standards, and the monitoring and enforcement of these measures. Actual practice reveals a rather strange and inconsistent amalgam of decision-making structures. In the United States, for example, we find that the setting of environmental standards themselves manifests some striking anomalies. Under the Clean Air Act Amendments of 1970, still the cornerstone of US policy for air-quality management, the US Environmental Protection Agency was directed to set standards for ambient air quality in terms of maximum permissible concentrations of pollutants applicable to every place in the nation. But only two years later, under the 1972 Amendments to the Clean Water Act, the US Congress directed the states to set standards for water quality within their own boundaries. It is not at all clear why standards for air quality should be set at a national level, while water quality standards are a matter for the states.

Likewise, in the European Union, there is a continuing tension between the EU commitment to the principle of subsidiarity that establishes a basic commitment to decentralized policymaking (where it is within the capacity of member states and their jurisdictional authorities) and the sense on the part of some that European-wide standards for environmental quality are needed.[1]

In this chapter, I will review the issue of environmental federalism with a focus on the setting of standards for ambient environmental quality. It is commonplace for environmental measures to take the form of centrally determined standards with the responsibility for implementation lodged with state or provincial governments. Environmental policy is thus often a joint activity in this limited sense. But the fundamental decision is one of just how stringent environmental measures are to be: meaningful decentralization thus entails 'local' determination over the stringency of the standards for ambient environmental quality.[2]

In the first section of the chapter, I approach this issue at the conceptual level by setting forth three 'benchmark models' of environmental circumstances. I find this helpful in thinking about where in the hierarchy of government the standard-setting function should be placed. After a preliminary consideration of the benchmark cases, the chapter examines in more depth the so-called 'race to the bottom' that has motivated sentiment in favour of the centralization of environmental management. The latter part of the chapter offers a survey of the empirical work on this matter. Some recent studies provide valuable insights into this issue. In the final section, I offer some reflections on all this for the structure of environmental decision making.

1.   THINKING ABOUT ENVIRONMENTAL FEDERALISM: THREE BENCHMARK CASES

For purposes of the analysis, let us envision a system with two levels of government: a 'central' government that may set ambient environmental standards to be met in each of the jurisdictions that make up the whole 'nation'. At the lower level are 'local' governments that make policies for their own local constituencies. In this setting, we consider three different kinds of pollutants.

Benchmark Case 1: Pure Public Good

The first case is one where environmental quality is a pure public good for the nation as a whole. It is important to understand just what this means. It does not mean that everyone, irrespective of his or her location, necessarily experiences the same level of environmental quality. Under global warming, for example, the predicted effects involve dramatic regional differentials. What I have in mind can be expressed as:

$$Q_i = f(E) \tag{1.1}$$

where Q_i is understood to be a *vector* of environmental quality, whose elements indicate pollutant concentrations at each of n places in the nation. I will associate place i with the ith local jurisdiction. Thus, environmental quality in general varies across the different locations, but it is a function of the aggregate level of emissions, E, where E is the sum of the emissions from all sources in the nation. The critical property of this case is that a unit of polluting emissions has the same effect on the vector of national environmental quality regardless of where it takes place; a unit of emissions in jurisdiction *i* is a perfect substitute in this sense for a unit of emissions in jurisdiction *j*.

In such a setting, it seems clear that central determination of environmental standards is in order. Decentralized, local jurisdictions simply do not have control over the level of environmental quality within their own boundaries, since Q_i, the level of environmental quality in the *i*th jurisdiction, depends on the aggregate level of emissions, *E*. Moreover, emissions in any given jurisdiction spill over by degrading the environment in other jurisdictions so that there exists a standard sort of interjurisdictional externality.

There is consequently a need for the central government to set standards. On efficiency grounds, the central environmental authority should set a standard for environmental quality that satisfies the basic Samuelson condition: one for which the marginal benefits (that is, benefits from a unit of improvement in environmental quality summed over everyone in the nation) equal marginal abatement cost. Efficiency would further require some kind of programme (such as a national uniform effluent charge or a nationwide system of tradeable emission permits) that results in an equating nationwide of marginal abatement costs across sources.

In fact, our first benchmark case is not widely applicable. But two important cases come to mind – both involving global environmental problems: global climate change and depletion of the ozone layer. For both of these matters, environmental degradation is, in the sense I have used it, a global public good. A unit of CO_2 emissions, or of CFC emissions in the second instance, has the same effect on global environmental quality irrespective of its location. And, as is universally recognized, these problems require a global solution.

Benchmark Case 2: Local Public Good

The second prototypical case is one for which environmental quality is a pure local public good. By this, I mean that polluting waste emissions within a given local jurisdiction have their effects solely within that jurisdiction. In more formal terms, we have:

$$Q_i = g(e_i) \tag{1.2}$$

so that the level of environmental quality in the *i*th jurisdiction, Q_i, depends only upon the level of waste emissions, e_i, in that jurisdiction. There are some instances in the real world that seem at least to approximate this case. For example, the determination of the quality of local drinking water and the collection and disposal of local refuse, with some minor qualifications, involve such circumstances.

For this case, the efficient level of environmental quality is that for which the sum of the benefits from reduced waste emissions (the summation taking place over the residents of the jurisdiction under consideration) equals marginal abatement cost. This, on the face of it, calls for a decentralized determination of environmental quality with each jurisdiction setting its own appropriate standard for environmental quality. The efficient outcome here will, in general, involve differing levels of environmental quality across the various localities. For Benchmark Case 2, assuming that local governments seek to maximize the welfare of their residents, we thus envision a system of decentralized standard setting and environmental management. This is the case where the principle of subsidiarity appears directly applicable.[3]

However, this may be too simplistic. I will return to this case in the next section to take up a forceful objection that has been raised in the literature that suggests the presence of a 'race to the bottom' in a setting of decentralized environmental decision making, even for the case of a pure local public good.

Benchmark Case 3: Local Spillover Effects

The third Benchmark Case is the most common in practice. Here the effects of local waste emissions entail both local pollution and some external effects on other (most likely neighboring) jurisdictions. We thus have:

$$Q_i = h(e_1, e_2, ..., e_n). \tag{1.3}$$

Here the level of environmental quality in jurisdiction i depends on the particular pattern of emissions in all n localities. There are numerous instances of both air and water pollution where polluting activities in one jurisdiction flow across boundaries (sometimes over long distances, like acid rain).

As is widely recognized, such interjurisdictional externalities are likely to be the source of distorted outcomes, typically involving excessive pollution, in a setting of decentralized decision making. Our natural response for this case is to invoke central intervention of some kind (although there may well be instances where Coasean-type negotiations can lead to an efficient resolution of the problem). Let me simply note here that the precise form of such central intervention is not entirely clear. But one thing is clear: the efficient outcome will *not* in general take the form of uniform national standards for environmental quality. The efficient pattern of pollution control will generally imply differing levels of environmental quality across jurisdictions.

The economist's usual response to such externalities is to prescribe a set of emissions taxes that internalize the social damages. But in an inter-governmental setting, this solution is less compelling. The central government must either specify some set of differentiated taxes directly on polluting sources across the nation, or it must offer an appropriate and differentiated subsidy to local governments to induce them to internalize the interjurisdictional benefits from pollution control. I will return to this issue in a later section. My point here is simply that this is both a common case in practice and a complicated one in principle for environmental federalism.

2. THE ISSUE OF A RACE TO THE BOTTOM

In this section, I want to re-examine Benchmark Case 2, our case of a local public good. This is the primary and strongest candidate for the decentralized setting of environmental standards. But there is a large literature that addresses both local public finance and environmental regulation that claims that even for this case, decentralized decision making is not appropriate – that it results in distorted outcomes which typically exhibit suboptimal outputs of local public goods or, in our case, excessive levels of local pollution.

The basic claim in this literature is that, in a setting of interjurisdictional economic competition, local officials, in their eagerness to attract new business investment and create new jobs, will introduce measures to reduce costs to local business in the form of low taxes and excessively lax environmental standards that result in suboptimal outputs of local public goods (including environmental quality). In one sense, such a claim is puzzling. If local governments seek to promote the well-being of their residents, then they should care about local environmental quality. If the benefits from a marginal improvement in the local environment exceed the costs, we should expect the improvement to receive support and be carried out. What is going on here?

There is now a large, in fact an enormous, theoretical literature on all this.[4] Let me first point out that it is straightforward to construct a standard kind of model of local public decision making in which competition among governments induces efficient local choices (for example, Oates and Schwab, 1988; Wellisch, 2000). In these models, local jurisdictions compete for mobile firms in order to increase local wage income and to expand the local tax base. The models generate what are effectively analogues to the purely competitive model for the private sector; they provide 'invisible-hand' theorems in which interjurisdictional competition guides local public choice into Pareto-efficient outcomes.

In these models, 'small' governments (small in the sense of being price takers in a national capital market) compete for a national stock of capital, making use of a rich array of policy instruments: they provide public inputs that raise the productivity of local private capital; they provide public services for local residents; they set environmental standards with associated measures to restrict the emissions of polluting firms; and they levy taxes on both local firms and residents. In the appendix to this chapter, I draw on a series of earlier papers by Robert Schwab and me to pull together just such a model and show how it produces efficient outcomes for both private sector activities and the local public economy (including local environmental quality).

But these models are restrictive. They not only assume that local governments are small in national capital markets; they also assume that these governments do not behave strategically with respect to their neighbours. In addition, the models postulate that local officials have the full range of needed tax and regulatory instruments so that they can effectively engage in benefit taxation by taxing residents for the public services they receive *and* firms for the public inputs they make use of. Not surprisingly, when we amend these conditions in various, often quite realistic, ways, the efficiency properties of their outcomes may no longer hold.

An important point of departure in this literature has been a series of models in which the local government has restricted access to tax instruments so that it cannot engage solely in benefit taxation. In the simplest case, such models assume that local governments can only tax mobile capital so that all public services (those for residents as well as local firms) must be financed by a tax on capital. In this framework, the seminal papers by Zodrow and Mieszkowski (1986), Wilson (1986) and Wildasin (1989) show that such non-benefit taxation of capital by local governments leads not only to a regional misallocation of capital, but to distorted local public finance. In particular, there arises a kind of 'fiscal externality'. From the perspective of an individual locality, the cost of providing local public services entails not only the resource cost, but also the loss of tax base to other jurisdictions that accompanies the raising of local tax rates. And this typically leads, at least in the most basic models, to suboptimal levels of local public services.

A corollary to this result is one for local environmental policy. Since more stringent environmental measures raise costs to firms and deflect capital elsewhere, there is an incentive for local governments to choose excessively lax standards for local environmental quality (for example, Oates and Schwab, 1988; Wilson, 1996). As Schwab and I have put it, environmental decisions in this setting have 'fiscal effects' that induce distorted local choices on pollution control.

Such inefficient outcomes can also emerge in certain cases where jurisdictions are not small and where they engage in strategic interactions with their neighbours. Making use of game-theoretic techniques, a substantial set of papers explores how strategic behaviour, aimed at gaining an economic advantage over rivals, can make use of excessively lax environmental measures as a competitive instrument. In some cases, the introduction of harmonizing measures can promise welfare gains relative to the uncoordinated equilibria. There is typically some kind of tradeoff here between the gains from coordination and the losses from more uniform levels of environmental quality across the jurisdictions. List and Mason (forthcoming) have explored such a case, making use of a dynamic game-theoretic model with asymmetric players to characterize outcomes in a setting with transboundary pollutants. In particular, they examine two subefficient policy alternatives: decentralized standard setting or a centrally determined uniform standard. Their numerical simulations of the model indicate that the decentralized setting of standards can dominate a centrally determined uniform standard if there are significant differences across the jurisdictions and if initial levels of pollution are not too high. Otherwise, central setting of standards yields a better outcome.[5]

This is a very large and complicated literature to which I have not begun to do justice in this admittedly terse summary. It treats a wide variety of quite realistic fiscal and regulatory institutions that can produce distorted outcomes in the presence of interjurisdictional competition. These include cases of multiple tax instruments, expenditure competition, and the explicit bidding for mobile firms. For a more systematic and comprehensive treatment of all this, let me again refer the reader to the excellent surveys by two leading contributors, Wellisch (2000) and Wilson (1996, 1999).

The point here is that once we depart from the 'competitive' case, the theoretical models typically produce distorted outcomes that involve overly lax local environmental policies. And from these models emerges the case on theoretical grounds for a 'race to the bottom' that takes the form of suboptimal provision of local public goods, one of which is environmental quality.[6]

The theoretical literature is, in my view, inconclusive on this issue. One can admittedly find support for the widely heard contention that local government cannot be entrusted with the responsibility for setting environmental standards because it will sacrifice the environment on the altar of economic development. But other parts of the literature reveal some efficiency-enhancing properties of such economic competition.

Let me offer two thoughts on this. First, the really important issue here is the *magnitude* of any distortions that result from interjurisdictional competition. If the deviations from efficient outcomes are small, then the race to the bottom may be a very short one and may not matter much. On this issue, we have scant evidence. But there are some tangential findings that I shall review later in the chapter. The problem here is that the measurement of the welfare losses from interjurisdictional economic competition is a formidable task. There is plenty of evidence suggesting that economic competition across states and localities is widespread and often intense (for example, Bartik, 1991). But this does not really address the question. The issue here is that under some circumstances, such competition may be efficiency-enhancing; in other settings, it can lead to distorted outcomes. Thus, the finding that such competition exists simply does not tell us much about the existence or the magnitude of the race to the bottom (Courant, 1994). We are badly in need of empirical estimates of these distortions.

Second, suppose that there are some tendencies toward distorted outcomes, perhaps in the form of excessively lax local environmental standards. What is the alternative? Standard economic theory would prescribe some sort of matching grant, or subsidy, from the central government to local governments to induce them to adopt somewhat more stringent environmental standards – and these subsidies would presumably vary across jurisdictions (Wildasin, 1989). But such a system of subsidies in practice seems remote. A more likely result is direct central intervention in the form of standards for environmental quality – most likely uniform standards (or at least a floor on environmental quality) on a nationwide scale. And this is clearly not an efficient, first-best outcome. In addressing this general issue, Farber (1997), a legal scholar, contends that even if decentralized decision making involves significant distortions, it is far from clear whether centralized measures will, in fact, improve matters. As Farber discusses at some length, the legal history of such measures, both in the United States and in the international arena, is at best a very mixed one. So, if there is a race to the bottom, we are left with a choice between two alternatives: suboptimal local decisions on environmental quality or inefficient uniform national standards. And which of these two alternatives leads to a higher level of social welfare is, in principle, unclear. Empirical studies of these alternative regimes are needed to shed light on this issue.

Finally, let me take up a related concern about decentralized environmental management that arises in an intertemporal context. Some have alleged that centralized control is required because local decision making tends to be myopic and fails to incorporate the interests of future generations. The argument here is that especially in the highly mobile modern world, current residents have a limited concern with the future quality of the local environment. Not only may they move elsewhere, but it is quite likely that their children will end up residing in some other jurisdiction. In consequence, local residents are likely to undervalue measures that promise to protect or enhance the local environment in the more distant future. In contrast, centralized decisions (so the argument goes) will tend to 'internalize' such concerns for the future; they will better preserve the environment for future generations.

This contention, however, is, in one very fundamental way, quite misleading. There is, in fact, a quite powerful market force that internalizes future benefits and costs in a decentralized setting: capitalization. So long as the future costs and benefits of environmental measures are known, future damages associated with current decisions will manifest themselves in *current* property values. Thus, the present residents of a local jurisdiction are effectively forced into taking into account the impact of their current decisions on the future state of the local environment.[7] Central decision makers do not face such a disciplining force; thus, it is conceivable that certain classes of local decisions may provide better safeguards for the interests of future generations than more centralized management.

3. SOME FURTHER THOUGHTS ON THE CASE OF LOCAL SPILLOVER EFFECTS

The case where polluting activities affect environmental quality in neighbouring jurisdictions presents, as we have seen, a complicated challenge *in practice* for environmental management. Policymakers in one jurisdiction will often have little incentive to worry about the costs that their actions impose on their neighbours. One form of policy response to this case is centralization. As we noted, the first-best policy measure in such a case is an effluent charge per unit of waste emissions equal to the marginal external damages. But this, in general, would be a differentiated tax that would depend on the particular location of the source and the 'victims'. Such differentiated tax rates are not easy for a central authority either to determine or, politically, to impose.

Moreover, as we noted earlier, centrally determined, uniform ambient standards for environmental quality are *not* an efficient policy response in such cases. The problem here is that a given jurisdiction is, in a sense, at the mercy of polluters elsewhere. The most efficient way of attaining the standard (whatever it may be) is likely to involve pollution controls in other jurisdictions over which the state or local authority has no control. An alternative approach is for the central authority to set emissions limitations on polluting activities with spillover effects. But even here, uniform regulations are unlikely to be very satisfactory. A fully efficient system of pollution control must take into account the particular patterns and magnitudes of the flows of pollutants across different borders; a system of uniform emissions standards is unlikely to be very efficient. In fact, Revesz (1996) shows that in the arena of air-quality management, federal measures in the US have not been very effective in addressing the issue of interstate externalities.[8]

In principle at least, regional cooperation offers the potential for an efficient, Coasean sort of resolution of jurisdictional spillover effects. The basic idea here is that so long as the polluting activities that are the source of the spillovers are not at their efficient levels, there exist potential gains-from-trade from an interjurisdictional programme to regulate these activities. The costs, in such cases, of pollution abatement are less than the benefits accruing *both* to residents of the home and neighbouring jurisdictions. The difficult problem in practice is the design of a set of cooperative decision-making institutions that can realize these gains-from-trade.

It is useful, I think, to approach this issue in terms of a typology of cases. There is at least one fundamental distinction to be drawn between forms of jurisdictional spillover effects. In the first class of cases, polluting flows are unidirectional. Thus, the polluting activities in one country or state generate environmental damages in a neighbouring jurisdiction, but not vice versa. In the second class of cases, there exists a reciprocal relationship: polluting activities in both jurisdictions spill over the common border.

The first class of unilateral spillover effects, while the simpler one in one sense, is probably the more difficult to deal with in a regional policy setting. This is because only one party stands to gain directly from the reduced flows of polluting waste emissions. One jurisdiction will need to undertake the costly activity of cutting back on its polluting activities, while the other jurisdiction will receive benefits from these controls. In the absence of any form of compensation, there is little in the way of incentives for the source-jurisdiction to adopt measures to reduce the flow of pollutants outside its borders. Some sort of compensatory mechanism is required here if there are to be mutual gains from regional cooperation.[9]

In the second class of interjurisdictional spillovers, there can exist mutual gains-from-trade without compensation. Here one state can agree to reduce its polluting activities and hence the damages its does to a neighbouring state in return for a similar programme in the adjoining state. For this class of cases, there exists a straightforward way for each party to compensate the other in terms of reduced transboundary pollution.

There are, incidentally, lots of actual cases of both of these classes of interjurisdictional pollution. One common case in the first class is that of a river that flows from one jurisdiction into another; the use of the river in the upstream jurisdiction imposes costs on the downstream users. Similarly, prevailing air currents often convey air pollutants from one set of jurisdictions to those downwind. There are also numerous cases of the second class of reciprocal interjurisdictional pollution flows. Such instances can involve bodies of water, such as bays or lakes, where different jurisdictions occupy segments of the shoreline.

Regional cooperation presents an appealing approach in principle to addressing some forms of interjurisdictional pollution. But such cooperation is not always easy to come by. I shall return to this shortly. But the basic point here is that cases of spillover effects across jurisdictions present us with a fairly complex set of policy alternatives in practice. The first-best measures of economic theory may simply not be feasible. The available alternatives then include not only centrally determined ambient or emissions standards, but regional programmes that involve cooperative management efforts. The second-best alternative may well vary from case to case, although we should be able to say something about the circumstances that tend to favour one approach over the other (List and Mason, forthcoming).

4. WHAT CAN WE LEARN FROM THE EVIDENCE?

Until quite recently, we have not had much in the way of evidence to bring to bear on the crucial issues in environmental federalism, but in the last few years some important studies (primarily for the US) have emerged. I find it helpful to organize the discussion of this work around three separate issues: the existence of a race to the bottom, the potential of cooperative regional measures for environmental management, and the estimation of the potential welfare gains from the decentralized setting of environmental standards.

Is There a Race to the Bottom?

Suppose that there is a race to the bottom. What should we expect to observe over time? If state and local officials have systematically sacrificed environmental quality in their jurisdictions on behalf of economic growth, we should expect to find a record of continuing environmental degradation until some point at which there is central intervention for environmental management. From such a point forward, centrally set standards should become the norm. States and localities would presumably not seek to introduce standards more stringent than those set by the central agency because this would put their jurisdictions at a competitive disadvantage in the market place.

Is this what we find? Let us begin with an examination of the US experience with air-quality management. This should be instructive inasmuch as most major programmes prior to the 1960s were at the state and local levels. Federal involvement took place in the 1960s, culminating with the Clean Air Act Amendments of 1970 under which the federal government, under the auspices of the Environmental Protection Agency, introduced a set of uniform national ambient air quality standards for a set of key (the so-called 'criteria') air pollutants.

The historical record both of emissions of air pollutants and ambient air quality is a rather mixed and complicated one. For some pollutants (for example, carbon monoxide and nitrogen dioxide), existing data indicate that there was continuing growth in aggregate national emissions through the decades prior to 1970 with significant reductions since then (Council on Environmental Quality, 1995, Ch. 10). However, for other air pollutants, there is clear evidence that things had been improving for a substantial period prior to an active federal role. Estimates of national emissions for particulate matter, for example, reveal a continuing decline since the late 1940s. And this translates into improved ambient air quality. Goklany (1999) provides a comprehensive review of trends in both emissions and ambient air quality insofar as the data will permit for periods prior to and after 1970. In one set of data based on about 80 urban and 20 rural areas beginning in 1957–58, Goklany (pp. 53–5) finds a substantial decline in the 'national' average concentration between 1958 and 1970. All this reflects efforts following World War II and extending through the 1960s in many urban areas to address their 'smoke' problems. These efforts resulted in dramatic improvements in air quality in a number of major cities including New York, Pittsburgh, Chicago and St. Louis. By 1956, there were some 82 local air pollution control programmes in place. There is likewise evidence of reduced emissions and concentrations of sulphur dioxide prior to the Clean Air Act Amendments of 1970. On another front, the State of California introduced vehicle emissions standards in 1967 which provided the basis for later federal standards. This is not to contest the real improvements in many dimensions of air quality since 1970, but simply to indicate that there were widespread and effective programmes in many areas for the control of at least certain forms of air pollution.

The record, in short, does not seem to support the view that prior to the Clean Air Act Amendments of 1970, state and local agencies were inactive in the realm of air pollution control. On the contrary, as public awareness and concern over air pollution mounted, there was, in fact, a real and substantial response at the state and local levels encompassing a wide range of programmes for the improvement of air quality.

In Goklany's view, the historical record as regards air-quality management is clearly inconsistent with the claims for a race to the bottom. The 'conventional wisdom' which attributes the marked improvements in air quality to federal intervention beginning with the Clean Air Act Amendments of 1970 is simply wrong. As Goklany documents, there were in fact 'broad improvements in air quality before federalization. The race, if any, seems to be in the opposite direction, particularly for those pollutants associated with . . . the greatest public health risks' (p. 150).

But there is a second part to my proposed test. Following the mandates of the CAA of 1970, the US EPA introduced ambient air quality standards consisting of maximum allowable concentrations of the criteria air pollutants applicable to every area in the country. If there were a race to the bottom, we might expect that such standards would not be tightened by the states. And, with a couple of minor exceptions, this is what we find. States and local environmental authorities have not adopted standards for these pollutants that are more stringent than the federal standards. However, while such behaviour is consistent with the existence of a race to the bottom, I think that, for the case of air-quality management, there is another explanation that is more compelling.

The standards set under the CAA of 1970 are *extraordinarily* stringent. Under the legislation, the EPA was directed to set uniform standards for air quality 'to protect the human health' and to do so in such a way as 'to provide an adequate margin of safety . . . from any known or anticipated adverse effects associated with such air pollutant(s) in the ambient air'. Moreover, these standards were to be set without regard to their cost of attainment. This has resulted in a very restrictive set of standards for air quality that many areas have been unable to attain after more than thirty years of continuing efforts.

This is admittedly a complicated issue. Existing benefit–cost studies suggest that the *total* benefits from air pollution control have substantially exceeded the *total* costs in the United States. But this, of course, does not really address the relevant question. It is still possible, and I think likely in view of the evidence, that for several of the criteria air pollutants (such as ground-level ozone), the standards have been pushed beyond the point where marginal benefits equal marginal cost. If this is so, then the federal standards (from an economic perspective) are excessive, and we would not expect to find state and local governments tightening these standards yet further. For this reason, I do not take the US experience with air quality standards to provide much support for the race-to-the-bottom view.

We do better, I think, to look to other areas of environmental regulation for more compelling evidence on this. Of the major environmental statutes, there are two that explicitly require that benefits and costs be weighed against one another in the setting of federal standards: the Toxic Substances Control Act (TSCA) and the Federal Insecticide, Fungicide, and Rodenticide Act (FIFRA).[10] And it is interesting that in these areas, we find lots of cases where the states have gone beyond the federal standards and, in some instances, have adopted much tougher regulations. Some states, for example, regulate pesticide use more stringently than required under the federal rules in FIFRA (see Grossman, 1996). Even under hazardous waste regulation which is not subject to a benefit–cost test, many states have introduced much tighter measures to regulate the disposal of hazardous wastes than required under the federal Resource Conservation and Recovery Act (RCRA) (see, for example, Lennett and Greer, 1985). All this admittedly requires closer scrutiny to determine the extent to which these tougher regulations impose higher costs on local business enterprise. But on the face of it, there are lots of cases where state and local authorities have introduced environmental measures that are significantly more restrictive than the minimum requirements established by federal regulations.

Some recent work has taken an altogether different tack on this. We do have a post-1970 experience in the US with an effort actually to decentralize a broad range of environmental decision making. Under the Reagan Administration in the 1980s, several actions were taken that moved the responsibility for environmental management on a variety of fronts back to the states. Indeed, one of Reagan's principles was to shift environmental responsibilities to the states 'whenever feasible'. Federal appropriations to federal environmental agencies such as the EPA were cut, and there were also large reductions in federal aid to the states for environmental programmes. This provides an opportunity, over an admittedly short span, to see how state and local governments responded to the task of taking greater control over their environmental programmes. In particular, can we see any evidence of an intensified race to the bottom? Three recent studies have looked at the record. List and Gerking (2000), using state-level data, examine both levels of environmental quality and abatement expenditures. Estimating a fixed effects model with both state-specific and time-specific effects, they employ as a test for the race to the bottom the signs of the time fixed effects during the years of the Reagan presidency. They find that the majority of the time effects are either insignificant or consistent with improved environmental quality and conclude that 'in this instance, the race to bottom did not appear to materialize' (p. 454).

In a second assessment of the Reagan experience, Millimet (2000) has undertaken a careful study of airborne emissions of nitrogen oxide and sulphur dioxide and of industry expenditures on pollution abatement. His technique is to estimate a model for a long period prior to the Reagan and Bush years and then to compare predictions of the model with actual outcomes during those administrations. This exercise finds support for a race to the top, rather than a race to the bottom – at least for abatement spending and nitrogen oxide emissions – as emissions and pollution control expenditures were significantly greater than those predicted by the model.

In a third study that covers a longer time period, 1977–94, a period that encompasses the Reagan years, Fredriksson and Millimet (forthcoming) have looked for strategic interaction in environmental management by the US states. And they find evidence of such interdependencies. In a series of regression equations that explains levels of abatement expenditure among the states, they find that spending for pollution control in a given state depends significantly on spending in neighbouring states. The form of this interdependency is especially interesting in that it exhibits a basic asymmetry. States appear to be 'pulled' to higher levels of abatement spending by more stringent measures in neighbouring states, but relatively lax regulations nearby appear to have no effect on such expenditures. Thus, in the spirit of the other two studies, this one likewise finds no evidence in support of a race to the bottom.

The historical evidence thus does not appear to provide compelling support for the race-to-the-bottom view of environmental federalism. But there are some other kinds of evidence that are of interest here. In particular, there exists a body of empirical work that looks directly at the response of industry location decisions to environmental regulations. The basic idea here is that areas with more stringent environmental regulations should find themselves at a competitive disadvantage that should manifest itself in relatively few new firms or plants in pollution-intensive industries. Some early empirical studies of this issue, both in a domestic and international context, found little support for this claim. In a study of motor-vehicle assembly plants in the US, for example, McConnell and Schwab (1990) found that regional differences in environmental regulations exerted no apparent influence on the locational choices of industry branch plants (see also Crandall, 1993 and Bartik, 1988). Similarly, in the international context, Tobey (1990) found that the relative stringency of environmental regulations in different countries had no discernible impact on patterns and levels of exports. Thus, this first wave or generation of research led to the conclusion that environmental regulations were themselves such a minor element in the location decisions of polluting firms that they had little impact on these decisions. In a well-known survey of this work, Jaffe and his colleagues (1995) concluded that 'Overall, there is relatively little evidence to support the hypothesis that environmental regulations have had a large adverse effect on competitiveness, however that elusive term is defined' (p. 157).[11]

There is, however, a second generation of research on the issue that, making use of richer and more recent data sets and a wide range of econometric techniques, has turned up measurable effects, in some cases sizeable ones, of the stringency of environmental regulations on location decisions in pollution-intensive industries. Henderson (1996), in a careful study of ground-level ozone regulation that employs a panel data set and fixed-effects analysis, found significant differences in industrial location patterns between attainment and nonattainment areas. Henderson found that polluting firms were more likely to stay in attainment areas or, if they relocated, to move to attainment areas where they would presumably be subject to less scrutiny and more lenient control measures than in non-attainment areas. Likewise, Becker and Henderson (2000) found that differentials in regulation affect levels of firm births in polluting industries; new plants in these industries exhibited birth rates in attainment areas that were estimated to be 26–45 percent higher than in nonattainment areas.

Other types of more recent studies have also found significant effects of environmental measures on location decisions. List and Mason (forthcoming), using a panel data set from the state of New York, find evidence suggesting that air quality regulations influence the choice of destination of relocating firms. List and Co (2000) study the location choices in the US of foreign multinational corporations and find that their location decisions for new plants are sensitive to the stringency of state environmental regulations. Examining the implications of these findings for economic growth, List and Kunce (2000) explore the impact of environmental regulations on the growth in manufacturing employment; they find that job growth in polluting industries is adversely affected by more stringent environmental measures. In a review and reassessment of this whole body of work, Jeppesen, List and Folmer (forthcoming) pull together estimates from a number of studies in a 'meta-analysis' that both documents the significance of these effects and suggests the importance of various methodological issues in estimating their magnitude.

We must, however, exercise some care in drawing out the implications of this research. First, a basic finding that polluting firms are responsive in their location decisions to area differentials in the stringency of environmental regulations does not in itself prove that states or localities actually use environmental measures as a competitive instrument. In fact, irrespective of the actual facts on the location decisions in polluting industries, whether or not officials use environmental regulations for competitive purposes depends largely on perceptions. If policymakers *think* that these regulations matter, then they may well craft environmental legislation in the light of their objectives for economic development. Perceptions matter here. As we have noted, the first generation of research on this issue found little evidence of the responsiveness of location decisions to the stringency of environmental regulations. But in their survey of this work,

Jaffe et al. (1995) pointed out that 'There appears to be widespread belief that environmental regulations have a significant effect on the siting of new plants in the United States' (p. 148). Likewise, Engel (1997) finds evidence in support of such perceptions. In a survey that she administered to state environmental agency officials, she found that some 88 percent stated that 'concern over industry relocation and siting affects environmental decision-making in their state' (p. 341).[12] But even this must be intepreted with care. For as the theory suggests (see the appendix for example), inter-jurisdictional competition can lead to efficient outcomes. The fact that such competition exists does not necessarily imply that environmental standards will be too lax.

Finally, there is an interesting and recent paper that finds evidence of free-riding behaviour on the part of the states. In a study of federal and state spending under the Endangered Species Act, List, Bulte and Shogren (forthcoming) examine a panel data set on expenditure patterns on endangered species. Their results suggest that states tend to spend less (relative to the federal government) on those species that demand a large habitat area and those whose preservation conflicts directly with economic development. But this is not contrary to expectations. The benefits from the conservation of species are largely non-use benefits that accrue to people everywhere. In terms of our earlier framework, this is a national (or global) public good – one for which centralized standard-setting is needed in order to avoid suboptimal measures.

Regional Cooperation as an Alternative to Centralization

As we noted earlier, for the case of environmental spillover effects across jurisdictional boundaries, centralization in the form of setting uniform national standards is, in general, not an efficient solution. Some kind of Coasean cooperative action may offer the opportunity for achieving a more efficient outcome. The difficult problem in practice is the design of a set of cooperative decision-making institutions that can realize the 'gains-from-trade' available from an efficient resolution of the externalities.

The record on the regional approach is a mixed one. Cooperation itself can present major challenges. The literature on such regional compacts is a very large one that cuts across the boundaries of several disciplines – and I cannot hope to encompass it all here. There are clear episodes of failure. One such early effort involved the creation of the Delaware River Basin Commission (DRBC) in 1961 as a new 'model regional agency' for the management of water quality on the Delaware River and Estuary. The DRBC, vested with broad decision-making powers, included constituencies from the four interested states (Pennsylvania, New York, New Jersey and Delaware) and the federal government. But the respective parties never seemed able to rise above their parochial interests to reach a 'regional' perspective. Ackerman et al. (1974), in their fascinating and insightful description and assessment of the early years of the DRBC experiment, make clear the formidable obstacles to interjurisdictional environmental management. But we may be learning from experience. With all the difficulties that it has encountered, the evidence suggests more in the way of success for the 'consortium' currently managing the Chesapeake Bay. Subsequent to a voluntary agreement in 1987 among the relevant jurisdictions (Maryland, Virginia, Pennsylvania and the District of Columbia) and the federal government to reduce pollution flowing into the Bay, there are a number of visible signs of improvement in water quality in the Bay.[13]

Another intriguing and important regional experiment in environmental management involves the control of air pollution. Scientific work in recent years has revealed that ground-level ozone pollution, once thought to be basically a localized problem, involves important elements of long-range transport. In the light of new evidence of the transport of ozone and its precursors, NO_x and VOC emissions, the US Congress in 1990 created an ozone transport region (OTR) with its commission (OTC) to address the nonattainment issue for ozone pollution in the Northeast states.[14] The OTC enacted two regional initiatives, one for the adoption of the California Low Emissions Vehicle programme and the other committing the states to pursue new emissions controls for power plants and other large boilers within their jurisdictions. A serious problem that became apparent is that OTR is not sufficiently large to encompass the full range of the transport problem. Analysis has indicated, for example, that the most cost-effective NO_x controls would involve reduced emissions in states outside the OTR, where such emissions reductions are more than an order of magnitude less expensive. This led to the formation of an expanded regional organization, the Ozone Transport Assessment Group (OTAG), to account for the full geographical scope of transport. An important facet of this programme is the explicit recognition of the particular spatial configuration of the ozone transport problem and the incorporation of these spatial features into the programme. The OTR states reached an important agreement on a system for the control of stationary source emissions that involves a 'NO_x Budget' and a 'Cap and Trade' system. Under this approach, there is an aggregate allowance to each state for its total level of emissions with the individual states being empowered to allocate their allowances within their states as they see fit. As Farrell, Carter and Raufer (1999) show, this system promises substantial savings relative to various command-and-control options. The trading system seems to be working well: Chartier (1999/2000) reports that the preliminary results for 1999 indicate that sources have achieved reductions in emissions well beyond required levels. Moreover, trading has been widespread (Farrell, 2000). It is especially noteworthy that much of the impetus for this programme has come from the concerned states themselves, not from federal intervention. The programme is still in the process of evolution, but it certainly appears quite promising. Finding efficient regional and interregional control strategies is complicated, but the potential returns seem quite large.

It is difficult to generalize from these experiences with regional environmental management. Both the circumstances and the institutions differ in important ways. But there is, I think, much to be learned here. A systematic study of such regional efforts that makes use of a sensible categorization into typologies of environmental interaction (for example, unilateral versus reciprocal pollution flows) and collective decision-making institutions might well reveal what sorts of structures and policy measures can work effectively for the regional management of environmental quality. There is an important research agenda here.

Estimates of the Gains from Decentralized Standards

Another empirical approach to environmental federalism is to compare in welfare terms the outcome under uniform national standards for a particular pollutant with that of a decentralized system that allows each jurisdiction to select its own optimal standard. There is only one such study that I know of. It is noteworthy not only for this reason, but also by reason of its striking findings.

The study by Dinan, Cropper and Portney (1999) considers the case in the US of setting uniform national standards for drinking water. This is an especially relevant case, since it approximates our Benchmark Case 2 of a pure local public good. With minor qualifications, standards for safe drinking water are of concern almost exclusively to the local population; they address contaminants that can be the cause of cancers or other chronic health effects when individuals are subject to long-term exposure. Both the benefits and also the costs of drinking water standards accrue almost wholly to local residents.

The US Congress passed in 1974 the Safe Drinking Water Act (SDWA), which mandated the first set of federally enforceable standards for drinking water (later amended and strengthened in 1986). Under these measures, the US EPA was directed to set maximum contaminant standards covering some 83 contaminants at a level at which 'no known or anticipated adverse effects on the health of persons occur and which allows for an adequate margin of safety'. Later amendments allow for some cost considerations in the determination of the standards, but these appear not to affect the standards as they apply to smaller systems that operate at much higher per capita cost.

As the authors discuss, the removal of contaminants from drinking water involves treatment procedures with very large economies of scale. In fact, for the particular contaminant they study (gross alpha emitters), which exhibits approximately linear benefits per household from reduced concentrations, the declining marginal costs imply corner solutions: welfare is typically maximized in a particular community either by zero treatment or complete removal of the contaminant. Their estimates indicate that for smaller systems, the costs of treatment far outweigh the benefits (even using a very generous assumption of $10 million for the value of avoiding a case of cancer). Welfare losses from the uniform standard vary widely across the size categories in their study; households served by the smallest systems incur estimated losses of $650 or more per annum, depending upon the initial level of contamination. In fact, only the very largest category of systems exhibits positive net benefits from the standard. *If* we assume that local systems adopt the level of treatment that maximizes such net benefits, the decentralized outcome would clearly be far superior to the universal attainment of the specified standard. This is a case where the costs of treatment per capita vary so dramatically across jurisdictions that uniform standards come at a very high welfare cost compared to the efficient pattern of local treatment.

5.   SOME CONCLUSIONS AND REFLECTIONS

Environmental federalism is a complicated issue. Both theory and practice suggest the existence of real tensions and a certain ambivalence about the roles of the different levels of government in environmental management. In concluding this lengthy treatment, let me offer a few thoughts on all this.

Turning first to the role of the central government, we find a major responsibility in supporting research and providing information on environmental matters. Basic knowledge concerning the nature and extent of environmental damages from polluting activities and methods of pollution control are pure public goods on a national (and international) scale. The discovery of a new and more effective technique for reducing polluting waste emissions, for example, can provide benefits to all jurisdictions. Following the standard arguments, we would expect a purely decentralized system to provide too little in the way of research and development activities because individual state, provincial, or local governments would typically ignore the benefits that such activities provide to residents in other places. The basic research function and, in addition, the dissemination of information on environmental damages and pollution-control techniques thus has a public-good character that points to a fundamental role for the central government.

It is important in this regard, however, to recognize that decentralization can provide a valuable dimension in policy innovation by offering the opportunity for experimentation with differing approaches to environmental management (Oates, 1999). Under so-called 'laboratory federalism', there are potential gains from learning-by-doing so that we can find out how certain kinds of policy measures work in practice without imposing untried systems on the entire nation. In addition, a variety of approaches to regulatory management across jurisdictions can sometimes turn up previously unrecognized methods or instruments. There is, in fact, a major and interesting case of this in the arena of US environmental policy: trading systems for emissions allowances. The introduction in the 1970s and 1980s of a variety of Emissions Trading Systems at the state level demonstrated the feasibility of such systems and some of their very appealing properties – as well as certain pitfalls. Without this experience, I doubt that the US would have introduced the national system of tradeable sulphur allowances under the 1990 Clean Air Act Amendments.

A second role for central government can arise in cases where standardization in pollution-control activities across jurisdictions involves large cost savings. The most obvious case here involves the determination of emissions standards for motor vehicles. It would obviously be very costly for auto manufacturers to have to produce 50 different variants of cars to satisfy the particular emissions standards of each state. There is clearly a case here for central standard-setting. At the same time, this may not mean a single standard only. It may prove worthwhile to have, say, two sets of standards that would allow jurisdictions some limited choice depending on their particular circumstances (as is the case in the US where California has set vehicle emissions standards that are more stringent than those required elsewhere).

When, however, we turn to the general issue of the setting of standards for environmental quality, things become murkier. The Benchmark Cases that I set forth in the first section of the chapter provide some guidance on this. There is the suggestion that for environmental matters that are strictly of 'local' interest (that is, Benchmark Case 2), a decentralized system of setting ambient standards seems appropriate. The 'one-size-fits-all' approach can result in large welfare losses compared to a system in which individual jurisdictions introduce standards that are the best suited to their own circumstances. The Dinan, Cropper and Portney study (1999), as discussed earlier, indicates, for a particular contaminant, the potentially significant magnitude of these losses from uniformity.

There are, as I see it, three major objections to this prescription.[15] The first is the race-to-the- bottom argument. As we saw, this argument is difficult to resolve at a purely theoretical level: different (and plausible) models can produce different results. There is an empirical literature beginning to emerge on this issue. And my reading of the findings is that they really do not provide much overall support for the existence of a race to the bottom. In fact, one can reasonably argue that they point more in the opposite direction – to a race to the top rather than to the bottom.[16]

The second objection is the need for expertise. Environmental management is a very complicated matter that involves sophisticated environmental science as well as skilled policy design and enforcement. A large central agency, so the argument goes, can pull together the critical body of 'experts' needed to carry out this work. State and local governments simply do not have the wherewithal to develop and administer effective systems of environmental regulation. Here again, I do not find the argument fully compelling. As discussed above, it makes good sense for a central agency to provide information and guidance on these matters. From this perspective, state and local governments do not have to go it alone. Moreover, there has been much written in recent years concerning the impressive improvement in the management capacities of state and local governments. Rivlin (1992, ch. 6), for example, describes the marked strengthening in recent decades of state and local governments in a whole range of fiscal and regulatory capabilities. There is considerable expertise now at decentralized levels of government, especially when seen against the background of centrally provided support. As an aside, the expertise argument surely carries little weight in the case for harmonization in the European context, where member states have plenty of experts.

The third argument against decentralization is more anecdotal in character. It has to do with political clout (and may, perhaps, be regarded as a variant of the race-to-the-bottom proposition). The claim is often set forth by visualizing a company town somewhere that is dominated by the company's representatives. Industrial interests inevitably prevail so that needed pollution-control measures never have a chance. There may be actual instances of this, although it is hard to know how prevalent it is in fact. But once again, while the argument may have some force under special circumstances at the level of relatively small, local jurisdictions, it is less likely to characterize outcomes at state or provincial levels – and again has little relevance to arguments for harmonization across the European Union.

My own sense is that where environmental quality is basically a local public good, the case for the setting of environmental standards at an appropriately decentralized level of government is quite compelling. At the same time, one can envision an essential informational and guidance role for the central authority. With the substantial scientific and policy expertise at its disposal, a central agency can effectively provide a menu of options for the stringency of standards and the choice among policy instruments. Such guidance would become an important resource for state and local officials and their constituencies in the actual design of decentralized environmental programs.

When we turn to Benchmark Case 3, however, things become yet more difficult. Here we have the case where local polluting activities degrade not only the immediate environment but spill over to some degree into neighbouring jurisdictions. A purely locally determined outcome in such circumstances cannot be expected to be an efficient one. But neither is an outcome where the central government establishes uniform standards across all jurisdictions. And yet a third alternative is some kind of cooperative or regional programme that involves joint decisions on the part of the relevant jurisdictions.

None of the three alternatives may be *generally* preferable to the other two. Local decision making, especially if the spillover effects are quite pronounced, is likely to result in excessive pollution. Centralized measures will typically exhibit a tendency toward national uniformity that will impose welfare losses relative to the efficient pattern of outcomes requiring local differentials in standards that reflect the varying benefits and costs across jurisdictions. Regional cooperation offers, in principle, opportunities to internalize interjurisdictional spillover effects with the design of policy measures that address particular conditions. But in practice such things as 'regional compacts' present a formidable challenge; it is hard to be sanguine about a general presumption that they will always produce superior outcomes.

I thus find it hard to reach a general conclusion for this quite pervasive class of cases. A better approach is probably one that tries to understand the particular circumstances that favour one of the three alternatives relative to the others. Such considerations may involve the extent of the interjurisdictional spillover effects, the geographical configuration of the relevant jurisdictions and pollutant flows, the ease of monitoring emissions, and the structure of environmental regulation within these jurisdictions. A blanket approach involving one alternative to the exclusion of the others is, in my view, unwise. My sense, for example, is that we may not have been well served in the United States by a system of air-quality management that imposes a uniform set of national ambient standards for all pollutants. Circumstances are simply too different to warrant such uniformity, as the persistence of so many non-attainment areas suggests. The efficient levels of concentration of different air pollutants in Los Angeles are surely very different from those in Buffalo – and for certain pollutants it will make sense to recognize those differences. Likewise for Paris and Venice.

APPENDIX

The model presented here is a consolidation of three earlier models of interjurisdictional competition that my colleague, Robert Schwab, and I have assembled (Oates and Schwab, 1988, 1991, and 1996). I thought it might be useful to pull together here such a consolidated model that is quite rich in terms of local public activity. In the model, local governments engage in an array of activities: they provide a local public good for their residents; they provide a local public input for firms that increases the marginal productivity of private capital in the jurisdiction; they set a standard for local environmental quality that translates into a limited allowance of polluting emissions for local firms; and they tax both residents and firms. We find in such a model that interjurisdictional competition leads to Pareto-optimal outcomes. Local governments effectively employ benefit taxes that lead to efficient private and public decisions.

Since the various elements of the model have been presented and discussed in detail elsewhere (Oates and Schwab, 1988, 1991, 1996), I simply summarize the expanded model in Table 1A.1 and discuss it briefly here. Its structure is embodied in the six equations in the first section of the table. In equation (1), we have the production function for the jurisdiction in which output is a function of the jurisdiction's *given* stock of labour, L, its endogenous stock of capital, K, the level of a publicly provided input, X, and the level of waste emissions, E. The publicly provided input (X) could consist of things like local roads, police protection, and refuse collection.[17] Waste emissions (E) are a byproduct of productive activity that result in pollution that causes disutility to residents (but such pollution is assumed, for now, to be wholly localized and not to spill over into other jurisdictions).[18] Assuming constant returns to scale, we can write the production function as $Lf(k, x, e)$, where k is the capital–labour ratio, x is the public input–labour ratio, and e is the emissions–labour ratio.

Equation (2) indicates that in a competitive labour market, the real wage equals the marginal product of labour. Workers, incidentally, are assumed to live and work in the same jurisdiction. In equation (3), r is the rate of return to capital in the national capital market; thus, in equilibrium, the capital stock in the jurisdiction will adjust until its *net* return there is r. As we see in (3), the net return to owners of capital is the return after adjusting for the enhancement of the productivity of capital from the locally provided public input (x) and from waste emissions (e), and after deducting the local tax on capital (t).

Table 1A.1   A model of interjurisdictional economic competition

---

The Model

(1) $Q = F(K, L, X, E) = Lf(k, x, e)$ Production function

(2) $w = f - kf_k - xf_x - ef_e$ Wages

(3) $f_k + (x/k)f_x + (e/k)f_e - t = r$ Rate of return to capital

(4) $u = u(c, g, e)$ Utility function

(5) $h + kt = p^g g + p^x x$ Public budget constraint

(6) $y + w = c + h$ Private budget constraint

Median-Voter Outcome: First-Order Conditions

(1) $MRS_{g,c} = p^g$

(2) $f_x = p^x$

(3) $MRS_{e,c} = f_e$

(4) $t = (x/k)f_x + (e/k)f_e$

First-Order Conditions for Social Optimality

(1) $MRS_{g,c} = p^g$ for each jurisdiction

(2) $f_x = p^x$ for each jurisdiction

(3) $MRS_{e,c} = f_e$ for each jurisdiction

(4) $f_k^i = f_k^j$ for all i, j

In equation (4), we find that the utility of each (identical) resident depends upon the level of private consumption, c, on the output of a publicly provided consumption good, g, and on the collectively consumed level of local pollution, e. Here e is a local public 'bad'. Finally, equations (5) and (6) describe the two relevant budget constraints in the system (expressed in per capita terms). In equation (5), public revenues consist of head tax receipts from residents (h) plus taxes on capital (kt), which together must equal public expenditures on the locally provided consumption good (g) and on the public input to local firms (x). I assume that the local government can purchase units of both g and x at predetermined prices of p^g and p^x. The individual's budget constraint in equation (6) indicates that income consisting of an exogenous component (y) plus wages (w) equals the sum of spending on private consumption (c), where the price of c is taken to be unity, and the individual's local tax payment (h). For simplicity, it is assumed that the revenues from taxes on capital are distributed equally among the jurisdiction's residents in the form of a credit against the resident's tax liability; thus, the head tax (h) is understood to be net of this credit.

The central interest in this model is on the various policy instruments available to the local government for competing in the national market for capital. The incentives in the model for encouraging an inflow of capital are straightforward. A larger capital stock increases the capital–labour ratio, thereby enhancing the productivity of labour and raising the level of real wages. In addition, the local capital stock constitutes a tax base from which local revenues can be raised.

Local government has, in the model, an array of policy instruments with which to influence local economic activity. There are five policy parameters to be determined: the level of the publicly provided input to private firms (x), the allowable level of polluting waste emissions (e), the output of the publicly provided consumption good (g), the tax rate on capital (t), and the head tax (h) on local residents.

Let us assume that the community operates under simple-majority rule. So the values of the policy variables are those that emerge from a median-voter model. Note that since all residents in a given jurisdiction have identical utility functions and income, this amounts simply to maximizing the utility of a representative resident (namely equation (4)) subject to the various constraints contained in the other equations.

The model captures the spirit of interjurisdictional competition in terms of the various tradeoffs that it presents to local residents and their public officials. As noted, it is in the jurisdiction's interest to encourage the inflow of capital both to raise wages and to augment the local tax base. Revenues can be realized from taxing capital at the rate, t. Of course, the larger is t, the more capital is deflected away from the jurisdiction resulting in a reduced level of wages. It is possible in the model for t to be negative, in which case the community would subsidize capital in the expectation of a higher level of wage income. A related tradeoff involves the level of publicly provided inputs (x). Increasing x enhances the productivity of capital and encourages an inflow of capital with resulting higher wages and tax revenues. However, these inputs are provided at a cost to the public treasury that must be balanced against the benefits from the associated inflow of capital.

Another set of tradeoffs arises in determining the level of local environmental quality. Residents, by reducing the level of waste emissions, e, can directly raise their utility level. However, this comes at a cost. Tougher environmental regulations reduce the productivity of capital and hence deflect capital to other jurisdictions. Thus, local residents must choose a level of environmental quality that balances their demands for cleanliness against their demand for private consumption.

The second section of Table 1A.1 summarizes the first-order conditions that must be met in setting these policy parameters in order to maximize the welfare of local residents. These reflect the outcomes under the median-voter model. We see (not surprisingly) in (1) that the output of the publicly provided consumption good should be extended to the point where the marginal rate of substitution of each resident equals the cost of providing another unit of the good. Equation (2) indicates that the publicly provided input to firms should be such that its marginal product equals its price. In (3), we find that the environmental standard should be set such that the marginal value of environmental quality equals foregone output. Finally, we see in (4) that the local tax per unit of capital has two components: it is equal to the increase in output of a unit of capital attributable, first, to the public input and, second, to its waste emissions. Or, in short, the community should employ a benefit tax on local business firms that essentially charges them for the value of the services that the jurisdiction provides to them in the form of public inputs and environmental 'services'.

Next, we find in the third section of the table that the conditions for social optimality are satisfied by the median-voter outcome in the second section. The first three conditions for optimality for society as a whole correspond directly to the corresponding first-order conditions for welfare maximization on an individual community basis. The fourth condition requires that the marginal product of capital be equated across jurisdictions. This will be satisfied if each community taxes capital on a benefit basis with t^i set equal to the contribution to the marginal productivity of capital afforded by the local publicly provided input and waste emissions.[19]

NOTES

* Professor of Economics, University of Maryland, College Park, MD, and University Fellow, Resources for the Future, Washington, DC. I am grateful for helpful comments on an earlier draft to Tom Crocker, David Evans, Per Fredriksson, Mitch Kunce, John List and Paul Portney.

1. More precisely, the Maastricht Treaty for European Union states that action at the community-wide level is justified 'only and insofar as the objectives of the proposed action cannot be sufficiently achieved by the Member States and can therefore, by reason of the scale or effects of the proposed action, be better achieved by the Community' (EC Treaty, 1992, Art. 36). For an excellent collection of papers on environmental decision making in a federal system that draws both on the US and European experiences, see Braden, Folmer and Ulen (1996).
2. The term 'standard' is somewhat ambiguous. It can refer, for example, to an emissions standard – that is, a limit on the emissions of a particular source or set of sources (sometimes called a 'performance standard') – or a technology standard that requires the use of a specified pollution-control technology. My focus here, however, is on an ambient standard: a standard for environmental quality (such as the allowable concentration of a pollutant in the atmosphere) that must be met through some kind of system of pollution control.
3. The case for the decentralized provision of local public goods has been formalized in terms of the so-called 'Decentralization Theorem' (Oates, 1972, ch. 2). In the treatment

       of this proposition, we find that the magnitude of the gains from decentralization (as compared to a uniform level of output across all jurisdictions) depends on the price elasticity of demand and on differences in costs across jurisdictions (Oates, 1997). In light of this, it may be useful to explore whatever information we have on the price elasticity of demand and on differentials in costs for various forms of environmental quality to get some sense of the potential welfare gains from the decentralization of environmental management. For a valuable study of this kind, see the Dinan, Cropper and Portney study (1999) of drinking water contamination that is discussed in Section 4 of this chapter.

4.   As I indicated, this literature extends beyond the issue of environmental federalism to the more general matter of decentralized public finance. On the broader issue of inter-jurisdictional economic competition, Wellisch (2000) has recently provided a superb, systematic and comprehensive treatment of the theoretical literature. Wilson (1999) has also given us an excellent explication and survey of tax competition in his recent paper. On the more specific theoretical issue of decentralized environmental decision making in a setting of economic competition, see again Wilson (1996) for a valuable review. There is, in addition, a very rich and illuminating literature on the race-to-the-bottom issue in the law journals. For some excellent contributions from legal scholars, see, for example, Revesz (1992, 1996), Esty (1996), Engel (1997), and the collection of essays edited by Esty and Geradin (2001).

5.   Ulph (1999), with a collection of his own important papers on this issue, provides an excellent treatment of another strand of this literature.

6.   This is not universally the case. In fact, there are some cases where market power for local governments may actually reduce the extent of distortions from interjurisdictional competition (Hoyt, 1991).

7.   Oates and Schwab (1996) show that in a simple two-period model with a housing market in which people move from one jurisdiction to the other at the end of the first period, there takes place the capitalization of environmental and fiscal differentials into housing (land) values which induces efficient intertemporal decisions regarding levels of environmental quality.

8.   For a careful treatment of this issue in the context of a study of ground-level ozone pollution in the United States and in Europe, see Braden and Proost (1996).

9.   See Baumol and Oates (1988, pp. 278–83) for a discussion of this issue.

10.   These standards, incidentally, are typically product, rather than ambient, standards. They govern such things as the ingredients that pesticides may or may not contain, or where and when pesticides can be used.

11.   There is, incidentally, some evidence suggesting that fiscal variables (such as taxes and certain kinds of public spending) have a modest effect on economic development (see Bartik, 1991).

12.   Engel finds from her survey that 'states strive to mimic the standards of other states' (p. 344). This sort of 'strategic' reaction to policies in neighbouring states has also been observed in fiscal matters (see, for example, the seminal paper by Case, Rosen and Hines, 1993). But it need not indicate the presence of a race to the bottom. As noted above, Fredriksson and Millimet (forthcoming) find in their study that such strategic interaction has appeared to work in the opposite direction; they find that it has either 'pushed' or 'pulled' states up to more stringent measures to enhance environmental quality.

13.   There is a need for a systematic study of the experience in regional management of the Chesapeake Bay. I know of none.

14.   Natalie Tawil and Terry Dinan (see Congressional Budget Office, 1997) provide an excellent description and assessment of the ongoing OTR experience that I draw on here. See also the insightful comparative study by Braden and Proost (1996) of the US and European efforts to regulate ground-level ozone.

15.   For a forceful statement of the case for the centralization of environmental management based on US experience, see Steinzor (2000).

16.   Even if there is some tendency toward laxity arising from economic competition, the important issue is its degree and extent. How large are the welfare losses from the race

to the bottom? While we have no direct evidence on this for the setting of environmental standards, Parry (2001) has recently estimated the welfare losses from tax competition with a computable general equilibrium model. In his model, regional governments have a single tax instrument: a tax on mobile capital. And this leads to distorted outcomes resulting from the fiscal interdependencies among jurisdictions. For the case of welfare-maximizing governments, Parry finds that these losses are, on the whole, quite modest – typically less than 3 percent of revenues. We cannot, of course, directly translate these findings to a setting of regulatory competition, but they do at least suggest that the distortions from interjurisdictional competition may not be very large.

17. I assume that the publicly provided input is not a Samuelsonian public good but is subject to congestion like a private good. The input is taken to be allocated among producers according to the size of their capital stock so that the public input–capital ratio is the same for all firms. The idea here is that larger private facilities receive proportionally more of such things as sewer and refuse services, police services, training programmes and so forth.

18. Waste emissions (like the public input) are taken to be allocated among firms in proportion to their capital stock. This assumption is not essential to the results, but it facilitates the analysis.

19. If there were no public inputs or environmental services to enhance the local productivity of capital, then the first-order conditions imply that the optimal tax on capital in each jurisdiction is zero. Gordon (1986) establishes this result for a small open economy in an international setting.

REFERENCES

Ackerman, Bruce, et al. (1974), *The Uncertain Search for Environmental Quality*, New York: The Free Press.

Bartik, Timothy J. (1988), 'The effects of environmental legislation on business location in the United States', *Growth and Change*, **22**, 22–44.

Bartik, Timothy J. (1991), *Who Benefits from State and Local Development Policies?*, Kalamazoo, MI: W.E. Upjohn Institute.

Baumol, William J. and Wallace E. Oates (1988), *The Theory of Environmental Policy*, 2nd edn, Cambridge: Cambridge University Press.

Becker, Randy, and Vernon Henderson (2000), 'Effects of air quality regulations on polluting industries', *Journal of Political Economy*, **108**, 379–421.

Braden, John B. and Stef Proost (1996), 'Economic Assessment of Policies for Combating Tropospheric Ozone in Europe and the United States', in J. Braden et al. (eds), *Environmental Policy with Political and Economic Integration: The European Union and the United States*, Cheltenham, UK and Brookfield, US: Edward Elgar, pp. 365–413.

Braden, John B., Henk Folmer and Thomas Ulen (eds) (1996), *Environmental Policy with Political and Economic Integration: The European Union and the United States*, Cheltenham, UK and Brookfield, US: Edward Elgar.

Case, Anne C., Harvey S. Rosen and James R. Hines, Jr. (1993), 'Budget spillovers and fiscal policy interdependence: evidence from the States', *Journal of Public Economics*, **52**, 285–307.

Chartier, Daniel (1999/2000), 'Trading NO_x in the North-East USA', *Environmental Finance* (Jan.–Feb.), 23.

Congressional Budget Office (1997), *Federalism and Environmental Protection: Case Studies for Drinking Water and Ground-Level Ozone*, Washington, DC: US Congress.

Council on Environmental Quality (1995), *Environmental Quality, 25th Anniversary Report, 1994–95* Washington, DC: Executive Office of the President.

Courant, Paul (1994), 'How would you know a good economic policy if you tripped over one? Hint: don't just count jobs', *National Tax Journal*, **47**, 863–81.

Crandall, Robert W. (1993), *Manufacturing on the Move*, Washington, DC: Brookings Institution.

Dinan, Terry M., Maureen L. Cropper and Paul R. Portney (1999), 'Environmental Federalism: Welfare Losses from Uniform National Drinking Water Standards', in Arvind Panagariya et al. (eds), *Environmental and Public Economics: Essays in Honor of Wallace E. Oates*, Cheltenham, UK and Northampton, MA: Edward Elgar, pp. 13–31.

Engel, Kirsten H. (1997), 'State environmental standard setting: is there a "race" and is it "to the bottom"?,' *Hastings Law Journal*, **48**, 271–398.

Esty, Daniel C. (1996), 'Revitalizing environmental federalism', *Michigan Law Review*, **95**, 570–653.

Esty, Daniel and Damien Geradin (eds) (2001), *Regulatory Competition and Economic Integration: Comparative Perspectives*, Oxford: Oxford University Press.

Farber, Daniel A. (1997), 'Environmental federalism in a global economy', *Virginia Law Review*, **83**, 1283–319.

Farrell, Alex (2000), 'The NO$_x$ budget: a look at the first year', *The Electricity Journal*, (March), 83–93.

Farrell, Alex, Robert Carter and Roger Raufer (1999), 'The NO$_x$ budget: market-based control of tropospheric ozone in the Northeastern United States', *Resource and Energy Economics*, **21**, 103–24.

Fredriksson, Per G. and Daniel L. Millimet (forthcoming), 'Strategic interaction and the determinants of environmental policy across US states', *Journal of Urban Economics*.

Goklany, Indur M. (1999), *Clearing the Air: The Real Story of the War on Air Pollution*, Washington, DC: Cato Institute.

Gordon, Roger (1986), 'Taxation of investment and savings in a world economy', *American Economic Review*, **76**, 567–86.

Grossman, Margaret Rosso (1996), 'Environmental Federalism in Agriculture: The Case of Pesticide Regulation in the United States', in J. Braden et al. (eds), *Environmental Policy with Political and Economic Integration: The European Union and the United States*, Cheltenham, UK and Brookfield, US: Edward Elgar, pp. 274–304.

Henderson, J. Vernon (1996), 'Effects of air quality regulation', *American Economic Review*, **86**, 789–813.

Hoyt, William (1991), 'Property taxation, Nash equilibrium, and market power', *Journal of Urban Economics*, **34**, 123–31.

Jaffe, Adam B., Steven Peterson, Paul Portney and Robert Stavins (1995), 'Environmental regulation and the competitiveness of U.S. manufacturing: what does the evidence tell us?' *Journal of Economic Literature*, **33**, 132–63.

Jeppesen, Tim, John A. List and Henk Folmer (forthcoming), 'Environmental regulations and new plant location decisions: evidence from a meta-analysis', *Journal of Regional Science*.

Lennett, David J. and Linda E. Greer (1985), 'State regulation of hazardous waste,' *Ecology Law Quarterly*, **12**, 183–269.

List, John A. and Catherine Y. Co (2000), 'The effects of environmental regulations on foreign direct investment', *Journal of Environmental Economics and Management*, **40**, 1–20.

List, John A. and Shelby Gerking (2000), 'Regulatory federalism and U.S. environmental policies', *Journal of Regional Science*, **40**, 453–71.

List, John A. and Mitch Kunce (2000), 'Environmental protection and economic growth: what do the residuals tell us?' *Land Economics*, **76**, 267–82.

List, John A. and Charles F. Mason (forthcoming), 'Optimal institutional arrangements for transboundary pollutants in a second-best world: evidence from a differential game with asymmetric players', *Journal of Environmental Economics and Management*.

List, John A., W. Warren McHone and Daniel L. Millimet (2001), 'Effects of Air Quality Regulation on the Destination Choice of Relocating Plants', working draft.

List, John A., Erwin H. Bulte and Jason F. Shogren (forthcoming), 'Beggar thy neighbor: testing for free-riding in state-level endangered species expenditures', *Public Choice*.

McConnell, Virginia D. and Robert M. Schwab (1990), 'The impact of environmental regulation on industry location decisions: the motor vehicle industry', *Land Economics*, **66**, 67–81.

Millimet, Daniel L. (April 2000), 'Assessing the Empirical Impact of Environmental Federalism', unpublished paper.

Oates, Wallace E. (1972), *Fiscal Federalism*, New York: Harcourt Brace Jovanovich.

Oates, Wallace E. (1997), 'On the welfare gains from fiscal decentralization', *Journal of Public Finance and Public Choice*, **2** (3), 83–92.

Oates, Wallace E. (1999), 'An essay on fiscal federalism', *Journal of Economic Literature*, **37**, 1120–49.

Oates, Wallace E. and Robert M. Schwab (1988), 'Economic competition among jurisdictions: efficiency-enhancing or distortion-inducing?', *Journal of Public Economics*, **35**, 333–54.

Oates, Wallace E. and Robert M. Schwab (1991), 'The Allocative and Distributive Implications of Local Fiscal Competition', in D. Kenyon and J. Kincaid (eds), *Competition Among States and Local Governments*, Washington, DC: The Urban Institute, pp. 127–45.

Oates, Wallace E. and Robert M. Schwab (1996), 'The Theory of Regulatory Federalism', in W. Oates, *The Economics of Environmental Regulation*, Cheltenham, UK and Brookfield, US: Edward Elgar, pp. 319–31.

Parry, Ian W.H. (2001), 'How Large Are the Welfare Costs of Tax Competition?', Resources for the Future, Discussion Paper 01–28.

Revesz, Richard L. (1992), 'Rehabilitating interstate competition: rethinking the "race-to-the-bottom" rationale for Federal environmental regulation', *New York University Law Review*, **67**, 1210–54.

Revesz, Richard L. (1996), 'Federalism and interstate environmental externalities', *University of Pennsylvania Law Review*, **144**, 2341–416.

Rivlin, Alice M. (1992), *Reviving the American Dream: The Economy, the States, and the Federal Government*, Washington, DC: Brookings Institution.

Steinzor, Rena I. (2000), 'Devolution and the public health', *Harvard Environmental Law Review*, **24**, 351–463.

Tobey, James A. (1990), 'The effects of domestic environmental policies on patterns of world trade: an empirical test', *Kyklos*, **43**, 191–209.

Ulph, Alistair M. (1999), *Trade and the Environment: Selected Essays of Alistair M. Ulph*, Cheltenham, UK and Lyme, US: Edward Elgar.

Wellisch, Dietmar (2000), *Theory of Public Finance in a Federal State*, Cambridge: Cambridge University Press.

Wildasin, David (1989), 'Interjurisdictional capital mobility: fiscal externality and a corrective subsidy,' *Journal of Urban Economics*, **25**, 193–212.

Wilson, John D. (1986), 'A theory of interregional tax competition', *Journal of Urban Economics*, **19**, 296–315.

Wilson, John D. (1996), 'Capital Mobility and Environmental Standards: Is There a Theoretical Basis for a Race to the Bottom?', in J. Bhagwati and R. Hudec (eds), *Harmonization and Fair Trade*, Vol. 1, Cambridge, Mass.: MIT Press, pp. 395–427.

Wilson, John D. (1999), 'Theories of tax competition', *National Tax Journal*, **52**, 269–304.

Zodrow, George and Peter Mieszkowski (1986), 'Pigou, Tiebout, property taxation, and the underprovision of local public goods', *Journal of Urban Economics*, **19**, 356–70.

2. Global environmental governance, political lobbying and transboundary pollution

Surjinder Johal and Alistair Ulph

1. INTRODUCTION

Recent 'anti-globalization' protests have focused on the perceived harmful effects of globalization, especially on the global environment. One aspect of this concern is that in a more competitive global market, nation states, acting independently, may engage in a 'race-to-the-bottom' in setting weak environmental standards in order to gain a strategic trade advantage, and in particular to respond to possible threats of delocation by transnational companies. Another reason why nation states acting independently may set environmental standards which are too weak from a global perspective is that they may be dealing with transboundary or global pollution. In both cases, to counter such weak standards, it is argued that environmental policies of nation states should be coordinated at a supranational level, perhaps through bodies such as the WTO or the proposed World Environmental Organisation (WEO). But this in turn raises concerns, also expressed in the protests, about the way such supranational agencies operate. First there is a concern that supranational bodies may not be as well informed about environmental conditions in different states as national governments. Second there is a concern that there is a 'democratic deficit' in decision making at the supranational level, with bodies such as the WTO being unaccountable and prone to being captured by special interests of transnational companies or northern governments, rather than by environmentalists or southern governments. The protests can thus be seen as a sign of frustration arising from the realization of a need to move international environmental governance beyond the nation state level, but with a distrust of the existing supranational agencies that might accomplish this.

In a previous paper, Johal and Ulph (2001b), we addressed the question whether deficiencies in political processes at the supranational level were sufficient to call into question the desirability of coordinating environmental policy at the supranational level. To answer the question we set up a model in which there was strategic environmental policy competition between nation states, policy could be set at national or supranational level, there was asymmetric information about environmental damage costs between state governments and the supranational agency, and both state governments and the supranational agency could be influenced by lobbying activities by both environmental and industrial special interest groups. By allowing for asymmetries in lobbying costs, we could vary the level of political influence between national and supranational levels (the 'democratic deficit' problem), between different nation states (the 'North–South divide') and between environmentalists and industrialists ('producer bias'). We analysed what effect these biases might have, and showed they were not always straightforward (for example, environmentalists might be better off with a democratic deficit, the South could be better off with less influence). More importantly we showed that no matter what asymmetries in political influence there might be, all parties were always better off when policy was set at the supranational level.

However, in Johal and Ulph (2001b) the only rationale for wanting to coordinate environmental policy at the supranational level was to overcome strategic trade considerations. In this chapter we extend that model to also allow for transboundary pollution. We show that transboundary pollution increases the extent of political lobbying and magnifies the effects of the various asymmetries in lobbying costs. However, it only changes a couple of our previous results: at high levels of transboundary pollution environmental groups are made worse off by a democratic deficit, and net welfare falls if there is producer bias. Our main result – that supranational coordination of environmental policy is desirable despite asymmetries in political influence – is strengthened by the introduction of transboundary pollution.

2.   THE MODEL

2.1.   The Economic Setting

We consider a partial equilibrium model of an industry with two identical firms each located in a different state, denoted $i = 1, 2$. These two states form a federation. The two firms produce a good, which is sold outside the two states. Firm i has total revenue and cost functions: $R(x_i, x_j)$, $C(x_i)$ respectively, with standard properties. The production of the good causes emissions of a pollutant. These emissions can be abated but only at a cost. By appropriate choice of units, emissions by firm i are: $x_i - a_i$ where a_i is its abatement level; total abatement costs are the strictly convex function $A(a_i)$. The only instrument available to control pollution by each firm is an emission limit, denoted e_i. Firm i takes as given its emission limit and the output of the other firm and chooses its own output (Cournot competition) and abatement to maximize profits, net of abatement costs: $\pi(x_i, x_j, e_i) \equiv R(x_i, x_j) - C(x_i) - A(x_i - e_i)$. Assuming that both emission limits bite, the resulting equilibrium profit function for firm i is denoted $\Pi(e_i, e_j)$.

Unabated emissions cause environmental damage in both states. Total pollution, T_i, in state i consists of domestic emissions plus some proportion $\alpha \in (0,1)$ of the other state's emissions: $T_i = e_i + \alpha e_j$. $\alpha = 0$ corresponds to the non-transboundary pollution case considered in Johal and Ulph (2001b), while $\alpha = 1$ would correspond to a global pollutant like CO_2. The value of α is common to both states and is public information. The damage cost function in state i is denoted $\delta_i D(T_i)$ where δ_i is a parameter and D is a strictly convex function. Welfare in state i is given by

$$W(e_i, e_j, \delta_i) \equiv \Pi(e_i, e_j) - \delta_i D(T_i).$$

To capture asymmetries of information between state and federal level, we suppose that the damage cost parameter, δ_i, in each state is known only to the state government in power.[1] To keep things simple, we suppose that in state $i = 1, 2$, δ_i can take one of only two values, δ_L and δ_H, $\delta_L < \delta_H$, with probabilities p and $1 - p$ respectively, independent of what happens to damages in the other state. Note that this implies that, *ex ante*, both states are identical. We denote the expected value of damage costs by $\bar{\delta} \equiv p\delta_L + (1-p)\delta_H$.

2.2. The Political Setting

In each country there is an environmental lobby group and an industrial lobby group; we denote the environmental lobby groups in states 1 and 2 by $g = 1, 2$, respectively, and the industrial lobby groups in states 1 and 2 by $g = 3, 4$, respectively. The two types of lobby group are distinguished by the importance they attach to environmental damage. This is represented by a parameter in the utility function γ, which can take two values. Environmentalists attach greater weight to environmental damage than in the welfare function ($\gamma_g = \gamma_H > 1$, $g = 1, 2$) whilst industrialists attach less weight than it has in the welfare function[2] ($\gamma_g = \gamma_L < 1$, $g = 3, 4$). The utility of group g in state i is given by

$$U(e_i, e_j, \delta_i, \gamma_g) \equiv \Pi(e_i, e_j) - \gamma_g \delta_i D(T_i).$$

Elections are held to elect the policymakers in both states and at the federal level[3] and electoral competition takes place between two parties that are representatives of the interests of the lobby groups.[4] It follows that the policymaker will be biased towards greater or less environmental protection than represented in the welfare function. So, state government i will set its policy to maximize its 'utility function'

$$U(e_i, e_j, \delta_i, \gamma_i) \equiv \Pi(e_i, e_j) - \gamma_i \delta_i D(T_i),$$

where once again γ_i can be either high or low depending on whether the government of state i is environmentally or industrially biased. Similarly, a federal government will set policy using its utility function

$$U_F(e_1, e_2, \delta_1, \delta_2, \gamma_F) = \Pi(e_1, e_2) + \Pi(e_2, e_1) - \gamma_F[\delta_1 D(T_1) + \delta_2 D(T_2)].$$

Whether the outcome of an election produces an environmental or industrial government is a random process, but the probability of electing, say, an environmental government is influenced by the amount of lobbying done in each election by each special interest group. We assume that each group can lobby in each election, but the environmental special interest groups lobby only for an environmental government and similarly for industrial special interest groups. Groups choose their lobbying effort to maximize their expected utility net of the costs of lobbying. We shall need to distinguish between *gross* and *net* utilities of special interest groups, where net utilities are gross utilities minus the costs of lobbying. In a similar way we shall distinguish between gross and net welfares of states.

To complete our broad description of the model, we assume that prior to any of the above activity taking place there will be a *constitutional* decision about whether environmental policy should be set at the state level, in which case policy will be set by the state governments acting independently to maximize utility, so we will have a non-cooperative equilibrium and environmental dumping; or whether it is to be set at the federal level, in which case the federal government acts to maximize its utility, but there will be no environmental dumping. This constitutional decision will be based on the expected *welfare* which each state expects to derive from the subsequent political process. We assume that policy will only be set at the federal level if both states derive higher expected net welfare from this constitutional choice.[5]

2.3.   The Game

Formally we have a six-stage game: in stage 1 there is a constitutional choice whether to set policy at state or federal level; in stage 2, lobby groups decide how much lobbying effort to undertake in each election; in stage 3 elections are held; in stage 4 state governments learn their true damage costs; in stage 5 either state or federal governments set emission limits; finally in stage 6 firms set their levels of output and abatement. We now describe each stage in more detail.

2.3.1.   Stage 6: Firms choose outputs and abatement

Firm i takes as given its emission limit, e_i, and the output of the other firm, x_j, and chooses its own output, x_i, and hence abatement, $a_i = x_i - e_i$, to maximize profits, net of abatement costs: $\pi(x_i, \ x_j, \ e_i) \equiv R(x_i, x_j) - C(x_i) - A(x_i - e_i)$. The first-order condition is: $R_1 - C' - A' = 0$, that is marginal revenue equals marginal cost plus marginal abatement cost. Solving the pair of first-order conditions for the two firms yields the equilibrium outputs $X(e_i, e_j), j = 1, 2, i \neq j$, and substituting back into the profit function yields the equilibrium profit function $\Pi(e_i, e_j)$. From the equilibrium profit function we can derive the equilibrium (gross) welfare function for each state $W(e_i, e_j, \delta_i) \equiv \Pi(e_i, e_j) - \delta_i D(T_i)$. Similarly, it is possible to define the equilibrium (gross) utility functions for each interest group: $U(e_i, e_j, \delta_i, \gamma_g) \equiv \Pi(e_i, e_j) - \gamma_g \delta_i D(T_i)$ and for each government; these have similar properties to the equilibrium welfare function.

2.3.2.   Stages 4 and 5: State governments learn damage costs and set emission limits

We take these stages together since at the end of stage 4 each state government knows only its own damage cost parameter δ_i and this affects how governments set their emission limits. We consider separately the cases where policy is set at the state and federal levels.

Policy set at the state level   For any given configuration of government types $\tilde{\Gamma}_s$, $s = 1, \ldots, 4$ the emission limits in the two states are set as the equilibrium of a Nash game in which each state government knows its own damage costs but not those of its rival. So each state has to take as given the emission limits set by the other state depending on whether it has high or low damage costs. This means there are four equilibrium emission limits to be determined: $\tilde{e}_1(\tilde{\Gamma}_s, \delta_L)$, $\tilde{e}_1(\tilde{\Gamma}_s, \delta_H)$, $\tilde{e}_2(\tilde{\Gamma}_s, \delta_L)$, $\tilde{e}_2(\tilde{\Gamma}_s, \delta_H)$, and correspondingly four first-order conditions to determine them. For example, if state 1 has low damage costs, it will take as given the low damage cost and high damage cost emission limits of state 2 and choose $\tilde{e}_1(\tilde{\Gamma}_s, \delta_L)$ to maximize expected utility:

$$pU[\tilde{e}_1(\tilde{\Gamma}_s, \delta_L), \tilde{e}_2(\tilde{\Gamma}_s, \delta_L), \delta_L, \gamma_1] + (1-p)U[\tilde{e}_1(\tilde{\Gamma}_s, \delta_L), \tilde{e}_2(\tilde{\Gamma}_s, \delta_H), \delta_L, \gamma_1].$$

There will be three other similar first-order conditions: for state 1 with high damage costs, state 2 with low damage costs and state 2 with high damage costs.

Knowing the four equilibrium emission limits we can now calculate for configuration s expected (gross) welfare of each state i, $\tilde{W}_{is}$, and expected (gross) utility for each group g, $\tilde{U}_{gs}$. For example, for environmentalists in state 1, we have:[6]

$$\tilde{U}_{1s} = p\tilde{U}_{1s}(\delta_L) + (1-p)\tilde{U}_{1s}(\delta_H)$$

Policy set at the federal level   For any configuration of three government types, $\hat{\Gamma}_f$, $f=1,\ldots,8$, the federal government needs to provide incentives for the state governments to reveal their private information. These incentives consist of both the choice of emission limits and the use of financial transfers, M. We assume that there is a cost of raising public funds to pay these transfers such that to raise 1 unit of the numeraire for public funds costs $(1+\sigma)$ units. Thus the federal government solves a standard mechanism design problem in which it asks state governments to announce their damage cost parameters, and depending on their announcements it will set each state an emission limit and a financial transfer. These are chosen to maximize the expected utility of the federal government, net of the cost of raising public funds, subject to both a set of incentive compatibility constraints to ensure the state governments reveal their true damage costs, and a set of individual rationality constraints so that no state government with its given political weight and damage cost parameter would be worse off than in the case where environmental policy was set at the state level. It is because these incentive compatibility constraints and individual rationality constraints are expressed in terms of the utilities of the state governments, and hence depend on the type of state governments elected, that the choice of emission limits depends on the types of all governments, and not just on the type of the federal government.

Formally, the federal government must choose the set of policy instruments[7]: $\hat{e}_{LL}^1$, $\hat{e}_{LH}^1$, $\hat{e}_{HL}^1$, $\hat{e}_{HH}^1$, $\hat{e}_{LL}^2$, $\hat{e}_{LH}^2$, $\hat{e}_{HL}^2$, $\hat{e}_{HH}^2$, M_L^1, M_H^1, M_L^2, M_H^2, to maximize:

$$\begin{aligned}
&p^2[U(\hat{e}_{LL}^1, \hat{e}_{LL}^2, \delta_L, \gamma_F) + M_L^1 + U(\hat{e}_{LL}^2, \hat{e}_{LL}^1, \delta_L, \gamma_F) + M_L^2] \\
&+ p(1-p)\,[U(\hat{e}_{LH}^1, \hat{e}_{HL}^2, \delta_L, \gamma_F) + M_L^1 + U(\hat{e}_{HL}^2, \hat{e}_{LH}^1, \delta_H, \gamma_F) + M_H^2] \\
&+ p(1-p)\,[U(\hat{e}_{HL}^1, \hat{e}_{LH}^2, \delta_H, \gamma_F) + M_H^1 + U(\hat{e}_{LH}^2, \hat{e}_{HL}^1, \delta_L, \gamma_F) + M_L^2] \\
&+ (1-p)^2\,[U(\hat{e}_{HH}^1, \hat{e}_{HH}^2, \delta_H, \gamma_F) + M_H^1 + U(\hat{e}_{HH}^2, \hat{e}_{HH}^1, \delta_H, \gamma_F) + M_H^2] \\
&- (1+\sigma)\,[pM_L^1 + (1-p)\,M_H^1 + pM_L^2 + (1-p)\,M_H^2]
\end{aligned}$$

subject to the incentive compatibility constraints:

$$pU(\hat{e}^1_{LL}, \hat{e}^2_{LL}, \delta_L, \gamma_1) + (1-p)U(\hat{e}^1_{LH}, \hat{e}^2_{HL}, \delta_L, \gamma_1) + M^1_L \geq$$
$$pU(\hat{e}^1_{HL}, \hat{e}^2_{LH}, \delta_L, \gamma_1) + (1-p)U(\hat{e}^1_{HH}, \hat{e}^2_{HH}, \delta_L, \gamma_1) + M^1_H \quad (2.1a)$$

$$pU(\hat{e}^1_{HL}, \hat{e}^2_{LH}, \delta_H, \gamma_1) + (1-p)U(\hat{e}^1_{HH}, \hat{e}^2_{HH}, \delta_H, \gamma_1) + M^1_H \geq$$
$$pU(\hat{e}^1_{LL}, \hat{e}^2_{LL}, \delta_H, \gamma_1) + (1-p)U(\hat{e}^1_{LH}, \hat{e}^2_{HL}, \delta_H, \gamma_1) + M^1_L \quad (2.1b)$$

$$pU(\hat{e}^2_{LL}, \hat{e}^1_{LL}, \delta_L, \gamma_2) + (1-p)U(\hat{e}^2_{LH}, \hat{e}^1_{HL}, \delta_L, \gamma_2) + M^2_L \geq$$
$$pU(\hat{e}^2_{HL}, \hat{e}^1_{LH}, \delta_L, \gamma_2) + (1-p)U(\hat{e}^2_{HH}, \hat{e}^1_{HH}, \delta_L, \gamma_2) + M^2_H \quad (2.1c)$$

$$pU(\hat{e}^2_{HL}, \hat{e}^1_{LH}, \delta_H, \gamma_2) + (1-p)U(\hat{e}^2_{HH}, \hat{e}^1_{HH}, \delta_H, \gamma_2) + M^2_H \geq$$
$$pU(\hat{e}^2_{LL}, \hat{e}^1_{LL}, \delta_H, \gamma_2) + (1-p)U(\hat{e}^2_{LH}, \hat{e}^1_{HL}, \delta_H, \gamma_2) + M^2_L \quad (2.1d)$$

and the individual rationality constraints:[8]

$$pU(\hat{e}^1_{LL}, \hat{e}^2_{LL}, \delta_L, \gamma_1) + (1-p)U(\hat{e}^1_{LH}, \hat{e}^2_{HL}, \delta_L, \gamma_1) +$$
$$M^1_L \geq \tilde{U}_{1s}(\delta_L) \quad (2.2a)$$

$$pU(\hat{e}^1_{LH}, \hat{e}^2_{HL}, \delta_H, \gamma_1) + (1-p)U(\hat{e}^1_{HH}, \hat{e}^2_{HH}, \delta_H, \gamma_1) +$$
$$M^1_H \geq \tilde{U}_{1s}(\delta_H) \quad (2.2b)$$

$$pU(\hat{e}^2_{LL}, \hat{e}^1_{LL}, \delta_L, \gamma_2) + (1-p)U(\hat{e}^2_{LH}, \hat{e}^1_{HL}, \delta_L, \gamma_2) +$$
$$M^2_L \geq \tilde{U}_{2s}(\delta_L) \quad (2.2c)$$

$$pU(\hat{e}^2_{HL}, \hat{e}^1_{LH}, \delta_H, \gamma_2) + (1-p)U(\hat{e}^2_{HH}, \hat{e}^1_{HH}, \delta_H, \gamma_2) +$$
$$M^2_H \geq \tilde{U}_{2s}(\delta_H) \quad (2.2d)$$

The utilities on the right-hand side of the individual rationality constraints are derived from the solution to the model when policy is set at the state level as set out in section 2.3.1 above; the configuration $\tilde{\Gamma}_s$ of types of state governments whose utilities are used on the RHS of equation (2.2) is the same as the configuration of state government types found in configuration $\hat{\Gamma}_f$ for which the mechanism design problem is being solved.

Incentive compatibility constraints (2.1a) and (2.1b) are for state 1 with low and high damage costs respectively, while (2.1c) and (2.1d) are for state 2 with low and high damage costs respectively. Similarly individual rationality constraints (2.2a) and (2.2b) are for state 1 with low and high damage costs, while (2.2c) and (2.2d) are for state 2 with low and high damage costs respectively.

So for any configuration of government types, f, we solve the mechanism design problem above. We can then calculate expected welfare for each state $i = 1, 2, \hat{W}_{if}$, and expected utility for each group $g = 1,...,4, \hat{U}_{gf}$. The calculation of the expressions is straightforward, but we omit the details because they are cumbersome to write out.

2.3.3. Stage 3: Elections

Let x_{gi} be the amount of lobbying done by group g in election $i = 1, 2, F$, and assume that the probability of electing an environmental government in election i is given by:

$$q_i = \frac{1 + x_{1i} + x_{2i}}{2 + X_i} \qquad \text{where } X_i = \sum_{g=1}^{g=4} x_{gi} \qquad (2.3)$$

Note that in the absence of lobbying the probability of electing an environmental government is 0.5. It is straightforward to show that that $0 < q_i < 1$ and that:

$$\frac{\partial q_i}{\partial x_{gi}} = \frac{(1 - q_i)}{(2 + X_i)}; \qquad \frac{\partial^2 q_i}{\partial x_{gi}^2} = -\frac{2(1 - q_i)}{(2 + X_i)^2}; \qquad g = 1, 2,$$

$$\frac{\partial q_i}{\partial x_{gi}} = -\frac{q_i}{(2 + X_i)}; \qquad \frac{\partial^2 q_i}{\partial x_{gi}^2} = \frac{2q_i}{(2 + X_i)^2}; \qquad g = 3, 4.$$

So q_i is an increasing, concave function of lobbying efforts by environmental groups and a decreasing convex function of lobbying efforts by industrial groups.

If policy is set at the state level, then, from the earlier stages of the game there will be four possible configurations of state government types, $\hat{\Gamma}_s$, each with probability $\hat{Q}_s$, $s = 1,...,4$. For each such a configuration, the previous section allows us to calculate expected (gross) welfares and utilities $\tilde{W}_{is}, \tilde{U}_{gs}$. So we can now take expectations over all possible configurations $\hat{\Gamma}_s$ to derive the expected gross welfare and utility for each state and group as:

$$\tilde{W}_i = \sum_{s=1}^{s=4} \tilde{Q}_s \tilde{W}_{is}; \qquad \tilde{U}_g = \sum_{s=1}^{s=4} \tilde{Q}_s \tilde{U}_{gs}$$

Similarly, if policy is set at the federal level we can calculate expected (gross) welfares and utilities across all configurations $\hat{\Gamma}_f, f = 1,..., 8$:

$$\hat{W}_i = \sum_{f=1}^{f=8} \hat{Q}_f \hat{W}_{if}; \qquad \hat{U}_g = \sum_{f=1}^{f=8} \hat{Q}_f \hat{U}_{gf}$$

2.3.4. Stage 2: Lobbying

Assume that if group g expends lobbying effort x_{gi} in election i then it incurs a cost $0.5\mu_{gi} \cdot (x_{gi})^2$ where μ_{gi} is a parameter which, as we shall see, can be varied to allow for the three asymmetries referred to in the introduction. We now determine the levels of lobbying effort by each special interest group in each election, and hence the probabilities of different types of government being elected.

Policy set at state level   It is clear that since the type of federal government has no influence on utilities or welfare, and since lobbying is costly, each interest group g will not lobby at the federal level. Denote by $\tilde{x} = (\tilde{x}_{11}, \tilde{x}_{12}, \ldots, \tilde{x}_{41}, \tilde{x}_{42})$ the vector of eight lobbying efforts $\tilde{x}_{gi}$ by interest group $g = 1, \ldots, 4$ in the election in state $i = 1, 2$. Denote by $\tilde{Q}_s(\tilde{x})$ the probability of electing configuration $\tilde{\Gamma}_s$ of state governments, given $\tilde{x}$. Then each special interest group will take as given the lobbying efforts by all other groups and choose $\tilde{x}_{g1}$ and $\tilde{x}_{g2}$ to maximize

$$\sum_{s=1}^{s=4} \tilde{Q}_s(\tilde{x})\tilde{U}_{gs} - \sum_{i=1}^{i=2} [0.5\mu_{gi}(\tilde{x}_{gi}^2)].$$

There will be eight first-order conditions, where for example the first-order condition for $\tilde{x}_{g1}$ is:

$$\{\tilde{q}_2(\tilde{x})(\tilde{U}_{g1} - \tilde{U}_{g3}) + [1 - \tilde{q}_2(\tilde{x})](\tilde{U}_{g2} - \tilde{U}_{g4})\}\frac{\partial \tilde{q}_1}{\partial \tilde{x}_{g1}} = \mu_{g1}\tilde{x}_{g1} \qquad (2.4)$$

(2.4) has a standard interpretation. The RHS is the marginal cost of lobbying by group g in state 1 and the LHS is the marginal benefit, where the term in square brackets is the difference in expected utility to group g from having an environmental rather than industrial government in state 1, and the remaining term is just the marginal effect on the probability of having an environmental government elected in state 1 from a bit more lobbying by group g. $\tilde{x}$ is the solution to the eight first-order conditions (4). Define equilibrium lobbying costs as $\tilde{K}_g(\tilde{x}) \equiv \sum_{i=1}^{i=2} 0.5\mu_{gi}(\tilde{x}_{gi})^2$. We can now establish the equilibrium levels of *gross* utility for each interest group and *gross* welfare for each state:

$$\tilde{U}_g^G = \sum_{s=1}^{s=4} \tilde{Q}_s(\tilde{x})\tilde{U}_{gs}, \qquad g = 1, \ldots, 4,$$

$$\tilde{W}_i^G = \sum_{s=1}^{s=4} \tilde{Q}_s(\tilde{x})\tilde{W}_{is}, \qquad i = 1, 2.$$

Similarly, equilibrium levels of *net* utility for each group and *net* welfare for each state are

$$\tilde{U}_g^N = \tilde{U}_g^G - \tilde{K}_g(\tilde{x}), \qquad g = 1,\dots,4.$$

$$\tilde{W}_i^N = \tilde{W}_i^G - \Sigma_g \tilde{K}_g(\tilde{x}), \qquad \text{for } i=1, g=1, 3; \text{ for } i=2, g=2, 4.$$

Policy set at the federal level We proceed in a similar way when policy is set at the federal level. $\hat{x} = (\hat{x}_{gi})$ is the vector of lobbying efforts by groups $g = 1, \dots, 4$ in elections $i = 1, 2, F$. $\hat{Q}_f(\hat{x})$ is the probability of electing configuration $\hat{\Gamma}_f$, $f = 1,\dots,8$ of government types given lobbying efforts $\hat{x}$. Interest group g takes as given the lobbying efforts by all other groups and chooses $\hat{x}_{g1}$, $\hat{x}_{g2}$ and $\hat{x}_{gF}$ to maximize

$$\sum_{f=1}^{f=8} \hat{Q}_f(\hat{x})\hat{U}_{gf} - \sum_{i=1}^{i=F} 0.5\mu_{gi}(\hat{x}_{gi}^2).$$

There will be 12 first-order conditions to determine $\hat{x}$ where, for example, the first-order condition for $\hat{x}_{gF}$ is:

$$\mu_{gF}\hat{x}_{gF} = \frac{\partial \tilde{q}_F(\hat{x})}{\partial \hat{x}_{gF}} \{\hat{q}_1\hat{q}_2(\hat{U}_{g1} - \hat{U}_{g5}) + \hat{q}_1(1-\hat{q}_2)(\hat{U}_{g2} - \hat{U}_{g6}) +$$

$$(1 - \hat{q}_1)\hat{q}_2(\hat{U}_{g3} - \hat{U}_{g7}) + (1 - \hat{q}_1)(1-\hat{q}_2)(\hat{U}_{g4} - \hat{U}_{g8})\} \qquad (2.5)$$

Equation (2.5) has exactly the same interpretation as equation (2.4). We solve these 12 first-order conditions simultaneously to determine the equilibrium vector of lobbying effort $\hat{x}$. Then define equilibrium lobbying costs for each group by $\hat{K}_g(\hat{x}) \equiv \Sigma_{i=1}^{i=F} 0.5\mu_{gi}(\hat{x}_{gi})^2$.

The equilibrium levels of *gross* utility for each interest group and *gross* welfare for each state are

$$\hat{U}_g^G = \Sigma_{f=1}^{f=8} \hat{Q}_f(\hat{x})\hat{U}_{gf}, \qquad g = 1,\dots,4,$$

$$\hat{W}_i^G = \Sigma_{f=1}^{f=8} \hat{Q}_f(\hat{x})\hat{W}_{if}, \qquad i = 1, 2,$$

and the equilibrium levels of *net* utility for each group and *net* welfare for each state are

$$\hat{U}_g^N = \hat{U}_g^G - \hat{K}_g(\hat{x}), \qquad g = 1, \dots, 4,$$

$$\hat{W}_i^N = \hat{W}_i^G - \Sigma_g \hat{K}_g(\hat{x}), \qquad \text{for } i=1, g=1, 3; \text{ for } i=2, g=2, 4.$$

2.3.5. Stage 1: Constitutional choice

States will only agree to yield environmental policy to a federal body if neither expects to be made worse off, that is iff $\hat{W}_i^N \geq \tilde{W}_i^N$. Furthermore this inequality is strict for at least one state, meaning that at least one state expects to be made better off. Note that the *ex post* individual rationality constraints defined in (2.2) do not guarantee that these *ex ante* individual rationality constraints will be satisfied, because the *ex post* constraints are expressed in terms of government utility, while the *ex ante* constraints are expressed in terms of expected welfare.

Given the complexity of this six-stage game it has not been possible to address the questions we posed in the introduction analytically, so in the next section we set out a special case of this model, for which we then report numerical results.

3.   A SPECIAL CASE

In this section we set out a special case of the model, extending the special case used in Ulph (1997) by allowing for transboundary pollution. In that model, the two firms produce a homogenous good and face a linear inverse demand function with intercept A and unit slope. There are no costs of production but there are quadratic abatement costs, $0.5a^2$ and the damage cost is a quadratic function of total pollution: $D(T_i) = 0.5(e_i + \alpha e_j)^2$. It is then straightforward to show that utility for state i is:

$$U(e_i, e_j, \delta_i, \gamma_i) = 3(2A - e_j)^2 + 18e_i(2A - e_j) - 37e_i^2 - 64\delta_i\gamma_i(e_i + \alpha e_j)^2 \tag{2.6}$$

We can use this formulation to calculate emission levels when policy is set at the state or federal levels. It is possible to derive explicitly the emission limits for the state case but not so for the federal case. However, what we are interested in is not emission limits for each configuration of government types but rather expected welfare and utilities over *all* configurations of government types. We now describe how we set the various parameters of our model.

3.1.   Choice of Parameter Values

There are five key parameters in our model, $\bar{\delta}$, γ, ν, μ and α. We use three values of expected damage costs, $\bar{\delta} = 0.1$, 0.3 and 0.5, implying that in a completely unregulated economy, expected pollution damage costs would lie between 7.5 percent and 37.5 percent of GNP. For the measure of dispersion in damage costs, v, and the dispersion in political weights, λ, we use the values 0.25, 0.5 and 0.75. The final figure, say in the case of v, implies that damage costs in the high cost country are seven times greater than in the low cost country.[9] The main qualitative results reported are not sensitive to variations in parameter values, so we report detailed results only for the mid-point case where $\bar{\delta} = 0.3$, $v = 0.5$, and $\lambda = 0.5$ and indicate which results do not carry over to other parameter values.[10] For the cost of lobbying parameter we have chosen the two values $\mu = 1$ and $\mu = 10$. By varying these we can capture the asymmetries of influence which are the focus of the chapter. The parameter reflecting transboundary pollution, α, takes values 0, 0.2, 0.4, 0.6, 0.8 and 1. The first of these corresponds to Johal and Ulph (2001b), the last reflects the 'global warming' scenario.[11]

3.2. Interpreting the Results of the Numerical Experiments

In Tables 2.1 to 2.5 we present results for a number of 'experiments' using different assumptions about lobbying costs for the central case set of parameters: $\bar{\delta} = 0.3$; $v = \lambda = 0.5$. For each experiment, whether policy is set at the state or federal level, we present the following results: the equilibrium lobbying efforts by the four interest groups, x11,...,x4F; the equilibrium probabilities of electing a green government in each election: q1,...,qF; the gross and net expected utilities for each group, gu1,...,gu4, nu1,...,nu4; and the gross and net welfares for each state, gw1, gw2, nw1, nw2.

The effects of variations in lobbying costs on net utilities and welfare can briefly be described as follows. Changes in lobbying costs will affect lobbying effort. This in turn will affect the probabilities of different configurations of government types, and consequently, expected gross utility and welfare. Combining these various effects enables us to calculate the changes on expected net utilities and welfare.

When changes in lobbying costs affect only some groups, the changes in lobbying behaviour will have a *direct effect* on the behaviour of groups whose costs have changed, and an *indirect strategic effect* on the response of other groups. In simple terms we could say it depends on whether lobbying efforts by different groups are strategic substitutes or strategic complements.

In terms of expected utilities there are going to be two types of effects.[12] First, for a given level of output by the rival producer, an interest group is going to be better off with a government of its own type setting environmental policy, at both the state and federal level. Second, though, there are the effects of strategic competition. When policy is set at the state level, profits are always higher when the other state's government is environmental. The simple reason is that an environmental government will restrict the

Table 2.1 (a) Low-cost symmetric case at state level (Experiment 1)

Alpha	0.0	0.2	0.4	0.6	0.8	1
x11	1.313	1.063	0.530	0.000	0.000	0.000
x21	4.567	5.694	7.110	8.678	10.119	11.713
x31	3.436	4.303	5.217	6.197	7.257	8.436
x41	0.000	0.000	0.000	0.000	0.000	0.000
x12	4.567	5.694	7.110	8.678	10.119	11.713
x22	1.313	1.063	0.530	0.000	0.000	0.000
x32	0.000	0.000	0.000	0.000	0.000	0.000
x42	3.436	4.303	5.217	6.197	7.257	8.436
q1	0.608	0.594	0.582	0.574	0.574	0.574
q2	0.608	0.594	0.582	0.574	0.574	0.574
gu1	1245.572	1186.289	1122.337	1055.981	990.087	922.200
gu2	1245.572	1186.289	1122.337	1055.981	990.087	922.200
gu3	1381.891	1363.800	1342.360	1318.620	1293.572	1266.213
gu4	1381.891	1363.800	1342.360	1318.620	1293.572	1266.213
nu1	1234.280	1169.513	1096.919	1018.324	938.890	853.604
nu2	1234.280	1169.513	1096.919	1018.324	938.890	853.604
nu3	1375.989	1354.543	1328.750	1299.416	1267.240	1230.630
nu4	1375.989	1354.543	1328.750	1299.416	1267.240	1230.630
gw1	1313.732	1275.044	1232.349	1187.300	1141.830	1094.206
gw2	1313.732	1275.044	1232.349	1187.300	1141.830	1094.206
nw1	1296.538	1249.012	1193.320	1130.439	1064.301	990.028
nw2	1296.538	1249.012	1193.320	1130.439	1064.301	990.028

rival firm's output, allowing the domestic firm to expand its output. Moreover, having two environmental governments may be better than two industrial governments if the environmental governments set emission limits which take outputs closer to the level which maximizes joint profits. Differences in state government types are obviously less important when policy is set at the federal level, but they do have some influence through the impact of the incentive compatibility and individual rationality constraints. Of course having policy set at the federal level eliminates environmental dumping, which is harmful not just to the environment, but also to profits, since it leads to too much output being produced.

The major effect of introducing transboundary pollution will be that for any given level of emissions, while profits remain unchanged, *total* pollution in each state will be higher the greater is the extent of transboundary pollution. This will make all groups worse off. Since environmental groups

Table 2.1 (b)   Low-cost symmetric case at federal level (Experiment 1)

Alpha	0	0.2	0.4	0.6	0.8	1
x11	0.000	0.000	0.000	0.000	0.000	0.000
x21	3.656	4.725	5.794	6.907	8.043	9.168
x31	4.081	5.157	6.183	7.213	8.229	9.173
x41	0.000	0.000	0.000	0.000	0.000	0.000
x12	3.656	4.725	5.794	6.907	8.043	9.175
x22	0.000	0.000	0.000	0.000	0.000	0.000
x32	0.000	0.000	0.000	0.000	0.000	0.000
x42	4.081	5.157	6.183	7.213	8.229	9.180
x1F	1.173	1.522	1.845	2.136	2.368	2.364
x2F	1.173	1.522	1.845	2.136	2.366	2.315
x3F	0.990	1.206	1.361	1.454	1.385	0.990
x4F	0.990	1.206	1.361	1.454	1.387	1.080
q1	0.478	0.482	0.486	0.490	0.495	0.500
q2	0.478	0.482	0.486	0.490	0.495	0.500
qF	0.529	0.542	0.557	0.574	0.603	0.649
gu1	1372.190	1344.065	1318.279	1295.193	1275.000	1252.519
gu2	1372.190	1344.064	1318.278	1295.192	1274.981	1251.721
gu3	1427.915	1410.031	1391.585	1373.155	1356.414	1343.588
gu4	1427.914	1410.030	1391.584	1373.153	1356.394	1342.798
nu1	1364.818	1331.745	1299.791	1269.060	1239.853	1207.638
nu2	1364.818	1331.744	1299.790	1269.058	1239.839	1207.013
nu3	1419.098	1396.007	1371.546	1346.083	1321.598	1301.024
nu4	1419.098	1396.005	1371.545	1346.082	1321.573	1300.082
gw1	1400.053	1377.048	1354.932	1334.174	1315.707	1298.053
gw2	1400.052	1377.047	1354.931	1334.173	1315.687	1297.259
nw1	1383.864	1350.704	1316.405	1280.969	1245.744	1210.608
nw2	1383.863	1350.703	1316.404	1280.968	1245.725	1209.836

place a greater weight on the environment their reduction in utility will be relatively greater than that of industrial groups. It is this factor, which at higher levels of transboundary pollution will reverse some of the results from the previous paper.

3.3. Symmetric Cases

Table 2.1 shows the results of our benchmark case, Experiment 1, for the symmetric case when lobbying costs are 1 for all groups in all elections. We

Table 2.2 (a)   High-cost symmetric case at state level (Experiment 2)

Alpha	0	0.2	0.4	0.6	0.8	1
x11	0.353	0.292	0.149	0.000	0.000	0.000
x21	1.235	1.565	1.980	2.451	2.902	3.402
x31	0.843	1.100	1.376	1.676	2.004	2.371
x41	0.000	0.000	0.000	0.000	0.000	0.000
x12	1.235	1.565	1.980	2.451	2.902	3.402
x22	0.353	0.292	0.149	0.000	0.000	0.000
x32	0.000	0.000	0.000	0.000	0.000	0.000
x42	0.843	1.100	1.376	1.676	2.004	2.371
q1	0.584	0.576	0.568	0.563	0.565	0.566
q2	0.584	0.576	0.568	0.563	0.565	0.566
gu1	1241.517	1182.475	1118.795	1052.591	986.606	918.674
gu2	1241.517	1182.475	1118.795	1052.591	986.606	918.674
gu3	1379.927	1362.182	1341.003	1317.413	1292.393	1265.057
gu4	1379.927	1362.182	1341.003	1317.413	1292.393	1265.057
nu1	1233.267	1169.802	1099.073	1022.556	944.497	860.802
nu2	1233.267	1169.802	1099.073	1022.556	944.497	860.802
nu3	1376.372	1356.136	1331.541	1303.372	1272.315	1236.947
nu4	1376.372	1356.136	1331.541	1303.372	1272.315	1236.947
gw1	1310.722	1272.329	1229.899	1185.002	1139.500	1091.865
gw2	1310.722	1272.329	1229.899	1185.002	1139.500	1091.865
nw1	1298.917	1253.609	1200.714	1140.926	1077.313	1005.883
nw2	1298.917	1253.609	1200.714	1140.926	1077.313	1005.883

first note the pattern of lobbying. When policy is set at the state level (Table 2.1(a)) and $\alpha = 0$, environmental groups lobby both states, but more intensively abroad. Industrial groups concentrate their lobbying effort at home. The reason, as noted in Johal and Ulph (2001b), is the effect of strategic competition: all parties are better off when the rival state has a green government, but, given our assumptions about lobbying behaviour, only environmental groups can increase the chance of the rival state being environmental. When $\alpha > 0$, there is an additional reason for groups to want the rival government to be green: to reduce emissions which result in transboundary pollution, but again only environmental groups can increase the chances of rival governments being green. As α rises, environmental groups increasingly lobby in the rival state, and reduce their lobbying at home, eventually to zero. Industrialists respond by increasing their lobbying at home. The reduction in lobbying by environmentalists in their

Table 2.2 (b)   High-cost symmetric case at federal level (Experiment 2)

Alpha	0	0.2	0.4	0.6	0.8	1
x11	0.000	0.000	0.000	0.000	0.000	0.000
x21	0.896	1.216	1.542	1.884	2.236	2.588
x31	1.023	1.348	1.662	1.980	2.295	2.592
x41	0.000	0.000	0.000	0.000	0.000	0.000
x12	0.896	1.216	1.542	1.884	2.236	2.590
x22	0.000	0.000	0.000	0.000	0.000	0.000
x32	0.000	0.000	0.000	0.000	0.000	0.000
x42	1.023	1.348	1.662	1.980	2.295	2.594
x1F	0.259	0.359	0.456	0.545	0.619	0.628
x2F	0.259	0.359	0.456	0.545	0.619	0.615
x3F	0.209	0.269	0.313	0.341	0.323	0.219
x4F	0.209	0.269	0.314	0.341	0.324	0.239
q1	0.484	0.486	0.488	0.492	0.495	0.500
q2	0.484	0.486	0.488	0.492	0.495	0.500
qF	0.517	0.528	0.540	0.554	0.576	0.606
gu1	1372.020	1343.716	1317.675	1294.255	1273.453	1249.984
gu2	1372.019	1343.715	1317.674	1294.254	1273.435	1249.239
gu3	1428.062	1410.277	1391.944	1373.629	1357.009	1344.162
gu4	1428.062	1410.276	1391.943	1373.628	1356.990	1343.424
nu1	1367.671	1335.676	1304.754	1275.026	1246.542	1214.478
nu2	1367.671	1335.675	1304.753	1275.024	1246.528	1213.862
nu3	1422.613	1400.828	1377.638	1353.442	1330.142	1310.334
nu4	1422.612	1400.827	1377.637	1353.441	1330.119	1309.503
gw1	1400.041	1376.997	1354.810	1333.942	1315.231	1297.073
gw2	1400.040	1376.996	1354.809	1333.941	1315.212	1296.332
nw1	1390.243	1359.507	1327.583	1294.526	1261.453	1227.739
nw2	1390.242	1359.506	1327.582	1294.524	1261.435	1227.033

own state causes the probability of electing an environmental government to fall.

When policy is set at the federal level (Table 2.1(b)) the basic pattern of lobbying remains the same regardless of the value of α, which reflects the fact that the federal government deals with the transboundary pollution. Environmentalists lobby in the rival state, industrialists lobby at home and all groups lobby at the federal level. Both groups expend most of their effort lobbying at the state level but environmentalists lobby relatively more at the federal level. This is reflected in the relative probabilities. The probability of

Table 2.3   The 'democratic deficit' (Experiment 3)

Alpha	0	0.2	0.4	0.6	0.8	1
x11	0.000	0.000	0.000	0.000	0.000	0.000
x21	3.649	4.713	5.778	6.887	8.020	9.149
x31	4.075	5.148	6.170	7.198	8.212	9.162
x41	0.000	0.000	0.000	0.000	0.000	0.000
x12	3.649	4.713	5.778	6.887	8.020	9.155
x22	0.000	0.000	0.000	0.000	0.000	0.000
x32	0.000	0.000	0.000	0.000	0.000	0.000
x42	4.075	5.148	6.170	7.198	8.212	9.167
x1F	0.259	0.359	0.456	0.545	0.619	0.628
x2F	0.259	0.359	0.456	0.545	0.619	0.615
x3F	0.209	0.269	0.314	0.341	0.324	0.219
x4F	0.209	0.269	0.314	0.341	0.324	0.239
q1	0.478	0.482	0.486	0.490	0.495	0.500
q2	0.478	0.482	0.486	0.490	0.495	0.500
qF	0.517	0.528	0.540	0.554	0.576	0.606
gu1	1372.005	1343.706	1317.671	1294.255	1273.455	1249.984
gu2	1372.005	1343.705	1317.670	1294.254	1273.436	1249.240
gu3	1428.054	1410.270	1391.940	1373.628	1357.009	1344.162
gu4	1428.053	1410.269	1391.939	1373.627	1356.990	1343.424
nu1	1365.014	1331.954	1299.940	1269.056	1239.378	1206.107
nu2	1365.013	1331.953	1299.939	1269.055	1239.363	1205.497
nu3	1419.534	1396.659	1372.411	1347.140	1322.771	1301.955
nu4	1419.533	1396.658	1372.410	1347.139	1322.748	1301.118
gw1	1400.029	1376.988	1354.806	1333.942	1315.232	1297.073
gw2	1400.029	1376.987	1354.805	1333.940	1315.213	1296.332
nw1	1384.518	1351.624	1317.546	1282.254	1246.916	1210.989
nw2	1384.517	1351.623	1317.545	1282.253	1246.898	1210.284

electing an environmental government at the state level is lower than at the federal level. As α increases, lobbying effort increases in all elections, except that at high values of α (>0.6) lobbying at the federal level falls, first for industrialists, then for environmentalists. However, unlike the state case, the higher the value of α the greater the probability of electing an environmental government at both levels, but significantly so at the federal level.

In Experiment 2 we assess the effect of increasing lobbying costs symmetrically to 10 for all groups in all elections. When policy is set at the state level (comparing Table 2.2(a) and Table 2.1(a)), the major change is that all

Table 2.4   Producer bias (Experiment 4)

Alpha	0	0.2	0.4	0.6	0.8	1
x11	0.000	0.000	0.000	0.000	0.000	0.000
x21	3.531	4.554	5.589	6.685	7.846	9.065
x31	3.985	5.028	6.028	7.044	8.080	9.110
x41	0.000	0.000	0.000	0.000	0.000	0.000
x12	3.531	4.554	5.589	6.685	7.847	9.069
x22	0.000	0.000	0.000	0.000	0.000	0.000
x32	0.000	0.000	0.000	0.000	0.000	0.000
x42	3.985	5.028	6.028	7.044	8.081	9.114
x1F	0.239	0.333	0.426	0.515	0.601	0.635
x2F	0.239	0.333	0.426	0.515	0.601	0.622
x3F	0.930	1.135	1.290	1.395	1.365	1.029
x4F	0.930	1.135	1.290	1.395	1.367	1.123
q1	0.476	0.480	0.484	0.489	0.493	0.499
q2	0.476	0.480	0.484	0.489	0.493	0.499
qF	0.341	0.338	0.341	0.349	0.371	0.417
gu1	1369.221	1338.982	1310.677	1284.814	1261.838	1238.853
gu2	1369.220	1338.981	1310.677	1284.813	1261.826	1238.342
gu3	1430.140	1413.424	1396.032	1378.394	1361.482	1346.684
gu4	1430.139	1413.423	1396.031	1378.393	1361.470	1346.177
nu1	1362.702	1328.058	1294.150	1261.141	1229.247	1195.713
nu2	1362.701	1328.057	1294.149	1261.139	1229.239	1195.322
nu3	1421.767	1400.138	1377.030	1352.613	1327.904	1304.655
nu4	1421.767	1400.137	1377.029	1352.611	1327.888	1304.011
gw1	1399.680	1376.203	1353.355	1331.604	1311.660	1292.768
gw2	1399.680	1376.202	1353.354	1331.603	1311.648	1292.260
nw1	1384.789	1351.994	1317.825	1282.149	1245.491	1207.600
nw2	1384.788	1351.993	1317.824	1282.147	1245.478	1207.073

groups reduce their lobbying, more so for environmental groups. Since environmentalists were previously lobbying more, the increase in μ implies a greater increase in their marginal lobbying cost. This results in a lower probability of electing an environmental government. When $\alpha = 0$ expected gross utilities of all groups fall. The greater possibility of having two industrial governments increases the chances of higher than optimal output, and hence lower profits. There is also a loss from higher pollution. Despite the increase in lobbying costs, the total cost of lobbying is lower for both groups since they expend much less lobbying effort. This means that in terms of net

Table 2.5   'North–south' divide (Experiment 5)

Alpha	0	0.2	0.4	0.6	0.8	1
x11	0.000	0.000	0.000	0.000	0.000	0.000
x21	3.655	4.723	5.791	6.903	8.039	9.167
x31	4.080	5.155	6.180	7.210	8.226	9.172
x41	0.000	0.000	0.000	0.000	0.000	0.000
x12	3.655	4.723	5.791	6.903	8.039	9.173
x22	0.000	0.000	0.000	0.000	0.000	0.000
x32	0.000	0.000	0.000	0.000	0.000	0.000
x42	4.080	5.155	6.180	7.210	8.226	9.179
x1F	1.489	1.955	2.389	2.781	3.095	3.080
x2F	0.149	0.195	0.239	0.278	0.309	0.302
x3F	1.245	1.534	1.741	1.866	1.776	1.268
x4F	0.125	0.153	0.174	0.187	0.178	0.138
q1	0.478	0.482	0.486	0.490	0.495	0.500
q2	0.478	0.482	0.486	0.490	0.495	0.500
qF	0.527	0.540	0.554	0.571	0.599	0.645
gu1	1372.156	1344.001	1318.172	1295.031	1274.738	1252.301
gu2	1372.155	1344.000	1318.171	1295.029	1274.718	1251.508
gu3	1427.941	1410.074	1391.647	1373.237	1356.515	1343.637
gu4	1427.940	1410.073	1391.646	1373.235	1356.495	1342.851
nu1	1364.369	1330.937	1298.550	1267.337	1237.636	1205.489
nu2	1365.365	1332.656	1301.117	1270.815	1241.929	1209.039
nu3	1418.843	1395.610	1371.033	1345.500	1321.106	1300.768
nu4	1419.541	1396.667	1372.395	1347.066	1322.502	1300.633
gw1	1400.048	1377.037	1354.910	1334.134	1315.626	1297.969
gw2	1400.048	1377.036	1354.909	1334.132	1315.607	1297.179
nw1	1383.164	1349.510	1314.673	1278.703	1243.115	1208.287
nw2	1384.859	1352.287	1318.604	1283.748	1248.824	1212.493

utility there is an offsetting benefit. For industrialists this is sufficient to cause net utility for industrialists to rise. When $\alpha > 0$ net utility is higher also for environmentalists. This reflects the fact that since greater lobbying takes place at higher values of α the marginal gain from reduced lobbying effort is greater also. At higher values of α this gain widens for both groups. The patterns in gross and net welfare mirror those of gross and net utility since the same factors are involved. Gross welfare in both states falls while net welfare rises. The pattern in gross welfare is also unaffected by transboundary pollution whereas the margin in net welfare widens as α increases.

When policy is set at the federal level, (comparing Table 2.2(b) with Table 2.1(b)), the increase in μ causes all groups to reduce lobbying in all elections, but the probability of a green government rises (slightly) at the state level and falls at the federal level. This, together with there being no environmental dumping, is reflected by lower gross utility for environmentalists and higher for industrialists. The reduction in total costs of lobbying is an additional benefit for both groups. For industrialists then their net utility always rises, while the reduction in lobbying costs is usually sufficient to also cause net utility for environmentalists to rise, except when there are high values of λ and ν. Gross welfare always falls but net welfare always rises. When $\alpha > 0$ we see the same pattern as at the state level. Gross welfares and utilities are largely unaffected and the disparities in net welfares and utilities are exacerbated.

Finally note that in both experiments, all interest groups and both states are better off when policy is set at the federal level. Not surprisingly, the gains to having policy set at the federal level increase as the level of transboundary pollution increases.

3.4.   Asymmetries in Influence at the Federal Level

3.4.1.   The 'democratic deficit' problem

We now try to capture the notion that decision making is less democratic when policy is set at the federal rather than state level. The way we capture such a difference in our model is to vary the cost of lobbying at state and federal level and so vary the probabilities of electing governments (or more generally 'capturing' agencies) that pursue policies in the interest of a particular group.

Even in the international relations literature it is not clear whether a 'democratic deficit' is consistent with more or less lobbying at the federal than state level (McGrew, 1999). The view we take is that, provided there were no asymmetries between interest groups, lobbying is part of the democratic process and a 'democratic deficit' arises at the federal level if there is less scope for lobbying at the federal than state level. In essence decisions at the federal level are taken by 'technocrats' with no consideration for the views of different groups in society.[13] Thus we shall take as our base case Experiment 1, where there are low costs of lobbying ($\mu = 1$) for all groups in all elections, and compare this with Experiment 3 (Table 2.3) where $\forall g = 1, \ldots, 4 \; \mu_{gi} = 1, i = 1,2; \; \mu_{gF} = 10$, so all groups now face higher costs of lobbying at the federal level. Obviously we only compare Experiments 1 and 3 when policy is set at the federal level (that is we compare Table 2.3 and Table 2.1(b)).

For $\alpha = 0$, the lobbying effort of all groups in all elections is reduced, very slightly at the state level, markedly at the federal level (very similar to Table 2.2(b)). Expected gross utilities of environmentalists fall, and expected gross utilities of industrialists rise, reflecting the lower probability of having an environmental federal government. Expected gross welfare also falls, again reflecting the fact that industrial governments generally increase environmental damage without necessarily increasing profits. Finally, the reduction in lobbying effort reduces total lobbying costs for both groups. For industrialists this reinforces the increase in gross utility. For environmentalists this benefit outweighs the lower probability of a green federal government. In terms of net utility then, when $\alpha = 0$, all parties are better off with a democratic deficit.

As α increases, the same qualitative effects are at work, but for higher values of α the reduction in lobbying costs for environmentalists is not sufficient to offset the reduction in the probability of electing a green federal government. This is rather different from the outcome in Experiment 2 where increasing lobbying costs in all elections led to environmentalists being significantly better off. The difference here is that because the reduction in lobbying costs takes place only at the federal level, the saving from reduced lobbying effort is lower and not sufficient to compensate for the reduction in the probability of electing a federal environmental government.

The lack of access to policymaking at a supranational level appears to be good for industrialists and good for environmentalists where transboundary pollution is low, but bad for environmentalists when transboundary pollution is high. In terms of net welfare though, both states seem to be better off, certainly not worse off. Note again that, despite the democratic deficit, all interest groups and both states are better off when policy is set at the federal level than at the state level.

3.4.2. Producer bias

We now explore the implications of the claim that industrialists exert more influence than environmentalists, particularly in the discussions about supranational bodies like the WTO. In Experiment 4 environmentalists face higher lobbying costs than industrialists but only at the federal level. Thus, we assume $\forall g \mu_{gi} = 1$, $i = 1, 2$, $\mu_{gF} = 10$, $g = 1, 2$ and $\mu_{gF} = 1$, $g = 3, 4$ and compare it with the base case (that is compare Table 2.4 with Table 2.1(b)).

For $\alpha = 0$, all groups reduce their lobbying in all elections: for environmentalists, very slightly in state elections but considerably in federal elections. The greater probability of having industrial governments at all levels implies laxer standards, which increase profit levels but also increase environmental damage. This hurts environmentalists more than it hurts industrialists. As a result, expected gross and net utilities fall for environmentalists but rise for industrialists. Gross welfare is slightly reduced but net welfare is higher.

With $\alpha > 0$ all the above effects go through, except that the magnitude of the gains and losses to industrialists and environmentalists are greater, and at high levels of transboundary pollution the losses in net welfare for environmentalists now outweigh the gains to industrialists, so that net welfare is lower. That is, high levels of environmental damages can outweigh gains from extra profits. This may give some credence to the fears of environmentalists that, with global pollutants, if policy is set at a federal level, their lack of influence may be damaging. It is important to note again though, that all interest groups, even environmentalists, and both states are better off when policy is set at the federal level.

3.4.3. 'North–south divide'

Finally, we study the effect of introducing significant differences between states in the costs of lobbying at the federal level, which we shall take to characterize the differences between the 'North' where lobbying is relatively cheap (perhaps reflecting longer-established interest groups, easier access to funds and so on) and the 'South' where lobbying is relatively expensive. We shall take state 1 to be the North and state 2 to be the South. In Experiment 5 the higher lobbying costs for the South are incurred only in federal elections so we assume that $\forall_i = 1, 2\mu_{gi} = 1$, for $g = 1,..,4$ but $\mu_{gF} = 1$ for $g = 3, 4$ and $\mu_{gF} = 10$ for $g = 1, 2$; again we compare this with the base case (that is, compare Table 2.5 to Table 2.1(b)).

We begin with the results for $\alpha = 0$. At the federal level Southern groups reduce their lobbying sharply, whilst Northern groups increase their lobbying (strategic substitutes effect dominates strategic complements). There is a small reduction in the probability of an environmental government at the federal level and this is reflected in lower expected gross utility for both environmental groups and higher gross utility for both industrial groups.[14] Indeed, in terms of net utilities these effects are dominated by the reduction in total lobbying costs. Reduced lobbying by the South results in a net utility gain for its groups whilst increased lobbying from the North results in a net utility loss. This pattern is repeated with welfare. Gross welfare is slightly lower for both nations but the North experiences a net welfare loss whilst the South experiences a net welfare gain. When the asymmetry between the North and the South occurs only at the federal level, since there is no great change in the balance of lobbying between groups there is no great change in the probabilities of different configurations of government types. Thus the main effect on net utilities and welfare comes from the change in lobbying costs, which benefits the South and harms the North.

The introduction of transboundary pollution increases the size of these effects, but not the pattern, so results of this experiment are robust to this introduction. Finally, we note again that all interest groups and both states, even in the South, are better off when policy is set at the federal level.

3.4.4. Summary

In this section we have considered three forms of asymmetry in lobbying costs at the federal level: a democratic deficit (less lobbying at federal than state level), producer bias (environmentalists have higher lobbying costs than producers at federal level) and North–South divide (the South faces higher lobbying costs at federal level than the North). Without transboundary pollution, the democratic deficit increased net utility for both industrialists and environmentalists, producer bias reduced net utility for environmentalists and increased it for industrialists, but with net welfare increasing, while the North–South divide increased net welfare for the South and reduced it for the North. Where these results are counterintuitive, it is because the effects of asymmetric lobbying costs on gross utilities and welfare are small, and outweighed by benefits of reduced lobbying costs, so groups (environmentalists, the South) can benefit from having less influence. With transboundary pollution the effects of asymmetries on both gross utilities and welfare and on lobbying costs get bigger, with effects on environmentalists being particularly marked. Now, at high levels of transboundary pollution, a democratic deficit does reduce the net utility of environmentalists, and producer bias does reduce net welfare. So some of the conclusions from Johal and Ulph (2001b) do get reversed when we introduce transboundary pollution.[15]

4. CONCLUSIONS

In this chapter we have analysed the question of how asymmetries in political influence between different special interest groups or between different nation states may affect the desirability of setting environmental policy at the supranational rather than national level, especially when these asymmetries in influence occur at the supranational level. More particularly, we have been concerned with the robustness of conclusions we reached on answers to this question in our previous paper (Johal and Ulph, 2001b) when we extend the rationale for having environmental policy set at the supranational level from simply dealing with strategic trade incentives for nation states to set too lax environmental standards to also allowing for transboundary pollution. Our general finding is that introducing transboundary pollution increases the level of political lobbying, and that the various asymmetries in lobbying costs we analyse have bigger effects in terms of gross and net utilities and welfares. However, in only two cases does this lead to any change in overall conclusion: with high levels of transboundary pollution then a democratic deficit at the supranational level of decision making can make environmentalists worse off, not better off, while producer bias at the supranational level can reduce net welfare. However, our main finding in Johal and Ulph (2001b) is strengthened by the introduction of transboundary pollution. That is, although transboundary pollution increases the effects of asymmetries in lobbying costs at a supranational level, it also substantially increases the gains to having policy set at this level. Our model remains simplistic. It would be worthwhile to test the robustness of our conclusions to other extensions, such as introducing consumer surplus, richer political models, joint setting of instruments between the two levels of government and different functional forms.

NOTES

*   This is an extension of a paper presented to the Workshop on Environmental Economics, University of Central Florida / Center Environmental Conference, held in Orlando, November 29–December 2 2000. We are grateful to participants, especially Michael Hoel, the editors and referees for comments on that earlier version. The usual disclaimer applies.

1. In some cases it may be inappropriate to assume that a federal government is less well informed than a state government about damage costs even if pollution is local. However even if that were true, there remains the issue of whether the information could be made verifiable in court. If not then the federal government will still need to design its environmental policy to be self-enforcing. This may change the formulation of the problem but not, we believe, the basic results of this chapter. We are grateful to Joe Swierbinski for this point.

2. We could think of the weight attached to environmental damages in the welfare function, 1, as the weight that might be attached by a utilitarian welfare function which added the utilities of all groups in a state, and if preferences are symmetrically distributed this would be the same as the utility of the median voter.

3. Although we refer to there being governments at state and federal level, we have in mind that the 'federal government' may refer more generally to some supranational agency such as NACEC or a putative WEO which is unlikely to be 'elected'. In this more general context we interpret 'elections' as some process by which special interest groups try to 'capture' the agency; this process is uncertain and depends on lobbying efforts by special interest groups just as described in the electoral process.

4. Having a government in power, which acts solely in the interests of the group that it represents, corresponds to what Roemer (1999) calls the 'militant' view of how special interest governments behave.

5. Note that if policy is set at the state level, then we need to track the types of governments elected in the two states. There are four configurations of state government types which we denote by $\tilde{\Gamma}_s = (\gamma_1, \gamma_2)$, $s = 1, \ldots, 4$, where: $\tilde{\Gamma}_1 = (\gamma_H, \gamma_H)$; $\tilde{\Gamma}_2 = (\gamma_H, \gamma_L)$; $\tilde{\Gamma}_3 = (\gamma_L, \gamma_H)$; $\tilde{\Gamma}_4 = (\gamma_L, \gamma_L)$; with probabilities: $\tilde{Q}_s$, $s = 1, \ldots, 4$, where $\tilde{Q}_1 = q_1 q_2$; $\tilde{Q}_2 = q_1(1-q_2)$; $\tilde{Q}_3 = (1-q_1)q_2$; $\tilde{Q}_4 = q_1(1-q_1)(1-q_2)$. If policy is set at the federal level then we need to

know the configuration of government types elected in the two states and the federal government. There are eight configurations denoted: $\hat{\Gamma}_f = (\gamma_1, \gamma_2, \gamma_F), f = 1, \ldots, 8$, where $\hat{\Gamma}_1 = (\gamma_H, \gamma_H, \gamma_H), \hat{\Gamma}_2 = (\gamma_H, \gamma_H, \gamma_L)$, and so on, with probabilities: $\hat{Q}_f, f = 1, \ldots, 8$ where $\hat{Q}_1 = q_1 q_2 q_F, \hat{Q}_2 = q_1 q_2 (1 - q_F)$, and so on.

6. Where $\tilde{U}_{1s}(\delta_L) = p U[\tilde{e}_1(\hat{\Gamma}_s, \delta_L), \tilde{e}_2(\hat{\Gamma}_s, \delta_L), \delta_L, \gamma_H] + (1 - p) U[\tilde{e}_1(\hat{\Gamma}_s, \delta_L), \tilde{e}_2(\hat{\Gamma}_s, \delta_H), \delta_L, \gamma_H]$ and $\tilde{U}_{1s}(\delta_H) = p U[\tilde{e}_1(\hat{\Gamma}_s, \delta_H), \tilde{e}_2(\hat{\Gamma}_s, \delta_L), \delta_H, \gamma_H] + (1 - p) U[\tilde{e}_1(\hat{\Gamma}_s, \delta_H), \tilde{e}_2(\hat{\Gamma}_s, \delta_H), \delta_H, \gamma_H]$.

7. To save notation we omit the dependence of these policy instruments on the configuration of government types $\hat{\Gamma}_f$.

8. Our justification for imposing these constraints even though a prior constitutional stage has decided that policy should be set at the federal level is that it may represent less formal structures such as the EU. Here, even at the implementation stage, state governments may have an incentive to defect from the constitutionally agreed decision. Actually, these constraints are frequently not binding, so we do not believe our result would be sensitive to dropping them.

9. δ, λ and ν can then be used to calculate $\delta_L = (1 - \nu)\delta$, $\delta_H = (1 + \nu)\delta$, $\gamma_L = (1 - \lambda)$ and $\gamma_H = (1 + \lambda)$.

10. These produce welfare losses when policy is set at the federal level between 0.8 percent and 1.3 percent of GNP, which is within the range found by Katz and Rosenberg (1989) who calculated the costs of rent seeking as a percentage of GNP for a number of countries, and showed that this varied from 0.19 percent to 5.43 percent.

11. Other parameters are p, A, and σ. Probability, p, is simply set as 0.5. A simply denotes the level of demand for the product and is just set equal to 10. The parameter σ denotes the social cost of raising a unit of the numeraire in taxes in order to fund transfers and is usually estimated in the range 0.2–0.4. Within this range results are relatively insensitive, so we report only for the case $\sigma = 0.3$.

12. See Johal and Ulph (2001a) for more details.

13. An alternative view is that the 'democratic process' consists of elections in which lobbying plays no influence so that the probabilities reflect the underlying distribution of environmental and industrial preferences in the population. This view leads to precisely the opposite effects of those we report.

14. Lobbying and hence probabilities are virtually unaffected at the state level.

15. In Johal and Ulph (2001b) we also considered producer bias and North–South divide where asymmetric lobbying costs between groups existed at both state and federal elections. These produced somewhat different results than with asymmetries only at the federal level but it turns out that the results carry through with transboundary pollution. To save space, we do not report the details of these.

REFERENCES

Johal, S. and A. Ulph (2001a), 'International Co-ordination of Environmental Policies, Harmonisation and Limiting Political Discretion', University of Southampton.

Johal, S. and A. Ulph (2001b), 'Globalisation, political lobbying and the design of international environmental governance', forthcoming, *Review of International Economics*.

Katz, E. and J. Rosenberg (1989), 'Rent-seeking for budgetary allocation: preliminary results for 20 countries', *Public Choice*, **60**, 133–45.

McGrew, T. (1999), 'The World Trade Organisation: "Technocracy Or Banana Republic"', in C. Thomas and A. Taylor (eds), *Global Trade And Global Social Issues*, London: Routledge, Chapter 10, pp. 227–49.

Roemer, J. (1999), 'The democratic political economy of progressive income taxation', *Econometrica*, **67** (1), 1–20.
Ulph, A. (1997), 'International Environmental Regulation When National Governments Act Strategically', in J. Braden and S. Proost (eds), *The Economic Theory of Environmental Policy in a Federal System*, Cheltenham, UK and Lyme, US: Edward Elgar, pp. 66–98.

3. Endogenous transfrontier pollution

Michael Rauscher*

1. INTRODUCTION

When environmental economists consider transfrontier pollution, they usually assume that the process of transboundary dissipation of pollutants depends on natural parameters only. Examples are the meteorological parameters and variables that influence the geographical distribution of pollutants, for example the direction of winds or patterns of precipitation. They are outside the scope of economic reasoning and can, therefore, be treated as exogenously given in economic models. Thus, the assumption of an exogenously given transfrontier pollution matrix which determines who pollutes whom to what extent appears to be justified in environmental economics. For many if not most purposes, the presumption that exogenous impacts determine the process of transfrontier pollution is reasonable. An example is the greenhouse effect. The impact of greenhouse gas emissions on the global climate is independent of the geographical location of the source of emissions. In this case, the elements of the transfrontier pollution matrix are identical and at present no way of changing them appears to be feasible. See Rauscher (2000a). However, there are situations where there is the choice to either solve an environmental problem by reducing or avoiding the emissions or to externalize it by discharging pollutants such that environmental harm occurs somewhere else.

European environmental policies in their infant stages of the 1960s and early 1970s provide examples of environmental policy by externalization. Re-industrialization after World War II led to severe environmental problems, particularly unprecedented local air pollution. The London smog catastrophe of December 1952 causing thousands of deaths is the most striking example. And other European cities and regions experienced similar problems – albeit with smaller numbers of casualties. The policy response was to tighten local air quality standards. There are two ways of meeting these tighter standards. One possibility is to reduce the emission of pollutants by the implementation of cleaner production processes or filter technologies. The other possibility is to leave emissions unchanged and reduce local pollution by distributing the pollutants over a wider area, for example by building higher smokestacks. In the early stages of European clean-air policies, the second approach was the dominant one. Local pollution was reduced substantially but only at the expense of an increase of new environmental problems generated by long-range air pollution. Probably the most prominent example is acid rain. Countries such as Norway and Sweden suffer from the high-smokestack environmental policies adopted elsewhere when they are subject to acid rain mainly generated by SO_2 emissions in central Europe and the British isles. Similar phenomena can be observed in the USA and Canada.

There are other examples of endogeneity of transfrontier pollution. One can locate environmentally intensive production close to a jurisdiction's border such that domestic damage remains moderate. Nuclear energy generation is an example. Nuclear power stations are often located close to national borders. Of course, this choice of a peripheral location does not reduce the risk of an accident but it externalizes a part of the damage, should an accident occur, to neighbouring jurisdictions. Another method of externalizing local pollution is to discharge pollutants into rivers such that the damage occurs in downstream jurisdictions. The negotiations on the cleaning-up of the Rhine river have recovered such practices, for example down-river water pollution caused by upstream potash plants located in Alsace.

This chapter addresses the externalization of local pollution and looks at endogenous transfrontier pollution in closed and open economies. The endogeneity of transfrontier pollution is a problem already in closed economies. Jurisdictions may face incentives to externalize pollution. From a supra-jurisdictional point of view, this is a waste of resources. Scarce goods and factors are used to merely redistribute pollution geographically without really solving environmental problems. That this is a waste of resources and a source of inefficiency, is probably uncontroversial. However, the chapter also derives some results that are surprising at a first glance. It is shown, for instance, that increases in transfrontier pollution are not necessarily harmful from a supra-jurisdictional viewpoint. Additional aspects related to endogenous transfrontier pollution arise if openness of the economies under consideration is explicitly considered. Policies directed at improving international competitiveness may aggravate the problem of externalization.

To keep matters simple, I will consider openness in terms of factor mobility. There is a mobile factor of production which moves to the jurisdiction where its remuneration is highest. These factor movements are affected by the strictness of environmental regulation. The literature on interjurisdictional competition and environmental pollution has shown that the mobility of factors of production across jurisdictions may aggravate environmental problems and lead to incentives to use suboptimal environmental policies. (See Wilson, 1996 and Rauscher, 2000b.) The conjecture is that these problems are aggravated if transfrontier pollution is endogenous, that is if resources can be used to merely redistribute pollution across jurisdictions. In order to make matters simpler and to rule out scenarios that are perhaps intellectually exciting but practically irrelevant, it is assumed that environmental pollution generates a pure consumption externality. Factor productivities are not affected by environmental damages. If they were, the competitiveness argument would get a sabotage component attached to it: domestic competitiveness could be increased by using transfrontier pollution to reduce foreign factor productivities. This possibility is disregarded here.

The chapter is organized as follows. The next section presents a simple model of endogenous transfrontier pollution and firm behaviour. I then consider optimal environmental policies in the closed-economy case. Situations in which jurisdictions cooperate are compared with situations in which they do not. Section 4 briefly looks at first-best cooperative and non-cooperative environmental policies in the small open economy case. Sections 5 and 6 deal with the second and third best, respectively, and Section 7 summarizes the results.

2. PRODUCTION TECHNOLOGY, EMISSIONS AND TRANSFRONTIER POLLUTION

Consider a jurisdiction in which an aggregate commodity is produced by means of several factors of production. One of them, for example labour or land, is immobile and constant and is, therefore, not modelled explicitly. The production function exhibits decreasing returns to scale in the remaining factors. These are capital and emissions. Usually emissions are thought of as being a harmful joint output of the production process rather than an input. If they enter the production function as an input, emissions can be interpreted as the share of natural capital that is used up during the production process and discharged into the ambient in terms of waste or contaminated air, water, or soil. This approach has become a standard tool in environmental economics (see Oates and Schwab (1988), for example).[1] Let K and E denote production capital (including a share of the capital stock used for abatement) and emissions, respectively. They are combined in a production process described by $F(K,E)$ which generates output, Q.

$$Q = F(K, E) \tag{3.1}$$

with

$$F_K > 0, \; F_{KK} < 0, \; F_{EE} < 0, \; F_{KE} > 0, \; F_{KK}F_{EE} - F_{KE}^2 > 0 \qquad (3.1a)$$

where subscripts represent partial derivatives. These assumptions are standard. The positive cross derivative, F_{KE}, implies that capital and emissions are substitutes, that is isoquants are convex. Moreover, assume that the Inada conditions for zero capital and emissions and for infinite capital are satisfied. As far as emissions are concerned, it makes sense to assume that for each level of the capital stock there exists a 'natural' or maximum level of emissions, $\tilde{E}$, such that

$$F_E(K, \tilde{E}) = 0 \quad \text{for} \quad \tilde{E} = g(K), \; g_K > 0, \; g(0) = 0. \qquad (3.1b)$$

$\tilde{E}$ is discharged in the absence of environmental regulation, that is if no abatement is undertaken.

Environmental pollution can be externalized. Immissions generated by local polluters, I, their emissions minus the quantity of pollutants deposited abroad, T.

$$I = E - T. \qquad (3.2)$$

The jurisdiction can increase T at a cost. For example, it can locate polluting plants in peripheral regions, that is close to the border, or build high smokestacks such that air pollutants are distributed over a wider area. However, such a policy is costly; resources that are used for the externalization of pollution cannot be used for other purposes. For example, the location of pollution-intensive activities in peripheral areas raises transportation and other transaction costs and the externalization of air pollution requires high smokestacks that tie in a part of the capital stock that could be used for commodity production otherwise. I model this by introducing an additional factor of production that is referred to as smokestack capital, S. Smokestack capital and normal capital are perfectly malleable, that is they can be added and this determines the total capital stock employed in the economy, A.[2]

$$A = K + S \qquad (3.3)$$

The externalization technology is represented by a production function $G(.,.)$ having emissions and smokestack capital as its arguments. Thus, transfrontier pollution, T, is

$$T = G(S, E) \qquad (3.4)$$

with

$$G_S > 0, \ G_E > 0, \ G_{SS} < 0, \ G_{EE} < 0, \ G_{SE} > 0, \ G_{SS}G_{EE} -$$
$$G_{SE}^2 \geq 0 \tag{3.4a}$$

Moreover, one cannot externalize more emissions than those that are discharged. This implies that

$$G(S, 0) = 0 \quad \text{and} \quad G_E(S, E) \leq 1. \tag{3.4b}$$

Moreover, as an Inada condition, assume that

$$G_S(0, E) = \infty. \tag{3.4c}$$

For the sake of simplification, I make the innocent assumption that no pollutants are discharged to extraterritorial areas. This simplifies notation a bit but does not affect the results. Thus, domestic pollution, P, is determined by domestic local emissions, $E - T$, plus transfrontier emissions coming from abroad, T^*:

$$P = E - T + T^*. \tag{3.5}$$

Pollution causes environmental damage and the marginal environmental damage is constant, D. This is a simplifying assumption. With increasing marginal damage, transfrontier pollution from abroad would have an impact not only on the level of domestic welfare but also on marginal welfare. This would affect the comparative statics of optimal environmental policies. The first-order conditions, however, would remain unaffected.

This concludes the presentation of the basic assumptions of the model. There are other jurisdictions that use similar technologies. We refer to them as 'the rest of the world', 'the foreign country', or 'abroad' and denote the corresponding variables and functions by asterisks. For example, E^*, S^*, and D^* are foreign emissions, smokestack capital, and marginal environmental damage, respectively, and $F^*(K^*, E^*)$ is the foreign production function.

Three policy instruments are considered:

- t^K, a source tax on mobile capital, relevant for all types of capital,
- t^E, an emission tax,
- t^I, an immission tax, relevant only for emissions deposited locally.

The environmental taxes can be translated into command-and-control instruments of environmental regulation. Since I assume perfect competition, that is price-taking behaviour of all agents except the government, command-and-control regulation of emissions and immissions would result in shadow prices that are equivalent to the taxes introduced here.

At the danger of stating the obvious, it shall nevertheless be mentioned that, of course, a jurisdiction cannot tax foreign firms. Thus, the domestic immission tax applies only to local emissions of domestic firms. Correspondingly, foreign immission taxes affect only foreign firms that discharge local pollutants but not domestic firms that contribute to foreign environmental pollution by externalizing part of their emissions.

A representative firm in the home jurisdiction maximizes its profits,

$$\Pi = F(K, E) - (r + t^K)(K + S) - t^E E - t^I[E - G(S, E)], \qquad (3.6)$$

where r is the rental rate of capital, subject to the constraint that $S \geq 0$. The first-order conditions for an interior solution are

$$F_K = r + t^K \qquad (3.7a)$$

$$G_S t^I = r + t^K, \qquad (3.7b)$$

$$F_E = t^E + (1 - G_E) t^I \qquad (3.7c)$$

The first condition is straightforward: marginal capital productivity equals the user cost of capital. The second condition states that the marginal productivity of smokestack capital equals its user cost, too. Together with the first one, it implies that in an optimum the firm is indifferent to whether to allocate the last unit of capital to production or to smokestacks. In the first case, the investment generates additional output, in the second case, it saves costs. The marginal cost saving equals the marginal output increase. In the third equation, the left-hand side can be interpreted as marginal abatement cost: a reduction of emissions by one unit causes an output loss of F_E units of output. The marginal tax saving corresponding to this emission reduction is on the right-hand side of equation (3.7c). It is the emission tax rate plus the immission tax rate where it has to be taken into account that the local emissions are reduced by G_E if E is increased. Thus equation (3.6c) states that the firm chooses its emission level such that marginal abatement cost equals the marginal tax payment.

For the case $t^I = 0$, we have $S = 0$ and condition (3.7c) is simplified such that $F_E = t^E$. This corresponds to the standard scenario in which transfrontier pollution is non-existent or exogenous and will, therefore, not be subject to further investigation. (See Rauscher (2000b) for the results.)

It should be noted that the environmental taxes can be expressed in an alternative fashion. Define σ as a subsidy on transfrontier pollution and θ as a tax on total emissions. Then the profit function of the firm can be rewritten

$$\Pi = F(K, E) - (r + t^K)(K + S) - \theta E + \sigma G(S, E), \qquad (3.6')$$

where

$$\theta \equiv t^E + t^I,$$

$$\sigma \equiv t^I.$$

With such a redefinition of tax rates, some of the results of this chapter are more easily to be interpreted, particularly in cases in which both types of taxes are used at the same time.

What are the effects of environmental and tax policies on firm behaviour? Total differentiation of (3.7a) to (3.7c) yields

$$\begin{vmatrix} F_{KK} & 0 & F_{KE} \\ 0 & t^I G_{SS} & t^I G_{SE} \\ F_{KE} & t^I G_{SE} & F_{EE} + t^I G_{EE} \end{vmatrix} \begin{vmatrix} dK \\ dS \\ dE \end{vmatrix} = \begin{vmatrix} 1 & 0 & 0 \\ 1 & 0 & -G_S \\ 0 & 1 & 1 - G_E \end{vmatrix} \begin{vmatrix} dt^K \\ dt^E \\ dt^I \end{vmatrix} \quad (3.8)$$

If the immission tax rate is positive, the determinant of the matrix on the left-hand side is negative. Diagonal elements are negative as well, and second principal minors are positive.[3] Thus, the second-order conditions are satisfied. The following results are obtained.

- A higher tax on capital reduces demand for both smokestack and production capital. This is not surprising. Moreover, it reduces emissions. The reason is that with less capital, emissions are less productive. The effect on transfrontier pollution is negative since less emissions plus less smokestack capital create less transfrontier pollution.
- A higher emission tax rate leads to less emissions and reduces demand for capital. The impact on transfrontier pollution is negative. The intuition behind these results is the same as in the case of capital taxation. The impact on immissions is ambiguous. This is due to the

fact that it is not clear whether emissions are reduced by more than transfrontier pollution.

• An increase in immission taxes has ambiguous effects on both types of capital and on emissions but an unambiguously negative effect on immissions, as expected. This follows algebraically from using the results derived from (3.7) in (3.2). The effect on transfrontier pollution is ambiguous. Thus, tighter environmental policies directed at immission reduction may increase emissions and transfrontier pollution.

Considering changes in environmental taxes is useful to get insights as to how firms react to economic incentives in environmental policy. However, real-world environmental policies predominantly use command and control. This was even more so in the 1970s, when high-smokestack environmental policies were initiated. Let us, therefore, consider two additional scenarios with changes in immission control. The first case is the command-and-control case, where emission and immission standards are given. With E being constant, it follows from $I = E - T$ that $dI = -dT$, that is tighter immission standards can only be met by increasing transfrontier pollution. The other scenario is a change in immission levels at a given emission tax rate. This tax rate may be zero. This case then corresponds to the clean-air policy approach adopted in the 1960s and 1970s: immissions rather than emissions were viewed as the major problem and immission standards (rather than emission taxes) were the appropriate instruments to solve it. In such a scenario, the firm's optimization problem is to maximize profits subject to the constraint that an immission target has to be met. Thus (3.2) is the constraint under which the firm optimizes its emission level and capital stock. The corresponding Lagrangean is

$$L = F(K, E) - (r + t^K)(K + S) - t^E E - \lambda[E - I - G(S, E)], \quad (3.9)$$

where λ is the Lagrangean multiplier associated with the immission constraint, (3.2). The first-order conditions are

$$F_K = r + t^K \quad (3.10a)$$

$$G_S(F_E - t^E) - (r + t^K)(1 - G_E) = 0, \quad (3.10b)$$

where λ has been eliminated already. Total differentiation of (3.10a), (3.10b), and (3.2) yields

$$
\begin{vmatrix}
F_{KK} & & 0 \\
G_S F_{KE} & G_{SS} & (F_E - t^E) - (r + t^K) G_{SE} \\
0 & & - G_S
\end{vmatrix}
$$

$$
G_S F_{EE} + G_{SE} \begin{pmatrix} F_{KE} \\ F_E - t^E \\ 1 - G_E \end{pmatrix} + (r + t^K) G_{EE} \Biggr) \begin{pmatrix} dK \\ dS \\ dE \end{pmatrix}
$$

$$
= \begin{pmatrix} 1 & 0 & 0 \\ -(1 - G_E) & G_S & 0 \\ 0 & 0 & 1 \end{pmatrix} \begin{pmatrix} dt^K \\ dt^E \\ dI \end{pmatrix}
$$

The determinant of the matrix on the left-hand side, Δ, is positive and it can be seen that tighter immission standards lead to less emissions and to an ambiguous effect on smokestack capital:

$$
\frac{dE}{dI} = \frac{F_{KK}}{\Delta}[G_{SS}(F_E - t^E) - (r + t^K)G_{SE}] > 0, \tag{3.11a}
$$

$$
\frac{dS}{dI} = \frac{-F_{KK}}{\Delta}[G_S F_{EE} + G_{SE}(F_E - t^E) + (r + t^K)G_{EE}] \tag{3.11b}
$$

That tighter immission standards induce less emissions, (3.11a), is straightforward. A reduction of immissions at a constant emission level would require an increase in smokestack capital. However, the marginal productivity of smokestack capital is diminishing. At an exogenously given opportunity cost of capital, this leads to a non-optimal situation, which can only be improved if emissions are reduced. Considering the impact of immissions on smokestack capital represented by (3.11b), one notes that the second term in brackets on the right-hand side is zero if there is no immission regulation in the initial situation.[4] The remaining terms in the brackets are negative and so is dS/dI. Thus, tighter immission standards lead to more smokestack investments if the initial stock of smokestack capital is small. If the stock of smokestack capital is large the converse is also possible.

The impact of tighter immission regulation on transfrontier emissions then is

$$
\frac{dT}{dI} = \frac{F_{KK}}{\Delta}\{G_E G_{SS}(F_E - t^E) - G_S[G_S F_{EE} + (r + t^K)G_{EE}] - G_{SE}(r + t^K)\}, \tag{3.11c}
$$

where (3.10b) has been used to simplify the term in brackets on the right-hand side. It is seen that the sign of dT/dI is ambiguous. Let us consider the special case where there is no initial regulation such that the immissions constraint does not bind and $S = 0$. Then it follows from (3.11a) and (3.11b) that

$$\left.\frac{dT}{dI}\right|_{S=0} = \frac{-F_{KK}}{\Delta}[G_S^2 F_{EE} + (G_S G_{EE} + G_E G_{SE})(r + t^K)], \quad (3.11d)$$

Given the assumptions on the $G(.,.)$ function, G_S is large and G_E is small if S is zero, a scenario is likely in which dT/dI becomes negative. This means that tighter immission standards lead to more transfrontier pollution. This is what happened in the 1960s and 1970s, when tighter immission policies were implemented that transformed local environmental problems into long-range transfrontier pollution problems.

Proposition 1
Tighter immission regulation can lead to more transfrontier pollution, particularly in the case of zero or very lax initial regulation.

3. OPTIMAL ENVIRONMENTAL POLICIES: THE AUTARKY CASE

In autarky, factors of production are immobile across jurisdictions. Thus, the resource constraint $K + S = A$ is binding with A being given exogenously. Two cases can be distinguished: cooperative and non-cooperative behaviour. In the first case, a federal government maximizes a weighted sum of welfare levels of individual jurisdictions. In the second case, each jurisdiction maximizes its own welfare function independently of what the rest of the world does.

As a starting point, consider cooperation and assume that domestic and foreign welfare enter the federal welfare function with equal weights. This welfare function is

$$W^{fed} = F(K, E) - D[E - G(A - K, E) + G^*(A^* - K^*, E^*)] + F^*(K^*, E^*)$$
$$- D^*[E^* + G(A - K, E) - G^*(A^* - K^*, E^*)]. \quad (3.12)$$

Maximization with respect to K, E, K^*, and E^* subject to the constraints that $S \geq 0$ and $S^* \geq 0$ yields

$$F_K = (D - D^*)G_S + \lambda, \quad (3.13a)$$

$$F_E = D(1 - G_E) + D^* G_E, \quad (3.13b)$$

$$F^*_K = (D^* - D)G^*_S + \lambda^*, \tag{3.13c}$$

$$F^*_E = D^*(1 - G^*_{E^*}) + DG^*_E, \tag{3.13d}$$

where the asterisks are omitted in the subscripts that represent derivatives of foreign functions. λ, $\lambda^* \geq 0$ are the Lagrangean multipliers associated with the non-negativity constraints. They are strictly positive if these constraints are binding.

Equations (3.13a) and (3.13c) state that capital should be allocated such that its productivities are the same in the production sector and in the smokestack utilization. Of course, one of the terms in brackets on the right-hand sides is negative unless $D^* = D$. Since neither F_K nor F^*_K can be negative, this implies a corner solution for at least one of the capital stocks: in at least one of the two jurisdictions, no smokestack capital is used. The condition for such a corner solution is

$$F_K(A, E) > (D - D^*)G_S(0, E),$$

that is in a situation with low smokestack productivity, the export of pollutants to the jurisdiction with low environmental costs is not desirable and, therefore, smokestack capital is zero. In the case of large differences in marginal environmental damage, it is optimal that one of the jurisdictions uses part of its capital for smokestacks. It is optimal to export some pollution to the other jurisdiction where the pollutants cause less environmental harm. Equations (3.13b) and (3.13d) state that marginal abatement cost equals marginal environmental damage.

Using the results on firm behaviour, (3.7a) to (3.7c), equations (3.13a) to (3.13d) can be translated into taxes. As far as taxes on capital are concerned, they are neutral since this factor is fixed. So the optimal tax on capital is ambiguous. For the interpretation of the results, it is useful to employ the alternative specification of environmental taxes, where σ is the transfrontier pollution subsidy and θ is the tax on total emissions. One obtains

$$\sigma = \begin{cases} D - D^* & \text{if } S > 0 \\ 0 & \text{if } S = 0. \end{cases} \tag{3.14a}$$

$$\theta = \begin{cases} D & \text{if } S > 0 \\ D(1 - G_E) + D^*G_E & \text{if } S = 0. \end{cases} \tag{3.14b}$$

In cases where domestic environmental damage exceeds foreign damage substantially, the optimal domestic environmental policy consists of taxing total emissions at a rate equalling domestic marginal damage. Moreover, a transfrontier pollution subsidy should be employed to externalize a part of the pollutants to jurisdictions where marginal damage is lower. If domestic environmental damage is not that large compared to foreign damage or even less, then high smokestacks should not be built. Then the emission tax rate equals domestic marginal damage and transfrontier pollution is subsidized such that the marginal damage of externalized emissions is the foreign marginal damage.

Proposition 2
In the case of similar environmental damages in the jurisdictions, a cooperative optimum is characterized by zero immission taxes and emission taxes equalling total marginal environmental damage. In the case of large differences in marginal damages, the high-damage jurisdiction exports its pollution by high smokestacks. This jurisdiction should tax emissions at a rate equalling the local environmental damage and it should subsidize transfrontier pollution.

The externalization of pollution is optimal since the environmental cost of additional environmental damage across the border is less than the marginal abatement cost at home. To implement such a cooperation across jurisdictions, side payments may be necessary. The jurisdiction receiving the pollution may be willing to accept this if it is compensated. This is closely related to trade in hazardous waste, where a jurisdiction accepts the waste generated elsewhere and receives a compensation. In first-best situations without other distortions of the economy and without informational asymmetries, this is optimal and in the interest of both the importing and the exporting jurisdictions. (See Rauscher, 2001, for instance.)

If both jurisdictions have equal marginal environmental damages, then emission taxes should be equal and immission taxes should be zero.

Now consider non-cooperative environmental policies. The function maximized by the domestic government is

$$W = F(K, E) - D[E - G(A - K, E) + G^*(A^* - K^*, E^*)]. \quad (3.15)$$

The first-order conditions in the case of an interior solution are

$$F_K = DG_S, \quad (3.16a)$$

$$F_E = D(1 - G_E), \quad (3.16b)$$

and the corresponding tax rates are

$$t^I = D, \quad (3.17a)$$

$$t^E = 0. \quad (3.17b)$$

These very straightforward results can be expressed as follows:

Proposition 3
In an interior non-cooperative optimum, the immission tax rates equal marginal local damage and emission tax rates are zero.

The economy behaves as if foreign marginal environmental damage were zero. A boundary solution is possible if smokestacks are unproductive in the externalization of environmental damage. Then the emission tax rate equals domestic marginal environmental damage like in the standard case where transfrontier pollution is not variable.

It is clear that combined welfare is larger in the cooperative than in the non-cooperative scenario. However, does this imply that emissions are lower if a government acts non-cooperatively than if it takes foreign environmental damage into account? Consider this issue by introducing a parameter a, measuring the degree of altruism, into equations (3.13a) and (3.13b). a measures the share of the environmental damage occurring on the other side of the border which is taken into consideration by the government. If $a=1$, there is perfect internalization; if $a=0$, the environmental policy addresses domestic damages only. Assume that a is small enough such that we have an interior optimum. For the home country:

$$F_K = (D - aD^*)G_S, \tag{3.18a}$$

$$F_E = D(1 - G_E) + aD^*G_E. \tag{3.18b}$$

The comparative static results are determined by applying Cramer's rule to

$$\begin{pmatrix} F_{KK} + G_{SS}(D - aD^*) & F_{KE} - G_{SE}(D - aD^*) \\ F_{KE} - G_{SE}(D - aD^*) & F_{EE} + G_{EE}(D - aD^*) \end{pmatrix} \begin{pmatrix} dK \\ dE \end{pmatrix} = \begin{pmatrix} -D^*G_S \\ D^*G_E \end{pmatrix} da.$$

Again using Δ to denote the determinant, which is positive in the optimum, and assuming that (3.17a) and (3.17b) have an interior solution, that is $D - aD^* \geq 0$, we obtain

$$\frac{dS}{da} = -\frac{dK}{da} \frac{D^*}{\Delta} \{G_S[F_{EE} + G_{EE}(D - aD^*)] + G_E[F_{KE} - G_{SE}(D - aD^*)]\} \tag{3.19a}$$

and

$$\frac{dE}{da} = \frac{D^*}{\Delta} \{G_E[F_{KK} + G_{SS}(D - aD^*)] + G_S[F_{KE} - G_{SE}(D - aD^*)]\}. \tag{3.19b}$$

For transfrontier pollution, this implies

$$\frac{dT}{dS} = \frac{D^*}{\Delta}[G_S^2 F_{EE} + 2G_S G_E F_{KE} + G_E^2 F_{KK} +$$

$$(D - aD^*)(G_S^2 G_{EE} - 2G_S G_E G_{SE} + G_E^2 G_{SS})]. \tag{3.19c}$$

It follows that altruism has ambiguous effects on emissions and on smoke-stack capital but an unambiguously negative effect on transfrontier emissions.[5]

Proposition 4
Starting from non-cooperative behaviour, altruism reduces transfrontier pollution. This can be due to lower emissions or less smokestack capital. It is possible that either smokestack capital or the level of emissions is increased by altruistic behaviour.

That smokestacks may be increased as a response to altruistic behaviour is a surprising result, but there is an underlying economic intuition. In equation (3.19a), the term causing this non-standard result is $D^* G_E F_{KE}$. An increase in the altruism parameter leads to an increase in marginal environmental damage by $D^* G_E$. (See equation (3.18b).) Emissions are reduced. This leads to a reduction in the marginal productivity of production capital, $F_{KE} dE$, such that the opportunity cost of smokestack capital is reduced and smokestacks are increased. Of course, there are other effects which may offset this effect but it is nevertheless possible that this effect dominates the other effects. Similar arguments explain the possibility of increased emissions after an increase in the cooperation parameter. The critical term in equation (3.19b) is $D^* G_S F_{KE}$. Cooperation reduces the marginal benefit of smokestack investment by $D^* G_S$ in equation (3.18a). Capital is relocated from smokestacks to production. This increases the marginal abatement cost by $F_{KE} dK$ and emissions tend to be increased. Like before, this is only one of several effects and all the other effects have the opposite sign. Thus, there is a theoretical possibility that altruism leads to either higher smokestacks or more emissions.

These results, that have been derived for a single country, carry over to a multi-country equilibrium in environmental policies. The reason is that marginal damages, D and D^*, are constant. Thus, the conditions for the optimal environmental policy in one country are independent of the levels of emissions, immissions and transfrontier pollution generated in the rest of the world.

4.   OPEN ECONOMIES: THE FIRST BEST

Openness means that the resource constraints of the individual jurisdictions are relaxed and there is only a global resource constraint

$$\bar{A} + \bar{A}^* = K + S + K^* + S^*, \tag{3.20}$$

where the left-hand side variables denote domestic and foreign factor endowments, respectively.[6] Consider first the cooperative outcome. Factor mobility, represented by equation (3.21), yields a slight modification of the welfare function and we have

$$F_K = F^*_K \tag{3.21}$$

as an efficiency condition. Marginal productivities are equal across countries. The first-order conditions of environmental policy remain unchanged. It should be noted, however, that emission and immission levels may be different since the allocation of capital may have changed compared to the autarky situations and, thus, the first-order marginal conditions are satisfied at different levels of the arguments of the functions. The countries are better off than in autarky since the federal government internalizes all externalities and capital mobility induces an efficiency gain from a better capital allocation.

Now consider non-cooperative environmental policies in open economies. Here I look at the first best, that is a small open economy with unrestricted access to the three policy instruments. To the small country the international rate of interest, r, and the level of transfrontier pollution coming from abroad are given. Thus the latter need not be considered. The small open economy thus maximizes

$$W = F(K, E) - r(K + S - \bar{A}) - D[E - G(S, E)] \tag{3.22}$$

with respect to K, S, and E. Maximization yields $F_K = r$, and

$$F_K = DG_S, \tag{3.16a}$$

$$F_E = D(1 - G_E), \tag{3.16b}$$

as an interior solution. The first condition is well known from the tax-competition literature: a small country should not tax the use of the mobile factor. The latter two conditions are the same ones as in the autarky case – with the only difference that the rate of return on international capital is determined on the international market rather than domestically. One can conclude that the marginal conditions governing the use of environmental resources in the open economy are the same in autarky and in the first-best scenario of a small open economy.

Proposition 5
The optimal environmental policies in open economies are determined by the same conditions as in autarky in the cases of cooperation and first-best non-cooperation, respectively.

This result is not surprising. It generalizes to all kinds of optimal environmental policies in open economies. What matters in the cooperative case, as well as in the first-best non-cooperative case, is marginal environmental damage. There are no other objectives of environmental policy but the internalization of environmental damage – global damage in the cooperative case and local damage in the non-cooperative case.

What is the impact of trade liberalization on emissions and transfrontier pollution in the non-cooperation case? To consider this, introduce a quantitative restriction on the capital imports or exports depending on whether the country under consideration is capital-poor or capital-rich. Let this restriction be denoted by R. Then $A = \bar{A} + R$. R is positive if the country is an importer of capital and negative if it is an exporter. Trade liberalization corresponds to an increase in A for the capital-importing country and to a reduction in A for the exporting country. Thus, from a point of view of a single country, the effect of factor-market liberalization on emissions and immissions is the same as that of a change in factor endowment in autarky if A were the autarky endowment. The first-order conditions, (3.16a) and (3.16b), can be differentiated totally using $(A - S)$ instead of K as the first argument of the $F(.,.)$ function. This yields:

$$\begin{pmatrix} DG_{SS} + F_{KK} & DG_{SE} - F_{KE} \\ DG_{SE} - F_{KE} & DG_{EE} + F_{EE} \end{pmatrix} \begin{pmatrix} dS \\ dE \end{pmatrix} = \begin{pmatrix} F_{KK} \\ -F_{KE} \end{pmatrix} dA \qquad (3.23)$$

and application of Cramer's rule gives $1 > dS/dA > 0$ and $dE/dA > 0$. An increase in available capital increases smokestack capital and emissions and, therefore, has a positive impact on transfrontier pollution. The intuition behind this result is straightforward. The increase in the total capital stock is shared among users of production capital and users of smokestack capital. This reduces marginal abatement cost. Thus, it is optimal to raise emissions. It can be shown that the effect on transfrontier pollution is stronger than in a scenario with exogenous transfrontier pollution.[7]

These results have the following implications for the environmental effects of trade liberalization. Note that liberalization of factor markets increases the availability of capital in the capital-poor country and reduces the capital stock in the capital-rich country. Then, the following proposition can be derived.

Proposition 6
The removal of restrictions on capital mobility leads to an increase in emissions and transfrontier pollution discharged by the capital-poor country and to a reduction in emissions and transfrontier pollution discharged by the capital-rich country. These effects are more pronounced than in a situation where smokestack capital is given exogenously.

The welfare effects then follow from the welfare function. There is an efficiency effect due to improved capital allocation plus an effect originating from changes in transfrontier pollution coming from across the border. The efficiency effect is $(F_K - r)dA$, which is always positive since the term in brackets and dA are either both positive or both negative. The transboundary-pollution effects are different for the two types of countries. A capital-poor country benefits from less transfrontier pollution. Capital-rich countries, in contrast, can lose from liberalization and the negative effect from transboundary pollution is more severe in a world with endogenous transfrontier pollution than in a world where transfrontier pollution is exogenous.

5.   NON-COOPERATION IN SMALL OPEN ECONOMIES: THE SECOND BEST

It is often argued that governments are restricted in their choice of policy instruments. The fiscal-federalism literature, for instance, introduces restrictions on the reductions of source taxes on capital. In tax-competition models, it is often assumed that the policymaker's discretion to reduce capital taxation is limited, that is that a zero tax on mobile capital, albeit optimal from a purely fiscal point of view, cannot be achieved in practice (see Wilson, 1986, and Zodrow and Mieszkowski, 1986). Thus, there is a lower limit on capital income tax rates that cannot be undercut. Given that the first best is characterized by zero taxation of the mobile factor, the lower bound on capital taxes becomes a binding restriction and can, therefore, be treated like a given and constant tax rate in the following analysis. For the small open economy, this implies $F_K = r + t^K$ as stated in equation (3.7a), and that the stock of production capital, K, depends on the level of emissions:

$$\frac{dK}{dE} = -\frac{F_{KE}}{F_{KK}} > 0. \tag{3.24}$$

Again, the welfare function (3.22) is maximized, but now only with respect to S and E. The first-order conditions are

$$G_S D = r \tag{3.25a}$$

$$F_E = (1 - G_E)D - t^K \frac{dK}{dE}. \tag{3.25b}$$

The first condition is an indifference condition: the marginal productivity of smokestack capital should equal its opportunity cost, which is the world market interest rate. The second condition is well known from the theory of environmental policy when capital markets are distorted (see Wilson, 1996). There is a wedge between the marginal productivity of emissions and the marginal environmental damage. This is due to a fiscal externality. Higher emissions than in the standard case are justified since they help to attract the tax base from abroad. From an international point of view this is inefficient, however, because the tax base as a whole is limited.[9,10] Using (3.7b) and (3.7c), these conditions can be rearranged such that

$$\sigma = t^I = \left(1 + \frac{t^K}{r}\right)D = D + \frac{t^K}{G_S}, \tag{3.26a}$$

$$t^E = -t^K \left(\frac{dK}{dE} + \frac{1 - G_E}{G_S}\right), \tag{3.26b}$$

$$\theta = D + t^K \left(\frac{DG_E}{r} - \frac{dK}{dE}\right) = D + t^K \left(\frac{G_E}{G_S} - \frac{dK}{dE}\right). \tag{3.26c}$$

The immission tax is larger than the marginal environmental damage and, according to equation (3.26b), the emission tax is negative: emissions should be subsidized. Behind this is the following economic intuition. Due to the source tax of capital, the private opportunity cost of using smoke-stack capital is larger than the opportunity cost for the economy as a whole. This implies that an incentive has to be given by the government such that the use of smokestack capital is increased. The instrument for doing this is an increase in the immission tax. However, this comes at the cost of a dis-torted environmental policy: immissions would be too low. Therefore, an additional incentive for emissions is given by a lower emission tax. Of course, if capital taxation vanishes, the emission tax rate is reduced to zero and the immission tax rate attains its Pigouvian level, where marginal envi-ronmental damage equals the emission tax rate. This has the following con-sequence:

Proposition 7
In a tax-competition framework with exogenously given source taxes on mobile capital, the optimal immission tax rate is higher than in autarky (and in the first-best world) and the emission tax rate is negative.

Alternatively, one can interpret the results in terms of σ and θ, that is a transfrontier-pollution subsidy and a tax on total emissions. If there were no capital taxation, then the optimal non-cooperative subsidy would be D. Since foreign damages are not considered in the home country, transfrontier pollution should be taxed at a zero rate; the corresponding subsidy is marginal environmental damage in the home country. However, there is an additional element in the subsidy if there is a capital-market distortion. To correct for the distortion, one should subsidize the use of domestic capital at least in the externalization sector. The tax on total emissions now consists of three components. The first one is the marginal damage. The second one is a correction term for the subsidy going to the smokestack industry. It is positive. The third one is the fiscal-externality term, which is negative as expected.

What is the impact of distortive capital taxation on emissions and transfrontier pollution? In other words: what would happen if the restriction on capital taxation were relaxed and lower taxes became feasible. In order to keep matters tractable, let us consider a situation in which all jurisdictions are identical. This is a standard assumption in the tax-competition literature and it allows one to disregard endowment effects and to concentrate on the fiscal externalities. Thus, capital – albeit mobile *ex ante* – does not move and the *ex-post* interjurisdictional capital allocation is the same as in autarky. Of course, in such a situation, the international capital rental rate is an endogenous variable. Thus, substitute $(F_K - t^K)$ for r in (3.25a). This implies

$$G_S D - F_K = -t^K. \tag{3.25a'}$$

$$F_E = (1 - G_E)D - t^K \frac{dK}{dE} \tag{3.25b}$$

Then, total differentiation of these equations and noting that in the tax-competition equilibrium $dK = -dS$ yields

$$\begin{pmatrix} DG_{SS} + F_{KK} & DG_{SE} - F_{KE} \\ DG_{SE} - F_{KE} & F_{EE} + DG_{EE} + t^K \dfrac{d^2K}{(dE)^2} \end{pmatrix} \begin{pmatrix} dS \\ dE \end{pmatrix} = \begin{pmatrix} -dt^K \\ -\dfrac{dK}{dE} dt^K \end{pmatrix} \tag{3.27}$$

Given that the (3.25a) and (3.25b) characterize a welfare maximum, the diagonal elements of the matrix on the left-hand side are negative and the determinant is positive.[11] Then, using (3.24), the following comparative statics results can be derived:

- Tax competition leads to an increase in smokestack capital. Given that the total capital stock in the economy remains constant if the jurisdictions are identical, this means that capital is relocated from productive to unproductive use.
- Tax competition leads to an increase in emissions. Laxer emission standards as a second-best instrument help to keep the tax base in the country.
- Given that emissions and smokestack capital are increased, transfrontier pollution rises as well.

It is seen that the endogeneity of transfrontier pollution aggravates the harmful consequences of fiscal externalities in an interjurisdictional tax-competition game. Not only are lax environmental policies used to attract the tax base; relocation of capital from productive to purely redistributive purposes causes additional inefficiencies – and pollution.

6. NON-COOPERATIVE OPEN ECONOMIES: THE THIRD BEST

Let us now consider situations in which the government has only one economic policy instrument: it can either regulate emissions or immissions. Capital taxes are assumed to be given as in the previous section.

In a first step consider a scenario in which the government regulates emissions only. This is closely related to what has been discussed by Wilson (1996) and Rauscher (2000b). The only difference is that in this model the share emissions crossing the border are not constant. The government maximizes (3.24) with respect to E and the first-order condition is

$$F_E = (1 - G_E)D - t^K \frac{dK}{dE} \qquad (3.25b)$$

as in the previous section. The difference compared to the earlier literature on environmental tax competition (for example Wilson, 1996) is that the share of transfrontier pollution, $(1 - G_E)$, is not constant. In all other respects, the interpretation of the result is the same. Tax competition has a negative impact on environmental quality since a lax environmental regulation is used to attract the mobile factor of production. The emission tax rate can be derived by setting $t^I = 0$ in equation (3.6c). Thus,

$$t^E = (1 - G_E)D - t^K \frac{dK}{dE}. \qquad (3.28)$$

The emission tax equals marginal environmental damage minus the fiscal-externality component. As a result, laxer environmental policies lead to more emissions than the optimal ones. The fiscal externality generates incentives to attract mobile capital by means of lax environmental policies. This confirms the result of the earlier tax competition literature: in a second-best world where the mobile factor of production is subject to positive taxes, public goods are under-provided.

Let us finally consider interjurisdictional competition with immission regulation as the only policy instrument. There are no restrictions on emissions such that $t^E = 0$. The first order optimality condition is

$$G_S D = r. \tag{3.25a}$$

as in the previous section and the corresponding immission tax rate is again determined by equation (3.26a). There is a surcharge on marginal environmental damage. Higher immission taxes are used to attract the mobile tax basis since they raise the profitability of investments into smokestacks. As before, r is endogenous in a tax-competition framework and is, therefore, substituted for in equation (3.25a):

$$G_S D - F_K = -t^K. \tag{3.25a'}$$

The immission tax rate is determined by equation (3.26a); it exceeds the marginal environmental damage. Moreover, combining (3.7a), (3.7b), and (3.7c) yields

$$F_E G_S = F_K (1 - G_E). \tag{3.29}$$

Total differentiation of these two equations, again noting that $dS = (-dK)$, yields

$$\begin{pmatrix} DG_{SS} + F_{KK} & DG_{SE} - F_{KE} \\ F_E G_{SS} - G_S F_{KE} + F_K G_{SE} + (1 - G_E)F_{KK} & F_E G_{SE} + G_S F_{EE} + F_K G_{EE} - (1 - G_E)F_{KE} \end{pmatrix} \begin{pmatrix} dS \\ dE \end{pmatrix} = \begin{pmatrix} -dt^K \\ 0 \end{pmatrix} \tag{3.30}$$

The signs of the second-row elements of the matrix on the left-hand side are ambiguous but the determinant, Δ, is unambiguously positive.[12] The comparative static results for smokestack capital and emissions are

$$\frac{dS}{dt^K} = \frac{1}{\Delta}[(1 - G_E)F_{KE} - F_K G_{EE} - G_S F_{EE} - F_E G_{SE}], \tag{3.31a}$$

$$\frac{dE}{dt^K} = \frac{1}{\Delta}[F_E G_{SS} - G_S F_{KE} + (1 - G_E)F_{KK} + F_K G_{SE}]. \tag{3.31b}$$

Both effects are ambiguous. The reason is that in a tax-competition equilibrium capital does not move *ex post*. The first-order effect of tighter immission regulation is a relocation of capital from production to smokestacks. With higher smokestacks, emissions cause less domestic environmental damage and the jurisdiction can afford to raise its emission level. However, the reduction in the production capital stock at the same time diminishes the productivity of emissions and this requires an emission reduction. Which one of these effects dominates depends on the parameters of the model. This is the second-order effect. The third-order effect results from repercussions of the change in emissions on capital allocation. If emissions are increased, this raises the marginal productivity of capital in output generation but also the marginal benefits from investing into smokestack capital. It depends on the parameters of the $F(.,.)$ and $G(.,.)$ functions whether capital moves from production to smokestacks or in the reverse direction. Of course, this ambiguity arises in the case of an emission reduction, too.

Proposition 8
In a third-best tax-competition framework with exogenous taxes on mobile capital, the immission tax rate is larger than the marginal damage. The capital market distortion has ambiguous effects on the allocation of capital inside the jurisdiction, on emissions and on transfrontier pollution.

The effects on transfrontier pollution are ambiguous as well since none of the terms cancel out when the smokestack and emissions impacts of the tax increase are combined via the $G(.,.)$ function.

7. FINAL REMARKS

The chapter has considered endogenous transfrontier pollution for autarkic and small open economies, the latter being subject to international tax competition. Some of the findings of this chapter confirm our a priori expectations; others are surprising. It can be shown, for instance, that tighter immission standards implemented in situations with low initial regulatory levels are likely to increase transfrontier pollution. This is in accordance with the stylized facts. However, if immission standards are restrictive already, then the converse may happen and transfrontier pollution may be reduced. It is a surprising result that tax competition does not necessarily result in more transfrontier pollution even if jurisdictions use environmental policies merely targeted at immissions.

Of course, an important question is whether countries really have measures for emissions and immissions. For many pollutants, the information is available. The problem, however, is to trace the observed immissions back to the polluters. Who is responsible and how should the polluters be regulated if immissions are targeted? Environmental policies in the 1960s and 1970s used command-and-control regulation in order to reduce immissions, which then could be traced back – more or less accurately – to local polluters. These polluters reacted by using high smokestacks. With high smokestacks, however, the relationship between emissions and immissions becomes much more fuzzy, and environmental policies have reacted by using emissions as the target variables rather than immissions. Nonetheless, in a very general sense, the incentives of externalizing environmental problems are still present as the existence of high smokestacks, the ongoing discussion on North Sea pollution and many other examples show.

Which extensions of the approach can be thought of? I wish to mention two:

- Since in the basic model without distortions, factor movements and international trade are substitutes (see Markusen (1983) for an overview), one might expect that the results derived here carry over to models with trade in final goods. Instead of capital moving from one country to the other, capital-intensive commodities would be exported. Whether or not this is true, may be shown by incorporating the idea of high smokestacks into trade models.
- A limitation of this model is the small-economy assumption. It simplifies the analysis and it helps to elaborate the results of this chapter very clearly. Nonetheless, it restricts the analysis to a limited number of questions. Other interesting issues must be disregarded. One of them is related to pollution leakage, that is to the phenomenon that stricter environmental policies in one jurisdiction lead to increases in emissions in other jurisdictions. The mechanism is the impact of domestic regulation on world market prices and the international allocation of factors of production (as in this model) and of tradable produced commodities. Stricter environmental regulation at home would lead to 'capital flight' to other countries, thus increasing foreign capital stocks and generating incentives to increase emissions there. It would be interesting to look at this issue in a world where environmental policy can actively influence the parameters of transfrontier pollution. This would, however, require a large-country model framework.

NOTES

[*] I wish to thank Cees Withagen, Gerald Willmann, Frank Stähler, Aart de Zeeuw, and an anonymous referee for helpful comments and suggestions. The usual disclaimer applies.

1. These two views, emissions as an input vs. emissions as an output are formally equivalent. A production function containing emissions as an argument can be interpreted as a reduced form of a more complex production process in which the other factors are used not only for production but also for abatement activities (see Rauscher, 1997, ch. 2).

2. Perfect malleability is a realistic assumption only in the long run. Thus, what this chapter does in its comparative static analysis is to compare long-run equilibria.

3. In the case $t^I = 0$, the second first-order condition cannot be used. S would be zero and would be unaffected by changes in capital taxes and emission taxes. All the other results would remain the same.

4. In this case $F_E = t^E$ since the constraint is not binding and the Lagrangean multiplier in (3.9) is zero.

5. Proof. The last term in brackets inside the squared brackets on the right-hand side is negative. That the first three terms together are negative can be shown as follows:

$$G_S^2 F_{EE} + 2G_S G_E F_{KE} + G_E^2 F_{KK}$$
$$= G_S^2 F_{EE} + G_E^2 F_{KK} + 2G_S G_E \sqrt{F_{EE} F_{KK}} - 2G_S G_E \sqrt{F_{EE} F_{KK}} + 2G_S G_E F_{KE}$$
$$= -\left(G_S \sqrt{-F_{EE}} - G_E \sqrt{-F_{KK}} \right)^2 - 2G_S G_E \left(\sqrt{F_{EE} F_{KK}} - F_{KE} \right) < 0.$$

6. In contrast, A and A^* denote the capital stocks employed in the two countries, which in the case of factor mobility can differ from the endowments.

7. The case of exogenous transfrontier pollution can be analysed by neglecting (3.16a) and considering (3.16b) only.

8. The last term on the right-hand side of this equation originates from the fact that the derivative of the welfare function contains the term $(F_K - r)dK/dE$ and $(F_K - r) = t^K$.

9. Consider for instance a situation with many small countries that are identical and use the same policies as the one considered here. Since all jurisdictions are identical, capital does not move *ex post*. Thus, the laxer environmental policy has no effect on capital allocation but only a detrimental impact on environmental quality.

10. Note that a similar result applies in the case of involuntary unemployment due to rigid wages, which may be more relevant in some countries than a capital market distortion. Then, it is optimal to use lax environmental policies to increase employment. The employment effect of laxer environmental standards is strengthened by capital mobility. This implies that there is a stronger incentive to use lax policies in open economies with capital mobility than in closed economies. However, like in the case of fiscal externalities, this has no effect on employment *ex post* since countries are identical and capital does not move.

11. Note that the Hessian does not contain the terms $(-F_{KE})$ and F_{KK}. These terms occur as a result of the identical actions taken by identical jurisdictions in the tax competition.

12. In order to establish the positive sign of the determinant, (3.25a') and (3.29) have to be utilized such that some terms cancel out.

REFERENCES

Markusen, J.R. (1983), 'Factor movements and commodity trade as complements', *Journal of International Economics*, **14**, 341–56.

Oates, W.E. and R.M. Schwab (1988), 'Economic competition among jurisdictions: efficiency enhancing or distortion inducing?', *Journal of Public Economics*, **35**, 333–354.

Rauscher, M. (1997), *International Trade, Factor Movements, and the Environment*, Oxford: Clarendon.

Rauscher, M. (2000a), 'Comment on "International Environmental Risk" by Jason Shogren', in H. Siebert (ed.), *The Economics of International Environmental Problems*, Tübingen: Mohr-Siebeck, pp. 20–25.

Rauscher, M. (2000b), 'Interjurisdictional Competition and the Environment', in H. Folmer and T. Tietenberg (eds), *International Yearbook of Environmental and Resource Economics 2000/2001*, Cheltenham, UK and Brookfield, US: Edward Elgar, pp. 197–230.

Rauscher, M. (2001), 'International Trade in Hazardous Waste', in G.G. Schulze and H.W. Ursprung (eds), *International Environmental Economics: A Survey of the Issues*, Oxford: Oxford University Press.

Wilson, J.D. (1986), 'A theory of interregional tax competition', *Journal of Urban Economics*, **19**, 296–315.

Wilson, J.D. (1996), 'Capital Mobility and Environmental Standards: Is There a Theoretical Basis for a Race to the Bottom?', in J. Bhagwati and R.E. Hudec (eds), *Fair Trade and Harmonization: Prerequisites for Free Trade? Volume 1: Economic Analysis*, Cambridge: MIT Press, pp. 393–427.

Zodrow, G.R. and P.M. Mieszkowski (1986), 'Pigou, Tiebout, Property Taxation, and the Underprovision of Public Goods', *Journal of Urban Economics*, **19**, 356–370.

4. Allocating greenhouse gas emissions among countries with mobile populations*

Michael Hoel

1. INTRODUCTION

In order to prevent dramatic climate changes in the next few hundred years, it is necessary to reduce greenhouse gas emissions from present levels (see for example Cline, 1992). To achieve significant reductions in emissions, it will be necessary to have some kind of international agreement on emission reductions.

In the negotiations towards any agreement to reduce greenhouse gas emissions, there will be at least two issues on which countries will have conflicting interests. These are

(a) how much should total emissions be reduced;
(b) how should the total emission reduction be allocated among countries.

These two issues are closely interrelated. For almost all rules of how to allocate emission reductions, countries will have different opinions about how much the total reduction should be. The reason for this difference in opinions is partly that different economies differ in several ways, so that most rules for sharing the emission reductions (including uniform cuts) will give countries different costs. The benefit from reducing emissions will also differ between countries, as the adverse effect of a given climate change will be different for different countries.[1]

If countries had agreed upon how much the total emission reductions should be, they would nevertheless usually disagree about how the emission reduction should be allocated among countries. In most analyses and policy discussions, it is usually taken for granted that each country would like their own share of the total permitted emissions to be as large as possible (see, for example, Kverndokk, 1993, 1995). As a main rule, this is probably correct. However, in this chapter I demonstrate that among countries where

84

there is a large degree of population mobility, each country might not want its own share of total emissions to be as large as possible.

The climate problem is a global problem involving all countries in the world. There is certainly far from full population mobility among all countries. The standard assumption used in most analyses, namely that there is *no* population mobility, might be a fair first approximation. However, between certain groups of countries there is a considerable degree of population mobility, and there is good reason to expect this to increase in the future. Examples of areas with a large degree of population mobility include USA and Canada, and most countries in the European Union. For these areas, analyses assuming no population mobility are obviously somewhat inaccurate. The opposite extreme assumption, namely perfect population mobility, is probably even more unrealistic. It is nevertheless useful to consider this extreme, since the real world lies somewhere in between the case of no mobility and perfect mobility.

2. EFFICIENT ALLOCATIONS OF EMISSIONS

We consider a simple model with one good and J countries. Production of this good in country j is given by a concave function $f_j(n_j, e_j)$, where n_j is the population in country j. It is assumed that labour input is an increasing function of the population, so that production is higher the higher the population is.[2] The production level is also assumed to be increasing in the greenhouse gas emission level e_j for the relevant sizes of emission levels. The interpretation is that the function $f_j(n_j, e_j)$ is a reduced form function, telling us that production is lower the lower are emissions, that is that abatement is costly.

Consumption per capita in country j is denoted by c_j. Total consumption summed over all countries cannot exceed total production, that is

$$\Sigma_i n_i c_i \leq \Sigma_i f_i(n_i, e_i). \tag{4.1}$$

Total emissions, denoted by E, are by assumption given, as in this chapter I wish to focus on the allocation of emissions among countries:

$$\Sigma_i e_i \leq E. \tag{4.2}$$

Finally, the total population in the group of countries we are studying is given at the level N, so that

$$\Sigma_i n_i = N. \tag{4.3}$$

There may be other constraints in addition to (4.1)–(4.3). In this chapter I discuss what is meant by efficient allocations of emissions under various additional constraints. Table 4.1 gives an overview over the different cases considered, denoted A–F. The cases with given populations in each country (that is A and B) have been extensively studied in the literature, and will be briefly treated in Section 3. Sections 4 and 5 treat the cases with endogenous populations (cases C–F).

Table 4.1   The six cases A–F studied in Sections 3–5

	Exogenous population	Population determined through optimization	Population mobility
No transfers between countries	A	C	E
Inter-country transfers permitted	B	D	F

3.   EXOGENOUS POPULATION

Consider first case A, that is the case in which population is fixed and we disregard the possibility of transfers (that is side payments) between countries. In this case *all* allocations of emissions across countries are Pareto efficient[3]: an increase in per capita consumption in one country can in this case only be achieved by increasing the permitted emissions in this country. But this must mean lower emissions in at least one other country, giving reduced per capita consumption there.

Case B is somewhat different. Since inter-country transfers in this case are permitted, an efficient outcome must imply that total consumption is maximized. The condition for this is that

$$f_{1e}(n_1, e_1) = \ldots = f_{Je}(n_J, e_J)\qquad(4.4)$$

that is, that the marginal abatement costs are equalized across countries. This condition is often referred to as the condition of cost-effectiveness, as it is the condition for minimizing abatement costs for a given amount of abatement.

In the simple model used here the efficiency condition (4.4) in combination with the given sum of emissions and the given population levels gives a unique allocation of emissions, and therefore also of production levels, across countries. The distribution of consumption between countries is however not determined by the efficiency condition. Any distribution of consumption is consistent with (4.4), given the appropriate transfers between countries.

An obvious way to introduce inter-country transfers is via a scheme of tradable emission quotas. Under such a scheme each country would be allocated a specific emission quota. However, countries would be free to trade quotas with other countries. In our simple model, the equilibrium competitive price of quotas will be equal to the common marginal abatement cost given by (4.4). Countries selling quotas will receive a 'transfer' equal to the amount of emission quotas they sell multiplied by this price; and vice versa for countries that buy quotas.

Under such a scheme one gets the efficient allocation of emissions no matter how the quotas are initially allocated. The initial allocation of quotas is thus simply the device that picks which of the efficient outcomes we obtain, and is thus a pure distributional issue.

4. POPULATION DETERMINED THROUGH OPTIMIZATION

In this section it is assumed that the location of people across countries is a policy choice, in the same way as we are considering the allocation of emissions as a policy choice. This scenario is not meant to be a description of a real world case. Nevertheless, it is useful as a hypothetical reference scenario.

When population levels are endogenous, one must take some care in the definition of efficiency. We define efficiency as any outcome that satisfies the constraints of the problem and maximizes some welfare function $W(c_1,\ldots c_J)$ that is increasing in all its arguments.

Consider first case D, that is the case with inter-country transfers. In this case (4.1)–(4.3) are the only constraints of the problem. Maximizing the function $W(c_1,\ldots c_J)$ subject to these constraints gives us (4.4) and the condition[4]

$$c_1 - f_{1n}(n_1, e_1) = \ldots = c_J - f_{Jn}(n_J, e_J). \tag{4.5}$$

Notice that unless all per capita consumption levels are equal in the efficient outcome considered, this condition implies that populations (and thus labour input) are not allocated so that total output is maximized. While this at first thought might seem counterintuitive, given the existence of inter-country transfers, it is in fact a direct consequence of the way we define efficiency. To see this, consider the two-country case. Imagine for a moment that the sum of income in the two countries was given, independent of where people live. Moreover, consider an outcome where per capita consumption is higher in country 1 than in country 2. In this case it would clearly be possible to increase per capita consumption in both countries by moving people from country 1 to country 2.[5] This would remain true even if this migration gave a slight reduction in the sum of income. How much the sum of income could go down without this conclusion being changed depends on the difference between the per capita consumption levels in the two countries. It is precisely this balancing of per capita consumption differences with the difference in marginal productivities that is implied by the efficiency condition (4.5).

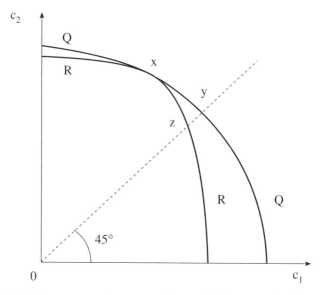

Figure 4.1   *The consumption per capita possibility space for the two-country case*

In the two-country case, the efficiency conditions (4.4) and (4.5) define a downward sloping curve in the consumption per capita space, illustrated by Q in Figure 4.1. All points along the frontier Q are efficient. Clearly, the residents of country 1 prefer the points further down and to the right.[6] Which point one reaches on Q depends on the size of the transfers. The more transfers country 1 receives from 2, the further to the right on the line Q will the outcome be. There will be one point along Q that transfers are zero; we have denoted this point by x.

Consider next case C. In addition to the constraints (4.1)–(4.3) we now have the additional constraints

$$n_i c_i \leq f_i(n_i, e_i) \quad i = 1, \ldots, J. \tag{4.6}$$

Maximizing $W(c_1, \ldots, c_J)$ now gives us

$$\frac{f_{1e}(n_1,e_1)}{c_1 - f_{1n}(n_1,e_1)} = \ldots = \frac{f_{Je}(n_J,e_J)}{c_J - f_{Jn}(n_J,e_J)}. \tag{4.7}$$

In this 'second-best' efficient case, the first-best conditions (4.4) and (4.5) are generally not satisfied. Since the second-best has more constraints than the first-best, the consumption per capita possibility curve for the former case lies inside Q. The consumption per capita possibility curve for the second-best case is denoted R in Figure 4.1. The curve R lies inside Q, except at the tangency point x, since in both cases there are no transfers between countries at x.

Case C has an important feature in common with case D: in both cases there is a conflict of interest between the different countries. In the two-country case, the residents of country 1 prefer the points further down and to the right on the curve R, just as they did with the curve Q in case D. There is, however, an important difference: while greenhouse gas emissions should always satisfy the cost-effectiveness condition (4.4) in case D, this is not true in case C. The reason is of course that since the possibility of using transfers to distribute consumption is ruled out in case C, the allocation of emissions now has an important distributional role.

Both of the cases C and D are unrealistic in one important way. They both require that the distribution of persons among countries is a policy choice. Although countries to some extent can limit immigration, this is nevertheless a rather strong assumption. In the next section I therefore consider the opposite extreme, where people choose freely where they want to live.

5. POPULATION MOBILITY

In this section I consider the case in which there are no restrictions on where people live. I also make the following strong assumption: people are identical and have no locational preferences. All they care about is their consumption level.[7] Given these strong assumptions, and ignoring corner solutions (see footnote 4), perfect population mobility will give an equilibrium where per capita consumption is the same in all countries, that is

$$c_1 = \ldots = c_J. \tag{4.8}$$

This equilibrium condition determines the allocation of populations between countries, in our cases E and F.

For the two-country case, the points along the 45° line in Figure 4.1 give the equilibrium condition (4.8). Consider first case E: all points along the 45° line between the origin and the point z, and no other points, are feasible outcomes in this case. Clearly, both countries have a common interest in achieving the point z. In this case there is thus no conflict of interest between different countries. They both (or all in the general case of J countries) would like greenhouse gas emissions to be allocated in a particular way, namely in a way that maximizes the common per capita consumption level.

At the point z, there are no transfers between countries. However, generally all countries can gain from inter-country transfers, thus enabling them to increase their per capita consumption levels from z to y in Figure 4.1. This somewhat counterintuitive result that a donor country may benefit from giving a transfer to another country was first pointed out by Myers (1990).

Notice that since per capita consumption levels are equalized at the point y, it follows from (4.5) that the marginal productivity of labour is also equalized at this point. Together with (4.4), this means that total output is maximized at this point.

In case E there are by assumption no transfers between countries. Since international trade of emission quotas serves as a type of transfer, case E is a case where such trade has been ruled out. In this case the final allocation of emissions will be identical to the initial allocation of emission quotas. Only one particular allocation of quotas will give the desired outcome z; any other allocation will make all countries worse off.

One interpretation of case F is that country j is given an emission quota e_j^* and simultaneously a transfer Y_j^* (where Y_j^* can be positive or negative). Obviously, the sum of transfers over all countries must be equal to zero. Since the allocation of emissions and transfers in case F implies that the cost-effectiveness condition (4.4) holds, marginal abatement costs are equalized across countries. Denote this common abatement cost by q^*. If the quotas of country j are distributed among private agents in country j, and domestic emission trading is allowed, the equilibrium quota price will be q^*. Since this price is the same in all countries, there will be no incentives for inter-country emission trading.

An alternative interpretation of case F is that each country j is given an emission quota equal to $e_j^{**} \equiv e_j^* + Y_j^*/q^*$, and no transfers. If actual emissions in each country were equal to the country's emission quota, marginal abatement costs would not be equalized across countries. If quotas are distributed among private agents in each country, there will thus be an incentive for inter-country quota trade. With no restriction on such trade, the equilibrium quota price will be q^*. Country j would in this equilibrium be selling an amount $e_j^{**} - e_j^*$ of quotas, and thus receiving an income

$q^* (e_j^{**} - e_j^*) = Y_j^*$ from its quota trade. It is therefore clear that this equilibrium is identical to the case in which country j receives an emission quota e_j^* and simultaneously a transfer Y_j^*.

From the discussion above it follows that the desired outcome in case F (point y in Figure 4.1) can be achieved whatever the initial allocation of emission quotas is, provided they are accompanied by a suitable set of transfers: Let country j be given an emission quota e_j^0 and a transfer $Y_j^0 = q^* (e_j^{**} - e_j^0)$. When these quotas are distributed to private agents, they will in equilibrium be selling an amount $(e_j^0 - e_j^*)$ of quotas, and thus receiving an income $q^* (e_j^0 - e_j^*) = q^* (e_j^{**} - e_j^*) - Y_j^0 = Y_j^* - Y_j^0$ from their quota trade. The net transfer to country j is thus Y_j^*, and its emissions will be e_j^*, that is the desired outcome is achieved.

Of the cases studied, B and F seem the most interesting cases: it is difficult to find good reasons to rule out the possibilities of inter-country transfers. Moreover, although countries can place some restrictions on immigration, population levels in each country are a long way from being policy variables.

Consider the cases B and F, and assume first that the only inter-country transfers are the payments related to inter-country trade of tradable emission quotas by private agents. In this context, cases B and F have very different properties. In B, that is, the traditional case without population mobility, there is a conflict of interest between countries regarding the appropriate initial allocation of emission quotas between countries. In fact, this allocation is a pure issue of income distribution between countries, as quota trade between private agents will give a Pareto-efficient allocation of final emissions no matter how quotas are initially distributed among countries. Case F, that is, the case with perfect population mobility, is quite different. Here all countries have a common interest in how emission quotas should be allocated. If they for some reason are allocated in a different way than this commonly shared optimum, the governments of the countries would either have to reallocate the emission quotas before distributing them to private agents, or introduce an appropriate set of transfers between countries, see the discussion above.

6. LOCATIONAL PREFERENCES

The model used in the discussion above is extremely simple in many respects. One of the simplifying assumptions used is that there are no locational preferences, that is people care only about their consumption levels, and not where they live. This is obviously unrealistic. Introducing locational preferences is, however, a simple modification of the model, as long as these preferences are shared by everyone. To see this let utility of a person living in country j be given by $u_j(c_j)$. Notice that this utility level does not depend on which person we are considering. If, for example, $u_j(c') > u_k(c')$ for an arbitrary consumption level c', this means that everyone prefers to live in country j rather than k. In order for anyone to choose to live in country k instead of j, they would need to be compensated, that is the consumption they could get in k would have to be higher than the consumption they could obtain in country j. In an equilibrium with population mobility and people living in all countries we would thus have the equilibrium condition

$$u_1(c_1) = \ldots = u_J(c_J) \tag{4.8a}$$

instead of (4.8).

In our discussion of Figure 4.1, the only change would be that instead of the 45° line, we would have an upward sloping line reflecting the locational preferences. If people preferred country 1 to country 2 (for the same consumption level) this line would lie somewhere above the 45° line. Apart from this change, all of our results from the previous discussion would remain valid.

Obviously, it is not particularly realistic to assume that everyone has the same locational preferences. In the next section I therefore consider the case of non-homogeneous populations, where differences in locational preferences could be one of the differences between people.

7.   NON-HOMOGENEOUS POPULATIONS

Assume that there are T distinct types or classes of people. There is homogeneity within a particular type, and the utility level of an individual of type *t* living in country j is as in the previous section assumed to depend on consumption and the country this person lives in. We denote this utility level by $u_j^t(c_j^t)$.

Consider first the case in which the only differences between people are their locational preferences. In this case the consumption for everyone living in the same country is the same, that is, $c_j^t = c_j$.

If there is no population mobility, differences in locational preferences are of course irrelevant. The present case is thus identical to the case discussed in Section 3 when there is no population mobility.

Consider next the case of population mobility, that is cases E and F in Table 4.1. Population mobility will imply that conditions of the type (4.8a) will hold for all types. However, we can no longer ignore the possibility of corner solutions, that is situations in which some types live only in a subset of all the countries. Formally, let $I(t)$ be the set of countries in which persons of type t will live (in equilibrium). Then instead of condition (4.8a) we will have

$$u_j^t(c_j) = u^t \text{ for } t \in I(t)$$
$$u_j^t(c_j) \leq u^t \text{ for } t \notin I(t) \tag{4.9}$$

where u^t is the equilibrium value of the utility level of type t.

Unless the differences in utility functions across persons are trivial, the equilibrium cannot have the property that all types live in all countries. This follows immediately from (4.9): if $I(t')$ is the set of all J countries for a particular type t', then it follows from (4.9) that there is a particular equilibrium consumption pattern across all countries. This consumption pattern can only make utility levels for other types be equal across all countries if the utility functions of other types differ from the function $u^{t'}$ in a trivial manner.

There is not much one can say in general about whether or not there will be a conflict of interest between countries regarding the allocation of emission quotas. There are, however, two special cases worth mentioning. First, consider the case in which, for all t, $I(t)$ consists of only one country. In other words, each type of person lives only in one country. In this case we are, in the neighbourhood of the equilibrium, in a situation where there is no population mobility. The standard results of Section 3 apply to this case (at least as long as only small reallocations of emission quotas are considered).

A second special case is the one where $I(t')$ is the set of all J countries for a particular type t', that is the equilibrium is characterized by people of type t' living in all countries. In this case it follows from (4.9) that any change in the allocation of emission quotas will change the per capita consumption levels of all countries in the same direction. Although most types of persons will be living in separate countries, all types therefore share a common interest in choosing the allocation of emission quotas that makes all consumption levels as high as possible.

Let us finally consider the case in which there may also be other differences among persons than differences in locational preferences. These differences could consist of differences in labour productivity and in ownership of other resources (for example capital and land).[8] To give a general discussion of these types of heterogeneity, let us introduce the following formal notation: Let $\mathbf{e} = (e_1, \ldots e_J)$ denote the vector of emissions from all countries (satisfying (4.2), that is $\Sigma_i e_i \leq E$). Let $\mathbf{s}_j$ be a vector describing the policy of country j, including this country's choice of all transfers within the country and (under F) to residents in other countries. The vector

$\mathbf{s} = (\mathbf{s}_1, \ldots, \mathbf{s}_J)$ thus gives a complete description of the policy choices in all countries.[9]

Once (e,s) is given, all other variables follow. In particular, the utility levels of all types and the number of each type living in each country follows.[10] Formally,

$$u^t = u^t\,(\mathbf{e},\mathbf{s}) \qquad\qquad (4.10)$$

and

$$n_j^t = n_j^t(\mathbf{e},\mathbf{s}) \qquad\qquad (4.11)$$

Among all emission and policy vectors $(\mathbf{e},\mathbf{s})$, the ones giving Pareto efficiency are of special interest. All types share a common interest in eliminating all vectors $(\mathbf{e},\mathbf{s})$ that do *not* give Pareto efficiency, since everyone can be made better off with appropriate policy changes if the initial vector $(\mathbf{e},\mathbf{s})$ does not give Pareto efficiency. In an economy resembling the one presented in Section 1 (except for heterogeneity in populations) all types would thus share the common interest in having the emission vector being cost-effective (see (4.4)), provided there are no restrictions on inter-country transfers.

We have already discussed the special case in which locational preferences are the only differences among types, and where there is one type that lives in all countries in equilibrium. For this case there is only one Pareto efficient outcome. Clearly, there is no conflict of interest in this case.

For the more general case there will be several vectors $(\mathbf{e},\mathbf{s})$ giving Pareto efficiency, and there will thus be pure conflict of interest: any change in the vector $(\mathbf{e},\mathbf{s})$ that increases the utility level for one group, will by definition reduce the utility level for another group.

In order to discuss whether or not there is a conflict of interest between *countries* as well as between types we must define what we mean by the welfare level of a country. Let us therefore introduce a welfare function in each country that weighs the interests of the different types. These weights may depend on the number of persons of each type that choose to live in the country. The welfare function for country j must therefore generally depend on the number of persons of each type living in the country as well as on the utility levels persons of each type have. Using (4.10) and (4.11) we thus have

$$V_j = \Phi_j[u^1(\mathbf{e},\mathbf{s}),\ldots, u^T\,(\mathbf{e},\mathbf{s}), n_j^1\,(\mathbf{e},\mathbf{s}),\ldots, n_j^T\,(\mathbf{e},\mathbf{s})] = V_j\,(\mathbf{e},\mathbf{s}) \qquad (4.12)$$

Notice that a special case of this function is where the population and utility levels of each type t enter only as the product $n_j^t\,u_j^t$.

The discussion above on common interests and interest conflicts among types is not affected by the properties of the welfare functions that countries have. No matter what properties these functions have, there will in most cases be a conflict of interests between different types regarding how emission quotas ought to be allocated. Whether or not there also is a conflict of interest between *countries* depends on the welfare functions of the countries. To see this, consider the special case analysed by Hoel and Shapiro (2000). Here we analyse the case in which each country has the same social welfare function. Moreover, this social welfare function is assumed to depend only on the utility level of each type, and not on how many people of each type are living in the country. In other words, in this case the welfare function (4.12) simplifies to

$$V_j = \Phi[u^1(\mathbf{e},\mathbf{s}),...,u^T(\mathbf{e},\mathbf{s})] = V(\mathbf{e},\mathbf{s}) \qquad (4.13)$$

In this special case all countries have the same welfare level, no matter what the vector $(\mathbf{e},\mathbf{s})$ is. They thus have a common interest in maximizing this common level. In other words, we get the same situation as we had with homogeneous populations: there is no conflict in interest regarding the allocation of emission quotas across countries. This is true independently of whether or not inter-country transfers are permitted, that is it is true both for case E and F.

For the more general welfare function (4.12), however, there will generally be an interest conflict among countries as well as among types. This follows directly from the fact that there is an interest conflict between types. If different countries weigh different types differently in their welfare functions, this interest conflict carries over to an interest conflict between countries. However, it is not necessarily true that each country would like to have as much as possible of the total emission quotas. Any change in the allocations of emission quotas will typically improve the utility levels of some types, and reduce it for other types. The effect on the welfare levels of countries will depend on the specification of the general welfare function given by (4.12).

8.   CONCLUDING COMMENTS

This chapter has challenged a common view in the literature discussing international climate agreements. The common view suggests that there is an interest conflict between countries, in the sense that for a given amount of total emissions, each country is better off the larger its share of the total number of emission quotas. This interest conflict is independent of whether or not the emission quotas are tradable.

In the chapter I show that if there is a perfectly homogeneous and mobile population in the countries considered, the interest conflict vanishes. In this simple case all countries have a common interest in a particular allocation of emission quotas.

The result is modified if one more realistically allows for population heterogeneity. In this case I show that there typically will be an interest conflict among countries regarding the allocation of emission quotas. However, it need no longer be true that each country is better off the larger its share of the total number of emission quotas.

NOTES

*   I have received useful comments from Aanund Hylland, Michael Rauscher, Aart de Zeeuv, and two anonymous referees. Financial support from the Research Council of Norway is acknowledged.

1. A recent study by Chao and Peck (2000) gives an explicit discussion of the relationship between the magnitude of the sum of emissions and how these emissions are allocated between countries.
2. Throughout the chapter, the analysis is simplified by assuming that the relationship between population and labour input is exogenous.
3. More precisely: all allocations giving a positive marginal productivity of emissions (that is a positive marginal abatement cost) in all countries.
4. Throughout the chapter, I shall assume that the production functions have properties implying that the population is positive in all countries in all efficient outcomes. The possibility of zero population in some countries is discussed by Hoel and Shapiro (2000).
5. Notice, however, that although such a change increases the value of W, it need not be a Pareto improvement: people moving from country 1 to country 2 may get a reduced consumption level when they move.
6. Strictly speaking, this need only be true for the persons who are residents in country 1 both before and after the move along the frontier.
7. Since people are identical, it is assumed that all residents of the same country have the same consumption level.
8. See Hoel and Shapiro (2000) for a more detailed discussion of how such differences can be explicitly modelled.
9. As previously, the vector **e** denotes actual emissions. If emission quotas are tradable, we thus interpret **e** as the final allocation of actual emissions. The vector **s** in this case includes payments for traded quotas. The choice of the initial allocation of emission quotas is thus reflected in **s**. (See also the discussion in the second half of Section 5.)
10. When types differ also in other respects than in locational preferences, consumption levels may differ across types as well as across countries. It is easily verified that an implication of this is that the equilibrium may be characterized by several or all types living in all countries.

REFERENCES

Chao, H.-P. and Peck, S. (2000), 'Greenhouse gas abatement: How much? And who pays?', *Resource and Energy Economics*, **22**, 1–20.

Cline, W. (1992), *The Economics of Global Warming*, Washington: Institute for International Economics.

Hoel, M. and M. Shapiro (2000), 'Transboundary environmental problems with a mobile population: Is there a need for central policy?', mimeo, University of Oslo.

Kverndokk, S. (1993), 'Global CO_2 agreements: a cost-effective approach', *The Energy Journal*, **14**, 91–112.

Kverndokk, S. (1995), 'Tradeable CO_2 emission permits: initial distribution as a justice problem', *Environmental Values*, **4**, 129–48.

Myers, G. (1990), 'Optimality, free mobility and regional authority in a federation', *Journal of Public Economics*, **43**, 107–21.

5. Environmental regulation and international trade: a general equilibrium approach

Chris Elbers and Cees Withagen

1. INTRODUCTION

There is ample evidence that in the debates on environmental policy the possibility of loss of competitiveness as a consequence of such policy plays a major role. For example, in the Netherlands there has been a fierce debate concerning the introduction of a carbon tax, where employers' unions predicted that many firms would leave the country if the tax were implemented. Similar debates with similar arguments occurred elsewhere in the European Union. NAFTA provides a good example as well, because of the fear that US firms would tend to move across the border. A recent example is provided by the Conference of Parties concerning the Kyoto agreement at The Hague and the meeting in Bonn in 2001, where the US made clear it would not commit to the protocol since that would endanger the profitability of US companies.

The argument used on the part of those advocating lax taxation of exporting firms can easily be sketched. Stricter environmental policy will cause an upward shift of the supply curves and on a competitive world market this will lead to fewer exports.

A related issue is 'ecological dumping'. Loosely speaking, governments, acting strategically, impose environmental taxes below the Pigouvian level on exporting firms in order to enhance the competitiveness of domestic firms in the world market.

Seminal work on the theory of ecological dumping and strategic behaviour in the context of international trade has been done by Rauscher (1994 and 1997) and Barrett (1994). Rauscher constructs a simple but full-fledged general equilibrium model of international trade involving externalities. In the absence of strategic considerations a first-best optimum is characterized by the use of two instruments: a tariff capturing the economy's market power and environmental taxes equal to marginal damage (or the corresponding emission quota). In the case of perfect competition there is no market power and therefore no tariff, whereas environmental quotas correspond to optimal marginal damage. In that case, contrary to popular views, ecological dumping is not optimal from a welfare perspective. In the case of a large country a first-best optimum cannot be obtained without the necessary instruments, namely tariffs. It is made plausible that in the case of a large country or in the case of an oligopolistic structure of the world market (first analysed by Barrett in the context of a partial equilibrium setting) ecological dumping might not be optimal from a social welfare point of view either. The underlying idea is that environmental taxes should be increased if that leads to better terms of trade, which might actually occur.

Rauscher considers environmental standards as the government's policy instrument, although some inferences are drawn for an optimal emissions tax policy as well. The analysis also is purely local around the point where emission standards are set at the level where marginal environmental damage equals marginal utility of the use of an environmentally unfriendly input factor. Except for the straightforward competitive case it turns out to be rather difficult to obtain general results, even with the Pigouvian case as point of departure. Indeed, particular assumptions with respect to the functions involved have to be made. Sometimes these assumptions do not refer to exogenous parameters but to the values of these functions, or their derivatives, in the presupposed equilibrium, or even to the value of determinants composed in a complex way from equilibrium values. This makes it hard to see from the primitives of an economy (that is the parameter values of the model) which conclusions are likely to hold. Regarding the oligopolistic case only a conjecture is stated.

The objectives of the present chapter are threefold. First, we aim at presenting a short account of the existing literature. Secondly, we construct a model similar to the one used by Rauscher with emission taxes rather than emission standards and show that unambiguous results can be obtained from a local analysis. In particular we show that the sheltered, non-exporting, sector should be taxed according to marginal damage. We also provide examples showing the optimality of higher emissions taxes on the export sector. Finally, we present numerical exercises to calculate the global second-best optimum under different market structures, including oligopoly, and other characteristics of the economy. The main novelty of the chapter lies in the treatment of oligopoly.[1] The conclusion is that we do not find support for a lax treatment for the export sector in general, at least from a utilitarian social welfare perspective.

2.   THE MODEL

The models discussed throughout this chapter have several characteristics in common. These are outlined in the present section. The models are all inspired by the model used by Rauscher (1994). A difference is that we consider emission taxes as a policy instrument instead of standards.

In the economy there are three *consumer commodities*, *capital* and a *raw material*.

The first consumer commodity is produced and consumed domestically only. Domestic consumption is denoted by c_1 Production takes place according to a technology described by an aggregate constant returns to scale production function (F_1) with capital (k_1) and raw material (y_1) as inputs. The raw material can be thought of as energy from fossil fuel. The second consumer commodity is produced domestically, according to a constant returns to scale production function (F_2), mapping capital (k_2) and the raw material (y_2) into output. Part of output is consumed domestically (c_2), part of it is exported (x). The export price is denoted by p_2. The third consumer commodity cannot be produced domestically. Its consumption (c_3) is imported at the given world market price, which is taken to be unity.

An important aspect of the type of models used in the related literature is that there is an internationally immobile factor. In the present model we have chosen to label this factor as capital. Capital is immobile internationally but mobile between domestic sectors. Empirical as well as theoretical support for the assumption of international immobility of capital can be found in Gordon and Bovenberg (1996). The economy's endowment is given by $\bar{k}$. The domestic rate of return on capital is denoted by r.

The raw material is freely available in unlimited amounts. However, processing the raw material causes pollution, for instance CO_2 or NO_x emissions. To alleviate the negative external effect associated with emissions the government levies taxes τ_1 and τ_2 per unit of raw material used by the firms in the domestic sheltered industry and the exposed sector, respectively. These taxes can differ between sectors. Tax revenues are recycled to the consumers in a lump sum fashion.

There is one representative *consumer.* The budget consists of the value of the capital endowment $r\bar{k}$ tax revenues $\tau_1 y_1 + \tau_2 y_2$ plus possibly revenues from the tariff, and the aggregate profits of the *firms.* The latter amount to $p_1 F_1(k_1, y_1) - rk_1 - \tau_1 y_1$ and $p_2 F_2(k_2, y_2) - rk_2 - \tau_2 y_2$, for the sheltered and the exposed sector, respectively, assuming for the moment that the domestic price of the second commodity equals its world market price. Under the assumptions of constant returns to scale and of full employment of capital (in a situation where firms maximize profits) national income boils down to (in shorthand) $p_1 F_1 + p_2 F_2$. The consumer maximizes utility, taking prices and income as given. Preferences of the consumer refer to two types of commodities. First, they depend on the consumption of the consumer goods. This is represented by a utility function, denoted by $U(c_1, c_2, c_3)$, which is assumed to have all the usually imposed properties such as concavity, differentiability and monotonicity. As explained above, the use of the raw material brings along pollution (in a proportional way). This part of the preferences is given by the (convex and increasing) damage function $D(y_1 + y_2)$.

In the sequel of the paper we restrict ourselves to environmental taxes. It has been pointed out by Ulph (1997), among others, that in a setting of strategic behaviour the choice of instruments matters. We do not go into this important matter in the present chapter, because we want to concentrate on the issue of partial versus general equilibrium. Another issue that is not dealt with in this chapter is transboundary pollution. In the model pollution is only local, following Rauscher (1994).

An assumption made in the initial sections of the chapter is that in each sector of the economy there is a large number of price-taking competing firms, identical per sector, which are all profit maximizing.

3. FIRST-BEST OPTIMUM: FULL COMPETITION AND THE LARGE COUNTRY CASE

Several steps will be taken in the framework developed above. The first step is to calculate the social optimum subject to the condition that equilibrium prevails on the current account: $c_3 = p_2 x(p_2)$. Here $x(p_2)$ is world demand for the exported commodity. Subsequently we discuss the instruments needed to implement the first-best optimum in a decentralized setting. These exercises are quite standard in the international trade literature and the results are well known, but we provide a detailed analysis for later reference.

Mathematically, the problem to be solved by the government is to find rates of consumption, inputs in production and exports such that the social welfare function

$$U(c_1, c_2, c_3) - D(y_1 + y_2)$$

is maximized, subject to the constraints imposed by technology, the equilibrium condition on the current account and the initial endowment of capital:

$$c_1 = F_1(k_1, y_1) \tag{5.1}$$

$$c_2 = F_2(k_2, y_2) - x(p_2) \tag{5.2}$$

$$c_3 = p_2 x(p_2) \tag{5.3}$$

$$k_1 + k_2 = \bar{k} \tag{5.4}$$

The Lagrangian of the problem reads:

$$L = U(c_1, c_2, c_3) + D(y_1 + y_2) - \varphi_1[F_1(k_1, y_1) - c_1] + \varphi_2[F_2(k_2, y_2) - x(p_2) - c_2]$$
$$+ \varphi_3[p_2 x(p_2) - c_3] + \mu[\bar{k} - k_1 - k_2].$$

Assuming an interior solution and differentiability, in the equilibrium, of the functions involved, we find as necessary conditions

$$U_{c_1} = \varphi_1$$
$$U_{c_2} = \varphi_2$$
$$U_{c_3} = \varphi_3$$
$$\varphi_1 F_{1k} = \mu; \ \varphi_1 F_{1y} = D'$$
$$\varphi_2 F_{2k} = \mu; \ \varphi_2 F_{2y} = D'$$
$$-\varphi_2 x'(p_2) + \varphi_3[x(p_2) + p_2 x'(p_2)] = 0$$

where primes and subscripts refer to (partial) derivatives. In the sequel asterisks will denote the solution of this problem: $(c_1^*, c_2^*, c_3^*, p_2^*, k_1^*, k_2^*, y_1^*, y_2^*, x^*)$. The optimal multipliers are denoted by asterisks as well.

The next step is to investigate how the first-best optimum can be realized in a decentralized setting. It suffices

a. to set emission taxes equal to the marginal damage of emissions;
b. to set the domestic price of the exported commodity equal to the world market price;
c. to impose an import tariff on the third imported commodity.

Recall that it is assumed that the exporting industry consists of many price-taking firms, but that the economy *as a whole* can influence prices on the world market by manipulating supply, at least in the case of a large country. More specifically, let (p_1, p_2, p_3, τ, r) be the vector of domestic prices for consumer goods, emissions and capital respectively. Denote by t the import tariff on the third commodity. Take

$$t = -1/(1 + \varepsilon^*), \ p_1 = \frac{\varphi_1^*}{\varphi_3^*}(1 + t), \ p_2 = \frac{\varphi_2^*}{\varphi_3^*}(1 + t) = p_2^*, \ p_3 = (1 + t),$$

$$\tau_1 = \tau_2 = \frac{D'(y_1^* + y_2^*)}{\varphi_3^*}(1+t), \ r = \frac{\mu^*}{\varphi_3^*}(1+t)$$

Here ε^* is the price elasticity of world market demand for the second commodity which, evaluated at the optimum, should be smaller than minus unity. Due to the concavity/convexity assumptions on the functions involved the necessary conditions corresponding with the first-best social optimum are also sufficient.

The pair (k_1^*, y_1^*) maximizes profits $p_1F_1(k_1, y_1) - rk_1 - \tau y_1$ of (aggregate) firm 1, because it maximizes

$$\varphi_1^*F_1(k_1, y_1) - \mu^*k_1 - D(y_1 + y_2^*).$$

For the same reason (k_2^*, y_2^*) maximizes profits of (aggregate) firm 2, which takes the world market price p_2 as given. The triplet (c_1^*, c_2^*, c_3^*) maximizes

$$U(c_1, c_2, c_3)$$

subject to

$$p_1c_1 + p_2c_2 + p_3c_3 = F_1 + p_2F_2 + T$$

where T denotes recycled import tariff revenues. The triplet satisfies the first-best necessary conditions for optimality; the latter are also sufficient in view of the concavity of the utility function. Furthermore, the consumption bundle is affordable.

Finally, all markets clear at the proposed prices.

This result about implementation is well known from the general theory of international trade (see also Neary, 1999). It implies that in the case of full competition on the world market for the exported commodity $(\varepsilon^* = -\infty)$, it is optimal not to impose an import tariff and to tax emissions according to their marginal damage. Moreover, in the case of a large country (with a finite price elasticity of world demand) the first-best optimum can be mimicked in a decentralized economy by setting emissions taxes equal to marginal damage, as in full competition, and by using a tariff on the imported commodity.

Instead of using an import tariff, the government could also use a tariff on exports. The optimal tariff equals $-p_2/\varepsilon^*$. Of course the effect of an export tariff is equivalent to an import tariff, but it might add intuition for the case of the second-best optimum to be discussed below.

4.   SECOND-BEST POLICY IN THE LARGE COUNTRY CASE

This section assumes that, due to international regulations, it is not feasible to use tariffs as an instrument. Then a second-best solution is in order. It was shown in the previous section that tariffs are not needed to implement the first-best optimum when there is perfect competition. Therefore, attention will be restricted to the large country case.

The questions addressed are whether it is optimal to differentiate between domestic sectors with respect to the emission taxes and whether taxes are below the marginal damage or not. We analyse the second-best optimum where the government conducts environmental policy by means of emission taxes as an instrument rather than standards. The attractiveness of this approach lies in the observation that a model with this characteristic has more structure because, due to the assumption of constant returns to scale, factor prices should lie on the factor price frontier. In this case unambiguous results can be obtained. First we follow an analytical approach. Later we shall perform some numerical experiments.

Suppose the government has set optimal emission taxes, subject to the constraints that the tax rates do not differ between sectors and such that they equal marginal damage. We are interested in the question how welfare changes if the government marginally deviates from this policy, given the market behaviour by individual agents. In a competitive economy the representative consumer maximizes utility subject to the budget constraint. Domestic prices equal world market prices. This yields

$$U_{c_1}/p_1 = U_{c_2}/p_2 = U_{c_3}$$

It follows from profit maximization and the fact that emission taxes equal marginal damage that

$$p_1 F_{1k} = p_2 F_{2k} = r, \ p_1 F_{1y} = \tau_1 = p_2 F_{2y} = \tau_2 = D'/U_{c_3}.$$

Moreover, feasibility and equilibrium on the current account require

$$c_1 = F_1, \ c_2 = F_2 - x(p_2), \ c_3 = p_2 x(p_2).$$

In a general equilibrium social welfare can be expressed as a function of the tax rates τ_1 and τ_2. The change in welfare (dW) following a change in the tax rate for sector 1, keeping the tax rate in sector 2 unaltered, reads:

$$dW = \left\{ U_{c_1}\left[F_{1k}\frac{\partial k_1}{\partial \tau_1} + F_{1y}\frac{\partial y_1}{\partial \tau_1} \right] + \frac{U_{c_2}}{p_2}\left[p_2 F_{2k}\frac{\partial k_2}{\partial \tau_1} + p_2 F_{2y}\frac{\partial y_2}{\partial \tau_1} - p_2 x'\frac{\partial p_2}{\partial \tau_1} \right] \right.$$

$$\left. + U_{c_3}\left[x\frac{\partial p_2}{\partial \tau_1} + p_2 x'\frac{\partial p_2}{\partial \tau_1} \right] - D'\left[\frac{\partial y_1}{\partial \tau_1} + \frac{\partial y_2}{\partial \tau_1} \right] \right\} d\tau_1$$

Due to the properties of the general competitive equilibrium, including the fixed initial endowment of capital, this expression boils down to:

$$dW = U_{c_3} x \frac{\partial p_2}{\partial \tau_1} d\tau_1.$$

The same exercise can be performed for the tax rate in the other sector. As a result we obtain that, as expected, the effect of a policy change depends on its impact on the terms of trade:

$$dW = U_{c_3} x\left[\frac{\partial p_2}{\partial \tau_1} d\tau_1 + \frac{\partial p_2}{\partial \tau_2} d\tau_2 \right]. \tag{5.5}$$

For the case of standards Rauscher (1994) merely states that the terms of trade effect of a lower emission standard in the exporting sector is positive, *under normal circumstances.* And he argues that the effect is ambiguous for the standard in the sheltered sector. It is our aim to be more specific, for the case of emission taxation.

We first turn to a *local* analysis that allows us to be more concrete with respect to optimal taxation, starting from a situation where both taxes are equal to marginal damage. It cannot be hoped that this objective can be achieved without further specifying the functions involved, although it will be shown below that for the general case the tax rate in the sheltered sector should equal marginal damage. We propose the following specifications. Utility is logarithmically additive, environmental damage is quadratic, production functions are Cobb-Douglas and world demand for the exported commodity is iso-elastic. A modest defence for this choice is the relative ease with which calculations can be made and the fact that these specifications are widely used elsewhere in the literature.

$$U(c_1, c_2, c_3) = \ln c_1 + \ln c_2 + \ln c_3 \tag{5.6}$$

$$F_1(k_1, y_1) = k_1^\alpha y_1^{1-\alpha} \tag{5.7}$$

$$F_2(k_2, y_2) = k_2^\beta y_2^{1-\beta} \tag{5.8}$$

$$D(y_1 + y_2) = \tfrac{1}{2}[y_1 + y_2]^2 \tag{5.9}$$

$$x(p_2) = p_2^\varepsilon, \ \varepsilon < 0 \tag{5.10}$$

It follows from utility maximization subject to the budget constraint that

$$p_1 c_1 = p_2 c_2 = c_3 = \tfrac{1}{3}[p_1 F_1 + p_2 F_2].$$

Together with the conditions for market equilibrium, $F_1 = c_1$, $F_2 = c_2 + x(p_2)$, this yields:

$$p_1 c_1 = p_2 x(p_2), \ c_2 = x(p_2), \ c_3 = p_2 x(p_2)$$

It follows from profit maximization that equilibrium prices are on the factor price frontiers, corresponding with zero profits, defined by:

$$p_1 = \left(\frac{r}{\alpha}\right)^{\alpha} \left(\frac{\tau_1}{1-\alpha}\right)^{1-\alpha} f_1(r, \tau_1) \tag{5.11}$$

$$p_2 = \left(\frac{r}{\beta}\right)^{\beta} \left(\frac{\tau_2}{1-\beta}\right)^{1-\beta} = f_2(r, \tau_2) \tag{5.12}$$

Factor demands are:

$$k_1(r, \tau_1, p_1, p_2) = \left(\frac{r}{\alpha}\right)^{\alpha-1} \left(\frac{\tau_1}{1-\alpha}\right)^{1-\alpha} F_1 = \left(\frac{r}{\alpha}\right)^{\alpha-1} \left(\frac{\tau_1}{1-\alpha}\right)^{1-\alpha} \frac{p_2 x(p_2)}{p_1} \tag{5.13}$$

$$y_1(r, \tau_1, p_1, p_2) = \left(\frac{r}{\alpha}\right)^{\alpha} \left(\frac{\tau_1}{1-\alpha}\right)^{-\alpha} F_1 = \left(\frac{r}{\alpha}\right)^{\alpha} \left(\frac{\tau_1}{1-\alpha}\right)^{-\alpha} \frac{p_2 x(p_2)}{p_1} \tag{5.14}$$

$$k_2(r, \tau_2, p_2) = \left(\frac{r}{\beta}\right)^{\beta-1} \left(\frac{\tau_2}{1-\beta}\right)^{1-\beta} F_2 = \left(\frac{r}{\beta}\right)^{\beta-1} \left(\frac{\tau_2}{1-\beta}\right)^{1-\beta} 2x(p_2) \tag{5.15}$$

$$y_2(r, \tau_2, p_2) = \left(\frac{r}{\beta}\right)^{\beta} \left(\frac{\tau_2}{1-\beta}\right)^{-\beta} F_2 = \left(\frac{r}{\beta}\right)^{\beta} \left(\frac{\tau_2}{1-\beta}\right)^{-\beta} 2x(p_2) \tag{5.16}$$

Use (5.13) and (5.15) in $k_1 + k_2 = \bar{k}$, solve for r and substitute in (5.12) to obtain the following expression

$$\bar{k} = \left(\frac{1}{\beta}\right) \left(\frac{\tau_2}{1-\beta}\right)^{\frac{1-\beta}{\beta}} p_2^{\frac{\beta(1+\varepsilon)-1}{\beta}} (\alpha + 2\beta). \tag{5.17}$$

In this case it is clearly optimal to raise the tax on emissions from the exporting sector above the level corresponding with marginal damage, because that will raise the price of the exported commodity (see (5.5)).

We also observe that the price of the exported commodity depends on the emission tax of the exporting sector only. Hence, marginally decreasing or increasing the tax on emissions in the sheltered sector does not yield higher social welfare. It can be shown that this is a general result, going beyond the specific functional forms used in this exercise. The argument runs as follows. In equilibrium we have from profit maximization in the sheltered sector $p_1 F_{1y} = \tau_1$. In equilibrium we also have $U_{c_1}/U_{c_3} = p_1$. Therefore

$$\frac{U_{c_1}}{U_{c_3}} F_{1y} = \tau_1$$

Consider a marginal variation of y_1 only. In an optimum this variation should not allow for a welfare improvement. Hence

$$\frac{d}{dy_1}[U(c_1, c_2, c_3) - D(y_1 + y_2)] = 0$$

Stated otherwise

$$U_{c_1} F_{1y} = \tau_1 U_{c_3} = D'(y_1 + y_2)$$

We conclude that it is optimal to have an emission tax in the sheltered sector equal to marginal damage.

In what follows we perform a *global* analysis of the problem. This allows for a calculation of globally optimal environmental taxes, rather than calculating the effect of a marginal deviation from taxes equal to marginal damage. Global welfare optimization on the part of the government requires maximization of utility minus damage, taking the constraints outlined above into account. After straightforward substitutions the Lagrangian can be written as follows:

$$\ln \frac{p_2 x(p_2)}{p_1} + \ln x(p_2) + \ln p_2 x(p_2) - \tfrac{1}{2}[y_1(r, \tau_1, p_1, p_2) + y_2(r, \tau_2, p_2)]^2$$

$$+ \lambda[k_1(r, \tau_1, p_1, p_2) + k_2(r, \tau_2, p_2) - \bar{k}] + \mu_1[p_1 - f_1(r, \tau_1)] + \mu_2[p_2 - f_2(r, \tau_2)]$$

This poses a well-defined mathematical programming problem that can in principle be solved. Even the simple functional forms we selected do not allow for much analytical work. Therefore we perform several numerical experiments. All the calculations were done in *Mathematica* (see Wolfram, 1996, and Cool, 1999). We use $\bar{k} = 10$ throughout.

For the Netherlands the production elasticities of energy are crudely estimated to be 3.5 percent and 20 percent in the sheltered and the exposed sector, respectively. For demand elasticity $\varepsilon = -2$ we obtain $\tau_1 = 0.8$ and

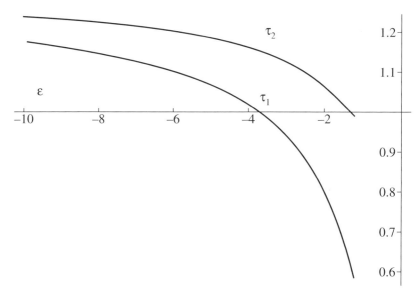

*Figure 5.1   Second-best emission taxes (τ_1 and τ_2) and demand elasticity
(ε)*

$\tau_2 = 1.06$. Hence the emission tax on the exposed sector is considerably higher. For a price elasticity of –6 the values are 1.1 and 1.2 respectively. In Figure 5.1 we have displayed the optimal taxes for a large range of demand elasticities. As was to be expected, for lower elasticities the difference between emission taxes is lower. In Figure 5.2 we have plotted the sectoral emission taxes as a function of the production elasticity of capital in the exposed sector.

5.   OLIGOPOLY: PARTIAL EQUILIBRIUM

In this section we consider the case where the country under investigation is an oligopolist on the world market. The analysis takes place within a partial equilibrium framework along the lines developed by Barrett (1994), based on Brander and Spencer (1985). It serves as a benchmark for the general equilibrium approach of the next section. A distinction can be made between Stackelberg competition by means of quantities (Cournot) and Stackelberg competition by means of prices (Bertrand). In a partial equilibrium analysis the two approaches to competition yield opposite results. In the sequel attention is paid to Cournot competition only.

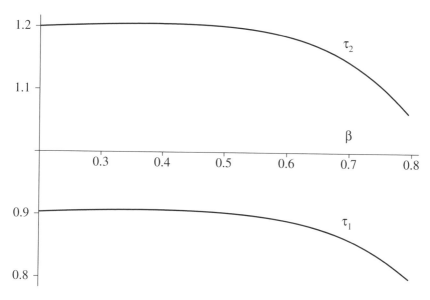

Figure 5.2   Second-best emission taxes (τ_1 and τ_2) and production elasticity (β)

In the model domestic and foreign firms compete on a third market: the exported commodities are not consumed domestically. The symbol x^f denotes total supply by foreign firms and x_i, $i=1,2,\ldots,n$ is supply by domestic firm i. Total domestic production is $x=\Sigma x_i$.

In the Barrett model the firm's costs consist of production costs, depending only on production, and abatement costs, depending on production as well as on the emission standard set by the government. Since we want to stay as close as possible to the general equilibrium model outlined in the previous sections, our model does not incorporate abatement nor emission standards. Instead, we restrict ourselves to emission taxes.

In the partial equilibrium approach the government takes as given all that occurs in the domestic sheltered sector. The government is not interested in total social welfare *per se*: pollution by the domestic sectors is not taken into account except for the exporting sector. Hence the government seeks to maximize export revenues minus social costs, the latter consisting of capital costs (which are exogenous) and the external damage costs caused by emissions of the exporting sector. Social welfare can be written as

$$W = \sum_{i=1}^{n} p(x+x^f)x_i - D(y_1+y_2+\ldots+y_n).$$

Here $p(x + x^f)$ is the inverse demand function. In Barrett's benchmark scenario the government takes output of domestic firms as given. In such circumstances the optimal standard arises from the equality of marginal abatement costs and marginal damage. Implementation of this rule requires information about the abatement cost function. In our model with taxes an analogous approach would be to assume that the government takes output of the domestic as well as the foreign firms as given. But it knows the cost function, from which demand for the raw material (and hence emissions) can be derived. It is then easily shown that it is optimal to set emission taxes equal to marginal damage.

Suppose now that the government acts strategically. Taking into account that the firms maximize their profits, that the government sets the emission tax equal to marginal damage, that total capital available for the sector is fixed and assuming that all firms are identical, it can be shown that

$$\frac{dW}{d\tau} = p'x\frac{n-1}{n}\frac{dx}{d\tau} + p'x\frac{dx^f}{dx}\frac{dx}{d\tau}. \tag{5.18}$$

The direction of the effect of lowering the emission tax rate is ambiguous in general. However, if additional assumptions are made the effect can be determined as negative. Assume that there is one domestic producer. Then the first term on the right-hand side vanishes. In the second term on the right-hand side three factors appear. Clearly $p' < 0$, because demand is downward sloping. Under mild assumptions, for example, with linear demand, the reaction curves are downward sloping so that $dx^f/dx < 0$. Moreover, $dx/d\tau < 0$ since the reaction curve of the domestic firm shifts outward as the tax rate decreases. Hence, in these circumstances it is optimal to set the emission tax below marginal damage. It is also seen from (5.18) that if the government takes foreign supply as given it is not optimal to deviate from the 'environmentally optimal' tax.

With multiple domestic producers $(n > 1)$ it might be optimal to have higher emission taxes, because two types of impacts can be distinguished due to a decrease in the emission tax rate. On the one hand, the government has an incentive to relax the tax rate below marginal damage because in doing so production will be increased, thereby enhancing profits from exports on the world market, at least as long as the reaction curves are downward sloping. On the other hand, the domestic firms are also competing amongst each other and consequently produce more than in the case of a domestic monopoly. The total effect is therefore ambiguous. This is also found by Barrett (1994) and by Ulph (1997), who employ a somewhat different model, but to which the same type of argument applies.

To illustrate the results obtained above we return to the example of a Cobb–Douglas technology and a quadratic damage function of Section 4, with a single domestic producer. To guarantee downward sloping reaction curves we employ a linear world demand schedule: $p(x + x^f) = 1 - a(x + x^f)$. Demand for the raw material is

$$y = \left(\frac{r}{\beta}\right)^{\beta} \left(\frac{\tau}{1 - \beta}\right)^{-\beta} x.$$

Without strategic behaviour on the part of the government the emission tax rate equals marginal damage: $\tau = D'(y) = y$. Combining the two equations we get a relationship between the emission tax and output:

$$\tau = \left(\frac{r}{\beta}\right)^{\frac{\beta}{1+\beta}} \left(\frac{1}{1 - \beta}\right)^{\frac{-\beta}{1+\beta}} x^{\frac{1}{1+\beta}}.$$

Paraphrasing Barrett this schedule can be called the *environmentally optimal emission tax*. Next we consider the possibility of strategic behaviour on the part of the government. Given the tax rate the exporting firm maximizes its profits with respect to the raw material, yielding

$$1 - 2ax - ax^f = \left(\frac{\tau}{1 - \beta}\right)^{1 - \beta} \left(\frac{r}{\beta}\right)^{\beta}.$$

Note that the reaction curve is downward sloping for all tax rates. The next question is what happens when the emission tax is lowered, below the 'environmentally optimal' one. Clearly, given the foreign country's output, the domestic firm's reaction curve shifts outward and the new equilibrium has higher domestic production and less foreign production. What is the implication for social welfare? According to (5.18) with $n = 1$ we have

$$\frac{dW}{d\tau} = -ax \frac{dx^f}{dx} \frac{dx}{d\tau}.$$

Taking into account that

$$\frac{dx}{d\tau} < 0 \text{ and } \frac{dx^f}{dx} < 0,$$

we conclude that it is indeed optimal for the government to set an emission tax lower than the environmentally optimal one. This is not only true under the assumption that the foreign government does not react strategically, but the conclusion holds as well if the foreign government does react strategically.

A more realistic case is one where domestic consumption of the exported commodity is allowed for. It has received only minor attention in the literature. According to Ulph (1997), if there is domestic consumption and the domestic market is oligopolistic, there is an additional incentive for the government to impose less stringent taxation. The reason is that imperfect competition will in general lead to too low output levels from the point of view of social welfare. Hence production for the domestic market should be stimulated.

6.   OLIGOPOLY: GENERAL EQUILIBRIUM

In this section a general equilibrium model is constructed with a single domestic producer acting as an oligopolist on the world market. As in the previous section we abstract from domestic consumption of the exported commodity ($c_2 = 0$).

The motivation for analysing oligopoly in a general equilibrium setting is that the strategy of increasing domestic production by relaxing emission standards has an effect on the allocation of capital in the economy through the rate of return. This effect is neglected in a partial equilibrium setting. It will be shown below that the effect can be important and may imply a policy recommendation opposite to the one obtained for the partial equilibrium discussed in the previous section.

We first show that with one oligopolist and Cournot–Nash as the equilibrium concept on the world market the first-best optimum is realized within a market economy, as was the case in the partial equilibrium approach. The underlying idea is simple. In the economy there are two distortions: one is the environmental distortion and the second is the fact that the world market is non-competitive. The latter distortion is fully exploited if the domestic firm can act as an oligopolist on the world market, which is the case at hand, contrary to the model of Section 3, where all domestic firms were competitive. Subsequently the first distortion can be solved independently, using uniform emission taxes equal to marginal damage. The formal proof of this is quite similar to the exercise performed in Section 3. It is given for the sake of completeness. The first-best optimum is the solution of maximizing social welfare

$$W = U(c_1, c_3) - D(y_1 + y_2)$$

subject to $c_1 = F_1(k_1, y_1)$, $c_3 = p_2(x)x$, $x = F_2(k_2, y_2)$ and $k_1 + k_2 = \bar{k}$. The necessary conditions are

$$U_{c_1} = \varphi_1$$
$$U_{c_3} = \varphi_3$$

$$\varphi_1 F_{1k} = \mu;\ \varphi_1 F_{1y} = D'$$
$$\varphi_2 F_{2k} = \mu;\ \varphi_2 F_{2y} = D'$$
$$\varphi_3 [p_2(x)x + p_2] = \varphi_2$$

The multipliers φ_1, φ_2, φ_3, μ correspond with the three commodities and capital, respectively. It is easily seen that the first-best optimum is realized in a decentralized setting if $p_1 = \varphi_1/\varphi_3$, $p_3 = 1$, $r = \mu/\varphi_3$ and $\tau = D'/\varphi_3$.

Next we calculate the welfare impact of a deviation from setting emission taxes equal to marginal damage, taking into account

- utility maximization on the part of the consumer: $U_{c_1}/p_1 = U_{c_3}$;
- profit maximization in the competitive sheltered sector: $p_1 \partial F_1/\partial k_1 = r$ and $p_1 \partial F_1/\partial y_1 = \tau_1$;
- profit maximization in the exporting sector: $(p_2 + p'_2 x)F_{2k} = r$ and $(p_2 + p'_2 x)F_{2y} + \tau_2$;
- the total fixed availability of capital.

Then

$$dW = U_{c_3} x p'_2 \frac{dx^f}{dx} \left[\frac{dx}{d\tau_1} d\tau_1 + \frac{dx}{d\tau_2} d\tau_2 \right]$$

Therefore, if the domestic exporting firm as well as the government takes as given the output of the foreign firm on the world market the impact of a deviation of a tax rate from the initial state is zero.

The more interesting case is where the domestic firm can be made to supply as a Stackelberg leader in equilibrium. This is achieved through the government's tax policy as in Brander and Spencer (1985). In order to perform the analysis we assume that the other country is a Stackelberg follower but is otherwise identical to the country under consideration, except possibly in size, measured by means of total available capital. The first step is to derive the other country's reaction function and to incorporate it into the objective function of the leader. We use the same specifications of the functions involved as before with iso-elastic demand: $x + x^f = 2p_2^\varepsilon$.

National income equals $p_1 F_1 + p_2 F_2$. In view of the utility functions and in the absence of domestic consumption of the exported commodity, it follows from utility maximization on the part of the consumers that:

$$p_1 c_1 = \tfrac{1}{2}[p_1 F_1 + p_2 F_2],\ c_3 = \tfrac{1}{2}[p_1 F_1 + p_2 F_2]$$

Equilibrium on the current account implies that $c_3 = p_2 F_2 = p_2 x$. Hence $p_1 c_1 = p_2 F_2 = p_2 x$.

Profit maximization in the sheltered sector requires that the equilibrium prices lie on the factor price frontier given by: $p_1 = f_1(r, \tau_1)$ (see equation (5.11)). Assuming a world demand function with constant elasticity, profit maximization on the part of the exporting sector implies

$$p_2'(x + x^f)x + p_2(x + x^f) =$$

$$2^{1/\varepsilon}(x + x^f)^{-1/\varepsilon}\left[1 - \frac{x}{\varepsilon(x + x^f)}\right] = \left(\frac{r}{\beta}\right)^\beta \left(\frac{\tau_2}{1 - \beta}\right)^{1-\beta} = f_2(r, \tau_2)$$

(see equation (5.12)). The capital and raw material inputs are given by (5.13)–(5.16), where it must be taken into account that we work with inverse demand now, giving rise to a slightly altered notation below. The mathematical problem faced by the government can be stated as:

$$\text{Max } \ln p_2(x + x^f)x/p_1 + \ln p_2(x + x^f)x - \tfrac{1}{2}[y_1 + y_2]^2$$

subject to

$$k_1 = k_1(r, \tau_1, p_2(x + x^f)x/p_1) \tag{5.19}$$

$$y_1 = y_1(r, \tau_1, p_2(x + x^f)x/p_1) \tag{5.20}$$

$$k_2 = k_2(r, \tau_2, x) \tag{5.21}$$

$$y_2 = y_2(r, \tau_2, x) \tag{5.22}$$

$$p_1 = f_1(r, \tau_1) \tag{5.23}$$

$$p_2'(x + x^f)x + p_2(x + x^f) = f_2(r, \tau_2) \tag{5.24}$$

$$k_1 + k_2 = \bar{k} \tag{5.25}$$

This problem cannot be solved in such a way that the sensitivity with respect to the parameters can be determined analytically, as one would wish to do in order to find out how to set optimal taxes in different circumstances. For that reason a number of numerical optimizations will be executed. The results are summarized in the figures displayed below. In the calculations the capital endowment of the home country is 10, for the foreign country the initial endowment is 5. The price elasticity of world demand is −8. The production elasticity of capital in the sheltered sector is 0.965 in both countries and 0.8 in the export sector.

In Figure 5.3a the Cournot–Nash equilibrium is depicted. This is a situation in which the sheltered firms in both countries maximize their profits given the market output price and the input prices and where the exposed sectors in both countries maximize profits given input prices, the market demand schedule and supply by the competing firm. Moreover, the tax rates are such that given the other country's supply on the world market social welfare cannot be increased. Both home country and foreign country's reaction functions include the optimal tax setting by the government. Fixing these tax rates at the Cournot equilibrium values leads to minuscule tilting of the reaction functions. Of course, the equilibrium itself is not affected by this. It is found that the optimal emission tax rates are 1.03 for the exposed as well as the sheltered sector, equalling marginal damage, as derived already above.

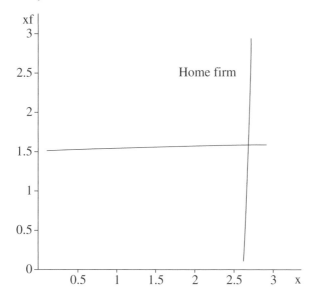

Figure 5.3a   Reaction curves and Cournot equilibrium

In Figure 5.3b we depict the shifted reaction function leading to the strategic Stackelberg equilibrium, along with the original reaction function. In both equilibria firm behaviour is the same but in the Stackelberg equilibrium the home government sets the emission tax rates so as to maximize social welfare, taking the reaction schedule of the foreign (following) exposed sector into account.[2] For the numerical example chosen the differences between the reaction functions are extremely small. Figure 5.3b therefore contains a cutout zooming in on the relevant part of the figure. The

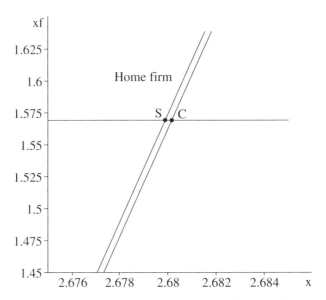

Figure 5.3b   Reaction curves, Cournot and Stackelberg equilibria

Stackelberg equilibrium is characterized by slightly contracted supply of the export good and a very small increase in the home country's welfare. For our set of parameter values we find optimal tax rates of 1.03 for the sheltered sector and 1.05 for the exposed sector. Hence we have provided an example where in a general equilibrium it is optimal to tax the exposed sector more heavily than the sheltered sector, contrary to what would be the case in a partial equilibrium setting.

7.   CONCLUSION

This chapter has addressed the issue of ecological dumping. We have developed a model with emission taxes as policy instruments to analyse several market structures: full competition, monopoly and oligopoly. It has been shown that it is indeed possible that in a second-best world where import tariffs are not allowed, it is optimal to tax the exposed export sector more heavily than the sheltered sector. This holds in a situation of monopoly on the world market as well as in the case of an oligopoly on a third market. Hence the results obtained in partial equilibrium exercises need modification.

Possible extensions of the analysis are the inclusion of transboundary pollution and multiple domestic exporting firms. Moreover, it would be interesting to consider a full-fledged general equilibrium model calibrated to a real world economy. It is also worthwhile to go more deeply in the sensitivity of the outcomes for changes in the parameters in order to evaluate the robustness of the results. From our analysis we do not wish to recommend stricter environmental policy with regard to exporting sectors. It was argued earlier by Barrett (1994) that other policy instruments might be more efficient. Moreover, our model is rather specific. Our purpose has been more modest in showing that things might be less straightforward than is sometimes suggested by a partial equilibrium analysis.

ACKNOWLEDGEMENTS

The authors wish to thank two anonymous referees, the editors, Jeroen van den Bergh, Erwin Bulte, Henk Kox, Daan van Soest and participants in the workshop on Environmental Policy and Competitiveness (Schiermonnikoog, 8–10 October 1998), in seminars at Tilburg University and Maastricht University and conferences of the European Association of Environmental and Resource Economists (Oslo, June 1999), the International Economic Association (Buenos Aires, August 1999) and the European Economic Association (Santiago de Compostela, September 1999). Martijn Vromans (CPB) was so kind to provide information on production elasticities.

NOTES

1. The case of monopolistic competition is treated by Pflüger (2001), who also finds ambiguous results.
2. For the home firm's reaction functions taxes were fixed at the respective equilibrium values. Changing taxes along with the home firm's output leads to slightly tilted curves, but leaves equilibria unchanged.

REFERENCES

Barrett, S. (1994), 'Strategic environmental policy and international trade', *Journal of Public Economics*, **54**, 325–38.
Brander, J. and B. Spencer (1985), 'Export subsidies and international market share rivalry', *Journal of International Economics,* **18**, 83–100.
Cool, T. (1999), 'The Economics Pack. User Guide', Thomas Cool Consultancy and Econometrics, www.gopherpublishers.com.
Gordon, R. and L. Bovenberg (1996), 'Why is capital so immobile internationally? Possible explanations and implications for capital income taxation', *American Economic Review*, **86**, 1057–75.

Neary, P. (1999), 'International trade and the environment: theoretical and policy linkages', paper presented at the annual conference of the European Association of Environmental and Resource Economists, Oslo, June.

Pflüger, M. (2001), 'Ecological dumping under monopolistic competition', *Scandinavian Journal of Economics*, forthcoming.

Rauscher, M. (1994), 'On ecological dumping', *Oxford Economic Papers*, **46**, 822–40.

Rauscher, M. (1997), *International Trade, Factor Movements, and the Environment*, Oxford: Clarendon Press.

Ulph, A. (1997), 'International Trade and the Environment: a Survey of Recent Economic Analysis', in H. Folmer and T. Tietenberg (eds), *The International Yearbook of Environmental and Resource Economics 1997/1998*, Cheltenham, UK and Lyme, US: Edward Elgar, pp. 205–42.

Wolfram, S. (1996), *The Mathematica Book*, Cambridge: Cambridge University Press.

6. The ups and downs of the environmental Kuznets curve

Arik Levinson

INTRODUCTION

Almost ten years ago, Grossman and Krueger (1993) and the World Bank (1992), publicized evidence that some measures of environmental quality appear to deteriorate with countries' economic growth at low levels of income per capita, and then to improve with economic growth at higher levels of income. Poor countries' environments get more polluted with economic growth, while rich countries' environments improve. Because this pattern of pollution and income bears superficial resemblance to the pattern of inequality and income documented by Kuznets (1955), the pollution–income relationship has been labeled an 'environmental Kuznets curve'.

Both Grossman and Krueger's paper, and the World Bank paper take the same strikingly simple approach. They regress average ambient levels of pollution on a polynomial in GDP per capita, across different countries and different time periods. They then plot the fitted values of pollution levels as a function of GDP per capita, and show that many of the graphs appear inverse-U-shaped, with peak pollution levels somewhere in the range of middle-income countries.

This observation, that pollution increases and then decreases with economic growth, has become a widely accepted truth, cited by op-ed pages and policy briefings worldwide. Simultaneously, it has sparked empirical and theoretical academic research. The empirical branch of the environmental Kuznets curve literature attempts to find similar patterns for additional pollutants, such as carbon, lead, hazardous waste, and indoor air pollution, and to test the sensitivity of the findings to functional form assumptions, specifications, time periods, countries, and additional control variables. The literature now includes papers with dynamic panel data models, fixed and random effects, splines, semi-parametric and non-parametric specifications, and includes controls for numerous country characteristics such as democratization, trade liberalization and corruption. Some papers confirm inverse-Us with other pollutants, countries, and time periods. Others argue that the result is spurious, and is highly sensitive to functional form assumptions and specifications.

The theoretical branch of the environmental Kuznets curve literature has attempted to model the pollution–income relationship. Models range from simple statics to complex dynamics with overlapping generations and endogenous policy determination. Some have welfare maximizing solutions that generate smooth inverse-U-shaped pollution–income paths, others rely on discrete jumps among multiple equilibria, while still others switch abruptly from constrained 'corner solutions' to interior optima in a sort of 'inverse-V-shaped' pollution–income path. Some even have multiple changes of direction and are 'N-shaped', or 'sideways-mirrored-S-shaped'.

The thesis of this chapter is that both the empirical and theoretical branches of the literature have lost sight of the fundamental questions raised by the original observation, and have obscured those questions in a thicket of mathematics and econometrics. First, the fundamental empirical observation is that, as Grossman and Krueger (1995) note, there is 'no evidence that environmental quality deteriorates steadily with economic growth'. Demonstrating this point does not require sophisticated econometrics. All one needs to do is show that there are some countries and some pollutants for which a time series of pollution plotted against GDP per capita shows a downward trend. Pooled estimates with fixed effects or random effects, polynomials, lagged values of GDP, and multiple control variables distract from the fundamental empirical question: are there pollutants that have declined with economic growth for some countries? In what follows I demonstrate that the answer to this question is unambiguously yes. For the few industrialized countries with sufficiently long time series in the data set used by Grossman and Krueger, one can document steady declines in ambient levels of urban air pollution, concurrent with economic growth.

The second area in which the environmental Kuznets curve literature has lost sight of the environmental forest for the mathematical trees involves the theory. It seems to me that the fundamental theoretical question raised by Grossman and Krueger's observation is whether the inverse-U-shaped pattern has normative implications for policy. We would like to know, for example, whether the upward-sloping portion of the pollution–income path, which is eventually reversed, is sufficient evidence that poor countries are enacting bad policies and would benefit from international guidance in setting local pollution standards. Alternatively, some have claimed that the downward sloping portion of the curve is evidence that local pollution problems are somehow 'self-correcting', and that the best environmental policy for developing nations is to grow wealthy as fast as possible.

These questions can be answered with the simplest of economic models, without dynamics, endogenous policies, or multiple equilibria. In what follows, I argue that an inverse-U-shaped pollution income path can be consistent with either Pareto-efficient policies, or sub-optimal behaviour with market failures. In other words, an observed inverse-U-shaped pollution–income path is neither sufficient evidence that poor countries' policies are inefficient, nor sufficient evidence to justify laissez-faire pollution regulations.

Most economics papers begin with theory, and support that theory with econometric evidence. This literature has proceeded in the opposite direction: first developing an empirical observation about the world, and then attempting to supply appropriate theories. Accordingly, I will follow the unconventional pattern and begin with the empirical evidence.

EMPIRICAL EVIDENCE FOR AN ENVIRONMENTAL KUZNETS CURVE

Since Grossman and Krueger's paper, the empirical literature has multiplied. Table 6.1 briefly outlines some of that literature. The papers in Table 6.1 apply various approaches to a wide variety of environmental problems. The original Grossman and Krueger paper regressed ambient pollution on a cubic polynomial in GDP per capita and lagged values of GDP per capita, using a random-effects specification, while the World Bank (Shafik and Bandyopadhyay, 1992) regressed those same pollutants on a quadratic in GDP per capita with fixed effects. Both found robust inverse-U-shaped relationships.

Since then, the literature has taken two directions. One tests the robustness of the early findings to functional form assumptions and specifications. Because this empirical literature is based on no underlying theory, it is particularly susceptible to such critiques. Harbaugh et al. (2002), for example, find that some of the original findings in this literature are changed dramatically by updates to the underlying data, and by the use of slightly different functional forms, and that confidence bands around the predicted pollution–income paths are wide enough to accommodate almost any pattern, inverse-U-shaped or otherwise.

A second, and far larger, set of papers seeks to expand these early results to other pollutants, including carbon (Holtz-Eakin and Selden, 1995; Taskin and Zaim, 2000), lead (Hilton and Levinson, 1998), automobile emissions (Kahn, 1998), toxic waste (Wang et al., 1998; Millimet and Stengos, 1999; Arora and Cason, 1999), and indoor air pollution (Chaudhuri and Pfaff, 1998). This last is notable because indoor air pollution is arguably entirely internalized. If households make rational, fully-informed decisions, then there are no market failures associated with indoor air pollution, and the

Chaudhuri and Pfaff result suggests that an inverse-U-shaped pollution–income path is consistent with Pareto-optimality.

None of the papers in this literature attempt to estimate structural parameters of the pollution–income relationship. Grossman and Krueger (1995) are explicit about this in their original work, 'reduced form equations that relate the level of pollution . . . to a flexible function of current and lagged income per capita in the country and to other covariates'. While researchers have included covariates in their regressions, none can claim to be estimating the direct, *ceteris paribus*, effect of income on pollution, for two important reasons. First, GDP is endogenous, and second, all of the studies omit unobservable variables we know are correlated with both income and pollution, such as environmental regulatory stringency, citizen preferences for clean air, and technological progress. Consequently, the only sensible interpretation of the results is as a correlation in the data, albeit one that is conditional on some related country characteristics.

By and large, the papers in this literature manage to find inverse-U-shaped patterns for most pollutants. The exceptions have reasonable explanations. Carbon emissions, for example, seem to increase at ever decreasing rates, but predicted peaks are far outside reasonable income levels. As a global pollutant involving cross-border externalities, no one country has sufficient incentive to regulate emissions. The free rider problem may simply be more troublesome with carbon than any other pollutant.

Some researchers find an 'N-shaped' path relative to income – increasing at low levels of income, decreasing at high levels, and then increasing again at even higher levels of national income. Grossman and Krueger dismiss the upper tail of this pattern as an artificial construct of the fact that they use a cubic functional form. The upper tail contains sparse data, and its shape is driven by the pattern of data at lower incomes. Millimet and Stengos, on the other hand, find a similar pattern with a semi-parametric specification, and so take the result seriously.

Finally, some pollutants appear only to decline with income, but this must by definition be a result of the data available. The researchers merely do not have data from earlier periods in which the pollution presumably increased, and only document the period of decline. In other words, in those cases documenting monotonic declines in pollution, the long-run pollution–income path must be roughly inverse-U-shaped. Environmental quality that is improving must once have degraded. Or, to abuse the cliche, 'what goes down must once have gone up'.

Ironically, this last point may be the most important insight of the literature. If we assume that countries cannot improve their environments beyond some primitive natural state, then environmental problems are only of consequence in those cases where economic growth has at some point been associated with increasing pollution. The upward sloping portion of the environmental Kuznets curve, in other words, is really not of interest. What is interesting, and perhaps policy relevant, is whether pollution eventually stops increasing with economic growth and begins to decline. In other words, economists have long argued that pollution is not an inevitable consequence of economic growth, but without convincing evidence. Now it appears that for the first time we have long-term panel data describing various pollutants in different countries, and can back up that claim. The original papers in this literature (Grossman and Krueger, Shafik and Bandyopadhyay) began to make this point – that pollution does not deterministically increase with growth – but were side-tracked by their functional form specifications into searching for inverse-U shapes.

To make the point slightly differently, what we would like to know is whether in fact there is convincing evidence that some forms of pollution decline with economic growth for some countries. This, it turns out, is a far simpler point to make than predicting an entire inverse-U-shaped pollution–income path.

NON-ECONOMETRIC EVIDENCE THAT POLLUTION CAN DECLINE WITH ECONOMIC GROWTH

To make the point that pollution can decline with income per capita, all one needs to do is plot pollution levels against GDP per capita for some sample pollutants and countries. As an example, consider SO_2, the pollutant most frequently found to have an inverse-U-shaped pattern, and internationally the best-monitored pollutant.

The GDP per capita data come from Summers and Heston's (1991) Penn World Tables. Data on ambient pollution levels used by the World Bank and Grossman and Krueger in their original work were collected by the Global Environmental Monitoring System (GEMS), sponsored by the World Health Organization (WHO) and the United Nations. The EPA maintains these data in its Aerometric Information Retrieval System (AIRS). For SO_2, the GEMS data contain 2401 annual observations from 285 monitoring stations in 102 cities in 45 countries, from 1971 to the present. Because the Summers and Heston data only extend to 1992, this analysis stops at that date.

It is useful to begin by separately examining the cross-section and time-series variation in pollution. Figure 6.1a depicts a cross-section of mean SO_2 readings from each monitoring station in 1980, plotted against GDP per capita. The observations are stacked up because there are multiple readings from each country, each with a single value of GDP per capita in

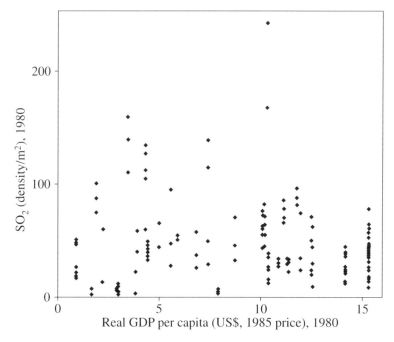

Figure 6.1a   Monitoring stations

1980. These are the numbers used to run the regressions plotted by Grossman and Krueger, and by the World Bank. By looking at Figure 6.1a, one can see the difficulty inherent in discerning any particular pattern. The data are roughly consistent with an environmental Kuznets curve, with the highest pollution readings coming from middle-income countries. However, middle-income countries also have monitoring stations with low SO_2 readings, so one cannot draw immediate conclusions from this figure.

Figure 6.1b plots the average SO_2 reading across all monitoring stations within a country, against GDP per capita. So by contrast to Figure 6.1a, Figure 6.1b has only one observation per country. One has to squint a little harder at this diagram to make the claim that cross-section evidence supports any particular decline in pollution levels at high incomes.

However, if the fundamental point to be made by this literature is that pollution does not inevitably increase with income, then cross-sectional evidence is irrelevant. Five of the studies reviewed in Table 6.1 contain only cross-sections of pollution and incomes at single points in time. While such evidence may suggest that richer countries are cleaner than middle-income countries, it does not necessarily show that richer countries have become cleaner over time. For that, we need time-series evidence.

Figure 6.1b   Country cross-sections

Most of the studies in Table 6.1 do use panels of data, but they typically pool time-series and cross-section evidence. Grossman and Krueger, for example, estimate panel data models with random effects. The coefficients on GDP per capita are thus identified partly from cross-sectional comparisons of countries within a given year, and partly from time-series comparisons within given countries. Again, however, if the fundamental point to be made by this literature is that pollution does not deterministically increase with income, then all we need do is show some countries whose pollution levels have declined with economic growth.

Take airborne sulphur pollution in the US, for example. Showing that a decline in pollution levels has occurred contemporaneously with economic growth is slightly more complicated than merely plotting average monitoring station readings against GDP per capita. That is because over time, countries have expanded the number of monitoring stations. If new stations are added in successively cleaner locales (the dirtiest places are targeted first), then the averages will display a spurious downward trend.

To avoid the bias inherent in the selection of monitoring station locale, in Figure 6.2 I have plotted average SO_2 readings from the monitoring stations in the US that were continuously active from 1979 through to 1992.

Table 6.1 Selected empirical papers on the environmental Kuznets curve

Paper	Pollutants	Data	Specification	Findings
Grossman and Krueger (1995)	SO_2, TSP, water quality.	Various countries, years	Cubic in logs, random effects, with lagged GDP	Most pollutants peak before GDP/capita reaches $8000.
Shafik and Bandyopadhyay (1992)	SPM, SO_2, faecal coliform in rivers, sanitation, municipal waste, carbon emissions, deforestation	149 countries 1960–1990	Panel regression based on OLS log linear, quadratic, cubic	Water and sanitation pollution peak earliest. Urban air pollution peaks for middle income countries.
Selden and Song (1994)	Panel of NO_xCOSPMSO_2$	30 countries, three periods (1973–75, 1979–81, 1982–84)	Pooled x-section, fixed effects, random effects	Substantial support for the inverted-U hypothesis, but with turning points at higher incomes.
Holtz-Eakin and Selden (1995)	CO_2	Uneven panel of data on 130 countries 1951–86	Quadratic in levels and natural logs	Concave emissions–income path, but no peak within reasonable range of incomes.
Roberts and Grimes (1997)	CO_2	US for 1962–91	OLS with linear and curvilinear effects of level of economic development on CO_2 emissions	Concavity of carbon emissions–income curve due to a relatively small number of wealthy countries becoming more efficient. No peak emissions at reasonable income levels.
Hilton and Levinson (1998)	Automotive lead emissions	48 countries. Leaded gasoline data from Octel	Quadratic in levels and logs, splines	Predicted peak lead emissions is sensitive to functional form and time period. Decomposes scale and technique effects.

Study	Variable	Data	Method	Findings
Kahn (1998)	Automotive hydro-carbon emissions	1993 California, USA	OLS	Finds inverted-U-shaped emissions–income relation peaking at $25000.
Wang, et al. (1998)	Exposure to toxic waste	Cross section of US counties in 1990	Tobit estimation	Inverted-U-shaped relationship between toxic waste and county income.
Chaudhuri and Pfaff (1998)	Indoor air pollution	Household level data in Pakiston	Tobit estimates of fuel use, translated into air quality	Inverted-U-shaped relationship between household income and indoor air quality.
Millimet and Stengos (1999)	Toxic releases from TRI	US states 1988–96	Semiparametric partially linear log	N-shaped path, turning up at high incomes ($30000 per capita)
Arora and Cason (1999)	Toxic releases from TRI	1993 cross section of 30000 zip codes.	2-stage maximum likelihood sample selection model where the first stage estimates a probit model	Variables that proxy for collective action significantly reduce local releases.
Harbaugh et al. (2002)	SO_2, TSP	Various years and countries	Fixed effects, panel, with polynomials in GDP and lagged GDP	Grossman and Krueger's (1995) findings are sensitive to countries studied, years covered, functional form, and econometric specification. Confidence bands around the pollution–income path render its shape uncertain.
Taskin and Zaim (2000)	CO_2 emissions (millions of tons)	Cross-section data on 52 countries 1975–90	Nonparametric kernel regression technique	Improved environmental quality at the initial phases of growth (up to GDP/ capita of $5000), followed by a phase of deterioration (up to $12000), and then improvement again.

Table 6.1 – continued

Paper	Pollutants	Data	Specification	Findings
Bradford et al. (2000)	13 different air and water pollutants	Various years and countries	New variant on cubic function with fixed effects	Similar to Grossman and Krueger: some pollutants exhibit inverse-Us, others do not.

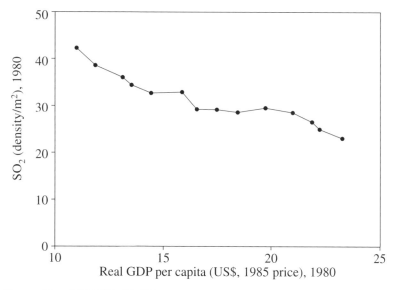

Figure 6.2   US 1979–92 (22 monitoring stations)

As is clear from the picture, economic growth and environmental cleanup are not mutually exclusive. Though other countries have fewer monitoring stations and fewer years of continuous data, the same trends are notable among industrialized countries.[1]

In sum, aggregate panel data on pollution levels across countries over time are noisy, and patterns are difficult to discern in the raw data. A large variety of empirical specifications attempting to detect such patterns have, in the literature, yielded an equally large variety of predictions. Nevertheless, for some pollutants it is quite easy to document steady improvements in ambient air quality, concurrent with economic growth. This is consistent with the claim that economic growth does not necessarily degrade the environment.

Although initially no economic theory provided foundations for understanding these data, in the past 10 years that gap has begun to be filled.

THEORETICAL EXPLANATIONS FOR THE ENVIRONMENTAL KUZNETS CURVE

To interpret the empirical observations outlined in Table 6.1, an equally diverse theoretical research has sprung up, each paper with its own normative implications. Several of these papers are summarized in Table 6.2.

Table 6.2   Theoretical models of growth and the environment

Paper	Model	Cause of non-monotonicity	Results
John and Pecchenino (1994)	Overlapping generations model. Environmental quality is a stock resource that degrades over time unless maintained by investment in the environment.	An economy that begins at the corner solution of zero environmental investment degrades its environment with economic growth until positive environmental investment is desired. Then environmental quality begins improving.	Inverse-V-shaped, peaking when the dynamic equilibrium switches from a corner solution of zero environmental investment to an interior optimum with positive investment.
Jaeger (1998) Stokey (1998)	Static model, choice of production technologies with varying degrees of pollution.	Below a threshold level of economic activity, only the dirtiest technology can be used. With economic growth, pollution increases linearly with income until the threshold is passed and cleaner technologies can be used.	Inverse-V-shaped pollution–income path, with a sharp peak at the point where a continuum of cleaner technologies becomes available.
Kelly (1999) Jones and Manuelli (2000)	Overlapping generations model, with endogenous formation of political institution.	Economy needs threshold income to establish institutions for correcting externalities.	Monotonic increasing pollution, inverted-U, or 'sideways mirrored S'.
Andreoni and Levinson (2001)	Robinson Crusoe model (static, one good, one person, one period)	Returns to scale in pollution abatement technology.	Pollution increases or decreases with income.

Perhaps the simplest, though least conclusive, interpretation of the empirics is that the inverse-U-shaped pollution–income path is merely the natural progression of economic development, from clean agrarian economies to polluting industrial economies to clean service economies (Arrow et al., 1995). This interpretation is inconclusive because it has no normative or predictive power. Since we cannot say what the *next* phase of economic development will bring us; we cannot predict the future pollution–income path.

One troubling corollary to the 'natural progression' theory is that the economic cleanup by rich nations may be facilitated by advanced economies exporting their pollution-intensive production processes to less-developed countries (Suri and Chapman, 1998). If so, then the economic improvement noted in industrialized countries will not be indefinitely replicable, as the world's poorest countries will never have even poorer countries to which they can export their pollution.

An alternative explanation with strong normative implications is in Jones and Manuelli (2000). They note that poor countries may not have the advanced institutions necessary for internalizing externalities. Their model consists of overlapping generations in which the younger generation sets pollution regulations. Depending on the collective decision-making institution, the pollution–income relationship can be an inverted-U, monotonically increasing, or even a 'sideways-mirrored-S' (what others have called 'N-shaped'). One normative implication of their paper is that poor countries' inability to self-regulate leads to inefficiently high pollution, and that international aid organizations could improve everybody's welfare by insisting on, or assisting with, regulatory standards and enforcement.

Still another set of models depicting inverse-U-shaped pollution–income paths relies on some constraint being relaxed at a threshold level of income. Stokey (1998), for example, describes a static model with a choice of production technologies with varying degrees of pollution. Her critical assumption is that below a threshold level of economic activity, only the dirtiest technology can be used. With economic growth, pollution increases linearly with income until the threshold is passed and cleaner technologies can be used. The resulting pollution–income path is therefore inverse-V-shaped, with a sharp peak at the threshold income where cleaner technologies become available.

Similarly, Jaeger (1998) assumes that at low levels of pollution consumers' taste for clean air is satiated, and that the marginal benefit of additional environmental quality is zero. Consequently, with few firms and few individuals, the environmental resource constraint is non-binding. More pollution does not result in lower utility. With economic growth represented by a growing population of individuals and polluting firms, once the satiation threshold of consumers' preferences is passed, depending on the parameters, growth may be accompanied by improved environmental quality. Jaeger's pollution–income relationship is also inverse-V-shaped, peaking when the optimum moves from a corner solution to an interior solution.

Finally, John and Pecchenino (1994) present an overlapping generations model in which environmental quality is a stock resource that degrades over time unless maintained by investment. An economy that begins at the corner solution of zero environmental investment will see its environmental quality decline with time and with economic growth until the point at which positive environmental investment is desired, when environmental quality will begin improving with economic growth. John and Pecchenino's pollution–income relationship also exhibits an inverse-V shape, peaking when the dynamic equilibrium switches from a corner solution of zero environmental investment to an interior optimum with positive investment.

Each of these 'constraint-relaxation' stories, or 'threshold' stories, involves the conclusion that at low levels of income, countries are somehow endowed with an *excess* of environmental quality. Stokey's producers would like to use an even more polluting technology, were one available. Since it is not, they use the dirtiest available technology and pollution increases steadily with production, until such time as they begin to value the environment and switch away from that dirtiest technology. Similarly, John and Pecchenino's citizens would like to trade environmental quality for other goods, but cannot, so they slowly degrade their environment with polluting production until they reach an income threshold beyond which they care about pollution and begin to invest in environmental quality.

The normative implication of these papers is just the opposite of the Jones and Manuelli paper. Here, low-income countries' degradation of their environments is efficient. In fact, if we could somehow relax the technology or endowment constraints in these models, they would get more polluted even faster.

The ultimate conclusion of the literature must be that, at least to date, there are no normative implications of the observed inverse-U. Some models generate inverse-Us that are Pareto-efficient, others generate inverse-Us that are market failures. Since inverse-Us can be generated with a variety of assumptions, and the normative implications depend on the assumptions, the observed inverse-U tells us nothing. The thesis of this chapter is that we do not need most of the mechanics in the existing literature to come to that conclusion. To make that point, in the next section I summarize the results of a simple model that neatly generates both efficient and inefficient inverse-U-shaped pollution–income paths.

A ONE-PERSON, ONE-GOOD, ONE-FACTOR, ONE-PERIOD MODEL OF THE ENVIRONMENTAL KUZNETS CURVE

Consider the following Robinson Crusoe-style model, from Andreoni and Levinson (2001). Imagine Robinson Crusoe, alone on his island, picking coconuts for food. Each coconut generates one coconut shell, which Crusoe can either toss aside as unsightly litter, or dispose of properly in a dump. Crusoe gets utility from consumption of coconuts, C, and disutility from pollution, P (coconut shell litter).

$$U = U(C,P) \tag{6.1}$$

where $U_C > 0$ and $U_P < 0$.

Suppose that Crusoe can dispose of his litter properly, but at the cost of foregone consumption. Pollution is then a function of consumption, C, and effort spent hauling coconuts to the dump, denoted E.

$$P = P(C,E) \tag{6.2}$$

where $P_C > 0$ and $P_E < 0$.

Finally, suppose Crusoe has an endowment, M, of time that can be spent on C or E. For simplicity, normalize the relative costs of C and E to be 1. So C denotes one hour's worth of coconuts, and E denotes one hour's worth of clean up effort. The resource constraint is therefore simply $C + E = M$.

For example, consider a version of (6.1) and (6.2):

$$U = C - P \tag{6.3}$$

$$P = C - C^\alpha E^\beta \tag{6.4}$$

Utility in (6.3) is additive and linear, and the marginal disutility of pollution is one. Pollution in (6.4) has two parts. The first term, C, is gross pollution before any abatement and is proportional to consumption. The second term of (6.4), $C^\alpha E^\beta$, represents abatement. So consumption in this model causes pollution one-for-one, but clean-up effort abates pollution with a standard concave production function.

The nice feature of this Robinson Crusoe model, with only one economic agent, is that without externalities, any private optimum is by construction economically efficient. To solve for Crusoe's optimum consumption and pollution level, substitute (6.4) into (6.3) and maximize $C^\alpha E^\beta$ subject to

$C + E = M$. Consumption and effort then have standard Cobb–Douglas solutions

$$C^* = \frac{\alpha}{\alpha + \beta} M \quad \text{and} \quad E^* = \frac{\beta}{\alpha + \beta} M. \tag{6.5}$$

Substituting (6.5) into (6.4), the optimal quantity of pollution is then

$$P^*(M) = \frac{\alpha}{\alpha + \beta} M - \left(\frac{\alpha}{\alpha + \beta} \right)^{\alpha} \left(\frac{\beta}{\alpha + \beta} \right)^{\beta} M^{\alpha + \beta}. \tag{6.6}$$

Equation (6.6) represents optimal pollution as a function of Crusoe's endowment. If it is inverse-U- shaped, it would be called an environmental Kuznets curve.

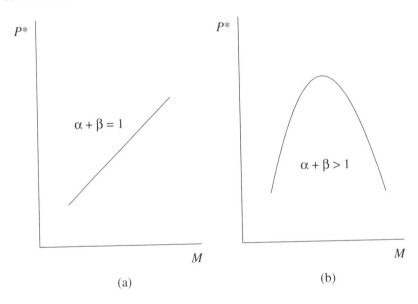

Figure 6.3   *Two parameterizations of equation (6.6)*

What shape does (6.6) have? When $\alpha + \beta = 1$, effort spent abating pollution has constant returns to scale, and $\partial P^*/\partial M$ is constant, as in Figure 6.3(a). However, if $\alpha + \beta > 1$, abatement has increasing returns to scale, and $P^*(M)$ is concave as in Figure 6.3(b). This is what has been described as an environmental Kuznets curve.[2]

The normative implication of this one-person model is that an inverse-U-shaped pollution–income path can be entirely consistent with Pareto-optimality. Because there is only one person, his optimum is necessarily socially optimal. There are no market failures, and yet Crusoe's world gets dirtier with income at low levels, and cleaner at high levels.

So observing an inverse U is not sufficient evidence for a market failure. What about the converse? Might an observed inverse U be sufficient evidence that the market is efficient? To examine this question, consider a multi-person version of the above model:

$$U_i = C_i - P, \qquad i = 1, \ldots, N,$$

$$P = C - C^\alpha E^\beta, \qquad C = \sum_i C_i, E = \sum_i E_i, \tag{6.7}$$

$$M_i = C_i + E_i, \qquad \alpha, \beta \in (0,1).$$

Suppose individuals, indexed $i = 1, \ldots, N$, take others' consumption and effort as given. Solving the first-order condition for consumer i yields the best response function:

$$C_i^* = \frac{\alpha}{\alpha + \beta} M_i + \left[\frac{\alpha}{\alpha + \beta} \sum_{j \neq i} M_j - \sum_{j \neq i} C_j \right]. \tag{6.8}$$

If all individuals maximize utility this way, the symmetric Nash equilibrium is

$$C_i^* = \frac{\alpha}{\alpha + \beta} M_i \quad \text{for all } i. \tag{6.9}$$

In this decentralized case, pollution follows the same path as in the one-person Robinson Crusoe example in equation (6.6) – the pollution–income path is concave and peaked when $\alpha + \beta > 1$.

To examine the Pareto-efficiency of this outcome, compare this Nash equilibrium to the centrally planned optimum. The centralized solution maximizes the sum of utilities

$$\max \sum_i U_i = \sum_i C_i - NP. \tag{6.10}$$

Note that this aggregate utility function is identical to (6.3), where C is replaced by $\sum C_i$ and the marginal social disutility of pollution is $-N$ rather than -1. This is just like the model in (6.3) except that when $N > 1$, the disutility of pollution is greater. In the centralized solution,

$$C^* = \frac{\alpha}{\alpha + \beta} M + \frac{1 - N}{N(\alpha + \beta)(C^*)^{\alpha-1}(M - C^*)^{\beta-1}} \qquad (6.11)$$

The second term of (6.11) is negative if $N > 1$, so C^* must be smaller than the Nash equilibrium C in equation (6.9), and the corresponding level of pollution is lower.

The larger is N, the higher the marginal social cost of a unit of pollution, and the lower will be optimal consumption C^*. Though the optimal levels of C^* and P^* at any income change in response to changes in N, the implications for the inverse-U-shaped pollution–income path remain the same – it is inverse-U-shaped so long as $\alpha + \beta > 1$.

The normative conclusion must be that observing an inverse-U-shaped pollution–income path is neither necessary nor sufficient evidence that environmental policy is efficient, because it can be consistent with either efficient policies or market failures.

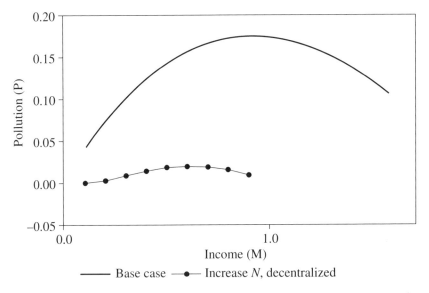

Note: For the base case scenario, $N = 1$, and $\alpha = \beta = 0.8$. For the 'Increase N' scenario, $N = 2$.

Figure 6.4   Pollution–income curves

Figure 6.4 depicts the results of a simulation of this model, with particular parameters. The base case has one person ($N = 1$), and $\alpha = \beta = 0.8$. Optimal pollution, P^*, is plotted against income M, and the curve peaks at around $M = 0.9$ and $P^* = 0.17$. By contrast, examine the case with identical parameters but two agents ($N = 2$). Here the decentralized solution is identical to the base case, peaking when $M = 0.9$ and $P = 0.17$. But the centralized solution peaks at much lower pollution and income ($M = 0.6$ and $P* = 0.019$). Though the decentralized result is 'self-correcting', it does so at excessively high income and pollution – too little too late. With two agents, the marginal social damage from pollution is greater, and given returns to scale in abatement, more abatement and less pollution would be optimal.

From the theory outlined in Table 6.2, we can see that inverse-U-shaped pollution–income paths can be generated in a wide variety of models. Some are Pareto-efficient, some are not. The conclusion must be that an inverse-U is neither necessary nor sufficient for Pareto-optimality. However, most of the theoretical mechanics and assumptions in the literature are unnecessary to make this point. Figure 6.4 depicts two inverse-U-shaped pollution–income paths. The top path is the decentralized result with two agents. The bottom path is the Pareto-optimal path for two agents. So the empirical observation is uninformative as to the efficiency or inefficiency of various countries' environmental policies.

A FINAL POINT: THE ENVIRONMENTAL KUZNETS CURVE IS UNRELATED TO THE ENVIRONMENT

The model outlined in the previous section generates an inverse-U-shaped pollution–income curve for a simple Robinson Crusoe economy, with no externalities. The phenomenon, therefore, would seem to be unrelated to pollution, and would be present any time a market good is associated with an undesirable side effect that can be mitigated. Take, for example, the case of driving. The good – transportation – is associated with accident risk. But accident risk can be mitigated by purchasing cars with anti-lock brakes, side-impact air bags, and by proper vehicle maintenance, all of which cost resources that could be spent in other ways. If safety is a normal good, and the cost of vehicle safety improvements do not increase faster than the marginal utility of the associated safety, then we should expect accident risk to have an inverse-U-shaped relationship to household income.

Figure 6.5 uses data from the 1995 Nationwide Personal Transportation Survey and the 1995 Fatality Analysis Reporting System, both collected by US Department of Transportation, to predict annual fatal accident risk by household income. The predictions are based solely on (a) make, model, and year of vehicle driven, and (b) how far it is driven. For each household income range (for example $45 000 to $50 000), I estimate the ownership of each type of vehicle, and mileage. For each vehicle type, I estimate likelihood of a fatal accident, per mile driven. Multiplying this second term by the proportions for each household income class generates the likelihood of a fatal accident.

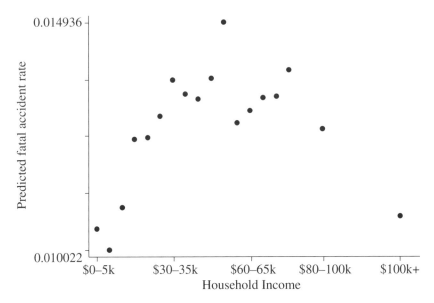

*Figure 6.5   Predicted fatal automobile accident rates and household
incomes*

The shape of the accident-rate versus income plot in Figure 6.5 is inverse-
U-shaped for the same reasons the environmental Kuznets curve is inverse-
U-shaped. Poor people either do not own cars, or do not drive them much.
Rich people own cars and drive them, but own late-model, well-maintained
vehicles with extra safety features. Middle-income people, who drive more
miles in less-safe vehicles, suffer the highest risk. The plot of Figure 6.5, like
the environmental Kuznets curve literature, describes a reduced-form correlation, not a causal relationship. Figure 6.5 cannot tell us why income and
fatal accident risk, or income and pollution, are related in this U-shaped
manner. However, it does suggest that this relationship, the technological
link between desirable goods and undesirable outcomes, is broader and more
general than might be suggested by the term 'environmental' Kuznets curve.

CONCLUSION

Grossman and Krueger (1995), who helped spark this literature, wrote in
their abstract that most pollution problems appear to begin improving
before countries' per capita incomes reach $8000. This description of an
inverse-U-shaped pollution–income pattern set off an empirical hunt for

other inverse-U-shaped patterns, and a theoretical hunt for general theories of this pattern. Meanwhile, in the text of their paper is the less eye-catching conclusion that there is 'no evidence that environmental quality deteriorates steadily with economic growth'. Though unsurprising to economists, who can demonstrate the result using simple theory, this finding is useful in policy circles where environmental and economic issues are often seen solely as a tradeoff.

Based on this brief perusal of the literature to date, the conventional wisdom on the state of knowledge on economic growth and the environment can be summarized as follows. Empirically, researchers have used a variety of specifications to tease inverse-U-shaped pollution–income patterns out of noisy aggregate data, though sceptics have argued that these results are not replicable and are sensitive to functional forms and specifications. Theoretically, inverse-U-shaped pollution–income paths can be the result of numerous causes, modelled in increasingly complex ways. In some cases, the inverse-U shape may be evidence for market failures. In other cases, the shape is consistent with efficient resource allocation.

The key insights therefore are that (a) pollution does not inevitably increase with growth, (b) inverse-U-shaped pollution–income paths are neither necessary nor sufficient evidence for market failures or efficiency, and (c) the inverse-U derives from a technological link between a desirable good and an undesirable side-effect, which is broader and more general than the environment.

All of these points can be made without most of the empirical and theoretical mechanics in the literature. To demonstrate the first point, all we need do is show that some pollutants have declined, even in rapidly growing countries. For the second point, all that is required is a static, one-good model, in which both the centralized (efficient) and decentralized (inefficient) pollution–income relationships are inverse-U-shaped. For the third, a few extensions into other applications suffice. As this literature inevitably proliferates, these three points will be important to keep in mind.

ACKNOWLEDGMENTS

The author gratefully acknowledges financial support by the National Science Foundation, grant #9905576, and research assistance from Esin Sile.

NOTES

1. See Greenstone (2001) for a more detailed analysis of these trends.
2. For a more general version of this model, see Andreoni and Levinson (2001).

REFERENCES

Andreoni, James and Arik Levinson (2001), 'The Simple Analytics of the Environmental Kuznets Curve', *Journal of Public Economics*, **80** (2).

Arora, Seema and Timothy N. Cason (1999), 'Do community characteristics influence environmental outcomes? Evidence from the toxics release inventory', *Southern Economic Journal*, **65**, 691–716.

Arrow, K., B. Bolin, R. Costanza, P. Dasgupta, C. Folke, C.S. Ho, B.O. Jansson, S. Levin, K.-G. Mäler, C. Perrings, D. Pimentel (1995), 'Economic growth, carrying capacity, and the environment', *Science*, **268**, 28 April, 520–521.

Bradford, David F., Rebecca Schliechkert and Stephen H. Shore (2000), 'The environmental Kuznets curve: exploring a fresh specification', NBER Working Paper #8001.

Chaudhuri, Shubham and Alexander Pfaff (1998), 'Household Income, Fuel Choice, and Indoor Air Quality: Microfoundations of an Environmental Kuznets Curve', mimeo, Columbia University Economics Department working paper.

Greenstone, Michael (2001), 'The Impact of the Clean Air Act Amendments on Sulfur Dioxide Concentrations', University of Chicago, working paper.

Grossman, G. and A. Krueger (1993), 'Environmental Impacts of a North American Free Trade Agreement', in P. Garber (ed.), *The U.S.–Mexico Free Trade Agreement*, Cambridge, MA: MIT Press.

Grossman, G. and A. Krueger (1995), 'Economic growth and the environment', *Quarterly Journal of Economics*, **110** (2) 353–77.

Harbaugh, William, Arik Levinson and David Wilson (2002), 'Reexamining the empirical evidence for an environmental Kuznets curve', *Review of Economics and Statistics*, **84**(3).

Hilton, F.G. Hank and Arik Levinson (1998), 'Factoring the environmental Kuznets curve: evidence from automotive lead emissions', *Journal of Environmental Economics and Management*, **35**, 126–41.

Holtz-Eakin, D. and T. Selden (1995), 'Stoking the fires? CO_2 emissions and economic growth', *Journal of Public Economics*, **57** (1), 85–101.

Jaeger, William (1998), 'Growth and Environmental Resources: A Theoretical Basis for the U-shaped Environmental Path', mimeo, Williams College.

John, A. and R. Pecchenino (1994), 'An Overlapping Generations Model of Growth and the Environment', *The Economic Journal*, **104**, 1393–410.

Jones, Larry E. and Rodolfo E. Manuelli (2000), 'Endogenous policy choice: the case of pollution and growth', *Review of Economic Dynamics*, **4** (2), 369–405.

Kahn, Matthew E. (1998), 'A household level environmental Kuznets curve', *Economics Letters*, **59** (2), 269–73.

Kelly, David (1999), 'On Kuznets Curves Arising from Stock Externalities', mimeo, University of Miami.

Kuznets, Simon (1955), 'Economic growth and income inequality', *American Economic Review*, **45** (1), 1–28.

Millimet, Daniel L. and Thanasis Stengos (1999), 'A Semiparametric Approach to Modeling the Environmental Kuznets Curve Across US States', mimeo, Southern Methodist University.

Roberts, J. Timmons and Peter E. Grimes (1997), 'Carbon intensity and economic development 1962–1991: a brief exploration of the environmental Kuznets curve', *World Development*, **25**, 191–8.

Selden, Thomas M. and Daqing Song (1994), 'Environmental quality and development: Is there a Kuznets curve for air pollution emissions?', *Journal of Environmental Economics and Management*, **27**, 147–62.

Shafik, N. and S. Bandyopadhyay (1992), 'Economic growth and environmental quality: Time series and cross-section evidence', World Bank Policy Research Working Paper #WPS904, Washington, DC: The World Bank.

Stokey, Nancy L. (1998), 'Are there limits to growth?', *International Economic Review*, **39** (1), 1–31.

Summers, R. and A. Heston (1991), 'The Penn World Table (Mark 5): an expanded set of international comparisons, 1950–1988', *Quarterly Journal of Economics*, 329–68.

Suri, Vivek and Duane Chapman (1998), 'Economic growth, trade and energy: implications for the environmental Kuznets curve', *Ecological Economics*, **25** (2), May, 195–208.

Taskin, Fatma and Osman Zaim (2000), 'Searching for a Kuznets curve in environmental efficiency using Kernel estimation', *Economics Letters*, **68**, 217–23.

Wang, Pingo, Alok K. Bohara, Robert P. Berrens and Kishore Gawande (1998), 'A risk-based environmental Kuznets curve for US hazardous waste sites', *Applied Economics Letters*, **5**, 761–3.

World Bank (1992), *World Development Report 1992*, New York: Oxford University Press.

7. Participation in industry-wide voluntary approaches: short-run vs. long-run equilibrium

Na Li Dawson and Kathleen Segerson[1]

1. INTRODUCTION

Traditionally policymakers have relied heavily on regulation to protect environmental quality. However, concerns about high costs and lack of flexibility have led to the search for less costly, more efficient means of achieving environmental protection goals. One alternative is the use of market-based policy instruments, such as emission taxes or tradable permit systems. The advantages and disadvantages of these instruments are well known. A less well-studied alternative to regulation, which also has the potential to increase flexibility and reduce costs for individual firms, is the use of voluntary approaches to environmental protection. Voluntary approaches (VAs) can be categorized into three types (EC, 1996; European Environment Agency, 1997; OECD, 1999; Carraro and Lévêque, 1999; Segerson and Li, 1999):[2] (1) unilateral initiatives by firms and industries (or 'self-regulation'), such as 3M's 3P programme, Dow Corporation's WRAP and CMA's Responsible Care programme;[3] (2) negotiated agreements between regulators and firms or industries, such as Project XL and the French agreement on the treatment of End-of-Life Vehicles (ELVs);[4] and (3) government-designed voluntary programmes, such as the 33/50 Program, the Conservation Reserve Program (CRP) and its successor, the Environmental Quality Incentives Program (EQIP).[5]

Although some VAs are firm-specific, many are concluded between governments and industries and involve an industry-wide environmental quality or emissions target (European Environment Agency, 1997; OECD, 1999). In addition, there is also implicitly a threat that if those targets are not met, some form of regulation or mandatory tax will be imposed on the industry as a whole. For example, in 1995 a group of German industry associations declared that by 2005 they would voluntarily reduce CO_2 emissions by 20 percent (relative to a 1990 baseline). The agreement was later updated to include more participating associations and defined targets for individual associations. The main goal of the declaration was to deter the passage of a waste heat ordinance and the implementation of a carbon/energy tax (Jochem and Eichhammer, 1999).

While VAs provide the potential for greater flexibility in the means by which individual firms achieve environmental improvement, an industry-wide VA can suffer from a potentially serious drawback, namely, the incentive for individual firms to free-ride. If the industry as a whole can avoid regulation or imposition of a tax with less than full participation in the VA, then individual firms that do not participate will reap the benefit of the avoided costly regulation or tax without incurring the associated cost of participation. In a recent paper Dawson and Segerson (2001) develop a model that analyses the free-rider incentive for individual firms in this context.[6] They show that, even if all firms are identical, it is possible to have an equilibrium in which a subset of firms in the industry participate in the VA and the remaining firms free-ride. In fact they show that an equilibrium of this type always exists if there is some potential cost savings for a firm from participation in the VA relative to the cost of the mandatory government policy (such as avoided tax payments). Thus the free-rider problem does not destroy the viability of industry-wide VAs.

However, the equilibrium examined in Dawson and Segerson (2001) is a short-run equilibrium in which the number of firms in the industry is fixed and no entry/exit occurs. Because in the short run equilibrium profits are higher for free-riders than for participating firms, a natural question is whether such a profit differential can be consistent with a long-run equilibrium in which firms can enter or leave the industry. In this chapter we extend the analysis in Dawson and Segerson (2001) to consider this question. We show that even with identical firms an industry-wide VA can achieve an exogenous emissions target not only in the short run but also in the long run. In addition, we characterize the nature of the long-run equilibrium participation rate and show that it is at least as high and can be higher than the short-run rate, depending on the magnitude of entry costs. More specifically, we show that when entry costs are zero the only long-run equilibrium involves full participation. This is in direct contrast to the short-run equilibrium, under which full participation is never an equilibrium outcome if potential savings for firms under the VA exist. However, with positive entry costs, even in the long run an equilibrium can involve less than full participation. Nonetheless, we show that the long-run participation rate is always at least as high as the short-run rate, which implies that the free-rider problem is no worse in the long run and can be reduced or even eliminated in long-run equilibrium.

The chapter is organized as follow. In Section 2 we describe the pre-policy equilibrium. Starting from this equilibrium, we then introduce the policy under which the regulator offers the industry an opportunity to meet the aggregate emissions limit voluntarily, with the understanding that if the voluntary approach is not successful, the regulator will impose an emissions tax on the entire industry. In Section 3 we describe the short-run equilibrium response to such a policy, focusing on equilibria under which the voluntary approach is successful. The equilibria in this section correspond to those in Dawson and Segerson (2001), which considers an industry with a fixed number of identical firms. In Section 4, we allow the industry to respond to the policy through entry/exit, that is, we endogenize the industry size. We characterize the long-run equilibrium as a function of entry costs, and compare it to the short-run equilibrium from Section 3. Section 5 summarizes the results and the implications for the use of industry-wide voluntary approaches.

2.   THE PRE-POLICY EQUILIBRIUM

We model the initial equilibrium based on a two-stage game. In the first stage each (identical) firm decides whether or not to enter the market. There is a fixed cost $K \geq 0$ that is incurred immediately upon entry. This cost is not recoverable in the event of exit. This sunk cost may be the cost of equipment that is specific to the industry whose value could not be salvaged if the firm decides to exit the industry (Tirole, 1988; Martin, 1993). It may also be the advertisement expenditure promoting the firm's product, which is sunk once spent (Kwoka and White, 1994). In the second stage those firms that chose to enter make output and emission decisions.

Stage Two Equilibrium

Given that a firm enters the market, it produces an output level y and emits at a level e. For simplicity, we assume that production and emission abatement costs are separable.[7] This allows us to model the output and emissions decisions separately and to write the firm's maximum net revenue R^* (revenue net of production costs) as a function of the number of firms that have entered the industry, that is, $R^* = R(N)$, where N is the number of firms in the industry. This net revenue function embodies the firm's optimal output decision[8] as well as the industry size. Under a standard Cournot oligopoly the firm's net revenue is given by $P(Ny)y - c(y)$, where $P(Ny)$ is the inverse demand function and $c(y)$ is the firm's production cost function.[9] With appropriate curvature assumptions,[10] the first order condition

$P'(Ny)y + P(Ny) - c'(y) = 0$ defines the optimal output level for each firm as a function of N, that is, $y^* = y(N)$, where $\partial y^*/\partial N < 0$. Substituting this into the expression for net revenue yields $R(N)$ for the case where the market structure is oligopolistic. Clearly $R(N)$ under perfect competition can be found simply by evaluating $R(N)$ for the case where N is very large.[11] Note that

$$R'(N) = P' \cdot y^{*2} + P' \cdot (N-1) \cdot y^* \cdot \partial y^*/\partial N$$

$$= P' \cdot y^{*2} \left\{ 1 - \frac{(N-1)(P''y^* + P')}{N(P''y^* + P') + P' - c''} \right\} < 0 \qquad (7.1)$$

that is, as the industry size increases, net revenues per firm decrease.

Given $R(N)$, the firm's profit is then given by $\pi(N,e) = R(N) - C(e)$, where $C(e)$ is the abatement cost function, with $C_e \leq 0$ and $C_{ee} > 0$. We assume that the cost functions under an emissions tax policy and the VA are the same. Thus there is no cost advantage *per se* from participating in a VA.[12] For firms the advantage of the VA comes from the avoided tax payments that they would have incurred under an emissions tax.[13]

It is assumed that firms do not derive any private benefit directly from their emissions reduction. Thus in the absence of any government policy the firm simply chooses e to maximize profit or, equivalently, to minimize costs. Let e_0 denote the unconstrained optimal emissions level, which is implicitly defined by $-C_e(e) = 0$. The corresponding profit level is denoted $\pi_0 = \pi(N,e_0) = R(N) - C(e_0)$. Without loss of generality we can set $C(e_0) = 0$, which implies $\pi_0 = R(N)$.

Stage One Equilibrium

Anticipating π_0, firms make a decision about whether to enter the industry. Entry will occur up to the point where

$$\pi_0 = R(N) = K. \qquad (7.2)$$

This defines an equilibrium number of firms in the industry, N_0, as a function of K, that is, $R(N_0) = K$ or, equivalently, $N_0 = N_0(K)$, where $\partial N_0/\partial K = 1/R'(N) < 0$, that is, an increase in the cost of entry reduces the equilibrium industry size. Note that if $K = 0$, then (7.2) is simply a zero profit constraint. Given an unanticipated change (such as the policy discussed below), the industry will continue to be in long-run equilibrium with N_0 firms, that is, there will be no incentive for entry or exit, if and only if the post-change profit given N_0 firms is not less than zero (which would induce exit) or greater than K (which would induce entry).

3.   SHORT-RUN EQUILIBRIUM UNDER A VA

We start from the long-run equilibrium described above in which there are N_0 firms, each emitting e_0 and earning a profit level of $\pi_0 = K$. We now introduce the following policy scenario. We assume that the regulator has an emissions target for the industry as a whole.[14] S/he first offers the industry an opportunity to achieve the target voluntarily. Should the industry fail to do so, the regulator will impose an emissions tax on all firms in the industry, with the magnitude of the tax set at the level necessary to achieve the goal.[15,16] In this section, we characterize the short-run equilibrium under this policy, where we assume the number of firms is fixed at N_0. In the following section we allow for endogenous entry/exit in response to the policy.

Let E denote the industry-wide emissions limit, where $E < N_0 e_0$. To characterize the equilibrium under the above policy, it is necessary first to characterize the equilibrium if the regulator were to use an emissions tax t to achieve this limit, since this defines the reservation profit level for the firms. Under the tax policy with N firms in the industry, each firm would choose its emissions level to maximize

$$R(N) - C(e) - te. \tag{7.3}$$

Let $e^*(t)$ denote the solution to this maximization problem. Note that, for a given t, with separability this solution is independent of N. In order to achieve the target using an emissions tax, the regulator would have to set the tax rate t^* such that $Ne^*(t^*) = E$, which yields $t^* = t(E/N)$, where $\partial t^*/\partial(E/N) = 1/(\partial e^*/\partial t) = -C_{ee} < 0$. Starting from an equilibrium with N_0 identical firms, $e^*(t^*) = E/N_0$. Thus in the short run the firm's profit under a tax rate of t^* would be $\pi_t^*(N_0) = R(N_0) - C(E/N_0) - t^*(E/N_0)\cdot E/N_0$. Clearly, in the short run no firm will be willing to undertake an amount of voluntary abatement that leads to a profit level lower than $\pi_t^*(N_0)$.

We next consider equilibria under which the industry meets the target voluntarily and thereby avoids the tax. As shown in Dawson and Segerson (2001), there are an infinite number of Nash equilibria under which the target would be met, including equilibria under which a subset of firms participate in voluntary reduction while the remaining firms do not (that is, they free-ride on the emission reductions of the participating firms).[17] Again following Dawson and Segerson (2001), we consider only the Nash equilibrium with the minimum participation rate, that is, the greatest degree of free riding. This is the only Nash equilibrium that is also a self-enforcing equilibrium (see Dawson and Segerson, 2001). The concept of a self-enforcing equilibrium has been widely used to study cartels and international environmental agreements (IEAs) (see, for example, Barrett, 1994; Becker and Easter, 1999; Carraro and Siniscalco, 1993; d'Aspremont et al., 1983; d'Aspremont and Gabszewicz, 1986; Donsimoni et al., 1986). Because a VA is not legally binding and hence not enforceable by an authority, to achieve the environmental goal, it has to be self-enforcing. In our context the self-enforcing equilibrium is one in which (i) no participating firm has an incentive to become a non-participating firm and (ii) no non-participating firm has an incentive to become a participating firm.

To characterize the short-run equilibrium under which the target is met voluntarily, let e_p represent the emissions level of a participating firm and let α denote the share of participating firms in the industry. Since a successful VA preempts the emissions tax, if a firm chooses not to participate, its problem is the same as in the absence of the policy and it thus continues to emit e_0. Given this, the conditions for a short-run equilibrium under which the target is met voluntarily are given by (see Dawson and Segerson, 2001):

$$e_p = \frac{E - (1 - \alpha)Ne_0}{\alpha N}, \text{ and} \qquad (7.4)$$

$$R(N) - C(e_p) = \pi_t^* (N), \qquad (7.5)$$

where in the short run N is set at N_0. Equation (7.4) ensures that the target is just met. Condition (7.5) ensures that participating firms are just as well off as they would have been if the target were not met and hence the tax were imposed. If they were worse off under the voluntary abatement, clearly they would not participate. On the other hand, if they were strictly better off, then an equilibrium with a lower participation rate would exist, implying that the original equilibrium was not self-enforcing.

Together (7.4) and (7.5) define the short-run equilibrium values of e_p and α (which we denote α_{SR}^*). Note that from (7.4)

$$\frac{\partial e_p}{\partial \alpha} = \frac{N(Ne_0 - E)}{(\alpha N)^2} > 0. \qquad (7.6)$$

Thus for a given industry size a higher participation rate implies a higher emissions level for each participating firm. Similarly,

$$\frac{\partial e_p}{\partial N} = \frac{- E\alpha}{(\alpha N)^2} < 0, \qquad (7.7)$$

that is, for a given participation rate, a larger industry implies a lower emissions level for each participating firm.

4.   LONG-RUN EQUILIBRIUM UNDER VA

In the long run firms can enter or exit the industry. Thus, in addition to conditions (7.4) and (7.5), in the long run the following conditions must also hold:

$$0 \le R(N) - C(e_0) \le K, \text{ and} \tag{7.8}$$

$$0 \le R(N) - C(e_p) \le K. \tag{7.9}$$

Conditions (7.8) and (7.9) ensure that neither non-participating nor participating firms have an incentive to either exit or enter the industry.

As in the short run, the long-run equilibrium depends, *ceteris paribus*, on the reservation profit level under the tax. In the short run, this is simply $\pi_t^*(N_0)$. Note that because N_0 is a function of K, this reservation profit level is also a function of K. Define $\tilde{\pi}_t(K) = \pi_t^*[N_0(K)]$. Then

$$\frac{d\tilde{\pi}_t}{dK} = \left\{ R' + \frac{\partial t^*}{\partial (E/N)} \cdot \frac{E^2}{N^3} \right\} \frac{\partial N_0}{\partial K} > 0. \tag{7.10}$$

Thus the short-run profit level under the tax is an increasing function of K. In particular, this profit is always negative when $K = 0$, that is, $\tilde{\pi}_t(0) < 0$, but can become positive for sufficiently large K. Let $\tilde{K}$ be defined by $\tilde{\pi}_t(\tilde{K}) = 0$. Then $\tilde{\pi}_t(K) \ge 0$ for all $K \ge \tilde{K}$, and $\tilde{\pi}_t(K) < 0$ for all $K < \tilde{K}$. We consider each of these possibilities in turn.

Case 1: $\tilde{\pi}_t(K) \ge 0$ ($K \ge \tilde{K}$). In this case $\pi_t^*(N_0) \ge 0$, that is, initial profits are sufficiently high that, given the stringency of the emissions limit, the emissions tax would not generate losses (and hence exit) for firms in the industry. Thus all of the conditions for a long-run equilibrium (that is, (7.4), (7.5), (7.8) and (7.9)) are satisfied at N_0, implying that the short-run equilibrium is also a long-run equilibrium. In this range the short-run minimum participation rate is also the long-run minimum participation rate. With K sufficiently large, that is, N_0 sufficiently small, there is enough of a profit margin for participating firms to absorb the abatement costs associated with the short-run participation rate without violating the conditions for long-run equilibrium. We would expect, however, that as K is reduced and the profit margin is correspondingly squeezed, the ability of the participating firm to absorb this cost is initially diminished and eventually eliminated. In these cases the long-run equilibrium would be expected to differ from the short-run equilibrium. We turn to this possibility in Case 2.

Case 2: $\tilde{\pi}_t(K) < 0$ ($K < \tilde{K}$). In this case $\pi_t^*(N_0) < 0$, implying that the tax would generate exit from the industry. Exit would continue until profits under the tax are zero. This occurs at an industry size of $N_t < N_0$, where N_t is implicitly defined by

$$\pi_t^*(N_t) \equiv R(N_t) - C(E/N_t) - t^*(E/N_t)\,(E/N_t) \equiv 0. \qquad (7.11)$$

Thus the reservation profit level is now zero. Note, however, that the existence of exit incentives under the tax does not necessarily imply that there will be exit under the voluntary approach. Under the VA if profits of participating firms are negative in the short run, it is possible to increase profits in the long run through an increase in participation. Nonetheless, when $\pi_t^*(N_0) < 0$ the conditions for long-run equilibrium ((7.8) and (7.9)) are not satisfied at the short-run equilibrium (defined by (7.4) and (7.5), with N equal to N_0).

To characterize the long-run equilibria, we look for combinations (α, N) that satisfy the conditions for both short- and long-run equilibrium. As before, we limit consideration to combinations that involve minimum participation rates given N, that is, self-enforcing equilibria. When $\alpha < 1$ the conditions defining the long-run equilibrium then become (7.4) and[18]

$$\pi_n \equiv \pi\,(N, e_0) \equiv R(N) - C(e_0) = K \qquad (7.12)$$

$$\pi_p \equiv \pi\,(N, e_p) \equiv R(N) - C(e_p) = 0. \qquad (7.13)$$

Using (7.4), (7.13) can be re-written as $\pi_p(N, \alpha) = 0$. This defines a locus of (α, N) combinations along which the profits of participating firms are zero, where along this locus,

$$\frac{\partial \alpha}{\partial N} = \frac{-\{R'(N) - C' \cdot \partial e_p / \partial N\}}{-C' \partial e_p / \partial \alpha} > 0. \qquad (7.14)$$

Above the locus, $\pi_p > 0$ while below it $\pi_p < 0$. Let $\bar{N}$ be the value of N at which this locus crosses $\alpha = 1$ (see Figure 7.1). $\bar{N}$ is then implicitly defined by

$$R(\bar{N}) = C(E/\bar{N}). \qquad (7.15)$$

While being on the locus in Figure 7.1 ensures that both (7.4) and (7.13) are satisfied, for a long-run equilibrium with $\alpha < 1$ equation (7.12) must be satisfied as well. However, (7.12) holds only at a single value of N, namely, N_0. The nature of the long-run equilibrium depends on the magnitude of N_0. We consider two possibilities.

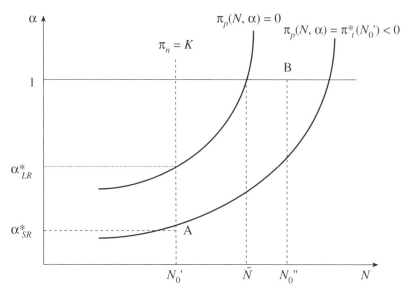

Figure 7.1   Determination of long-run equilibrium participation rate

Case 2a: $N_0 < \bar{N}$: If $N_0 < \bar{N}$ (as with N_0' in Figure 7.1), then at N_0 the profits of participating firms are negative. (Point A lies below the zero profit locus in Figure 7.1.) There are two ways to increase the profit of participating firms. The first is to decrease the industry size through exit, holding the participation rate constant at α_{SR}^*. However, such a change cannot be consistent with a long-run equilibrium, since the reduction in N would increase the profit of non-participants above K, and thereby induce entry. Thus as long as there are non-participants, increasing the profit of participants through exit cannot yield a long-run equilibrium.

The second way to increase the profit of participants is through an increase in the participation rate, given the industry size. If $N_0 < \bar{N}$, then the profit of participants can be increased to the reservation level (that is, to zero) through an increase in α. More specifically, in Figure 7.1 the intersection of the vertical line at N_0' and the zero-profit locus for participating firms defines the long run equilibrium participation rate, α_{LR}^*. Note that α_{LR}^* must be greater than α_{SR}^*, the short-run participation rate. This follows from the fact that at the short-run participation rate the profits of a participating firm were negative, while at the long-run participation rate these profits are zero. Since the number of firms is N_0 in both cases, it follows that the participation rate must be higher in the long run. In addition, as long as $N_0 < \bar{N}$, $\alpha_{LR}^* < 1$. Thus, although the extent of free-riding is reduced in the long run, with $N_0 < \bar{N}$ it is not eliminated.

Case 2b: $N_0 > \bar{N}$: Consider next the case where $N_0 > \bar{N}$ (see N_0'' in Figure 7.1). As with the case where $N_0 \leq \bar{N}$, profits for participating firms are negative at (α_{SR}^*, N_0) but can be increased through an increase in the participation rate. However, in this case, even with full participation, profits for participating firms would still be negative at the initial industry size, that is, $R(N_0) - C(E/N_0) < 0$. (The point B lies below the zero-profit locus in Figure 7.1.) Thus, a long-run equilibrium with N_0 firms does not exist. We show next that, when $N_0 > \bar{N}$, the only combination (α, N) that constitutes a long-run equilibrium in which the VA is successful is $(1, \bar{N})$, that is, a full-participation equilibrium with exit up to the point where the remaining firms earn zero profits.

Because a long-run equilibrium with N_0 firms does not exist, any long-run equilibrium must involve some exit, that is, a reduction in the number of firms in the industry. However, as noted above, if $\alpha < 1$, that is, if there are some non-participating firms, then this reduction in the number of firms will increase the profits of non-participants. Since $\pi_n = K$ initially, any increase in profits for non-participants would create incentives for entry, implying that the industry was not in long-run equilibrium. Thus, any long-run equilibrium with exit must involve full participation. Given full participation, exit must occur until the profits of participating firms are increased to the same level the firm would have earned by exiting or by not participating (and hence facing the tax). This occurs when the industry size is reduced to $\bar{N}$ and participating firms earn zero profits. Thus the new long-run equilibrium occurs at $(1, \bar{N})$. Note that, since $\alpha_{SR}^* < 1$, the participation rate is greater in the long run than in the short run.[19]

While we have characterized the long-run equilibrium based on the magnitude of N_0, N_0 is endogenously determined by entry costs, K. Thus variation in K induces variation in N_0. To characterize the equilibrium in terms of the magnitude of K, first note that $\bar{N}$ is independent of K. However, there exists a value of K, which we denote $\bar{K}$, at which the initial long-run equilibrium industry size is $\bar{N}$. Thus $\bar{K}$ is implicitly defined by $\bar{N} = N_0(\bar{K})$. For $K \geq \bar{K}$, $N_0(K) \leq \bar{N}$ while for $K < \bar{K}$, $N_0(K) > \bar{N}$. Our main results regarding self-enforcing equilibria under which the VA is successful can then be summarized as follows:

Proposition:
(i)   *If entry costs are sufficiently large relative to the aggregate emissions limit, that is, $K \geq \bar{K}$, then the short-run equilibrium (α_{SR}^*, N_0) is also a long-run equilibrium.*
(ii) *If entry costs are sufficiently small relative to the aggregate emissions limit, that is, if $K < \bar{K}$, then the VA induces exit in the long run and the long-run equilibrium is the full participation equilibrium given by $(1, \bar{N})$.*

(iii) *For intermediate values of K, that is,* $\bar{K} < K < \tilde{K}$, *the long-run equilibrium is given by* (α^*_{LR}, N_0), *where* $1 \geq \alpha^*_{LR} > \alpha^*_{SR}$.

Note that if entry costs are zero, as typically assumed in models of perfect competition, then (ii) implies that the long-run equilibrium involves full participation.[20] In this case the short-run equilibrium characterized by Dawson and Segerson (2001), under which there is free-riding and non-participants earn higher profits than participants, could not be an equilibrium in the long run as well. However, it would be consistent with long-run equilibrium under sufficiently high values of *K*.

The proposition immediately implies the following corollary:

Corollary: The long-run equilibrium participation rate is at least as high as the short-run equilibrium rate.

Thus in the long run the free-rider problem is no worse than it is in the short run and, depending on the magnitude of entry costs, the free-rider problem is reduced or eliminated in the long run.

5. CONCLUSION

Voluntary approaches have been widely used since the early 1990s as part of a search for more flexible and cost effective ways to protect the environment. Among the hundreds of voluntary agreements concluded throughout the world, many are between government and an industry or trade association. When firms in an industry share the responsibility of achieving a goal set in a VA, it creates an incentive for individual firms to free-ride. Dawson and Segerson (2001) show that, with industry-wide targets and the threat of imposition of a costly mandatory policy (such as an emissions tax), an equilibrium in which the aggregate target is met but free-riding occurs can emerge. Thus in equilibrium some firms (namely, free-riders) earn higher profits than others (participants). However, that analysis is strictly a short-run analysis in which the number of firms in the industry is fixed. Thus it cannot address the question of whether such an equilibrium can be sustained in the long run.

In this chapter we extend the Dawson and Segerson (2001) model to incorporate entry/exit incentives and examine equilibrium participation rates in the long run. We consider a two-stage game in which in the first stage firms make entry decisions and then in the second stage they choose output and emissions levels. We incorporate entry costs and show that the magnitude of these costs is an important determinant of the long-run equilibrium. Since entry costs determine firm profits in the pre-policy long-run equilibrium, they determine the profit 'cushion' that is available for absorbing the cost increase that results from voluntary abatement.

When entry costs are high, initial (that is, pre-policy) profits are high. If the aggregate emissions limit is not too stringent relative to these profits, the amount of voluntary abatement implied by the short-run equilibrium is not sufficient to generate losses for participating firms. Participating firms can absorb the associated cost increase and still earn a profit level that is no lower than their reservation profit.

However, as entry costs are reduced, initial profits are also reduced and eventually fall to a point at which participation in the VA at the short-run equilibrium generates losses for participating firms. If these losses are not too large, that is, if the emissions limit is not too stringent relative to entry costs, then the participation rate increases in the long run without any exit. At the long-run equilibrium the industry size remains unchanged but free-riding is reduced.

For large losses even full participation will not yield non-negative profits for firms under the VA. In this case the long-run equilibrium under the VA must involve a reduction in the industry size. However, exit is not consistent with long-run equilibrium except under full participation. Thus in this case the long-run equilibrium is a full-participation equilibrium with zero profit for all firms.

An implication of our results is that under perfect competition with zero entry costs the only participation rate consistent with long-run equilibrium is full participation. Although Dawson and Segerson (2001) show that full participation is not consistent with short-run equilibrium when the VA generates potential cost savings for the industry, we have shown here that full participation is consistent with long-run equilibrium under which price adjusts to ensure zero profits under either the emissions tax or the VA. In fact with zero entry costs full participation is the only participation rate that can exist in long-run equilibrium under which the VA is successful. Thus, while free-riding occurs in a short-run equilibrium, under perfect competition with zero entry costs it is eliminated in the long run.

However, free-riding is not necessarily eliminated in the long run when entry costs are positive. Depending on the stringency of the emissions reduction target relative to the entry costs, an emissions tax may preserve the size of the industry (case 1) or induce some firms to exit the industry (case 2). If the number of firms in the industry does not change under the emissions tax (case 1), the analysis is the same as in the short run, implying that the equilibrium participation rate and the extent of free-riding are the same in both the short run and the long run. However, when the emissions tax induces some firms to exit (case 2), the reservation level of profit is higher in the long run than in the short run, since firms can ensure at least zero profit by exiting the industry. As a result the equilibrium participation rate is higher in the long run than in the short run, although there may still be less than full participation. Thus with positive entry costs in the long run the free-rider problem is reduced but not eliminated.

The above results suggest that, despite the free-rider incentive, it is possible to meet emission targets using an industry-wide VA not only in the short run but also in the long run. In other words, the free-rider incentive does not destroy the viability of using this approach either in the short run or in the long run. In fact, the existence/extent of free-riding can be reduced or even eliminated in the long run.

NOTES

1. We would like to thank an anonymous referee for very useful comments that significantly improved this chapter.
2. The European Environment Agency (1997) categorizes VAs into 'target-setting' VAs and 'implementation' VAs. The difference between these two types of VAs lies in the way the environmental quality targets are determined. In 'target-setting' VAs governments and firms/industries negotiate the targets, while the targets for 'implementation' VAs are determined outside the agreements and are thus not subject to negotiation.
3. For the details of these programmes, see Schmidheiny (1992), Smart (1992), Strasser (1996) and Batie (1997).
4. For details of Project XL and its evaluation, see Davies and Mazurek (1996). For details of the French ELVs agreements, see Lévêque and Nadaï (2000) and European Environment Agency (1997).
5. For an evaluation of the 33/50 Program, see Davies and Mazurek (1996) and Khanna and Damon (1999). Babcock et al. (1996, 1997) and Wiebe et al. (1996) provide evaluations of the CRP and EQIP programmes.
6. The free-rider problem has also been examined by Maxwell et al. (2000), Millock and Salanié (2000) and Brau et al. (2000). However, these papers do not examine an equilibrium in which a subset of the firms in an industry participate. Thus the issues of concern in this chapter do not arise in these other studies.
7. In the notation of the model in Dawson and Segerson (2001), this implies $C_{ye} = 0$. For a model that examines the interaction between emissions and output decisions, see Brau and Carraro (1999).
8. Thus we do not need to consider output choices explicitly in the analysis below.
9. To simplify notation we anticipate the symmetry of the equilibrium and write aggregate output simply as Ny, although in deriving the first order condition the output of the other $(N-1)$ firms is assumed to be fixed.
10. Sufficient conditions are $P''y + P' < 0$ and $c'' > 0$. We assume these conditions hold throughout.
11. Alternatively we can find $R(N)$ for the case of perfect competition directly. Under perfect competition the firm will choose its output level y to maximize its net revenue, $py - c(y)$, where p is the output price. Market clearing then requires that $D(p) = Ny^*(p)$, where $D(p)$ is the market demand function and $y^*(p)$ is the firm's supply function. The market clearing condition defines an equilibrium price as a function of N, that is, $p^* = P(N)$. Substituting this into the supply function and the expression for net revenue then yields $R(N)$.

12. If the background threat is an inefficient regulation rather than a tax, the motivation for firms to participate in the VA is the potential savings in abatement costs under the VA. For such a model see Segerson and Dawson (2001).
13. Note, however, that the cost advantage does not necessarily need to stem from a legislative threat. The same principles apply to any situation where there is a potential private gain from the VA that would have been lost under alternative scenarios, for example, product differentiation (Arora and Gangopadhyay, 1995) or reduced citizen lawsuits and environmental liabilities (Batie, 1997).
14. This target can either be set exogenously, for example, as a part of a national plan, or as a result of negotiation between the regulator and the industry. We do not model the target setting stage in this chapter.
15. Examples of using an emissions tax as the background threat on a VA include the German industry's voluntary declaration on CO_2 reductions and a negotiated agreement in Switzerland for a 10 percent reduction of CO_2 emissions (OECD, 1999).
16. The scenario we consider here is similar to the provision point mechanism for the provision of public goods. Under that mechanism a public good is provided at a given cost if and only if voluntary contributions for its provision are sufficient to cover that cost. We are indebted to Bill Schulze for pointing this out to us. For a theoretical model of the provision point mechanism, see Bagnoli and Lipman (1989). For a recent experimental study of the effectiveness of the mechanism, see Rondeau et al. (1999).
17. This is consistent with the existence of multiple Nash equilibria in the provision point literature. See Bagnoli and Lipman (1989) and Bagnoli and McKee (1991).
18. Clearly (7.12) does not need to hold in an equilibrium where there are no non-participants, that is, where $\alpha = 1$.
19. This does not necessarily imply that the number of participating firms is greater, however, since the total number of firms in the industry is smaller.
20. This assumes the absence of adjustment costs. In the presence of adjustment costs, the reservation level of profit that triggers exit may be negative. In this case it is possible to get a long-run equilibrium under perfect competition with less than full participation, depending on the relative magnitude of the adjustment costs.

REFERENCES

Arora, S. and S. Gangopadhyay (1995), 'Toward a theoretical model of voluntary overcompliance', *Journal of Economic Behavior and Organization*, **28** (3), 289–309.

Babcock, B., P.G. Lakshminarayan, J. Wu and D. Zilberman (1996), 'The economics of a public fund for environmental amenities: A study of CRP contracts', *American Journal of Agricultural Economics*, **78** (4), 961–71.

Babcock, B., P.G. Lakshminarayan, J. Wu and D. Zilberman (1997), 'Targeting tools for purchase of environmental amenities', *Land Economics*, **73** (3), 325–39.

Bagnoli, M. and B.L. Lipman (1989), 'Provision of public goods: Fully implementing the core through private contributions', *The Review of Economic Studies*, **56** (4), 583–601.

Bagnoli, M. and M. McKee (1991), 'Voluntary contribution games: Efficient private provision of public goods', *Economic Inquiry*, **29** (2), 351–66.

Barrett, S. (1994), 'Self-enforcing international environmental agreements', *Oxford Economic Papers*, **46** (5), 878–94.

Batie, S.S. (1997), 'Environmental issues, policy, and the food industry', in B. Schroder and T.L. Wallace (eds), *Food Industry and Government Linkages*, Boston: Kluwer Academic Publishers, pp. 235–56.

Becker, N. and K.W. Easter (1999), 'Conflict and cooperation in managing international water resources such as the Great Lakes', *Land Economics*, **75** (2), 233–45.

Brau, R. and C. Carraro (1999), 'Voluntary approaches, market structure and competition', Note di Lavoro 53.99, Fondazione Eni Enrico Mattei, Milan, Italy.

Brau, R., C. Carraro, and G. Golfetto (2000), 'Endogenous VAs and market structure', paper presented at the 5th CAVA workshop on 'Voluntary Approaches, Competition and Competitiveness', May 25–26, 2000, Milan, Italy.

Carraro, C. and F. Lévêque (1999), 'Introduction: The Rationale and Potential of Voluntary Approaches', in C. Carraro and F. Lévêque (eds), *Voluntary Approaches in Environmental Policy*, Dordrecht, Boston, London: Kluwer Academic Publishers, pp. 1–15.

Carraro, C. and D. Siniscalco (1993), 'Strategies for the international protection of the environment', *Journal of Public Economics*, **52** (3), 309–28.

Commission of the European Communities (EC) (1996), 'On environmental agreements', Communication from the Commission to the Council and the European Parliament, Brussels.

d'Aspremont, C.A., A. Jacquemin, J.J. Gabszewicz and J.A. Weymark (1983), 'On the stability of collusive price leadership', *Canadian Journal of Economics*, **16** (1), 17–25.

d'Aspremont, C.A. and J.J. Gabszewicz (1986), 'On the Stability of Collusion', in J.E. Stiglitz and G.F. Matthewson (eds), *New Developments in the Analysis of Market Structure*, Cambridge, MA: The MIT Press, pp. 243–61.

Davies, T. and J. Mazurek (1996), 'Industry incentives for environmental improvement: Evaluation of US federal initiatives', prepared for Global Environmental Management Initiative, Resources for the Future, Washington, DC.

Dawson, N.L. and K. Segerson (2001), 'Voluntary agreements with industries: Participation incentives with industry-wide targets', Working Paper, Department of Economics, University of Connecticut.

Donsimoni, M.P., N.S. Economides and H.M. Polemarchakis (1986), 'Stable cartels', *International Economic Review*, **27** (2), 317–27.

European Environment Agency (EEA) (1997), *Environmental Agreements: Environmental Effectiveness*, Environmental Issues Series No. 3, vol. 1–2, Copenhagen.

Jochem, E. and W. Eichhammer (1999), 'Voluntary Agreements as an Instrument to Substitute Regulations and Economic Instruments: Lessons from the German voluntary agreements on CO_2 reduction', in C. Carraro and F. Lévêque (eds), *Voluntary Approaches in Environmental Policy*, Dordrecht: Kluwer Academic Publishers, pp. 209–27.

Khanna, M. and L. Damon (1999), 'EPA's voluntary 33/50 Program: Impact on toxic releases and economic performance of firms', *Journal of Environmental Economics and Management*, **37** (1), 1–25.

Kwoka, J.E. and L.J. White (1994), *The Antitrust Revolution: The Role of Economics*, New York: Harper Collins College Publishers.

Lévêque, F. and A. Nadaï (2000), 'A firm's involvement in the policy-making Process', in H. Folmer, H.L. Gabel and H. Opschoor (eds), *Principles of Environmental and Resource Economics*, 2nd edition, Cheltenham, UK and Northampton, MA, US: Edward Elgar, pp. 235–64.

Martin, S. (1993), *Advanced Industrial Economics*, Oxford and Cambridge: Blackwell.

Maxwell, J.W., T.P. Lyon and S.C. Hackett (2000), 'Self-regulation and social welfare: The political economy of corporate environmentalism', *Journal of Law and Economics,* **43** (2), 583–618.

Millock, K. and F. Salanié (2000), 'Are collective voluntary agreements ever efficient?', paper presented at the AERE workshop on 'Effectiveness of Resource and Environmental Regulation', June 11–13, 2000, La Jolla, CA.

Organisation for Economic Co-Operation and Development (OECD) (1999), *Voluntary Approaches for Environmental Policy: An Assessment*, Paris.

Rondeau, D., W.D. Schulze and G.L. Poe (1999), 'Voluntary revelation of the demand for public goods using a provision point mechanism', *Journal of Public Economics*, **72** (3), 455–70.

Schmidheiny, S. (1992), *Changing Course: A Global Business Perspective on Development and the Environment*, Cambridge, MA: MIT Press.

Segerson, K. and N.L. Dawson (2001), 'Environmental voluntary agreements: Participation and free riding', in E. Orts and K. Deketelaere (eds), *Environmental Contracts: Comparative Approaches to Regulatory Innovation in Europe and the United States*, Dordrecht: Kluwer Law International, pp. 369–88.

Segerson, K. and N. Li (1999), 'Voluntary Approaches to Environmental Protection', in H. Folmer and T. Tietenberg (eds), *The International Yearbook of Environmental and Resource Economics 1999/2000*, Cheltenham, UK and Northampton, MA, US: Edward Elgar, pp. 273–306.

Smart, B. (1992), *Beyond Compliance: A New Industry View of the Environment*, Washington, DC: World Resource Institute.

Strasser, K.A. (1996), 'Preventing pollution', *Fordham Environmental Law Journal*, **8** (1), 1–57.

Tirole, J. (1988), *The Theory of Industrial Organization*, Cambridge and London: MIT Press.

Wiebe, K., A. Tegene and B. Kuhn (1996), *Partial Interests in Land: Policy Tools for Resource Use and Conservation*, Agricultural Economic Report Number 744, US Department of Agriculture.

8. Irreversible development of a natural resource: management rules and policy issues when direct use values and environmental values are uncertain

Anastasios Xepapadeas*

1. INTRODUCTION

Uncertainty is an issue of considerable interest in the environmental and resource economics literature. When the analysis is carried out in a dynamic context the interactions between uncertainty and irreversibility are of special interest.[1] One fundamental proposition in the area of environmental economics, established by Arrow and Fisher (1974), is that an option value exists associated with refraining from an irreversible decision now, when next period benefits or losses resulting from the decision are uncertain, even if the decision maker is risk neutral. Closely associated with the above concepts is the concept of timing of the irreversible decision, and the question of whether or not the decision maker should postpone action until more information is acquired in the future.

Recent approaches to the solution of this type of stochastic control problem focus on the derivation of a free or exercise boundary derived from the solution of the associated Hamilton–Jacobi–Bellman (HJB) equation (for example Dixit and Pindyck, 1994; Soner, 1997). The basic property of the boundary is that it divides a certain strategy space into two regions which determine whether or not an irreversible action is undertaken.

The purpose of this chapter is to analyse the problem of resource management that entails the irreversible development of an exhaustible resource, when the benefits – or, more precisely, the values – of services generated by the resource in either the developed or the undeveloped state are uncertain. In analysing the structure of the benefits associated with the resource, a broad division of values into direct use values and indirect values or non-use values is considered. Direct use values are associated with the value of services generated by the resource after it has been developed. On the other hand indirect or non-use values are associated with the values of services generated by the resource when it is in an undeveloped state. Indirect or non-use values can be associated with services generated by the biodiversity of an undeveloped part of an ecosystem, or with passive values related mostly to ethical positions.[2] These indirect or non-use values are referred to, in the rest of the chapter, as the environmental or the intrinsic value of the undeveloped resource.

In the resource management problem, while the direct use values as defined above can in principle be approximated by market prices associated with the services generated by the developed resource, the non-use values are much harder to approximate because of the well-known missing market problems. In practice these values, especially for the cases of aesthetic or existence values, are approximated by state preference methods, such as contingent valuation, or revealed preference methods such as travel cost, hedonic models or random utility models. The difficulties associated with any attempt to approximate non-use values induce a relatively high degree of uncertainty in the estimates. On the other hand when environmental values are associated with services provided by intact ecosystems, which might undergo irreversible development, a more direct valuation might be possible. For example ecosystem services relate closely to the development of new products in biotechnology and pharmaceuticals. These services can be associated with the formation of market values for bioprospecting rights in locations representing biodiversity hot spots. Certain ecosystem services can have direct market values such as watershed services (Chichilnisky and Heal, 1998) or ecotourism services based on the preservation of intact eco-systems (Heal, 2000), which are ignored by private developers.

The problem of analysing the irreversible development of an environ-mental resource under use value and non-use value uncertainty is thus considered, by explicitly taking into account the facts that: (i) the resource can be developed by a private profit-maximizing decision maker that acquires profits by developing the resource involved in the problem or by a social planner or environmental regulator that seeks to maximize some appropriately-defined social welfare criterion; (ii) the undeveloped resource has an environmental value which is not taken into account by the individual developer, but is accounted for in the context of the social optimization problem faced by the social planner or environmental regu-lator; and (iii) there is simultaneous uncertainty both on profits from the resource development, that is market prices associated with direct use values, and the environmental value of the undeveloped resource, that is indirect non-use values.[3]

The resource management problem in this chapter is analysed by using an exercise barrier approach corresponding to the associated stochastic control problem and in particular by deriving the privately-optimal or unregulated free boundary and the socially-optimal free boundary. A free boundary is a curve which divides a space where development decisions are taken into two regions: the 'no development' region and the 'development region'. The unregulated and the socially-optimal free boundaries characterize the optimal resource development in the sense that, depending on the region of the space in which a stochastic variable associated with profit or/and environmental uncertainty is realized, the decision maker decides whether or not to undertake the irreversible resource development. The two boundaries are used to compare the pace of development under profit maximization or social optimization. It is shown that when uncertainty exists only with respect to the market prices associated with direct use values, the pace of development under social optimization is slower relative to the development pace under profit maximization, a result anticipated by the existing literature on resource management. However, when uncertainty is associated with both use and non-use values, the pace of development could be reversed under certain circumstances. This result is possible under a downward shift of the non-use values relative to use values. If this shift is sufficiently strong then the externality associated with non-use values that makes the socially-optimal development pace slower than the privately-optimal, works the other way round implying that in a given time interval the socially-optimal development should be faster than the privately-optimal one.

Having established the deviation between the unregulated and the socially-optimal free boundaries, the issue of policy design is addressed.[4] The idea is to introduce a regulatory scheme in the form of development taxes or command and control limits on development that will induce the profit-maximizing decision maker to behave in the same way as the social planner regarding development choices. We show that the optimal policy scheme is different in the case of use value uncertainty relative to the case of simultaneous use and non-use uncertainty.

In the context described above, one contribution of this chapter can be associated with using the concept of the optimal exercise boundary to compare development paths under socially-optimal and market solutions under simultaneous use and non-use values uncertainty. By using this exercise boundary comparison approach there is no need to compare expected equilibrium outcomes. Instead a deterministic function for the exercise boundary is used to compare development paths corresponding to the two solutions. Since the development paths are obtained by comparing the boundaries to the observed values of the stochastic variables, it is a straightforward process to compare the development paths by simply comparing the boundaries relative to the moves of the state variables. The comparison confirms the generally accepted results that the socially-optimal solution implies slower development than the market solution, but it also reveals the possibility, which to my knowledge has not yet been explored, that it might be socially optimal to develop the resource relatively faster at some time interval. This result is made possible by the use of the boundary comparison approach to the general problem of the simultaneous use and non-use value uncertainty.[5]

The chapter contributes also to the design of policy schemes under uncertainty. The main idea is that since the private profit-maximizing agent uses a boundary to design management strategies, if a policy regime shifts the boundary so that it coincides with the socially-optimal boundary, then the privately-optimal development path will be the same as the socially-optimal development path. Thus under uncertainty the policy objective is to develop policy schemes that will make the optimal boundary of the profit-maximizing agent the same as the optimal boundary for the social planner.

2. RESOURCE DEVELOPMENT UNDER IRREVERSIBILITIES

A resource or environmental asset of fixed size S which can be developed into a new use is considered. In the undeveloped state the asset has an environmental or intrinsic value associated with indirect or non-use values equal to $q_t S$, where q_t is the unit environmental value of the resource at time t.[6] The asset can be some landscape that could, for example, undergo industrial, housing or agricultural development, or a scenic land that can potentially undergo tourist development. At the undeveloped stage the land provides indirect or non-use value services, such as services related to biodiversity of the undeveloped landscape, aesthetic values of the undeveloped land, or more general existence values.

Assume that one potential developer[7] of the site exists and at each point in time he or she develops $h_t \geq 0$. Thus total cumulative development at time t is defined as:

$$D_t = \int_0^t h(s)ds, \; D_t \leq S. \tag{8.1}$$

Since $h_t \geq 0$, development is irreversible. After the development the environmental value of the asset is defined as:

$$q_t(S - D_t).$$

Thus the development of the site linearly reduces its intrinsic value.

However, the development generates a net flow of services for the developer, according to an increasing and strictly concave function:

$$f(D_t), f'(D_t) > 0, f''(D_t) < 0.$$

We assume that the developer is small relative to the market for the resource services, and that these services can be sold at some exogenously determined world price.[8] This price, P_t, evolves stochastically following a geometric Brownian motion:

$$dP_t = a_1 P_t dt + \eta_1 P_t dz_{pt} \qquad (8.2)$$

with $\{z_{pt}\}$ being a Wiener process.[9,10] Thus the developer's net revenues at each instant of time are defined as

$$P_t f(D_t).$$

Let the cost of developing one unit of the resource be c. If the decision is to develop the site by ΔD from the existing development level D_0, then

$$\Delta D = D_0^+ - D_0.$$

The cost of this change in the development is then defined as:

$$c\Delta D. \qquad (8.3)$$

Given this structure we seek an optimal development strategy which takes the form of a free boundary defined by an equation $P = P(D)$ relating price and cumulative development. When the realized price P^r at any point in time is such that $P^r < P(D)$, no development is undertaken, while when $P^r > P(D)$, enough development is undertaken to restore equality between the realized price and the value of the boundary.

3.   PRIVATELY-OPTIMAL DEVELOPMENT

Consider the case of the developer when the initial market price of the services generated by the developed resource is P_0 and the initial development is D_0. Given a private discount rate $\rho > 0$,[11] with $\rho > a_1$, the developer seeks the nondecreasing process D_t, that will maximize the present values of net revenues less the cost of development.

Let $\mathcal{D} = \{\Delta D_t: \Delta D_t \geq 0, \ \forall t \geq 0, \text{ and } \int_0^t \Delta D_u du < L, \ \forall t \geq 0\}$. The set of admissible controls which represent resource development is defined as:

$\mathcal{U} = \{\Delta D_t : \Delta D_t \in \mathcal{D}, \forall D \in [0, L)\}$. Then the developer's problem is defined as

$$\max_{\mathcal{U}} J(P_t, D_t; \Delta D_t) = \mathrm{E}_0 \int_0^\infty e^{-\rho t} [P_t f(D_t) - c\Delta D_t] dt$$

subject to (8.2).

The value function associated with this problem can then be defined as:

$$V(D_t, P_t) = \sup_{\mathcal{U}} \varepsilon_0 \int_0^\infty e^{-\rho t} [P_t f(D_t) - c\Delta D_t] dt \qquad (8.4)$$

By the concavity of $f(D)$ and the linear dynamics it can be shown that the value function is concave in D. The dynamic programming equation for the developer's problem takes the form (Soner, 1997):

$$\rho V = \max_{\Delta D_t} \{[\mathcal{L}_{\Delta D}^{PD}] V + f(D) - c\Delta D\}$$

where $\mathcal{L}_{\Delta D}^{PD} = \frac{1}{2}\eta_1^2 P^2 \partial^2 / \partial P^2 + a_1 P \, \partial / \partial P + \Delta D \, \partial / \partial D$ is the differential generator.

At each instant of time the developer has two choices: to preserve the site or to develop it. The time interval when no development is taking place and the previously acquired development is used to generate net revenues can be defined, following Dixit and Pindyck (1994), as the no action or the continuation interval. A stopping time is defined as a non-negative random variable τ at which new development is undertaken.

Let D_τ^* be the optimal development process at time τ. Following Fleming and Soner (1993) or Soner (1997), if τ is a stopping time then by the dynamic programming principle:

$$V(D, P) = \sup_{\mathcal{U}} \mathrm{E}_0 \left[\int_0^\tau e^{-\rho u} P_u f(D_u) du + e^{-\rho \tau} V(D_\tau^*, P_\tau) \right]. \qquad (8.5)$$

Assume that in the time interval $[0, \theta]$ the developer undertakes no new development, but keeps it constant at D_0. Then by the principle of dynamic programming, the value function should be no less than the payoff (continuation payoff) in the interval $[0, \theta]$, plus the expected value after θ, or:

$$V(D, P) \geq \mathrm{E}_0 \left[\int_0^\theta e^{-\rho u} P_u f(D_0) du + e^{-\rho \theta} V(D_\theta, P_\theta) \right] \qquad (8.6)$$

with equality if D_0 is the optimal policy in $[0, \theta]$. Applying the Itô lemma to the value function on the right-hand side of (8.6), dividing by θ and taking limits as $\theta \to 0$, we obtain:[12]

$$\rho V \geq \frac{1}{2}\eta_1^2 P^2 V_{PP} + a_1 P V_P + P f(D) \qquad (8.7)$$

with equality if $D_t = D_0$ in the interval $[0, \theta]$.

Consider now the decision to develop instantaneously by $\Delta D = D_0^+ - D_0$. Then the right-hand side of the dynamic programming equation becomes

$$\max_{\Delta D \geq 0}\left\{\left[\mathcal{L}_{\Delta D}^{PD}\right]V + f(D) - c\Delta D\right\} = \frac{1}{2}\eta_1^2 P^2 V_{PP} + a_1 P V_P + Pf(D) + \widehat{\mathcal{H}}(V_D)$$

where

$$\widehat{\mathcal{H}}(V_D) = \max_{\Delta D \geq 0}\{V_D\Delta D - c\Delta D\}$$

which implies

$$V_D - c \leq 0, \Delta D \geq 0, \text{ or}$$

$$\text{if } V_D - c < 0 \text{ then } \Delta D = 0 \tag{8.8}$$

$$\text{if } \Delta D > 0 \text{ the } V_D - c = 0. \tag{8.9}$$

Thus when no development is optimal, (8.7) is satisfied as equality, while when development is optimal, (8.9) is satisfied as equality. Combining the two the HJB equation can be written as:

$$\min\left\{\left[\rho V - \frac{1}{2}\eta_1^2 P^2 \, V_{PP} - a_1 P V_P - Pf(D)\right], -[V_D - c]\right\} = 0. \tag{8.10}$$

The HJB equation can be used to derive the free boundaries at the unregulated and regulated equilibrium.

3.1. The Free Boundary at the Private Optimum

The HJB equation (8.10) determines the conditions under which a profit-maximizing agent will undertake new development or not. Thus the HJB divides the (P, D) space into two regions. The curve $P = P(D)$ for the boundary between the two regions determines the profit-maximizing development process. This optimal exercise or free boundary will divide the (P, D) space into two regions: the 'no development' region, called region I, and the 'development region', called region II. In region I the first term of the HJB equation is zero since $\Delta D = 0$ and the second term of the HJB equation is positive by (8.8), thus

$$\rho V - \frac{1}{2}\eta_1^2 P^2 \, V_{PP} - a_1 P V_P - Pf(D) = 0. \tag{8.11}$$

The general solution of (8.11) can be obtained as:

$$V(D, P) = A_1(D)\, P^{\beta_1} + A_2(D)\, P^{\beta_2} + \frac{f(D)}{\rho - a_1} \tag{8.12}$$

where $\beta_1 = 1/2 - a_1/\eta_1^2 + \sqrt{(a_1/\eta_1^2 - \frac{1}{2})^2 + 2\rho/\eta_1^2} > 1$ is the positive root of the fundamental quadratic $Q = \frac{1}{2}\eta_1^2\beta(\beta - 1) + a_1\beta - \rho = 0$. We need to disregard the negative root in order to prevent the value from becoming infinitely large when the market size becomes very small, thus we set $A_2(D) = 0$.[13]

In region II the second term of (8.10) is satisfied as zero and $\Delta D > 0$, or

$$V_D(D, P) - c = 0. \tag{8.13}$$

Using (8.12) and (8.13), the constant $A_1(D)$ and the function $P = P(D)$ can be determined. To obtain this the 'value matching' and the 'smooth pasting' conditions are used.[14]

The value matching condition means that on the boundary separating the two regions the value functions should be equal. Solving (8.13) for P we can obtain the yet unspecified function for the boundary $P = P(D)$. Then we have, combining (8.12) and (8.13) and substituting for P,

$$V_D(D, P) = A_1'(D) P^{\beta_1} + P\frac{f'(D)}{\rho - a_1} = c, \ P = P(D). \tag{8.14}$$

The smooth pasting condition means that the derivatives of the value functions with respect to P on the boundary are equal or:

$$V_{DP}(D, P) = \beta_1 A_1'(D) P^{\beta_1 - 1} + \frac{f'(D)}{\rho - a_1} = 0 \text{ with } P = P(D). \tag{8.15}$$

Combining (8.14) and (8.15) we can solve for the unknown functions $P(D)$ and $A_1'(D)$ to obtain:

$$P(D) = \frac{\beta_1}{\beta_1 - 1}\frac{\delta c}{f'(D)} \tag{8.16}$$

$$A_1'(D) = -\left(\frac{\beta_1 - 1}{c}\right)^{\beta_1 - 1}\left[\frac{f'(D)}{\beta_1(\rho - a_1)}\right]^{\beta_1} \tag{8.17}$$

The optimal boundary is increasing in D by the assumption of diminishing returns and the convexity of the cost function,

$$\frac{dP}{dD} = \frac{-f''(D)\beta_1 (\rho - a_1)c}{(\beta_1 - 1) [f' (D)]^2} > 0.$$

In region I, (8.6) holds as a strict inequality and no development is undertaken. For any given D, random price fluctuations move the point (D, P) vertically upward or downward. If the point goes above the boundary then development is immediately undertaken so that the point shifts on the boundary. Thus optimal development proceeds gradually. In the terminology of

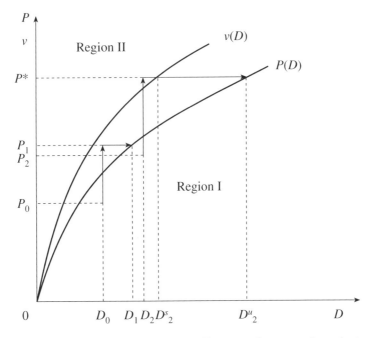

Figure 8.1   Privately-optimal and socially-optimal exercise boundaries

Dixit and Pindyck, this is a 'barrier control' policy. The free boundary is shown in Figure 8.1. If the price P moves from P_0 to P_1, the private developer will undertake $D_1 - D_0$ new development.

The equation describing the boundary can be interpreted in the following way. For a small development dD, its expected present value is defined as:

$$E[PV] = \left(\frac{Pf'(D)}{\delta} \right) dD$$

where $\rho - a_1$ is the real discount rate defined as the difference between ρ and the expected rate of growth of the price. Define the incremental cost of this development as $\Delta C = c$, then the benefit–cost ratio for this investment is defined as $BC = E[PV]/c$. As seen from the definition of the incremental benefits and the strict concavity of f, the benefit–cost ratio is lower, the higher the development level is. Using the equation of the boundary to substitute for P, the optimal investment rule requires:

$$BC = \frac{\beta_1}{\beta_1 - 1} > 1$$

The fact that the benefit–cost ratio for the marginal project exceeds one, as compared to the traditional rule of $BC=1$ in the no uncertainty/irreversibility case, reflects the option value of keeping the status quo development level.

By equation (8.14) the incremental development is justified if the discounted value of the incremental development marginal value product, $Pf'(D)/(\rho - a_1)$, covers development costs, c, plus the opportunity cost of the option to wait $A_1'(D) P^{\beta_1}$. By (8.17) the marginal option value $A_1'(D)$ is negative, that is, it represents a cost.[15]

4.   SOCIALLY-OPTIMAL DEVELOPMENT

Consider the case of a social planner or an environmental regulator that seeks to optimally develop the site by taking into account – in addition to the development benefits, that is the direct use values – the environmental losses arising from the irreversible destruction of the site during the development process.

In addition to price uncertainty, the regulator also faces uncertainty regarding the environmental or intrinsic value of the undeveloped resource. We assume that the environmental values associated with the resource in the undeveloped state evolve stochastically following a geometric Brownian motion

$$dq_t = a_2 q_t dt + \eta_2 q_t dz_{qt}. \tag{8.18}$$

The use of a geometric Brownian motion to model the evolution of environmental values fits better when these values are interpreted as reflecting values of ecosystem services which can be associated with market values, such as land values for bioprospecting,[16] watershed or ecotourism services.[17]

The instantaneous benefits of the regulator can then be defined as:

$$B(P_t, q_t, D_t) = P_t f(D_t) + q_t (S - D_t)$$

with the value function defined as:

$$w(P_t, q_t, D_t) = \sup_u \mathrm{E}_0 \int_0^\infty e^{-\rho^s t}[P_t f(D_t) + q_t(S - D_t) - c\Delta D_t]dt$$

subject to (8.2) and (8.18).

In the value function definition above ρ^s denotes the social discount rate used by the regulator. With perfect private capital markets and no divergence between private and social costs and benefits, the private and the social discount rates coincide.[18] The case of environmental losses due to irreversible development of a natural resource examined in this chapter, introduce a source of deviation between private and social benefits implying potential differences between the private and the social discount rates. In this context, Weitzman (1994) shows that environmental effects imply a lower social discount rate relative to the private one. Following Weitzman the environmental effect is modelled here by introducing a correction factor $\delta > 0$, and defining the social discount rate as

$$\rho^s = \rho(1 - \delta).$$

Following Davis and Norman (1990), the linear homogeneity of the benefit function in P and q implies that the value function is also linearly homogeneous.[19] Then the dimensionality of the social planner's problem can be reduced from three to two for $q_t \neq 0$. By taking the non-use values as the numeraire, the social planner's benefit function can be written as:

$$v_t f(D_t) + (L - D_t), \ v_t = \frac{P_t}{q_t}.$$

Linear homogeneity of the value function implies that

$$w(P, q, D) = qw(v, 1, D).$$

Then, it can be defined that:

$$W(v, D) = w(v, 1, D) = q^{-1}w(P, q, D),$$

where $W(v, D)$ is the value function associated with the problem:

$$W(v, D) = \sup_{u} E_0 \int_0^\infty e^{-\hat{\rho}t}[v_t f(D_t) + (L - D_t) - c\Delta D_t]dt$$

subject to

$$dv_t = \mu v_t dt + \sigma v_t dz_t$$

where:

$$\hat{\rho} = \rho^s - a_1 = \rho(1 - \delta) - a_1 > 0$$
$$\mu = a_1 - a_2$$
$$\sigma^2 = \eta_1^2 - 2\gamma\eta_1\eta_2 + \eta_2^2$$

and γ is the correlation coefficient of the Wiener processes dz_p, dz_q.

The stopping time for the regulator's problem satisfies:

$$W(D, v) = \max_{u} \mathrm{E}_0\left[\int_0^{\tau} e^{-\hat{\rho}u}\left[v_u f(D_u) - D + L\right]du\right]$$

$$+ e^{-\rho\tau}W(D^*_{\tau}, v_{\tau}). \qquad (8.19)$$

Then, following the same steps as in the section above, the HJB equation is defined as:

$$\min\left\{\left[\hat{\rho}W - \frac{1}{2}\sigma^2 v^2 W_{vv} - \mu v W v - [vf(D) - D + L]\right], -[W_D - c]\right\} = 0. \quad (8.20)$$

4.1. The Free Boundary at the Social Optimum

As before, the socially-optimal free boundary will divide the (v, D) space into two regions: the 'no development' region I and the 'development' region II. In region I the first term of the HJB is zero and the second term of the HJB equation is positive, thus the general solution for the value function is defined as:

$$W(D, v) = R_1(D)\, P^{\beta^s_1} + v\frac{f(D)}{\phi} - \frac{(D - L)}{\hat{\rho}} \qquad (8.21)$$

where $\phi = \hat{\rho} - \mu$ and β_1^R is the positive root of the fundamental quadratic, $Q^s = \frac{1}{2}\sigma^2\beta^s(\beta^s - 1) + \mu\beta^s - \hat{\rho} = 0$, with solution: $\beta_1^s = \frac{1}{2} - \mu/\sigma^2 + \sqrt{(\mu/\sigma^2 - 1/2)^2 + 2\rho/\sigma^2} > 1$

In region II the second term of the HJB equation is zero and $\Delta D > 0$ or

$$W_D(D, v) - c = 0. \qquad (8.22)$$

The constant $R_1(D)$ and the function $v = v(D)$ can be determined as before, using the value matching and the smooth pasting conditions, or

$$W_D(D, v) = R'_1(D)\, v^{\beta^s_1} + v\frac{f'(D)}{\phi} - \frac{1}{\hat{\rho}} = c, \; v = v(D) \qquad (8.23)$$

and

$$W_{Dv}(D, v) = \beta_1^s R'_1(D)\, v^{\beta^s_1 - 1} + \frac{f'(D)}{\phi} = 0 \text{ with } v = v(D). \qquad (8.24)$$

Combining (8.22) and (8.23) we obtain:

$$v(D) = \frac{\beta_1^s}{\beta_1^s - 1} \frac{\phi\left(\frac{1}{\rho} + c\right)}{f'(D)} \tag{8.25}$$

$$R_1'(D) = -\left(\frac{\beta_1^s - 1}{1 + c}\right)^{\beta_1^s - 1} \left(\frac{f'(D)}{\beta_1^s \phi}\right)^{\beta_1^s} \tag{8.26}$$

$$\phi = \hat{\rho} - \mu = \rho(1 - \delta) + a_2 - 2a_1 > 0 \tag{8.27}$$

As before the optimal boundary is increasing in D by the assumption of diminishing returns.

By equation (8.23) the incremental development is justified if the discounted value of the incremental development marginal value product adjusted for non-use values, $vf'(D)/\phi$, covers development costs, c, plus the present value of one unit of resource irreversibly developed, $1/\hat{\rho}$, plus the opportunity cost of the option to wait, $R_1'(D) \, v^{\beta_1^s}$. By (8.26) the marginal option value $R_1'(D)$ is negative, that is, it represents a cost.[20]

The benefit–cost rule for the regulated development is also determined as:

$$BC^s = \frac{\beta_1^s}{\beta_1^s - 1} > 1$$

5. COMPARISON OF EXERCISE BOUNDARIES AND MANAGEMENT RULES

The privately-optimal and the socially-optimal exercise boundaries determine the profit-maximizing and the socially-optimal management rules respectively, for the resource development. They are defined as:

$$P(D) = \frac{\beta_1}{\beta_1 - 1} \frac{(\rho - a_1) c}{f'(D)}$$

$$v(D) = \frac{\beta_1^s}{\beta_1^s - 1} \frac{(\hat{\rho} - \mu)\left(\frac{1}{\hat{\rho}} + c\right)}{f'(D)}$$

$$\mu = a_1 - a_2$$

$$\beta_1 = \frac{1}{2} - \frac{a_1}{\eta_1^2} + \sqrt{\left(\frac{a_1}{\eta_1^2} - \frac{1}{2}\right)^2 + \frac{2\rho}{\eta_1^2}}$$

$$\beta_1^s = \frac{1}{2} - \frac{\mu}{\sigma^2} + \sqrt{\left(\frac{\mu}{\sigma^2} - \frac{1}{2}\right)^2 + \frac{2\hat{\rho}}{\sigma^2}}$$

$$\sigma^2 = \eta_1^2 - 2\gamma\eta_1\eta_2 + \eta_2^2, \ \hat{\rho} = \rho(1-\delta) - a_1.$$

For $\lim_{D\to 0} f'(D) = \infty$, $P(0) = v(0) = 0$ and both boundaries pass through the origin; furthermore they are both increasing in D.

To compare the two boundaries we start with the simplest case where the environmental value of the undeveloped resource is fixed and normalized to one, implying $a_2 = \eta_2 = 0$. In this case $\mu = a_1$, $\sigma^2 = \eta_1^2$ while for $\delta \to 0$, $\beta_1 \to \beta_1^s$. In this case the difference $P(D) - v(D)$ is defined as:

$$v(D) - P(D) = \frac{\beta_1}{\beta_1 - 1} \frac{(\rho - a_1)}{f'(D)} > 0.$$

Thus the socially-optimal boundary is above the privately-optimal one. This means that there is a need for a higher upsurge in price in order to undertake development under social optimization. Thus the socially-optimal management rule in this case implies slower development of the resource. This slowdown in the development occurs because the non-use values are taken into account under maximization of social benefits, but are ignored under maximization of private profits. The result is shown in Figure 8.1. If the price moves from P_2 to P^*, the new private development is $D_2^u - D_2$, while the socially-optimal development is $D_2^S - D_2$.

When δ is greater than zero, so that the social discount rate takes into account the environmental correction factor and becomes lower than the private discount rate, the $v(D) - P(D)$ is more complex. However, numerical simulations indicate that $\partial v(D,\delta)/\partial\delta > 0$. Thus an increase in δ shifts the socially-optimal boundary upwards, implying further slowing down in the development of the resource. This result is in agreement with the central proposition in the theory of exhaustible resources that a reduction in the discount rate leads to greater conservation.

When, however, we consider the general case with $(a_2, \eta_2) \neq 0$, the comparison is not straightforward. To obtain some idea of the relative positions between the two exercise boundaries, we consider the following parameter values:

- $a_1 = 0.01$.
- $a_2 = 0$, this assumption implies that we do not expect the expected value of the resource's environmental value to change as compared to the current level.
- $\rho = 0.1$, $\delta = 0.2$.

- $\kappa = 0.5$, $c = 1$.
- $\eta_1 = 0.1$, $\eta_2 = 0.2$, these values reflect the assumption that the volatility of the resource's non-use values is likely to be higher than the price volatility associated with direct use values.
- It is difficult to make *a priori* assumptions regarding the sign and the size of the correlation coefficient γ between profit and environmental uncertainty, since the value of γ is most likely to depend on the specific problem. For example, an increase in the price of the resource's services indicating stronger demand might be accompanied by an increase in the undeveloped resource's indirect use values because at the same time more people might want to experience and preserve the undisturbed resource, yielding a *positive* corrrelation between profit and environmental uncertainty.[21]

For the chosen parameter constellation, the socially-optimal exercise boundary is uniformly above the privately-optimal exercise boundary.

However the relative pace of development can not be inferred from the relative positions of the exercise boundaries as in the case of profit uncertainty alone ($a_2 = \eta_2 = 0$). This is because the private agent chooses his/her development plan according to the movements of P_t, while the social planner chooses his/her development plan according to the movements of $v_t = P_t/q_t$. Thus unless P_t/q_t behaves exactly as P_t, we expect different responses, which can be summarized in the following proposition:

Proposition 1
Assume simultaneous uncertainty in the market price of resource services (use values) and the environmental value (non-use values) of the undeveloped resource. Then, if the relative price of resource services when the environmental value of the undeveloped resource is the numeraire or, P_t/q_t, evolves differently from the unadjusted price P_t, the development of the resource under social planning could be slower or faster relative to the profit-maximizing behaviour.

This proposition can be shown with reference to Figure 8.2, where the socially-optimal exercise boundary is drawn uniformly above the privately-optimal exercise boundary. Assume that from a given development level D_0, and market price of resource services P_0, the price moves to P_1, while the relative price moves from v_0 to $v_1 = P_1/q_1$. Then the social planner will undertake new development $D^s - D_0$, while the private developer will undertake development $D^U - D_0 > D^s - D_0$. Thus development is slower under the socially-optimal rule. Assume now that instead of moving to P_1 the price moves to P_2, while relative price still moves to v_1. Then while the social planner still undertakes new development $D^s - D_0$, the private developer undertakes *no* new development and development is *faster* under the socially-optimal rule.

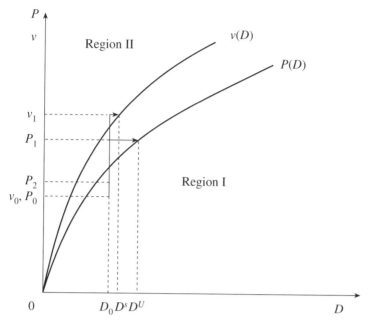

Figure 8.2   Development pace at the private and social optimum

This result goes contrary to the generally accepted view that taking into account environmental or intrinsic values, which are not taken into account under profit maximization, implies greater conservation. The driver of the result is the possibility of different evolution of market prices relative to non-use values. Under plausible parameter values, the socially-optimal exercise boundary is uniformly above the privately-optimal exercise boundary. This indicates that under similar movement of market prices and environmental values or under relatively faster growth of environmental values, the socially-optimal development is always slower than the privately-optimal development. However, if there is a downward movement of environmental values, then the externality effect goes the other way and, for a certain time interval, development at the social optimum is faster relative to the private optimum. This could happen for example if new information pushes down bioprospecting values of undeveloped ecosystems, or changes in preferences reduce the ecotourism value of the undeveloped landscape. In this case it would be socially desirable to develop the resource faster. This is because the private developer ignores, say, the drop in bioprospecting values, and thus the loss, from keeping an asset whose return is going down relative to the returns of the alternative,[22] is not internalized. This loss is internalized at the social optimum which takes into account the relative returns of both assets.

Socially desirable development is also faster if the undeveloped part is associated with negative intrinsic values, for example existence of a disease in the undeveloped state of the resource. In this case the private optimization problem might not fully internalize the external cost of the disease which is, however, internalized at the social optimum indicating relatively faster development, which eliminates the negative externality.

This result indicating the possibility of faster development at the social optimum can be related to a similar result obtained by Farzin (1984), where a reduction in the discount rate might lead to a faster and *not* slower development of an exhaustible resource, depending on the capital requirement for the production of a substitute and the size of the resource stock. In our case the *slow-down* effect induced by the environmental correction might be counterbalanced by the movement of environmental values relative to the market prices.

6. POLICY DESIGN

Since development at the private optimum is determined with reference to the privately-optimal boundary, the policy scheme should be chosen so that the private exercise boundary following the introduction of regulation coincides with the socially-optimal exercise boundary.

The case in which non-use values are fixed at the level $\bar{v}$, and uncertainty exists only with respect to the use values is considered first. In this case the socially-optimal development is always slower than the privately-optimal development and a possible policy instrument could be a development tax that will slow down private development. Consider a fixed tax $\mathcal{T}$ per unit of incremental development so that the unit development cost is $c + \mathcal{T}$. Then, the regulated privately-optimal exercise boundary is defined as:

$$P^R(D) = \frac{\beta_1}{\beta_1 - 1} \frac{(\rho - a_1)(c + \mathcal{T})}{f'(D)}$$

while the socially-optimal exercise boundary becomes:

$$P(D) = \frac{\beta_1^s}{\beta_1^s - 1} \frac{(\rho^s - a_1)\left(c + \dfrac{\bar{v}}{\rho^s}\right)}{f'(D)}.$$

It is clear that the optimal development tax which makes the two boundaries identical is defined for $\delta = 0$ as:

$$\mathcal{T} = \frac{\bar{v}}{\rho}.$$

Thus the optimal development tax is equal to the present value of the flow of one unit non-use value services which are lost by the irreversible development of the resource. It is interesting to note that by looking at the policy design problem as an issue of equating privately-optimal and socially-optimal free boundaries, the optimal tax is the same as the tax that would have been used under certainty. Since the private developer compares the regulated boundary, which is now identical to the socially-optimal boundary, with observed market prices, the regulation problem is solved by a simple deterministic tax without the need to use contingent instruments.

The appealing characteristic of what might be called *a barrier control policy design*, is that instead of choosing the optimal tax according to the realization of a random variable, the tax is set at a level such that the private developer is induced to behave like the social planner for *any* realization of the random variable. So the system is decentralized and once the tax is set the private developer is left to respond to price changes.

When $\delta > 0$ then the development tax is defined as:

$$T^s = \frac{(\beta_1 - 1)}{\beta_1(\rho - a_1)}[v(D) - P(D)].$$

The larger δ is, the larger is the difference $v(D) - P(D)$ and the higher the tax is. This is expected since the larger the difference $v(D) - P(D)$ is, the slower the development at the social optimum and the higher is the required tax to induce the private developer to slow down.

The general case with simultaneous use and non-use value uncertainty is now considered. In this case the development tax that equates the two boundaries is determined as:

$$T^* = \frac{(\beta_1 - 1)\,\beta_1^s}{(\beta_1^s - 1)\,\beta_1}\frac{(\hat{\rho} - \mu)\left(c + \dfrac{1}{\hat{\rho}}\right)}{(\rho - a_1)} - c.$$

However, under simultaneous uncertainty the private developer responds to changes in P_t while the social planner responds to changes in $v_t = P_t/q_t$. Thus although the regulated boundary coincides with the socially-optimal boundary, it is not certain that the private developer will follow the socially-optimal development. The socially-optimal development will be followed if P_t evolves in the same way as P_t/q_t. In all other cases the development tax will not induce the socially-optimal behaviour. This is summarized in the form of a non-existence result.

Proposition 2
Assume, under simultaneous use and non-use values uncertainty, that market prices for use values P_t evolve differently than the adjusted prices P_t/q_t. Then there is no

development tax that can induce the private developer to undertake the socially-optimal development.

The result can be shown with reference to Figure 8.3. Let the private boundary $P(D)$ shift after regulation to $v(D)$, and observed prices move from (P_0, v_0) to (P_1, v_1). The socially-optimal development is $D^s - D_0$, but since the private developer responds to the unadjusted price signal, the privately-optimal development after regulation is $D^R - D_0$. The unregulated development would have been $D^U - D_0$. Thus, although the tax does not achieve the socially-optimal development, it restricts the unregulated development towards the social optimum. This development tax can be regarded as a fixed second-best tax.

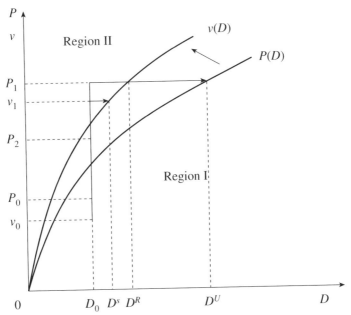

Figure 8.3 Regulation

The socially-optimal development can be secured by a proportional tax on the market prices equal to $1/q_t$ that will make the effective market price equal to v_t, and a subsidy for the undeveloped resource equal to $L - D_t$ per unit time. In this case the private solution exactly reproduces the social planner's value function. This scheme, however, is contingent on the realizations of the random variables and dependent on the current development state, and may be hard to implement, since it should be updated for changes in non-use values and development levels.

Another way to implement the socially-optimal rule is to use a system of quantity instruments, with a possible subsidy to correct for cases where the socially-optimal development should be faster than the privately-optimal one.

By inverting (8.24) the socially-optimal exercise boundary can be written as:

$$D^s = g(v) = v^{-1}(D).$$

Then the quantity instrument can be set as the limit $D_t \leq D_t^s$. Under the limit the HJB equation implies for the development region that:

$$V_D(D, P) - c - \lambda \leq 0, \Delta D \geq 0$$
$$\lambda(D^s - D) = 0, \lambda \geq 0$$

where λ is the Lagrangian multiplier associated with the quantity limit. Consider Figure 8.3, and suppose that prices move to (P_1, v_1). Then $D^s < D^U$, the constraint is binding and the limit secures the socially-optimal development. Suppose now that the market price moves to P_2, while the adjusted price remains at v_1. To secure the socially-optimal development, a subsidy s should be given, such that

$$(1 + s)P_2 = v_1.$$

Under the subsidy the private developer responds to the correct, from the social point of view, signal v_1 and undertakes the socially-optimal development D^s. The policy scheme can therefore be defined as follows:

- If $D_t^U > D_t^s$ then the development limit is set at D_t^s.
- If $D_t^U < D_t^s$ then the private developer receives a subsidy s_t: $(1 + s_t) = 1/q_t$.

The above scheme is also contingent on the realization of the random variable, q_t, and dependent on the development state.

The analysis of the policy schemes seems to suggest that under simultaneous use and non-use value uncertainty, a fixed development tax cannot achieve the social optimum but could have only a second-best character. The social optimum can be achieved by contingent, state development schemes which, however, might be difficult to implement.

7.   CONCLUDING REMARKS

In this chapter an exercise boundary approach has been used to analyse the problem of irreversible development of a natural resource under uncertainty in the use and non-use values associated with the resource.

This approach seems to have a number of advantages that could be useful in the analysis of dynamic management problems, not only in the field of environmental and resource economics. In particular it allows the characterization and comparison of development paths under privately-optimal and socially-optimal management rules. The comparison of development paths made possible by this approach provides a basis for exploring situations where, contrary to the generally accepted intuition, socially-optimal development might be faster than privately-optimal development for a certain time interval.

Furthermore the use of exercise boundaries indicates that regulation can be designed in such a way that the regulated boundary coincides with the socially-optimal boundary. For the case of uncertainty in use values only, this approach shows that a simple fixed deterministic development tax can induce the socially-optimal path. This is clearly an advantage since there is no need for contingent instruments. When, however, uncertainty affects both use and environmental values, the fixed tax can bring the regulated development closer to the socially-optimal one, but cannot achieve the socially-optimal path. To do this contingent and state-dependent schemes are required. It is an open issue, however, whether or not a fixed tax that approaches the optimal path should be preferred, on implementability and acceptability grounds, to a complicated scheme that achieves the social optimum.

NOTES

*   I am grateful to an anonymous referee for valuable comments on an earlier draft of this paper. Support from ELKE 1266 is acknowledged.
1.   See for example Arrow and Fisher (1974), or Fisher and Hanemann (1986, 1987). The same issue has also received considerable attention in the literature of finance and investment (for example Constandinidis, 1986; Dixit and Pindyck, 1994; Dixit, Pindyck and Sodal, 1998) or public finance (Hassett and Metcalf, 1999).
2.   For detailed definitions of these values and measurement issues see, for example, Perrings (1995).
3.   Scheinkman and Zariphopoulou (1999) have recently analysed a similar problem of resource management in a fairly general set up of simultaneous uncertainty on the returns from the resource development and the returns of the undeveloped resource. In the present chapter, by analysing a simpler model it becomes possible to completely characterize and distinguish optimal policies, under private profit maximization and social optimization, and furthermore to address regulation issues under simultaneous uncertainty and irreversibility.

4. Uncertainty on the benefit and cost side in environmental problems has been related to the choice between price or quantity environmental policy instruments (for example, Weitzman, 1974). Stavins (1996) analyses this issue under correlated benefit and cost uncertainty.
5. A boundary comparison method has been used by Xepapadeas (1998) in a simpler model of resource development with uncertainty only in prices.
6. This value could have been obtained by state preference or revealed preference methods.
7. The qualitative nature of the results will not change if we assume n idential developers.
8. This might be, for example, the case of services associated with the development of a scenic land which are sold in the world market of tourist services.
9. See for example Malliaris and Brock (1982) for definitions and more details.
10. It should be noted that the Brownian motion assumption causes price to move away from its starting point. If however price is related to long-run marginal costs, then a better assumption about price movements could be a mean-reverting process. Under this assumption price tends toward marginal costs in the long run and price movements can be modelled as

$$dP_t = a(\tilde{P}_t - P_t)P_t dt + \sigma P_t dz_{pt}$$

where $\tilde{P}_t$ can be interpreted as long-run marginal costs.
11. For a small open economy with negligible country risk it could be assumed that firms can borrow at a risk-free world interest rate.
12. Subscripts associated with the value functions denote derivatives.
13. See Dixit and Pindyck (1994).
14. For a presentation of these conditions, see Dixit and Pindyck (1994).
15. Integrating (8.17) we obtain $A_1(D)$ as:

$$A_1(D) = \int_D^\infty [-A'_{1s}]ds =$$

$$\left(\frac{\beta_1 - 1}{c}\right)^{\beta_1 - 1} \int_D^\infty \left(\frac{f'(D)}{\beta_1 \delta}\right)^{\beta_1}.$$

As shown by Dixit and Pindyck (1994) for the integral to converge with a Cobb–Douglas development function, $f(D) = D^\kappa$, $0 < \kappa < 1$, κ should be sufficiently small so that $\beta_1 > 1/1 - \kappa$.
16. Heal (2000) mentions that bioprospecting rights might be worth as much as $9000 per hectare in biodiversity hot spots.
17. This interpretation of the evolution of environmental values in this chapter as values of ecosystem services, is related to the diffusion formulation of environmental benefits at the undeveloped state used by Scheinkman and Zariphopoulou (1999). On the other hand, when environmental values are interpreted as unobserved existence values which are currently uncertain, the Brownian motion assumption might not be the most appropriate because of the dependency of its drift and volatility on uncertain current values.
18. The comparison between the private and the social discount rate is an issue that has been discussed extensively. See for example, Arrow and Kurz (1970, Ch. I.2), Lind (1982, 1990).
19. See also Scheinkman and Zariphopoulou (1999).
20. Furthermore,

$$R_1(D) = \int_D^\infty [-R'_1(s)]ds = \left(\frac{\beta_1^s - 1}{1 + c}\right)^{\beta_1^s - 1} \int_D^\infty \left(\frac{f'(D)}{\beta_1^s \phi}\right)^{\beta_1^s}.$$

where for the same Cobb–Douglas production function we must have $\beta_1^s > 1/1 - \kappa$.

21. When γ = 0 implying that the social returns of the resource are uncorellated with the private returns, then the Arrow and Lind (1970) result – that for small public investment uncorellated with the previous national income, the government should be risk neutral – implies that the environmental regulator should use a risk free discount rate, along with the potential environmental correction.
22. The alternative is to develop the resource.

REFERENCES

Arrow, K.J. and A. Fisher (1974), 'Environmental preservation, uncertainty and irreversibility', *Quarterly Journal of Economics*, **88**, 312–19.

Arrow, K.J. and M. Kurz (1970), *Public Investment, the Rate of Return, and Optimal Fiscal Policy*, Baltimore: Johns Hopkins University Press for Resources for the Future.

Arrow, K.J. and C. Lind (1970), Uncertainty and the evaluation of public investment decisions, *American Economic Review*, **60**, 364–78.

Chichilnisky, G. and G. Heal (1998), 'Economic returns from the biosphere', *Nature*, 629–30.

Constandinidis, G.M. (1986), 'Capital market equilibrium with transaction costs', *Journal of Political Economy*, **94**, 842–62.

Davis, M. and A. Norman (1990), 'Portfolio selection with transaction costs', *Mathematics of Operations Research*, **15**, 676–713.

Dixit, A.K. and R.S. Pindyck (1994), *Investment under Uncertainty*, Princeton NJ: Princeton University Press.

Dixit, A.K., R.S. Pindyck and S. Sodal (1998), 'A markup interpretation of optimal investment rules', *The Economic Journal*, **109**, 179–89.

Farzin, Y.H. (1984), 'The effect of discount rate on depletion of exhaustible resources', *Journal of Political Economy*, **92**, 841–51.

Fisher, A.C. and M. Hanemann (1986), 'Environmental damages and option values', *Natural Resource Modelling*, **1**, 111–24.

Fisher, A.C. and M. Hanemann (1987), 'Quasi-option value: some misconceptions dispelled', *Journal of Environmental Economics and Management*, **14**, 183–90.

Fleming, W. and H.M. Soner (1993), *Controlled Markov Process and Viscosity Solutions*, New York: Springer-Verlag.

Hassett, K.A. and G. Metcalf (1999), 'Investment with Uncertain Tax Policy: Does Random Tax Policy Discourage Investment?', *The Economic Journal*, **109**, 372–93.

Heal, G. (2000), 'Biodiversity as a Commodity', in S. Levin, G.C. Daily, J. Lubchenco and D. Tilman (eds), *Encyclopedia of Biodiversity*, Boston: Academic Press.

Lind, R. (1982), *Discounting for Time and Risk in Energy Policy*, Washington, DC: Resources for the Future.

Lind, R. (1990), 'Reassessing the government's discount rate policy in light of new theory and data in a world economy with high capital mobility', *Journal of Environmental Economics and Management*, **18**, S9–S28.

Malliaris, A.G. and W.A. Brock (1982), *Stochastic Methods in Economics and Finance*, Amsterdam: North-Holland.

Perrings, C. (1995), 'The Economic Value of Biodiversity', in H. Heywood and R. Watson (eds), *Global Biodiversity Assessment*, UNEP, Cambridge University Press.

Scheinkman, J.A. and T. Zariphopoulou (1999), 'Optimal environmental management in the presence of irreversibilities', *Journal of Economic Theory*, forthcoming.

Soner, H.M. (1997), 'Controlled Markov Processes, Viscosity Solutions and Applications to Mathematical Finance', in I. Capuzzo Dolcetta and P.L. Lions (eds), *Viscosity Solutions and Applications*, Berlin: Springer-Verlag.

Stavins, R.N. (1996), 'Correlated uncertainty and policy instrument choice', *Journal of Environmental Economics and Management*, **30**, 218–33.

Weitzman, M.L. (1974), 'Prices vs. quantities', *Review of Economic Studies*, **41**, 477–91.

Weitzman, M. (1994), 'On the environmental discount rate', *Journal of Environmental Economics and Management*, **26** (3), 200–209.

Xepapadeas, A. (1998), 'Optimal resource development and irreversibilities: cooperative and noncooperative solutions', *Natural Resource Modelling*, **11**, 357–78.

9. A model of neighbourhood conditions and internal household environments

Mark Agee and Thomas Crocker*

INTRODUCTION

An extensive economic literature in the past decade has applied rational choice theory to traditional sociological and developmental psychology concerns with the conditioning of individuals' behaviour by their physical neighbourhoods and by their neighbours. This literature asks how local physical features, information networks and behavioural prescriptions affect the choices of people who live with them.[1] The features, networks and prescriptions are said to alter the types, terms and scopes of transactions in which individuals engage. Ambient environmental conditions, public legal, political and physical infrastructures, school quality, ethnic composition and their effects on welfare roll incidence, crime, labour supply, teenage pregnancy and so on have all attracted considerable analytical and empirical attention.[2] But nearly all this literature treats the impact of neighbourhood circumstances upon family members' household investments as a black box.[3] Consider, for example, the famous Tiebout (1956) proposition in which neighbourhood attributes determine household location choice without altering internal household investments in any manner whatsoever. This chapter begins to remedy this deficiency by linking two relationships: the contribution of the home environment to adult work performance; and the impact of neighbourhood circumstances upon the home environment. Incorporating the linkage into an otherwise standard model of household behaviour directs attention to a richer set of issues.

Internal household investments may amplify or may temper the influence a neighbourhood attribute has upon the behaviour of an individual family member. Exchange possibilities within the home environment may expand the individual's adjustment opportunities just as constraints this environment imposes may restrain them beyond those available to the stand-alone individual. Thus, for example, the ethnic socialization efforts of family adults may counter the 'melting pot' cultural pressures with which the larger society confronts a child (Bissin and Verdier, 2000). Or parents may alleviate the impact of neighbourhood environmental pollution upon a child's health by not allowing it near the pollution source or by purchasing medical help (Agee and Crocker, 1996). Alternatively stated, neighbourhood attributes which influence internal household investments and home time decisions may differ across households with the relative benefits and costs the households face, though the properties of the attributes which trigger these decisions may apply equally to all households in a locale. It follows that attempts to explain the impact of neighbourhood attributes upon the behaviour of individuals as if all people live in households which behave internally in identical ways may be highly misleading.[4]

If biology is not destiny, the effects of parents' home investments and home time on a child's development may depend crucially on how these investment and time allocations combine with neighbourhood circumstances. We use the image of a single custodial parent with her offspring to carry forward our analysis of the linkage between neighbourhood circumstances and the child's home environment. The offspring are presumed to be young enough such that neighbourhood circumstances do not directly affect them, nor do the offspring affect these circumstances. Instead, the neighbourhood circumstances (for example, abandoned industrial sites) affect the investments the custodial parent makes in the household and thus the household environment in which the child resides.[5]

In the next section, we define the basic model. A third section develops its comparative statics. The fourth section allows the parent's rate of time preference to have a role in determining internal household responses to neighbourhood circumstances. We introduce stochastic home investment payoffs caused by neighbourhood circumstances in a fifth section. A sixth section talks in general terms about testing the model. Finally, we conclude that situations may readily exist where neighbourhood circumstances exercise leverage over the home environment a parent chooses to provide for herself and her child.

THE BASIC MODEL

Consider a single period, two-generation setting consisting of a custodial parent, the mother and a preschool child. The mother derives utility, $U(Y, l)$ in a weakly separable fashion from her consumption, Y and from her home time, l, during which she is available to provide security and predictability for her young child. Inclusion of l in $U(\cdot)$ implies it is the process of interacting with the child which provides the mother joy and satisfaction

(Juster, 1995).[6] $U(\cdot)$ is twice differentiable and concave in both its arguments. So as to remove fertility issues, the number of children in the home is predetermined. Children are passive with respect to the mother's consumption and investment decisions.

The mother's net wealth is a function of the physical environment, g, she provides herself and her child and the time, L, she spends away from home and the child, given her total available hours, H, and the money equivalent of her exogenous wealth, X. This exogenous wealth includes government transfers to her and whatever mandated child support payments she can collect from a former spouse. Investment in the home environment includes devices which protect the household from neighbourhood dangers or which enhance positive neighbourhood effects upon the household. Her net wealth is then

$$Y = X + f(g,L) - c(Q;\alpha)g, \qquad (9.1)$$

where f (.) is the mother's earning function. A better home environment (cleaner, warmer, more food stocks, and so on) and more work time increase the mother's earnings as well as enhancing her child's well-being. In contrast then to the textbook labour–leisure choice framework, this model takes home (leisure) time as enhancing both the utility and the earnings and childcare productivity of the mother. Childcare productivity can be interpreted in terms of enhancements in the child's future earnings and thus the mother's potential old age income security.

Paid work is only available to the mother away from home. The $c(Q;\alpha)$ is the mother's unit cost of investing in the home environment. The c varies inversely with a scalar index, Q, of neighbourhood circumstances. A cleaner, more secure neighbourhood reduces the unit cost of providing a clean, secure household environment. Since we are not conducting an empirical investigation of the influence of neighbourhood circumstances upon household environments, nothing is to be gained by delineating the nuanced forms these circumstances and environments may take. The c also varies inversely with a vector, α, of predetermined household members' genetic and cultural attributes, the household phenotype. For example, Grossman (1999) shows that a more educated parent produces a healthier home environment. Expression (9.1) together with U (.) basically say that neighbourhood circumstances affect the home environment the mother supplies herself and her child and that this home environment influences the mother's work and childcare performances. That is, neighbourhood circumstances influence the child only through their effects upon parental home time and parental investments in the home environment. The social science literature suggests that three features of the home environment – maternal warmth, home physical environment and home learning – are critical for child development (Klebanov et al., 1997, p. 142). Maternal warmth and home learning involve the presence of a parent.

Let f (.)/g denote the mother's rate of return to investing in the home environment. Also, let $s[v\,(Q, n), \alpha]$ be the mother's highest possible rate of return to g, conditional upon the share, v, of resident to nonresident investment in the neighbourhood. Given that residents are liquidity constrained, this resident share will decline as improvements in the neighbourhood circumstances attract outside investors from a less constrained national capital market. Then

$$f(.)/g \leq s[v\,(Q, n), \alpha] \qquad (9.2)$$

where $\partial s\,/\,\partial v > 0$, $\partial v / \partial Q < 0$, and n is the rate of return in the national capital market. If $r > l < n$ is the highest rate of return the mother could obtain by moving from the neighbourhood, then $c\,(.) < s\,(.) \geq r$ must occur for the mother to stay put. We assume throughout that the mother does not move and that her choice of where to live is predetermined. We thus focus on short-run adjustments. In the absence of very large X, expression (9.2) thus implies strictly positive investment by the mother in the home environment, g.

If expression (9.1) is substituted into U (.), the Lagrangian for the mother's decision problem is

$$£ = U[X + f(g,L) - c(Q;\alpha)g, H - L] + \lambda[sg - f(g,L)], \qquad (9.3)$$

where g and $L = H - l$ are the mother's decision variables. Given that expression (9.2) is binding such that the mother stays put, her Kuhn–Tucker necessary conditions are

$$\textbf{g:}\ f_g(U_Y - \lambda) = U_Y c - \lambda s, \qquad (9.4)$$

$$\textbf{L:}\ f_L(U_Y - \lambda) = U_l, \qquad (9.5)$$

and the constraint. A subscript denotes a partial derivative. Inspection of (9.4) reveals that $\lambda \neq U_Y$, given that $c < s$. Upon dividing (9.4) by (9.5) and setting $w = U_l/U_Y$, the mother's marginal value of home time or marginal cost of work effort, one obtains

$$f_g/f_L = c/w - \lambda s/U_l. \qquad (9.6)$$

Because the last term in (9.6) is positive, $f_g/f_L > c/w$ which violates the market efficiency condition requiring marginal rates of substitution to be equal to relative market prices. Insight into the form of this violation can be gained be rewriting (9.4) and (9.5) as

$$f_g - c = \lambda(f_g - s)/U_Y, \qquad (9.7)$$

$$f_L - w = \lambda f_L/U_Y. \qquad (9.8)$$

Since $f_g < s$ (see Appendix A), these expressions imply that the mother will invest in the home environment such that $f_g < c$ and will therefore spend time at the home such that $f_L > w$. That is, relative to a person who views work (production) and family life as separable, and who is therefore driven to equate her marginal earnings to her marginal cost of work effort, this mother will invest more in the home environment and spend less time away from home.[7] Her shadow price of home time is less than her market wage because working long hours reduces her earnings productivity (Crocker and Horst, 1981). That is, her home time consumption decisions and her home environment investment decisions influence her earnings decisions. Cesario (1976) showed in the context of travel cost approaches to recreational demand that the shadow price of time and marginal earnings could not be equal at the optimum if a time variable appeared in the recreationist's utility function. If one grants that people have home lives not entirely separable from their outside lives, expressions (9.7) and (9.8) imply that a similar caution be applied to any research which would employ analytical devices such as full income constraints to model issues like the impact of environmental pollution upon human health. Most people like to be at home and their home environment contributes to their productivity away from home. An acknowledgment that people have home lives causes shadow prices and full income to be endogenous.

NEIGHBOURHOOD DIFFERENCES

Neighbourhoods differ – some are newer than others, some have violence, crime, inferior public services and others have pristine environments rather than polluted, crowded streets. Consider now the impacts of neighbourhood differences upon a mother's optimal mix of home time and investment in the home environment.

First consider the consequences of an exogenous change in the mother's costs due to a change in the money price of investing in the home environment. By the Implicit Function Theorem the effects upon the decision variable g and L are

$$\partial g/\partial c = U_Y f_L^2/|\mathbf{B}| < 0 \qquad (9.9)$$

$$\partial L/\partial c = U_Y(s-f_g)f_L/|\mathbf{B}| < 0 \qquad (9.10)$$

where $|\mathbf{B}| > 0$ the determinant of the bordered Hessian matrix, satisfies the sufficient second order conditions for a maximum. Expressions (9.9) and (9.10) state that an increase in the mother's cost of investing in the home environment will reduce these investments while also increasing her home time and reducing her work time. Moreover, since $\partial L/\partial c = (\partial g/\partial c)(s-f_g)/f_L$ from (9.9) and (9.10) which, upon substitution from (9.7) and (9.8), becomes $\partial L/\partial c = (\partial g/\partial c)(s-c)/w$, the relative magnitude of her increase in home time depends upon the magnitude of $(s-c)/w$. The larger the marginal value, w, of her home time, l, the larger her cost of investing in the home environment, g, and the smaller her highest possible rate of return, s, from this investment, the more responsive will her home time be to a change in her costs of investing in the home environment.

Now presume a change in neighbourhood circumstances due perhaps to the arrival or the shutting down of a factory which pollutes the neighbourhood air with fine particulates that seep into the mother's home. The effects of this change in neighbourhood circumstances upon the decision variables g and L are given by

$$\partial g/\partial Q = \{[U_Y(\partial c/\partial Q) - \lambda(\partial s/\partial Q)]f_L^2 + \mathbf{B}_{31}(\partial s/\partial Q)g\}/|\mathbf{B}| \qquad (9.11)$$

$$\partial L/\partial Q = -\{[U_Y(\partial c/\partial Q) - \lambda(\partial s/\partial Q)](s-f_g)f_L^2 + \mathbf{B}_{32}$$
$$(\partial s/\partial Q)g\}/|\mathbf{B}|. \qquad (9.12)$$

$\mathbf{B}_{jk}$ is the cofactor of the jkth element of $\mathbf{B}$ and $\partial s/\partial Q = (\partial s/\partial v)(\partial v/\partial Q) < 0$. The sign of $\partial L/\partial Q$ in (9.12) depends on the sign of $1 + f_g - c$ and is ambiguous. Nevertheless, a large cost of investing in the home environment and a small contribution of this investment to earnings will, with a decline in neighbourhood circumstances, reduce the mother's home time.

The sign of $\partial g/\partial Q$ in (9.11) depends on the signs of $U_Y(\partial c/\partial Q) - \lambda(\partial s/\partial Q) \equiv \Gamma$ and the cofactors $\mathbf{B}_{31}$, the signs of both of which can be determined with some reasonable assumptions. First, given that neighbourhood circumstances are a normal good, from the Lagrangian in (9.3) we have

$$\partial U^*/\partial Q = \partial \pounds/\partial Q = -g[U_Y(\partial c/\partial Q) - \lambda(\partial s/\partial Q)] \geq 0, \qquad (9.13)$$

by the Envelope Theorem, which implies $\Gamma \leq 0$ for all $g > 0$. Expression (9.13) thus states that the household's direct gains from improvement in the neighbourhood will be at least as great as its indirect gains from the outside investment the neighbourhood improvement attracts.

Additional algebraic manipulation (see Appendix B) shows that

$$\mathbf{B}_{31} = - w(s-f_g)[(U_{YY}f_L - U_{IL} + U_{ll} - U_{lY}f_l)/w]$$
$$- (U_Y - \lambda)[f_{LL}(s-f_g) + f_L f_{Lg}]. \tag{9.14}$$

Since $w(s-f_g)>0$ and $U_Y - \lambda > 0$, the sign of $\mathbf{B}_{31}$ depends on the signs of the second and fourth bracketed terms in (9.14). Let $F(Y, l; w)$ implicitly define the marginal value of home time, $w = U_l/U_Y$. Then

$$\partial w/\partial Y = - F_Y/F_w = (U_{YY} - U_{lY}/w)/U_Y \tag{9.15}$$

by the Implicit Function Rule which implies

$$U_{lY}/w \geq U_{YY} \tag{9.16}$$

if $\partial w/\partial Y \geq 0$, that is, if the marginal value of home time increases as household wealth increases. With the inequality in (9.16), the second bracketed term in (9.14) is negative.

Finally to sign the fourth bracketed term in (9.14), divide (9.7) by (9.8) to obtain an analogy of the standard tangency condition

$$(f_g - c)/(f_l - w) - (f_g - s)/f_L = 0. \tag{9.17}$$

The derivative of (9.17) in respect to the marginal value of home time gives

$$f_g + wf_{gL}(dL/dw) + sf_{LL}(dL/dw) - cf_{LL}(dL/dw) - s = 0, \tag{9.18}$$

which can be rewritten as

$$(dL/dw)[f_{LL}(s-f_g) + f_L f_{gL}](w/f_L) = s - f_g > 0. \tag{9.19}$$

Since $w/f_L > 0$, the sign of $\mathbf{B}_{31}$ in (9.14) and hence the sign of $\partial g/\partial Q$ in (9.11) depends upon the slope, dL/dw, of the curve relating the mother's home time to her marginal value of home time. If $dL/dw < 0$, then the fourth bracketed term in (9.14) is negative and the mother will change her investment in the home environment in the same direction as any change in the neighbourhood circumstances, that is, $\partial g/\partial Q > 0$ in (9.11). The comparative static result in this basic model is[8]

$$\partial L/\partial w = - (s - f_g)^2/|\mathbf{B}| < 0, \tag{9.20}$$

which is similar to the traditional result of textbook labour–leisure analysis: as the marginal value of home time increases, the mother achieves greater well-being by substituting home time for time away from home (work time). This of course assumes convexity of the mother's indifference curves between home time and work time, an assumption justified by the everyday observation of diversification between work-related income and home time. But a mother very well endowed with exogenous wealth, X, might choose just to stay home. In terms of the geometry of this result, such a 'corner solution' would be preferred if the mother's indifference curve were steeper than her budget surface at endowment level X.

In short, $dL/dw < 0$ and thus $\partial g/\partial Q > 0$ make intuitive sense. Consider an exogenous deterioration of neighbourhood circumstances which raises the mother's unit cost of investing in the home environment and thus by (9.1) lowers the mother's net wealth. In order to compensate for her loss, she might try to increase her earnings. But trying to do so by investing in her home environment, g, will not help since f_g, the marginal contribution of this environment to her earnings, is already less than c, the unit cost of improving the home environment. Her remaining option is to work more – to increase L. But increasing L means less home time which is the fundamental tradeoff.

Finally, note that as in Bowles (1998), preferences, as expressed by $w = U_l/U_Y$, are endogenous in this model. These preferences reflect both personal characteristics and the circumstances of the neighbourhood in which the mother resides.

RATE OF TIME PREFERENCE

The results of the basic model presume that the mother's net benefits of investments in the home environment accrue instantaneously. Yet some realizations of these benefits can take time, especially if they involve a young child's adult prospects and the mother's old-age security. Thus a mother's decisions to invest in the home environment can affect her future as well as her present net wealth. Here we ask how these temporal considerations impact the propensity established in the basic model for households who do not treat the worlds of work and home as separable to invest more in the home environment and to be at home more than would a person who lives according to $f_g/f_L = c/w$, that is, a person who equates her marginal rate of substitution between home investment and away-from-home (work) time to their relative prices.

To set the argument, initially suppose at present date, t, the mother invests g_t in the home environment but finds herself at the return

$$f(g_t, L_t)/g_t < s[v(Q, n), \alpha] \tag{9.21}$$

which, by (9.6), implies $\lambda = 0$ and $f_{gt}/f_{Lt} = c/w$. That is, perhaps because of an unanticipated change in household particulars, the mother is not maximizing her net wealth. But repositioning her home and work lives can take time, say $t + \tau$ periods. To maximize her wealth with the new household particulars she must increase her investments in the home environment by $\Delta g = g_{t+\tau} - g_t$ and reduce by $\Delta L = L_t - L_{t+\tau}$ her work effort, thus increasing her home time by $\Delta l = l_{t+\tau} - l_t$. Let the difference

$$(c \cdot \Delta g) - (w \cdot \Delta L) > 0 \tag{9.22}$$

be the opportunity cost of this repositioning, the costs incurred at each instant prior to $t+\tau$ when the benefits of restoring (9.6) are realized. Restoration of the condition in (9.6) raises the mother's net wealth by $(s - c)\Delta g$. The mother's discounted future benefits $B(\tau)$, are then given by

$$B(\tau) = [(s - c) \cdot \Delta g] \sum_{z=t}^{t+\tau} (1 + \rho)^{-z} - [(c \cdot \Delta g) - (w \cdot \Delta L)] \sum_{\gamma = t+z}^{\infty} (1 + \rho)^{-z} \tag{9.23}$$

where ρ denotes the mother's rate of time preference, her intertemporal marginal rate of substitution.

A positive value for expression (9.23) requires that $\lambda s/U_l$ in expression (9.6) be positive, that is, expression (9.23) must be such that

$$B(\tau) = [(s - c) \cdot \Delta g](1/\delta)(1 + \rho)^{-t+\tau}$$
$$- [(c \cdot \Delta g) - (w \cdot \Delta L)](1/\delta)[1 - (1 + \rho)^{-(t+\tau)}] > 0 \tag{9.24}$$

where $\delta = \rho/(1 + \rho)$. Expression (9.24) will be positive provided

$$[(s \cdot \Delta g) - (w \cdot \Delta L)](1 + \rho)^{-(t+\tau)} > (c \cdot \Delta g) - (w \cdot \Delta L) \tag{9.25}$$

Inspection of (9.25) reveals that the mother will not succumb to treating her work and family life as separable worlds when: (i) there is a high return to investing in the home environment; (ii) the unit cost of investing in the home environment is small; (iii) home time has a high marginal value; (iv) the waiting period for the benefits of investing in the home environment is short; and (v) the mother has a low rate of time preference. It is common to associate a high time preference rate with a low level of investment in the home environment, for example, Becker and Tomes (1989). Holden et al. (1998) even conclude that high rates of time preference cause environmental disinvestments. Note, however, that expression (9.25) suggests the positive home environment impacts of strength of the mother's preference for home investment and for home time could dominate any negative impact from a high rate of time preference.

Expression (9.24) portrays the condition that must be fulfilled if it is to be worthwhile for the mother not to separate her work and her home lives. But how far will she take this nonseparability? Maximization of (9.24) provides an insight. Note that any change in the mother's work time is likewise a function of the change in her investment in the home environment, that is, $\Delta L = \Delta L(\Delta g)$. Differentiation of expression (9.24) then yields

$$\frac{dB(\tau)}{d(\Delta g)} = \{s - w[d(\Delta L)/d(\Delta g)]\}(1/\delta)(1 + \rho)^{-(t+\tau)}$$

$$- \{c + w[d(\Delta L)/d(\Delta g)]\}(1/\delta) = 0, \tag{9.26}$$

where $d(\Delta L)/d(\Delta g)$ is the slope of the mother's earnings function at her optimum degree of nonseparability between her home and work lives. However, when expression (9.10) is divided by expression (9.9), the relationship

$$dL/dg \cong (s - f_g)/f_L \tag{9.27}$$

is obtained for the mother who is maximizing her net wealth. Solving the first-order condition in (9.26) for $d(\Delta L)/d(\Delta g)$, substituting (9.27) into the result and rearranging terms yields

$$f_g/f_L = c/w - \beta f_g(s - c)/(1 - \beta)w(s - f_g), \tag{9.28}$$

where $\beta = (1 + \rho)^{-(t+\tau)}$. Further substitution from the tangency condition in (9.17) reduces expression (9.28) to

$$f_g/f_L = (1 - \beta)c/w. \tag{9.29}$$

Expression (9.29) says that the mother's preferred degree of nonseparability of her work and home lives is a function of the time, $t + \tau$, at which the benefits of the degree of nonseparability will be realized and of her rate of time preference. The degree of nonseparability is defined by the extent to which $f_{gt}/f_{Lt} > c/w$. A larger waiting period or a higher rate of time preference pushes β closer to zero and thus reduces the mother's incentive to invest in the home environment and increases her incentive to work more and spend less time at home. Briefly, the mother's investment in home environments which involve payoffs distant from the present are less likely to be made when outside investments with short-term payoffs increase in the neighbourhood.

UNCERTAINTY ABOUT HOUSEHOLD PROSPECTS

Previous sections have shown that a mother who does not separate her work and home lives has an incentive to invest more in her home environment and to be at home more than would a person who treats work and home as separate worlds. However, neighbourhood decay reduces this incentive. Long delays in payoffs from home environment investments and high rates of time preference do likewise. It follows that economic evaluation of a change in neighbourhood circumstances requires an accounting of the impact of the change on behaviour within the home. In this section, we ask whether a mother's uncertainty about what investment in the home environment will do for her earnings will alter any of the results in the previous sections.

To begin, assume the mother's earnings to be susceptible to some exogenous family event such as having her child become ill. The illness could be caused by ambient pollution in the neighbourhood. Because she does not know whether or not illness will strike her family, she is unsure about the best rate of return she can obtain from investing in her home environment. Consequently, her decision to invest recognizes that her realized best return may, depending on whether illness strikes her child, be less than, equal to or exceed $s(\cdot)$ in expression (9.2). Let k denote her *ex ante* home investment and have u be a random health variable distributed over $[0, \infty)$. Then $g = g(k,u)$ is the more or less imperfect correlation of this investment with the realized home environment. That is, illness inhibits the ability of the mother to bring about the environment she expected from a given *ex ante* home investment. Her net wealth is the sum

$$Y = X + f\{L[g(k,u)]\} - c(Q;\alpha)k. \tag{9.30}$$

Our previous formulation where certainty prevailed had the mother simultaneously selecting labour and home time and her investment in the home environment. Because the realized efficiency of this investment is now uncertain, the formulation in (9.30) says that she initially selects an investment in the home environment, then observes the exogenous event and only then generates earnings, $f(\cdot)$, by selecting her labour time and her home time. This formulation is most applicable to home investments expected to produce lagged changes in the home environment. A mother might, for example, procure equipment to provide respiratory care for an ill child only to find that the child recovers before the equipment is exhausted. Given the recovery, she can then adjust her labour and home times but, absent ready access to a market for used, specialized medical equipment, she is stuck with it.

Let u correspond to the mother's assessment of the distribution of the uncertain event

$$D(\bar{u}) = \int_0^{\bar{u}} m(u)du. \tag{9.31}$$

This implies the mother estimates the likelihood of attaining her best rate of return, $s(\cdot)$, for any particular level, k, of her *ex ante* home investment. This specification allows a chance constrained programming approach to her decision problem.

Let the function

$$h(u,k) = f\{L[g(k,u)]\}/k, \tag{9.32}$$

represent the mother's uncertain return from k; that is, $h(\cdot)$, a function of u and the parameter k, is monotonically increasing in u and has the range (c, s). Once the mother chooses k, her $h(\cdot)$ depends on the realization of the exogenous event. Moreover, by the inverse function rule, $u = u(k)$. Given that the mother thinks in terms of the distribution $h(\cdot)$ and hence the probability that her $h \leq s$ or $h \geq s$, her problem is to select a level, k, of *ex ante* investment in the home environment which maximizes her expected utility

$$\max_k U\langle X = f\{L[g(k,u)]\} - c(\cdot)k, H - L[g(k,u)]\rangle \tag{9.33}$$

subject to her recognition that the probability of exceeding $s, P\{h \geq s\}$ is less than some value, γ:

$$\rho\{h \geq s\} \int_{u(k)}^{\infty} m(u)du \leq \gamma \tag{9.34}$$

In other words, the mother tries to achieve her best rate of return, s, with at least probability γ. Assuming a solution exists for $k > 0$ and invoking Leibniz's rule, the first-order condition with respect to k is

$$f_k/f' = [(c - \vartheta)/w][w/(f' - w)], \tag{9.35}$$

where $f' = df/dL$, $f_k = f'L_g g_k$, $\vartheta = \lambda(dw/dk)m[u(k)]/U_Y$, and λ is a Lagrangian multiplier. The ratio ϑ is positive when returns to k conform to expression (9.34). If $0 \leq \vartheta < c$, expression (9.35) states that the mother, uncertain about the benefits of investing in her home environment will, parallel to the result in (9.6), choose to be at home more than would a person who views her work life and her home life as separable. Conversely, if $\vartheta = c$, the mother sacrifices even more home time for work time than would the person who treats the two as separable. That is, $f' < w$ for her. Thus, whether or not the mother will invest more or less in her home environment than $f_k = c$ is unclear; however, whenever $\vartheta = c$, she will invest such that $f_k = 0$ and choose home time such that $f' = w$.

On the other hand, when $\lambda = 0$, such that the mother regards her work life and her home life as separable, she might not behave according to the efficiency condition under separability of $f_k/f' = c/w$. This is because when $\lambda = 0$, ϑ is zero and expression (9.35) simplifies to

$$f_k/f' = (c/w) \cdot (f' - w) \tag{9.36}$$

which says that if the mother who views her lives as separable chooses her home time such that $2w > f' > w$, she will be at home more and will invest less in her home environment than she would under conditions of certainty about the benefits of her investment. In other words, if the marginal productivity of the mother's work time is less than twice her marginal value of home time, the mother with separable lives will behave like a mother with nonseparable lives: she will be at home more than the $f_k/f' = c/w$ condition demands. However, this mother will also have a lesser incentive than does the mother with the nonseparable lives to invest in her home environment. Without further restrictions, this model gives no insight as to whether the wealth consequences of this reduced investment in the home environment outweigh the consequences of spending more time at home. What is clear is that conditions can exist in which a person with separable lives can have incentives to spend time at home similar to those of a person with nonseparable lives. Conditions for the mother with separable lives to behave in this fashion are ripe when this mother, just like her peer with nonseparable lives, places a high value on her home time and/or when the marginal contribution of her work time to her earnings is low.

TESTING THE MODEL

Any empirical finding that the home environment is not responsive to changes in neighbourhood conditions or that a mother's work and child-care performances do not respond to differences in the home environment would justify rejection of the model here set forth. Similarly, empirical results which say that the shadow price of a mother's home time is equal to or less than her market wage or that the shadow price of the home physical environment is equal to or greater than the money cost of providing it, are inconsistent with the model.

To fix ideas on issues involving empirical implementation of the model, suppose that child health, θ, is the focus. The child health technology function in a given period is given by $\theta^* = \theta(g,l,b)$, where g and l respectively remain the physical environment of the child's home and the mother's home time and $b = \mu + e$. The μ represents the child's phenotype, that set of biological and cultural traits with which the child is endowed. Not all of these traits are observable to the researcher. Random shocks such as an unanticipated change in neighbourhood circumstances are given by e.

When no other changes occur, the response of child health to a change in mother's home time is given by $\partial\theta/\partial l$. But the observed or reduced form effect of a change in mother's home time is

$$d\theta^*/dl = \partial\theta/\partial l + (\partial\theta/\partial g)(dg/dl). \tag{9.37}$$

Thus the relation between child health and the mother's home time depends not only on $\partial\theta/\partial l$, the direct child health productivity of the mother's home time. It depends as well on the response of the child's home environment to the mother's home time. If, for example, $(dg/dl) > 0$, such that more of the mother's resources are devoted to the child's home environment when the mother is at home more, then, given $(\partial\theta/\partial g) > 0$, the expression (9.37) version of the health function will exaggerate the contribution mother's home time makes to child health. To overcome biases like this which appear in simple specifications of the child health function where the arguments are treated as exogenous, one must embed the health technology in a behavioural model which predicts the mother's utility–maximizing values for g and l. Simple correlations between inputs and health outcomes cannot be used to determine causality.

The behavioural model developed in this chapter suggests that if neighbourhood circumstances influence a mother's investments in her home time and environment, then her household shadow prices will not be given exogenously by the market but will instead be determined endogenously by the interaction between household supply and demand.

Endogenous household shadow prices require that structural rather than reduced form versions of models be estimated if technological and economic contributions to observed outcomes are to be distinguished. They also raise complex estimation issues of identification and of unobserved heterogeneity associated with terms like μ, the child's phenotype. In general, empirical implementation requires estimation of a system of demand equations for outcomes of interest and related inputs that allows cross-price effects to be distinguished from the effects of price-induced changes in input consumption upon outcomes. Because error terms are likely correlated across equations and because of unobserved heterogeneity across sample households, ordinary least-squares estimators are inconsistent. According to the particulars of the structure to be estimated, resort must be had to some form of instrumental variable or maximum liklihood estimators. If selection (participation) features are present, appeal to semi-parametric and non-parametric methods is sometimes made. Strauss and Thomas (1995) provide a thorough review of most of these estimation issues.

SUMMARY AND CONCLUSIONS

This chapter embeds individuals in families as well as in neighbourhoods. The impact of neighbourhood circumstances, including neighbourhood pollution, upon individuals' health states and prospects has been widely studied. A similar remark holds for the impact of home environments. We show that neighbourhood circumstances and what individuals choose to do in the home can be related. A mother who treats her home and work lives as nonseparable in the sense of recognizing that her choices of home environment affect her earnings will invest more in the home environment and be at home more than would a person who separates her work and her home lives. A mother who is at home more and who invests more in her home environment simultaneously contributes to the well-being of her children. But when the mother's rate of return from investing in the home environment declines, she will reduce her investment *and* reduce her time at home. These behaviours will, with minor exceptions, be accentuated when her investment payoffs are more delayed, more uncertain or are founded upon lower quality neighbourhood circumstances. We thus conclude that many of the statistical correlations between individual outcomes and neighbourhood circumstances (for example, human health and air pollution) reported in the literature may be biased by a failure to embed the individual in a family.[9] This bias is likely to be especially serious when children are at issue since their health and their prospects are widely acknowledged to increase with the quality of their home environment and the time their mother is available to them.

APPENDIX A

The Kuhn–Tucker necessary conditions (9.4) and (9.5) require

$$g > 0 : U_Y(f_g - c) + \lambda(s - f_g) = 0 \tag{9.A1}$$

$$L > 0 : U_Y f_L - U_l - \lambda f_L = 0 \tag{9.A2}$$

where

$$\lambda = U_Y(f_g - c)/(f_g - s) \tag{9.A3}$$

by (9.A1) and

$$U_Y - \lambda = U_l/f_L > 0 \tag{9.A4}$$

by (9.A2), given non-satiation. Combining (9.A3) and (9.A4) yields

$$U_Y > U_Y(f_g - c)/(f_g - s)$$

which implies

$$(f_g - c)/(f_g - s) < 1. \tag{9.A5}$$

Further manipulation of (9.A5) yields

$$(s - c)/(f_g - s) < 0.$$

Since $s > c$ if the mother is not to change residence, then $f_g < s$.

APPENDIX B

From the Lagrangian in (9.3)

$$\begin{aligned}
\mathbf{B}_{31} &= \pounds_{gL}\pounds_{L\lambda} - \pounds_{LL}\pounds_{g\lambda} \\
&= -f_L[f_{Lg}(U_Y - \lambda) + (f_g - c)(U_{YY}f_L - U_{lY})] \\
&\quad - (s - f_g)[f_{LL}(U_Y - \lambda) + f_L(U_{YY}f_L - 2U_{lY} + U_{ll})]. \tag{9.B1}
\end{aligned}$$

Substituting $-(f_g - c) = \lambda/U_Y(s - f_g)$ from (9.4) and rearranging terms yields

$$\begin{aligned}
\mathbf{B}_{31} &= -(U_Y - \lambda)[f_{LL}(s - f_g) + f_L f_{Lg}] + (s - f_g)(U_{YY}f_L - U_{lY})(\lambda/U_Y - 1)f_L \\
&\quad + (s - f_g)(U_{YY}f_L - U_{ll}). \tag{9.B2}
\end{aligned}$$

Substituting $\lambda/U_Y = 1 - w/f_L$ from (9.5) yields

$$\begin{aligned}
\mathbf{B}_{31} &= -(U_Y - \lambda)[f_{LL}(s - f_g) + f_L f_{Lg}] - (s - f_g)(U_{YY}f_L - U_{lY})w \\
&\quad + (s - f_g)(U_{lY}f_L - U_{ll}). \tag{9.B3}
\end{aligned}$$

Further manipulation yields

$$\mathbf{B}_{31} = -(U_Y - \lambda)[f_{LL}(s - f_g) + f_L f_{Lg}]$$
$$- w(s - f_g)[U_{YY} f_L - U_{lY} + (U_{ll} - U_{lY} f_L)/w].$$

(9.B4)

APPENDIX C

Strict quasiconcavity of the utility function requires

$$|\mathbf{B}| = -U_l^2 U_{YY} + 2U_Y U_l U_{YL} - U_Y^2 U_{ll} > 0.$$

(9.C1)

Dividing through by U_Y^2 and by substituting $w = U_l/U_Y$ yields

$$-w[U_{YY} w - U_{Yl} + (U_{ll} - wU_{Yl})/w] > 0.$$

which implies

$$U_{YY} w - U_{Yl} + (U_{ll} - U_{Yl})/w < 0.$$

(9.C2)

If

$$U_{YY} f_L - U_{Yl} + (U_{ll} - U_{Yl} f_L)/w < 0,$$

(9.C3)

it is likewise true that

$$\frac{U_{YY} f_L - U_{Yl} + (U_{ll} - U_{Yl} f_L)/w}{U_{YY} w - U_{Yl} + (U_{ll} - wU_{Yl})/w}$$

(9.C4)

is positive. Expansion of (9.C4) yields

$$\frac{U_{YY} w - U_{Yl} + (U_{ll} - wU_{Yl})/w + U_{YY} f_L + U_{YY} w - (f_L/w)U_{Yl} + U_{Yl}}{U_{YY} w - U_{Yl} + (U_{ll} - wU_{Yl})/w}$$

(9.C5)

which simplifies to

$$\frac{(f_l - w)(U_{YY} - U_{Yl}/w)}{U_{YY} w - U_{Yl} + (U_{ll} - wU_{Yl})/w} + 1$$

(9.C6)

Since $f_L > w$ by (9.8) and $\partial w/\partial Y \geq 0$ by assumption, (9.C6) is positive and therefore

$$U_{YY} f_L - U_{Yl} + (U_{ll} - U_{Yl} f_L)/w < 0.$$

(9.C7)

NOTES

* Corresponding author. Although the research described in this article has been funded by the United States Environmental Protection Agency through Grant #R82871601 to the University of Wyoming, it has not been subjected to the Agency's required peer and policy review and therefore does not necessarily reflect the views of the Agency and no official endorsement should be inferred.

1. Club (Sandler and Tschirhart, 1980) and local public good (Oates and Schwab, 1991) theories provide an analytical foundation for this economic literature. For theoretical work on informational networks in social assemblages, see Ellison and Fudenberg (1995); for a rational choice treatment of the role of behavioural prescriptions, see de Bartolome (1990). Jencks and Mayer (1990) review the descriptively-oriented earlier sociological literature; the articles in Brooks-Gunn et al. (1997) update this sociological literature. Ginther et al. (2000) review the empirical economics as well as the empirical sociological and developmental psychology literature.

2. Manski (1993) criticizes some of the empirical literature, noneconomic as well as economic, for failing to discriminate between people whose behaviour is influenced by group behaviour and people who behave in the same ways because they are subjected to similar correlated exogenous effects.

3. Case and Katz (1991) is an exception.

4. Empirical studies of neighbourhood influences which fail to embed individual behaviour in internal household choices may therefore be biased by inattention to considerable unobserved heterogeneity.

5 The presumption of a single parent household is not just an artifact for analytical tractability. The number of single parent households nationwide is now about one-quarter of total households. About half the children in the United States spend part of their childhood in households headed by a single parent, typically the mother (Bureau of the Census, 1998). Analytical tractability could also be achieved by adopting Becker's (1981) paradigm of a non-paternalistic, altruistic head in a household with multiple adults. The head earns all household income and decides how to invest it. Alternatively, multiple adults who have somehow unified their preferences could be assumed. Yet another story consistent with our formulation is to have the father influence the mother's choices only through the income he contributes.

6 The literature is unclear on what combination of mother's home time and household income or environment maximizes a child's adult prospects. But there is a consensus that some combination does – home time by itself or money income devoted to provision of household environment by itself are inadequate. We are not aware of any work which estimates how the parental elasticity of substitution between money resources and home time varies with parental attributes.

7. See also Suen and Mo (1994). The assumption of separability between production and consumption is very attractive to empirical researchers because it implies a two-stage model for an individual's behaviour. A person initially uses information on wages and technology to select her income-maximizing level of production effort. Only after having solved this problem does she decide her utility-maximizing level of consumption on the basis of relative prices and her predetermined income. This two-stage approach narrows the focus, reduces data requirements and conserves statistical degrees of freedom in empirical work. If production is not separable from consumption, empirical studies with this narrow separability focus are misspecified.

8. The comparative static result for investing in the home environment is
$\partial g/\partial w = (s - f_g)f_L/|\mathbf{B}| < 0$.

9. The words 'family' or 'home' do not appear in the index of a recent 1300 page compendium (van den Bergh, 1999) on the state of environmental and resource economics.

REFERENCES

Agee, M.D. and T.D. Crocker (1996), 'Parents' discount rates for child quality', *Southern Economic Journal*, **63**, 36–50.

Becker, G.S. (1981), *A Treatise on the Family*, Cambridge, MA: Harvard University Press.

Becker, G.S. and K.M. Murphy (2000), *Social Markets*, Cambridge, MA: Harvard University Press.

Becker, J.S. and N. Tomes (1989), 'Human capital and the rise and fall of families', *Journal of Labor Economics*, **4**, 677–91.

Bernheim, R.D. (1994), 'A theory of conformity', *Journal of Political Economy*, **102**, 841–77.

Bissin, A. and T. Verdier (2000), 'Beyond the "Melting Pot": cultural transmission, marriage, and the evolution of ethnic and religious traits', *The Quarterly Journal of Economics*, **115**, 955–88.

Borjas, G. (1995), 'Ethnicity, neighbourhoods and human capital externalities', *The American Economic Review*, **85**, 365–90.

Bowles, S. (1998), 'Endogenous preferences: the cultural consequences of market and other institutions', *Journal of Economic Literature*, **36**, 75–111.

Brooks-Gunn, J., G.J. Duncan and J.L. Aber (eds) (1997), *Neighbourhood Poverty*, Vols I and II, New York, NY: Russell Sage Foundation.

Bureau of the Census (1998), *Statistical Abstract of the United States*, Washington, DC: U.S. Department of Commerce.

Case, A.C. and L.F. Katz (1991), 'The Company You Keep: The Effects of Family and Neighbourhood on Disadvantaged Youths', NBER Working Paper No. 3705.

Cesario, F.J. (1976), 'Value of time and recreational benefit studies', *Land Economics*, **52**, 32–41.

Crocker, T.D. and R.L. Horst, Jr. (1981), 'Hours of work, labor productivity, and environmental conditions', *The Review of Economics and Statistics*, **63**, 361–8.

de Bartolome, C.A.M. (1990), 'Equilibrium and inefficiency in a community model with peer group effects', *Journal of Political Economy*, **98**, 110–33.

Ellison, J. and D. Fudenberg (1995), 'Word-of-mouth communication and social learning', *The Quarterly Journal of Economics*, **110**, 93–126.

Ginther, D., R. Haveman and B. Wolfe (2000), 'Neighbourhood attributes as determinants of children outcomes', *Journal of Human Resources*, **35**, 603–42.

Grossman, M. (1999), 'The Human Capital Model of the Demand for Health', NBER Working Paper 7078.

Jencks, C. and S. Mayer (1990), 'The Social Consequences of Growing Up in a Poor Neighbourhood', in L. Lynn and M. McGeary (eds), *Inner City Poverty in the United States*, Washington, DC: National Academy Press, pp. 111–86.

Juster, F.T. (1995), 'Preferences for Work and Leisure', in F.T. Juster and F.P. Stafford (eds), *Time Goods and Well-Being*, Ann Arbor, MI: Survey Research Center, University of Michigan.

Holden, S., B. Shiferaw and M. Wik (1998), 'Poverty, market imperfections and time preference: of relevance for environmental policy?', *Environment and Development Economics*, **3**, 105–30.

Klebanov, P.K., J. Brooks-Gunn, P.L. Chase-Lansdale and R.A. Gordon (1997), 'Are Neighbourhood Effects on Young Children Mediated by Features of the Home Environment?', in J. Brooks-Gunn, G.J. Duncan and J.L Aber (eds), *Neighbourhood Poverty*, Vol. I, New York, NY: Russell Sage Foundation.

Manski, C.F. (1993), 'Identification of endogenous social effects: the reflection problem', *Review of Economic Studies*, **60**, 531–42.

Oates, W. and R. Schwab (1991), 'Community composition and the provision of local public goods: a normative analysis', *Journal of Public Economics*, **44**, 217–38.

Sandler, T. and J. Tschirhart (1980), 'The economic theory of clubs: an evaluative survey', *Journal of Economic Literature*, **18**, 1481–521.

Strauss, J. and D. Thomas (1995), 'Human Resources: Empirical Modeling of Household and Family Decisions', in J. Behrman and T.W. Srinivasan (eds), *Handbook in Development Economics*, Vol. 3A, Dordrecht, The Netherlands: Elsevier Academic Publishers.

Suen, W. and P.H. Mo (1994), 'Simple analytics of productive consumption', *Journal of Political Economy*, **102**, 372–83.

Tiebout, C.M. (1956), 'A pure theory of local expenditures', *Journal of Political Economy*, **64**, 416–24.

van den Bergh, J.C.J.M. (ed.) (1999), *Handbook of Environmental and Resource Economics*, Cheltenham, UK and Northampton, MA: Edward Elgar Publishing, Ltd.

10. Environmental policy and the timing of drilling and production in the oil and gas industry*

Mitch Kunce, Shelby Gerking and William Morgan

1. INTRODUCTION

The literatures on tax and regulatory competition, recently surveyed by Wilson (1999) and Oates (1999), look at choices of local taxes and public service levels in situations when owners of capital can choose where to locate. Firms maximize profits and view alternative locations offering different combinations of taxes, government regulations, and public services as imperfect substitutes. Theoretical studies in this area ask whether choices of fiscal and regulatory instruments are efficient and empirical studies measure the extent to which capital actually moves as these instruments are applied. Stylized facts about tax and regulatory competition often involve examples of manufacturing firms. On the other hand, when capital is immobile, firms either cannot relocate or at least cannot take capital with them if they move. One option for firms subject to serious impediments to mobility is to use time, rather than location, as the dimension across which to substitute as taxes and government regulations change. This option is particularly important to firms extracting nonrenewable resources that attempt to optimize the timing of exploration and production in a dynamic framework. At a point in time, of course, such firms make choices between different reserves to exploit that may be based in part on public policy decisions. Yet, timing of exploration and production is the essential feature of the problem and information about location choice decisions can be recovered by comparing development paths of different reserves.

This chapter estimates the extent to which firms in the oil and gas industry adjust the timing and intensity of their activities in the face of changes in environmental regulations. Many studies have examined the geographic responsiveness of manufacturing to these regulations. Jaffe et al. (1995) and Tannenwald (1997) have written surveys of this literature and Levinson

(1996), Henderson (1996), Becker and Henderson (2000), and Greenstone (2000) have contributed recent papers. However, relatively few empirical studies of effects of public policy changes on nonrenewable resource firms have been conducted. Econometric studies of oil and gas supplies, such as the one conducted by Pesaran (1990), frequently do not consider effects of public policies. Those that do look at public policies (Deacon et al., 1990 and Moroney, 1997) focus only on taxes. Different types of tax policies, but not environmental regulations, have been considered in simulation studies such as those conducted by Yücel (1989) and Deacon (1993). These studies, however, are aimed mainly at assessing the generality of theoretical results obtained in more limited settings and numerically illustrating key propositions using representative parameter values. In any case, little evidence is available to guide policy formulation regarding effects of environmental regulations and public land management practices by all levels of government.

The remainder of the chapter is divided into four sections. Section 2 presents the conceptual framework for the study, which is an adaptation of Pindyck's (1978) widely applied model of nonrenewable resource exploration and production. Section 3 describes empirical estimates that are used to estimate parameters of the model so that it can be used to simulate drilling and production in major oil- and gas-producing US states. The central focus of this analysis is on estimating cost functions from a unique and extensive panel data set covering more than 319 000 on-shore oil and gas wells drilled in the US over the period 1987–98. Section 4 presents simulation results showing how oil and gas exploration and production in Wyoming and New Mexico respond over time to changes in stringency of environmental regulation. While other major oil- and gas-producing states could have been used for a case study, Wyoming and New Mexico are of particular interest because both have a high percentage of federal land ownership (see Table 10.1). As discussed later on, environmental regulations in the oil and gas industry appear to be more stringently applied on federal property than on other types of land. Thus, results presented have the advantage of showing how exploration and production might be expected to change over time if stringency of environmental enforcement on federal property is reduced to the standard of enforcement prevailing on private property. Implications and conclusions of this analysis are drawn in Section 5.

2. CONCEPTUAL FRAMEWORK

Background

It is useful to begin by reviewing evidence of added environmental compliance costs paid to explore for and extract oil and gas on federal property vs. other types of property. Oil and gas field activity in the US is regulated by various government agencies, such as the Environmental Protection Agency, under federal statutes such as the National Environmental Policy Act, the Toxic Substances Control Act, the Resource Conservation and Recovery Act, the Comprehensive Environmental Response, Compensation, and Liability Act, the Antiquities Act, and the Threatened and Endangered Species Act. Additionally state agencies such as oil and gas conservation commissions and game and fish commissions have had increasingly broad rule-making authority since the early 1980s. Whereas the regulations listed apply to all land types, evidence suggests that these regulations are more stringently applied to federal land thus increasing operators' costs. Two sources of evidence, petroleum engineering studies and interviews with market participants, confirm this cost differential.

Several engineering studies have been conducted in which operators are questioned about cost differences related to drilling on federal land versus other types of land. Although environmental contamination can occur at any stage in the life cycle of oil and gas wells, these studies focus mainly on drilling (exploration and development) because of the comparatively high risks associated with bringing large volumes of potentially hazardous gases and fluids to the surface (Carls et al., 1994). These studies have found that drilling regulations are more stringently enforced on federal land than on other types of land (see Godec and Biglarbigbi, 1991; Harder et al., 1995; Kudia and McDole, 1996; Bureau of Land Management, 1997, and Schulz, 1998) leading to higher drilling costs ranging from tens of thousands to hundreds of thousands of dollars per well. These cost estimates, however, are difficult to interpret because in each case they consider only a small number of drilling sites and do not adjust for differences in remoteness or in the types of environmental resources present on properties analysed. Also, federal land managers apparently have considerable discretion in deciding what steps should be taken to maintain environmental quality, so the premium may vary substantially from one site to another.

Nevertheless, these studies still suggest that incremental costs associated with drilling on federal property arise from four sources: (1) permitting procedures, (2) well and site construction and supervision, (3) drilling waste disposal, and (4) restrictions on site access. Permitting procedures include development of impact studies and operation plans as well as plans for liability mitigation (influenced by the Oil Pollution Act of 1990). Well and site construction and supervision includes added labour costs needed to meet regulatory stipulations, as well as costs of site inspections, pit liner monitoring, separating and flaring gases. Drilling waste disposal costs include payments to third party contractors for handling mud and cuttings in addition to installation of closed-loop drilling systems designed to reduce waste generation. Site access restrictions apply mainly to route planning and road construction, although on rare occasions access to federal land drilling sites has been limited to aerial site drops (Harder et al., 1995).

We have also conducted our own interviews with government agencies, industry officials, and landowners familiar with exploration for and development of oil and gas resources in Wyoming (see Kunce et al., 2000). Respondents indicated that drilling costs on federal land are generally higher than on private land. Factors identified in the studies above were cited, although respondents tended to focus more heavily on differences in protection of cultural and biological resources. Regarding cultural resources, federal land managers are obligated under the Antiquities Act to identify and preserve Native American artefacts (that is, arrowheads, pottery shards) and historic sites, such as those along the Overland Trail. Private landowners, in contrast, have an incentive to view items of historical significance as their own and in some cases have refused to allow archaeological surveys on their property. Thus, cultural resources that might be protected on federal property simply are never identified on private property. Also, federal land managers require greater precautions than private landowners to protect biological resources. Conflicts between endangered species protection, private property rights and economic activity are well documented (Innes et al., 1998; Turner and Rylander, 1998), but federal land managers appear to show greater concern for more prevalent species as well. Intrusions into antelope ranges in winter and protection of flowering plants in spring were examples cited in this regard.

Extra precautions taken on federal property translate into delays and added expense, but vary greatly from one location to another. McDonald (1994) has discussed delays in issuing permits and suggests that the federal government has been slow to release drilling areas on public land. Yet, the issue appears to be broader because the permits themselves frequently narrow the window of time in which drilling can occur to as little as a few months per year, thereby disrupting drilling programmes. Moreover, if drilling is permitted only in winter, higher labour and equipment costs would be expected as crews must deal with subzero temperatures and windy conditions. Also, cultural and biological resources are not distributed evenly over space and federal land managers appear to have broad discretion in determining protection requirements. Thus, additional costs of environmental compliance on federal land can vary considerably between locations. As a consequence, it is not possible to develop an estimate of the difference in drilling costs on federal versus private property that would be universally applicable to all parcels of land.

Additionally, selected stylized facts give credence to the view that cost differences may be large enough to shift drilling from federal property to

Table 10.1   Data on drilling rates: selected states, 1996

State	Total wells drilled	Oil and gas reserves (in quads of BTUs)	Ratio of wells to reserves	% Wells drilled on federal land	% Federal land acreage to total state acreage
California	1399	22.08	63.36	7.86	44.45
Kansas	1403	9.48	148.07	0.08	1.31
Louisiana	1289	13.66	94.40	0.06	2.58
New Mexico	1084	21.31	50.87	43.70	33.11
Oklahoma	2036	17.14	118.75	0.75	1.95
Texas	8258	72.73	113.55	0.16	1.69
Wyoming	615	16.20	37.96	50.90	48.77

other types of property. Table 10.1 shows data on total wells drilled in each of seven major oil and gas producing states for a representative year (1996) along with data on oil and gas reserves for that same year stated in quadrillions of BTUs. The table also shows the ratio of wells drilled to reserves, the percentage of wells drilled on federal land (which is taken from the data set used in this study and is discussed momentarily) and the percentage of federal land acreage in a state. Of course, many possible factors can explain the substantial differences across these states in the ratio of wells drilled to reserves including geological conditions, the amount of environmental resources to be protected, local attitudes toward development, and whether deposits are located in remote areas. However, it is nonetheless interesting that the two states (Wyoming and New Mexico) with the lowest well-to-reserve ratios are those with the greatest percentages of drilling on federal property and correspondingly are those with large federal ownership of land. This example proves little, but it does provide a basis for speculation that differences in environmental compliance costs could be partly responsible, and further analysis of the issue is warranted.

Model

This chapter adapts Pindyck's (1978) model of nonrenewable resource industries to develop a simulation model that can be applied to seven major oil and gas producing states in the US (California, Kansas, Louisiana, New Mexico, Oklahoma, Texas and Wyoming). Both the model and example simulations for each of these states are more fully described in Gerking et al. (2000). The adaptation explicitly accounts for the interaction between environmental compliance costs and taxes levied at various levels of government. This model explicitly treats both exploration and production, but ignores aspects such as uncertainty and grade selection (see Krautkraemer, 1998 for a recent survey of these issues). Perfectly competitive producers maximize discounted present value of future profits from the sale of resources. Their problem, essentially, is to take (known) future output prices, taxes and environmental regulations as given, and then choose optimal time paths for exploration and production. For simplicity, exploration here is defined to include resource development and a single firm is used to represent the industry. The aim of exploration is to add to the reserve base, which in the model represents a form of (immobile) capital. Oil and gas are treated jointly in the analysis, rather than as separate industries. Wells are classified as oil or gas (or dry) only after the outcome of drilling is known and oil fields sometimes produce so-called associated gas. Problems of aggregating across fields (ignored here) and the treatment of joint production are discussed more fully by Bohi and Toman (1984) and Livernois (1987, 1988).

Incorporating taxes and environmental regulations into the model is not difficult conceptually, but requires some judgement and institutional knowledge. Environmental regulations are the easier of the two to handle and our treatment of them is described momentarily. Taxation of oil and gas production, however, is quite complex, and tax rules vary among the lower 48 states responsible for most US production (that is, California, Kansas, Louisiana, New Mexico, Oklahoma, Texas and Wyoming). Tax bases also interact between the local, state, and federal levels. Most states levy severance taxes on the value of production (California does not), but most states do not levy property taxes on the value of reserves in the ground (Texas and California do). Most states treat royalty payments for production on public land as deductible items in computing severance tax liabilities (Louisiana does not). For a given state, severance tax rates for oil and gas can differ. Most states levy a corporate income tax (Wyoming and Texas do not). All states define tax bases differently and grant innumerable exemptions and credits (which differ by state) for special situations encountered by operators. Within states, counties apply their own mill levies to compute property taxes on above-ground and down-hole equipment at different rates. However, taxation of structures and equipment are usually less important sources of revenue and are ignored below. Regarding federal taxes, all incorporated producers file federal corporate income tax returns. Independent producers (those without downstream refining or retail interests) are permitted to take a percentage depletion allowance, which amounts to a credit against this tax. Major producers can take only cost depletion, which is less generous and is ignored in the analysis below. All operators can expense certain intangible drilling costs on their federal corporate income tax returns. The fact that some smaller producers are not incorporated and may therefore face alternative state and federal tax treatment also is ignored. Expenses for environmental compliance frequently are deductible in computing federal and state corporate income tax liabilities.

The firm's problem is to

$$\max_{q,w} \Omega = \int_0^\infty [qp - C(q,R) - (1+\tau)D(w)]e^{-\delta t}\, dt \tag{10.1}$$

subject to

$$\dot{R} = \dot{x} - q \tag{10.2}$$

$$\dot{x} - f(w,x) \tag{10.3}$$

$$q \geq 0,\ w \geq 0,\ R \geq 0,\ x \geq 0 \tag{10.4}$$

where a dot over a variable denotes a rate of change per unit of time, q denotes the quantity of the resource extracted measured in barrels of oil equivalent (BOE), p denotes the exogenous market price per BOE net of all taxes and royalties, $C(\cdot)$ denotes the total cost of extracting the resource net of all taxes, which is assumed to depend on production (q) and reserve levels (R), $D(w)$ denotes total cost of exploration for additional reserves net of taxes, w denotes exploratory effort, τ denotes the percentage addition to drilling cost arising from environmental and land use regulations,[1] δ denotes the discount rate, x denotes cumulative reserve discoveries, $f(\cdot)$ denotes the production function for gross reserve additions ($\dot{x}$), and $\dot{R}$ denotes reserve addition net of production (q).

In this formulation, the net-of-tax price per BOE is related to the well-head (pre-tax) price (p^*) according to $p = \alpha_p p^*$, where α_p is a function of federal, state, and local tax rates such that $0 < \alpha_p < 1$. Correspondingly, $C(q,R) = \alpha_c C^*(q,R)$ and $D(w) = \alpha_D D^*(w)$, where α_c and α_D also are functions of tax rates and lie on the unit interval. Additional discussion of the derivation of tax parameters for Wyoming and New Mexico is provided in Appendix A. Also, τ, which either can be positive or negative, denotes the percentage change in drilling costs due to a change in environmental and land use regulations. Thus, the treatment of taxes and regulations is simplified by assuming that firms take them as exogenous. Making tax rates and regulations endogenous to the problem considered here would be a logical and important extension of this research. Also, to simplify the remaining discussion in this section, taxes and regulations are assumed fixed for all time at the beginning of the programme. As the model is manipulated, time derivatives of the tax and environmental regulation parameters are set equal to zero.

The Hamiltonian for this problem is

$$H = qpe^{-\delta t} - C(q,R)e^{-\delta t} - (1+\tau)D(w)e^{-\delta t} + \lambda_1[f(w,x) - q]$$
$$+ \lambda_2[f(w,x)] \tag{10.5}$$

Properties of $C(\cdot)$ and $f(\cdot)$ include $C_q > 0$ $C_{qq} > 0$, $C_R < 0$, $C_{RR} > 0$, $f_x < 0$, $f_w > 0$, and $f_{ww} < 0$. These conditions imply that marginal extraction costs are positive and increase with q, and extraction costs rise as the level of reserves declines. Also, $f_w > 0$ and $f_{ww} < 0$ capture the idea that the marginal product of exploratory effort is positive and decreases with w, and $f_x < 0$ indicates that it becomes increasingly difficult to make new discoveries of reserves as exploration effort cumulates. The cost of exploratory effort, $D(w)$, increases with w at a constant rate, $D_{ww} = 0$. Increasing marginal cost of exploration ($D_{ww} > 0$) would presume a monopsonistic rather than a perfectly competitive firm.

Differentiating H with respect to R, q, x, and w yields

$$-C_R e^{-\delta t} + \dot{\lambda}_1 = 0 \tag{10.6}$$
$$pe^{-\delta t} - C_q e^{-\delta t} - \lambda_1 = 0 \tag{10.7}$$
$$f_x(\lambda_1 + \lambda_2) + \dot{\lambda}_2 = 0 \tag{10.8}$$
$$-(1+\tau)D_w e^{-\delta t} + f_w(\lambda_1 + \lambda_2) = 0 \tag{10.9}$$

In equation (10.7), λ_1 is the discounted shadow price of the reserve state. It is easily shown that this shadow price can be decomposed into two components where $\lambda_1 = (p - C_q)e^{-\delta T} - \int_t^T C_R e^{-\delta s} ds$. The term, $(p - C_q)e^{-\delta T}$, represents the present value of *future* operating profits at the margin. These are zero if $\lambda_1(T) = 0$ (see the boundary condition discussion below). The second term, $-\int_t^T C_R e^{-\delta s} ds$, denotes the present value sum of future extraction cost increases resulting from marginally reducing the reserve stock today (Levhari and Leviatan, 1977). In equation (10.6) $\dot{\lambda}_1 < 0$ because $C_R < 0$. From equation (10.8) and equation (10.9), $(\lambda_1 + \lambda_2)$ equals the discounted value of the marginal cost of adding another unit of reserves by exploration (discoveries) $(1+\tau)(D_w/f_w)e^{-\delta t}$. If τ initially is set higher (environmental regulations on federal land are more stringent), the after-tax marginal cost of reserve additions also is higher, but this effect is attenuated because $0 < \alpha_D < 1$. The shadow price of cumulative reserve discoveries, λ_2, is negative because current reserve finds increase the amount of exploration needed in the future. The evolution of this shadow price is increasing, $\dot{\lambda}_2 > 0$, because $f_x < 0$.

The time path of w can be determined by manipulating the optimality conditions. Using equation (10.7) and equation (10.9) to solve for λ_2, differentiating with respect to time to obtain an expression for $\dot{\lambda}_2$ equating the result to equation (10.8) and rearranging terms yields equation (10.10) that describes the time path of exploratory effort.

$$\dot{w} = \frac{(1+\tau)D_w\{[(f_{wx}/f_w)\cdot f - f_x] + \delta\} + C_R f_w}{[-(1+\tau)D_w(f_{ww}/f_w)]} \tag{10.10}$$

Equation (10.10) can be simplified by choosing a functional form for f such that the quantity $[(f_{wx}/f_w)\cdot f - f_x] = 0$. A suitable choice turns out to be

$$\dot{x} = Aw^\theta e^{-v\cdot x} \tag{10.11}$$

which is similar to an equation describing the discovery process proposed by Uhler (1976) and later adopted by Pesaran (1990). Additionally, the denominator of equation (10.10) is f_w times the derivative of the marginal cost of reserve additions with respect to w, $[\partial(1+\tau)(D_w/f_w)/\partial w]$. Thus, the trajectory of exploratory effort is determined by a tradeoff between the cost of finding new reserves (D_w) and the extraction cost savings this new level of reserves brings. As specified in the model, environmental regulations, then, increase the cost of finding new reserves and do not alter the costs of extraction. Therefore, these regulations work against the extraction cost savings effect and push exploration into the future. Tilting drilling activity to the future, in turn, affects reserve levels and production as described below.

The evolution of q is obtained by differentiating equation (10.7) with respect to time and setting the result equal to equation (10.6) to eliminate $\dot{\lambda}_1$. This yields equation (10.12).

$$\dot{q} = \frac{-\delta(p - C_q) + \dot{p} - C_{qR}\dot{R} - C_R}{C_{qq}}. \tag{10.12}$$

In equation (10.12), the term $-\delta(p - C_q) < 0$ denotes the effect of discounting on the rate of change in production over time. Incentives to increase production in early periods prevail because future revenues, net of extraction costs, are discounted. If prices increase over time, $\dot{p} > 0$, the negative discounting effect can be at least partially offset, but even when $\dot{p} = \delta p$, where price rises with the discount rate, extraction still can decline over time depending on the relative magnitudes of the cost derivatives in the numerator of (10.12). The term $- C_{qR}\dot{R}$ represents the marginal impact of reserve depletion over time. If reserves fall over time, marginal extraction costs rise, thus attenuating production. The term $- C_R$ relates to the negative effect of the decline in the shadow price of new reserves.

Transversality conditions can be established by first assuming that $D_w/f_w = 0$ when $w = 0$ (see Pindyck, 1978, pp. 846–7). In this situation, when production ceases at some terminal time, T, exploration ceases at the same time because it is of no further value. Also, $\lambda_2(T) = 0$ as long as there are no terminal costs associated with cumulative discoveries. In consequence, from equation (10.9), $\lambda_1(T) = 0$ implies that operating profit on the last unit of reserves extracted is zero, $p = C_q$. An alternative terminal state centres on the case where $(1+\tau) D_w/f_w = \Phi > 0$, when $w = 0$. In this situation, production will continue after exploratory effort ceases. Let $T_1 < T$ denote the time when $w = 0$. If exploratory effort is zero, $f_x = 0$, hence $\dot{\lambda}_2(T_1) = 0$ and $\lambda_2(T_1) = 0$. From (10.7) and (10.9), $p - C_q = \lambda_1(T_1)e^{\delta t} = \Phi = (1+\tau) D_w/f_w$ which indicates that exploration will stop just as $p - C_q$ approaches marginal discovery cost, Φ.

To simulate effects of changes in environmental policies using the model just described, estimates are needed for τ, the tax rates in α_p, α_c, and α_D as well as for the equations for extraction costs, C, exploration costs, D, and reserve additions, f. Estimates for τ are obtained in the next section using results from an econometric study of drilling costs in the US. As mentioned previously, estimates of the tax rate terms are presented in Appendix A and are also discussed in connection with the simulations presented in Section 4. Estimates of the three equations (C, D, and f) are taken from Gerking et al. (2000) where they are described in detail.

3.   ESTIMATION OF τ

Available evidence cited in Section 2 regarding the cost premium paid to drill on federal property vs. other types of property does not establish a convincing value for τ for at least two reasons. First, engineering studies have only compared costs at a small number of sites. These sites were not randomly chosen and studies do not appear to have controlled for differences in attributes such as remoteness or the quantity of environmental resources to protect. Second, the interviews that we conducted (referred to earlier) were aimed at assessing why drilling costs on federal land might be higher than on private land, rather than at estimating the dollar value of the cost premium. Kunce et al. (2000) used data from the Wyoming Checkerboard to estimate the drilling cost premium on federal property as compared with private property. In this study, the randomized pattern of land ownership, resulting from the Pacific Railway Acts of 1862 and 1864, serves as a crucial control in identifying differences in environmental compliance costs on the two types of property. However, a limitation of this study is that the Checkerboard is a relatively small area and the drilling cost premium on federal property there may not be a useful guide to the corresponding cost premium elsewhere in the US. In consequence, this section presents results on the added cost associated with drilling on federal property in the lower 48 states. Separate analyses are performed for Wyoming and New Mexico because these two states have comparatively large fractions of drilling activity on federal property.

Data

Data used in this study to estimate costs were obtained from two major information providers. First, the American Petroleum Institute (API), through the Joint Association Survey on Drilling Costs (JAS), tabulates cost data, obtained from a survey of operators, on each completed well drilled in the United States, including dry holes. Total costs are reported for each well drilled that include variable cost items such as labour, materials, supplies, machinery and tools, water, transportation, fuel and power. Also, costs of direct overhead for operations such as permitting and site preparation, road building, drilling pit construction, erecting and dismantling derricks/drilling rigs, hauling and disposal of waste materials, and site restoration are included in total cost as well. Thus, costs reported appear to include major elements of environmental costs discussed in Section 2, however, components of total cost are *not* individually itemized. Second, limited additional information on well completions is compiled by Petroleum Information/Dwights LLC d/b/a I.H.S. Energy Group, Inc. from drilling data reported to the US government. This information includes well depth, type of well (oil, gas or dry) and surface land ownership (private, Native American (tribal), federal government, state government and local government). I.H.S. Energy Group, Inc. has merged the information from these two sources and made them available for use here.

This study uses data on 319 475 onshore well completions in the contiguous 48 US states between 1987 and 1998 aggregated to the county level. Similar data to those just described also are available from I.H.S. Energy Group on wells drilled prior to 1987; however, these were not used because information about surface ownership is incomplete for this earlier period. Also, because I.H.S. Energy Group charges by the record, it was considerably less expensive to obtain aggregate data for counties as compared with data on individual wells.[2] The data set measures average total cost per completed well drilled by county by year. In addition, well depth, in feet, is measured as a county-wide average, too. Surface land ownership is measured as the percentage of wells drilled on each type of land in each county in each year. Data on types of wells are measured as the percentage of each by county by year. The number of wells drilled in each county in each year also is provided. Over the period 1987–98, there were 1073 counties in the US in which at least one well was drilled; however, no drilling occurred in

Table 10.2   Variable definitions and means

Explanatory variable	Definition	US sample mean	Wyoming mean	New Mexico mean
Drilling cost	Drilling cost per foot in $1992.	51.48	69.46	70.50
Depth	Average well depth in thousands of feet.	4.873	6.586	4.617
Private	Fraction of wells in a county/year drilled on private land.	0.919	0.399	0.297
Federal	Fraction of wells in a county/year drilled on federal land.	0.045	0.508	0.437
State	Fraction of wells in a county/year drilled on state land.	0.029	0.076	0.184
Tribal	Fraction of wells in a county/year drilled on tribal land.	0.004	0.016	0.070
Other	Fraction of wells in a county/year drilled on other land.[a]	0.003	0.001	0.012
Oil	Fraction of wells drilled in a county/year that are oil producers.	0.299	0.412	0.298
Gas	Fraction of wells drilled in a county/year that are gas producers.	0.283	0.246	0.283
Dry	Fraction of wells drilled in a county/year that are dry.	0.418	0.342	0.419

Note: [a] Other lands are those for which ownership is contested or for which ownership is not reported in the data.

many of these counties for one or more years. As a result, the entire data set for the US forms an unbalanced panel and contains 10 710 observations. This number of observations is smaller than the number that would be present if the panel were balanced ($1073 \times 12 = 12876$). The data sets (both unbalanced panels) for Wyoming and New Mexico, of course, are smaller, containing 238 and 135 observations, respectively.

In any case, data used in this study come from 33 of the 48 contiguous US states. Table 10.2 presents definitions and means of variables used in the analysis. In the entire sample, mean constant dollar ($1992) per foot drilling costs across all states and time periods is $51.48/ft and average well depth is 4873 feet. About 4.5 percent of all wells are drilled on federal land. In Wyoming and New Mexico, cost per foot drilled is somewhat higher (about $70/ft. in each state) than the national average. Wells in Wyoming tended to be deeper than those in New Mexico. Both states had a much higher fraction of wells drilled on federal property, 44 percent in New Mexico and 51 percent in Wyoming, reflecting large federal land ownership in the two states (see Table 10.1). Wells drilled in Wyoming are more likely to find oil than wells drilled either nationally or in New Mexico.

Cost Functions and Estimation Procedures

Cost functions are estimated for the US, Wyoming and New Mexico in order to measure the cost premium for drilling on federal land. Available data are not detailed enough to permit drilling costs to be estimated as a function of input prices; thus, standard methods applied in the empirical cost function literature cannot be used. An alternative approach, taken here, is to characterize wells by depth and then to recognize that depth is produced by applying capital, labour, and other inputs, subject to both geological and technological constraints. For given geological and technological conditions, deeper wells require greater applications of productive inputs. Thus, at any particular location, the total cost of a well is expected to increase (probably at an increasing rate) with depth. Moreover, the total cost of drilling wells of the same depth varies across space because of differences in geological conditions and well drilling infrastructure (availability of well service firms, for example) as well as over time in light of advances in technology. Total drilling costs may also be affected by environmental and land use regulations that apply to surface land. For example, as discussed above, such regulations appear to be more onerous on federal land as compared with land under different ownership. This approach has the advantage of effectively utilizing a rich data set, but the disadvantage that substitution possibilities between inputs cannot be explored.

The cost functions estimated extend Greene's (1997, pp. 432–4, 555–7) analysis of weighted least squares when using grouped data. Greene's analysis considers the case in which an equation is estimated from a single cross-section or time series of grouped data and the number of micro observations in a group is known. The situation encountered here is quite similar, except that panels are unbalanced and the number of wells drilled in each county varies over time. Thus, appropriate weights computed are more complex than the square root of the number of underlying micro units in each group. More specifically, the drilling cost functions for the US, Wyoming and New Mexico can be derived from equation (10.13).

$$TC_{jkt} = (\mu_k + \phi_t)\, \mathfrak{D}_{jkt} + \beta_1\, \mathfrak{D}^2_{jkt} + \beta_2 S_{jkt}\, \mathfrak{D}_{jkt} + \beta_3 \mathfrak{W}_{jkt}\, \mathfrak{D}_{jkt}$$
$$+ U_{jkt}\, \mathfrak{D}_{jkt} \tag{10.13}$$

Thus, total cost (TC) of well j, in county k, in year t is a quadratic in depth ($\mathfrak{D}$) and the cost function obeys the constraint that if $\mathfrak{D} = 0$, $TC = 0$. The dummy variable S indicates the surface ownership of land on which the well is drilled and the dummy variable $\mathfrak{W}$ indicates the type of well drilled. As shown in Table 10.2, several land and well type measures are used in the empirical analysis presented in the next section; however, this aspect is suppressed at this point to economize on notation. Also, the μ_k are dummy variables to account for net effects of county-specific factors such as geological conditions and well drilling infrastructure (which may be difficult to enumerate and measure) and the ϕ_t are dummy variables capturing time-specific factors such as technical progress. The β_i are slope coefficients and U_{jkt} is a disturbance term that is assumed to be independent and identically distributed with mean of zero and variance of σ^2.

Notice that equation (10.13) is specified at the level of the individual well and anticipates use of two-way fixed effects estimation. This approach was chosen because it controls for both the net effect of unique aspects of counties that may affect drilling cost, such as geological conditions, as well as heterogeneity over time arising from technical change and possibly other factors. An advantage of the fixed effects approach is that coefficients estimated are interpreted as conditional effects of the various explanatory variables on cost. In the context of this study, conditional effects are thought to be of greater interest than unconditional effects that might be obtained in a random effects framework.

Dividing both sides of equation (10.13) by $\mathfrak{D}_{jkt}$, and re-expressing the result in terms of county averages to maintain consistency with available data yields equation (10.14).

$$\mathfrak{C}_{\cdot kt} = (\mu_k + \phi_t) + \beta_1 \mathfrak{D}_{\cdot kt} + \beta_2 S_{\cdot kt} + \beta_3 \mathfrak{W}_{\cdot kt} + U_{\cdot kt} \qquad (10.14)$$

In equation (10.14), $\mathfrak{C}$ denotes cost per foot drilled, the notation $X_{\cdot kt}$ denotes the county average of a variable, and information about the number of wells drilled in a county/year is lost. Next, rewrite equation (10.14) in terms of averages over time for each county and subtract the result from equation (10.14). This yields

$$c_{\cdot kt} = \gamma_t + \beta_1 d_{\cdot kt} + \beta_2 s_{\cdot kt} + \beta_3 w_{\cdot kt} + u_{\cdot kt} \qquad (10.15)$$

where the notation $x_{\cdot kt}$ denotes the difference between a county average and its time mean and $\gamma_t = \phi_t - [(1/T)\Sigma_t \phi_t]$. Least squares applied to equation (10.15) is equivalent to two-way fixed effects estimation. Notice that subtracting the time means for each county eliminates the county-specific effects (μ_k), leaving the γ_t to be explicitly estimated. The slope coefficients

(β_i) would therefore be interpreted as conditional effects of depth, land type, and well type on average cost per foot drilled, given μ_k and γ_t.

The error term in equation (10.15) exhibits heteroskedasticity because it arises from averaging U_{jkt} over different numbers of wells drilled in each time period. In particular, given the assumptions about U_{jkt} outlined previously, the variance of $u_{.kt}$ is

$$var(u_{.kt}) = \sigma^2\{(1/n_{kt}) - (2/T_k n_{kt}) + (1/T_k^2)[\Sigma_t(1/n_{kt})]\} \qquad (10.16)$$

where n_{kt} denotes the number of wells drilled in county k in year t and T_k denotes the number of sample years in which a positive number of wells were drilled there. Thus, the observations for each county/year should be weighted by the reciprocal of the square root of the term in square brackets in equation (10.16). This approach has the advantage of incorporating information about wells drilled by county/year that was lost in computing average values of variables. Also, for each grouped observation, weights are an increasing function of the amount of information (number of wells) about the group.

Empirical Results

In the regression results shown in Table 10.3, the column (1) regression uses all observations from the contiguous US states. Columns (2) and (3) present results for Wyoming and New Mexico. In the regressions shown, the dependent variable is average real drilling cost per foot (in $1992), computed from nominal values using the GDP deflator. Surface land ownership is divided into five categories (private, federal, state, tribal, other). The variables oil, gas and dry, control for well type. The R^2 in the transformed US regression was 0.18 and the R^2 values for the transformed Wyoming and New Mexico regressions were 0.13 and 0.53, respectively.

All three regressions show that cost per foot drilled rises with well depth. Also, in the US regression, natural gas wells appear to be more expensive than oil wells, and dry wells are less expensive than oil wells. This result might be expected because gas wells are frequently drilled in areas with different geological conditions than are oil wells. Also, gas well rigs must be constructed to handle greater underground pressures and, as a consequence, safety precautions at the surface must be intensified. Dry wells are less expensive than oil wells partly because of the incentive to give up when core samples suggest that further drilling will not yield a positive result. In the Wyoming and New Mexico regressions, however, coefficients of the well type variables are not significantly different from zero. These imprecise estimates may arise because of the relatively small sample sizes available for

Table 10.3   Two-way fixed-effects drilling cost estimates[a]

Explanatory variable	US sample	Wyoming	New Mexico
Depth	4.84	8.62	4.43
	(11.57)	(2.09)	(2.71)
Private	_[b]	_[b]	_[b]
Federal	18.14	22.02	19.81
	(3.00)	(2.31)	(2.63)
State	−5.29	34.28	8.06
	(−0.91)	(1.00)	(0.31)
Tribal	−11.88	17.53	−4.50
	(−1.79)	(0.20)	(−0.13)
Other	14.65	10.20	26.93
	(0.91)	(0.83)	(0.30)
Oil	_[b]	_[b]	_[b]
Gas	18.54	13.67	3.14
	(8.62)	(0.76)	(0.12)
Dry	−13.28	−2.67	−2.76
	(−6.99)	(−0.11)	(−0.11)
R^2	0.18[c]	0.13[c]	0.53[c]
N	10710	238	135

Notes:
[a] t-statistics in parentheses beneath coefficient estimates. Estimates are corrected with White's (1980) general correction for heteroskedasticity. County- and time-specific effect estimates are suppressed.
[b] Denotes omitted variable.
[c] R^2 of the transformed regressions.

the two states in comparison with the sample size used in the US regression.

The three regressions also suggest that drilling on federal land is significantly more expensive than drilling on other types of land. In fact, because both county- and time-specific effects are controlled, these results have a particularly interesting interpretation: Within a county, a shift in drilling activity from private land to federal land will result in an increase in average drilling costs.[3] More specifically, using results from the column (1) regression, the average real cost per foot of drilling a well on federal property is $18.14 more than on private property. As a consequence, the average real cost of drilling a 4873 foot well (the sample mean of well depth for the US) is $88 396 more expensive on federal property than on private property. Corresponding values for Wyoming and New Mexico, evaluated at each state's average well depth, are $145 004 and $91 458. These estimates of extra costs paid to drill on federal vs. private land are at least broadly consistent with those obtained in the previously referenced study of the Wyoming Checkerboard. That study found a federal land drilling cost premium of about $111 000 using data from I.H.S. on 1390 individual wells drilled in Southwestern Wyoming over the period 1987–98.

In light of effects controlled in the present study, the cost premiums estimated are cautiously interpreted as the result of differences in stringency of application of environmental and land use regulations on federal and private property. This interpretation, however, is subject to at least five qualifications. First, many county-level control variables potentially important to the analysis are not available. For example, including a variable for drilling intensity (cumulative wells drilled divided by county land area) would likely capture scale economies in drilling effort; however, data on cumulative wells drilled are only available at the state level. Additional county-level variables, possibly important but currently unavailable, include proved reserves, federal and private land lease (access) costs, and cumulative production. Second, unmeasured heterogeneity between federal and private property may remain in spite of the county-specific, time-specific and other controls included in the analysis. For example, within a given county, there may still be more environmental resources to protect on federal property than on private property and/or federal property may be more remotely located than private property. Third, as previously discussed, environmental resources to protect vary greatly over space, so the estimates presented represent an average cost premium, rather than an extra cost applicable to all drilling sites on federal property. Fourth, when a number of wells are drilled in a particular lease area, operators may have difficulty in allocating fixed costs (including those associated with environmental compliance) between wells. This problem arises on both federal and private property, but is a factor that would reduce the precision of the estimates presented. Fifth, the specification used here implicitly assumes that the federal land drilling cost premium varies with well depth, whereas it may in reality be a component of fixed cost. Evaluating the premium at average well depth, however, may partially ameliorate this problem.

4.   SIMULATION RESULTS

This section applies the model described in Section 2, calibrated to the estimates found in Gerking et al. (2000), and estimates of τ from Section 3 to simulate removal of the more stringent environmental and land use regulations on federal property for oil and gas drilling in the states of Wyoming and New Mexico. Solution values reflect a situation where environmental regulations on federal and private property are equally stringent. Because the simulations envision a reduction in regulation in the two states, $\tau<0$. In effect, the term $(1+\tau)$ will net out any estimated drilling cost premium and allows a comparison to a simulated base case where $\tau=0$. Wyoming's value of τ is determined by, $\tau=(-\$145\,004/(\$600\,931-(0.51\times\$145\,004)))0.51=-0.14$, where $\$145\,004$ represents the incremental estimated cost, from Section 3, of drilling a Wyoming well, $\$600\,931$ is the average cost of drilling a well in the state in 1997, and 0.51 represents the fraction of wells drilled on federal property in 1997. Correspondingly, New Mexico's value is determined by $\tau=(-\$91\,458/(\$503\,474-(0.44\times\$91\,458)))0.44=-0.09$.

A discussion of four key base case assumptions regarding prices and initial values of variables in the model is warranted. First, oil and gas producers are assumed to receive $\$19.22$ per BOE gross-of-tax at the wellhead (in real terms) in each year of the extraction and drilling programme. This figure is the 1970–97 US national mean for the real price per BOE. It is roughly the equivalent of assuming a national real oil price of $\$25$/barrel and a national real gas price of $\$2.25$/Mcf. Second, the perspective taken is that Wyoming and New Mexico represent only a small fraction of total world (or US) oil and gas supply. Thus, taxes levied and regulations imposed are assumed to have no impact on prevailing prices faced by other producers in other states or countries. Third, in the simulations reported, the initial values of reserves and cumulative wells drilled were fixed at year-end 1997 levels and the discount rate, δ, was set at 4 percent to reflect the risk-free real rate of long-term borrowing. This figure for δ is comparable to discount rates used in prior simulation studies of effects of taxation on nonrenewable resource exploration and extraction (see Yücel, 1989). Fourth, federal, state and local tax treatment of oil and gas exploration and production were modelled using *effective* tax rates, as described in Appendix A.

To obtain numerical solutions for the time paths of drilling, production and reserves, difference equation approximations were derived for the optimal first-order differential equations (10.10) and (10.12) along with the state variable evolution equations (10.2) and (10.3). For example, the evolution of reserves, equation (10.2), can be approximated by the simple difference, $R_t-R_{t-1}=f_{t-1}-q_{t-1}$. These difference equations then are solved recursively by varying (iterating over) the initial values of the control variables, q and w, until transversality conditions are satisfied. Because of the functional form assumed for the extraction cost function (see Gerking et al., 2000), production approaches zero only asymptotically. Thus, the programme horizon was arbitrarily set at $T_1=60$ years, because after that time very little exploration and extraction occurs. Simulated time paths for

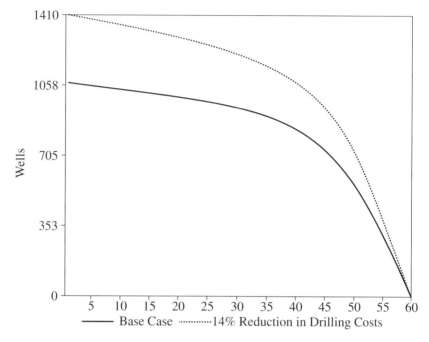

Figure 10.1 Wyoming (drilling)

drilling and production depict the outcome of an initial decrease in drilling costs (14 percent in Wyoming and 9 percent in New Mexico) held constant over the 60-year programme. The specific method used to obtain solutions for the set of numerical difference equations that form the model involves the Generalized Reduced Gradient (GRG2) nonlinear optimization algorithm found in Microsoft Excel.

Results showing the simulated differences in timing and intensity of drilling and production are presented in Table 10.4 for both Wyoming and New Mexico. The first six rows of each state's results report individual programme year activity (drilling cost reductions compared to the base case) divided into 10-year increments of the 60-year simulated programme. The next six rows report cumulative drilling and production comparisons. For Wyoming, individual year and cumulative results in Table 10.4 show that removing the more stringent environmental drilling regulations on federal property would substantially increase this activity and tilt it to the present. The 14 percent cost reduction increases drilling by approximately 32 percent in the first year and adds 14 388 wells drilled (29.3 percent above the base case) over the entire 60-year horizon. As shown graphically in Figure 10.1, the increase in drilling activity is tilted toward the present, reflecting

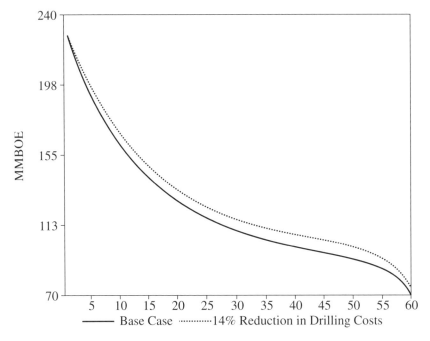

Figure 10.2   Wyoming (production)

the fact that a constant real cost saving is worth more today than in the future. With intensified drilling in the early years of the programme, 624 million BOE of new reserves are identified and production gradually rises above that found in the base case as shown in Figure 10.2. During the life of the programme, eliminating the added environmental regulatory costs on federal property in Wyoming increases extraction of oil and gas by about 557 million BOE or 7.6 percent above the base case. To put these simulated values into perspective, Wyoming's actual drilling and production activity averaged (annually) approximately 1028 wells and 206 million BOE over the period 1970–97.

The smaller drilling cost reduction in New Mexico (9 percent) increases wells drilled in year 1 by 20.6 percent and tilts drilling to the present as shown in Figure 10.3. Over the 60-year life of the programme, the decreased regulatory costs would result in additional drilling of 16700 wells. This figure represents an 18.4 percent increase in total wells drilled as compared to the base case. During the first half of the simulated programme, 10400 or roughly 63 percent of the additional wells are drilled. As in Wyoming, increased early period drilling activity enhances New Mexico's reserve base by 442 million BOE and production rises over time

Table 10.4 *Timing and intensity of drilling and production*

		Individual Programme Year:					
Wyoming	Year 1	Year 10	Year 20	Year 30	Year 40	Year 50	Year 60
Drilling (base case, in wells)	1070	1037	998	945	837	561	8
Drilling (14% cost cut, in wells)	1411	1355	1293	1217	1072	716	9
Change from base case (%)	31.87	30.67	29.56	28.78	28.08	27.63	12.50
Production (base case, in MMBOE)	228.4	162.7	127.1	109.6	100.2	93.3	74.9
Production (14% cost cut, in MMBOE)	229.6	170.9	137.8	120.7	110.8	103.0	82.4
Change from base case (%)	0.53	5.04	8.42	10.13	10.58	10.40	10.01
Cumulative to:							
Drilling (base case, in wells)		10535	20696	30409	39343	46411	49069
Drilling (14% cost cut, in wells)		13823	27036	39575	51042	60077	63457
Change from base case (%)		31.21	30.63	30.14	29.74	29.45	29.32
Production (base case, in MMBOE)		1922.1	3331.8	4496.9	5537.3	6501.8	7358.3
Production (14% cost cut, in MMBOE)		1973.5	3481.7	4757.3	5906.0	6971.7	7915.7
Change from base case (%)		2.67	4.50	5.79	6.66	7.23	7.58

Individual Programme Year:

New Mexico	Year 1	Year 10	Year 20	Year 30	Year 40	Year 50	Year 60
Drilling (base case, in wells)	1934	1851	1769	1688	1562	1186	13
Drilling (9% cost cut, in wells)	2332	2214	2100	1992	1834	1388	14
Change from base case (%)	20.58	19.61	18.71	18.01	17.41	17.03	7.69
Production (base case, in MMBOE)	384.8	202.6	137.8	116.1	106.9	101.3	78.8
Production (9% cost cut, in MMBOE)	386.3	210.5	146.7	124.2	114.0	107.3	83.1
Change from base case (%)	0.39	3.90	6.46	6.98	6.64	5.92	5.46
Cumulative to:							
Drilling (base case, in wells)		18914	36966	54223	70491	84427	90550
Drilling (9% cost cut, in wells)		22714	44213	64624	83765	100101	107252
Change from base case (%)		20.09	19.60	19.18	18.83	18.57	18.45
Production (base case, in MMBOE)		2789.5	4398.3	5639.6	6744.8	7782.7	8714.4
Production (9% cost cut, in MMBOE)		2843.3	4539.0	5864.9	7045.1	8147.9	9133.1
Change from base case (%)		1.93	3.20	3.99	4.45	4.69	4.80

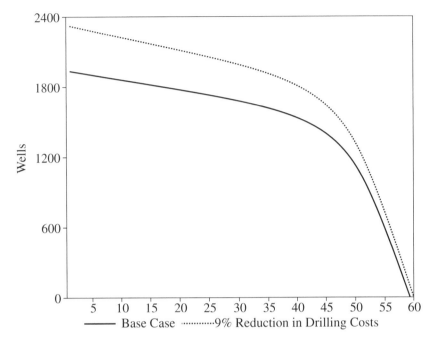

Figure 10.3   New Mexico (drilling)

as shown in Figure 10.4. Interestingly, latter year production increases (see rows 6 and 18 of Table 10.4) begin to diminish earlier and in larger magnitude as compared to the Wyoming case. This outcome reflects the difference in size of reserves added by reducing regulatory cost and highlights the estimated differences in the marginal product of drilling across the two states (see Gerking et al., 2000). Total cumulative production in New Mexico increases by 419 million BOE or 4.8 percent above the base condition. For the period 1970–97, New Mexico's actual drilling and production averaged (annually) 1210 wells and 285 million BOE.

In both states, results show that earlier period drilling is more sensitive than production to regulatory changes affecting drilling cost. A reduction in environmental compliance cost increases incentives to drill, but in any given year the marginal product of drilling falls with the increased number of wells drilled. As discussed in Section 2, increased production occurs when increased drilling adds to reserves, thus lowering future extraction costs (see Pindyck, 1978; Levhari and Leviatan, 1977). In consequence, production, which is influenced mainly by the size of the reserve base, changes by a smaller percentage than drilling activity during the 60-year programme.

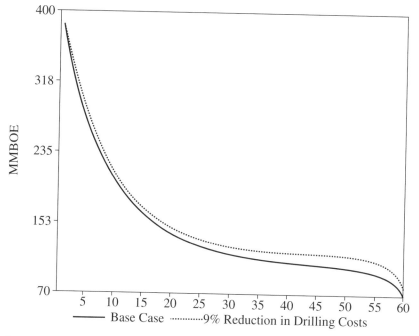

Figure 10.4 New Mexico (production)

5. CONCLUSION

This chapter assesses the relationship between environmental and land use regulation and the timing and intensity of oil and gas drilling and production. One key issue is whether drilling costs for oil and natural gas are higher on federal land than other types of land, including private land. The analysis is focused on Wyoming and New Mexico, two important energy producing states with substantial federal land. The data set on drilling costs consists of observations from drilling 319 475 oil and gas wells in 33 states during the period 1987–98 and subsets for Wyoming and New Mexico. The empirical analysis developed in this study suggests that drilling on federal land is significantly more expensive than drilling on other types of land, which is consistent with information based on engineering studies and interviews with market participants. Additionally, it is consistent with information on drilling costs for the Wyoming Checkerboard, located in the southwestern corner of that state. The evidence indicates that the differential cost of drilling on federal land is due largely to more stringent application of environmental regulations, in particular the protection of cultural, wildlife and plant resources.

A second key issue is the extent to which higher drilling costs affect the timing and cumulative production of oil and natural gas over time. The empirical analysis was conducted by calibrating and simulating an adaptation of Pindyck's (1978) widely applied model of nonrenewable resource exploration and production. The model was calibrated to estimates developed by Gerking et al. (2000), and the estimates of drilling costs mentioned above. The higher costs of drilling on federal land in Wyoming and New Mexico are shown to substantially reduce drilling in earlier periods, tilting exploration, development and production towards the future, and to a lesser extent reduce cumulative production over time. In fact, some oil and natural gas resources may not be explored (over one billion BOE estimated for the two states) because of the stricter application of environmental and land use regulations on federal land, shifting exploration from federal to private land.

The central conclusion of this study, therefore, is that drilling regulations appear to be more stringently enforced on federal land than on privately owned land, resulting in higher drilling costs on federal land, substantially lower rates of drilling in earlier periods and somewhat less cumulative production over time. A broader issue to consider in this context is whether or not it is appropriate for drilling regulations to be more stringently enforced on federal land than on other types of land. It is assumed that the purpose of the regulations is to internalize the negative externalities associated with drilling so that marginal social benefits equal marginal social costs at the equilibrium rate of drilling. If relatively stringent protection of cultural, plant and wildlife resources on federal land is appropriate, then it may well be appropriate to apply the same standards to drilling on private land. In any case, the economic rationale for the consistently stricter enforcement of environmental regulations on federal land than on other types of land in the United States remains to be established.

APPENDIX A

Tax parameters introduced in Section 2 are more fully specified in this appendix. In general, $\alpha_j = (j = p, C, D)$ can be specified using equations (10.A1) – (10.A3).

$$\alpha_p = [(1 - \tau_{us})(1 - \tau_s)(1 - \tau_r)(1 - \tau_p) + \tau_{us}(1 - \tau_r)\Psi] \qquad (10.\text{A1})$$

$$\alpha_c = [(1 - \tau_{us})(1 - \tau_s)] \qquad (10.\text{A2})$$

$$\alpha_D = [(1 - \tau_{us})(1 - \tau_s)\eta] \qquad (10.\text{A3})$$

In these equations, τ_{us} denotes the federal corporate income tax rate on operating profits, τ_s denotes the state corporate income tax rate on operating profits, τ_r denotes the royalty rate on production from public (state and federal) land, τ_p denotes the production (severance) tax rate, Ψ denotes the federal percentage depletion allowance weighted by the percentage of production attributable to eligible producers (nonintegrated independents), and η denotes the expensed portion of current and capitalized drilling costs attributable to current period revenues. η is the sum of: (1) the percentage of current period drilling costs expensed, and (2) the estimated present value share of depreciation deductions for the capitalized portion of current and past drilling expenditures. Producers are allowed to expense costs associated with drilling dry holes along with certain intangible costs (for example, labour and fuel) for completed wells as they are incurred. All direct (tangible) expenditures for completed wells must be capitalized and then depreciated over the life of the producing well (Bruen et al., 1996).

This formulation assumes that: (1) public land royalty payments are deductible in computing state production tax liabilities; (2) public land royalty payments, state production taxes, state reserve taxes, extraction costs, and certain drilling costs (described below) are deductible in computing both state and federal corporate income tax liabilities, (3) the federal percentage depletion allowance is applied to the production value net of royalties, and (4) state corporate income taxes are deductible against federal corporate income tax liabilities. Some of these assumptions do not apply universally across all states and in situations such as these, of course, equations (10.A1) – (10.A3) are modified.

Also, notice that this treatment incorporates the entire tax structure into the model and highlights the interactions between tax rates and tax bases. All tax parameters are interpreted as effective rather than nominal rates. As previously noted, states and the federal government grant numerous incentives, credits, and exemptions against tax levied, so nominal rates generally overstate amounts actually paid. Thus, effective rates fully account for all tax breaks granted. State tax collection data required for the calculation of the tax parameters are not compiled in a common format, therefore all data were obtained directly from local tax officials of Wyoming and New Mexico. Estimates of both state tax parameters are representative of the mid to late 1990s. A more complete description of specific tax parameters and how they entered the simulations is contained in the discussion of each state's institutional structure below.

At the federal level, an analysis of data from the US Treasury, Statistics of Income for the oil and gas sector shows that federal corporate taxes paid averaged about 10 percent of net operating income in 1997. This estimate is used in simulations for both states. Also, following Deacon (1993), the expensed portion of current period drilling costs is estimated at 40 percent for the industry in all states and the present value of depreciation deductions for capitalized drilling cost is approximated by $(q/R) / [\delta + (q/R)]$, a formulation that assumes the ratio of production to reserves is constant. The expensed share of current period drilling costs used here is 5 percentage points lower than Deacon's (1993) industry estimate. Dry hole costs were proportionally lower in the mid to late 1990s as compared to prior 1987 industry estimates (U.S. Census Bureau, 1997 Economic Census, Mining Industry Series). The ratio of production to reserves (q/R) will vary across states but the industry expense share of 40 percent is used in each state simulation.

Wyoming

Royalty rates (computed as the sum of state and federal royalty payments divided by the gross value of production) averaged 10 percent in 1997. This percentage is higher than for other oil and gas producing states because of the comparatively large share of Wyoming's production on public lands. Production tax rates are computed as total production tax collections divided by the gross value of production net of public land royalties. The sum of the two average effective rates in the mid to late 1990s totalled approximately 12 percent (local 6.5 percent and state 5.5 percent). Also, the current nominal percentage depletion rate of 15 percent applied to about 53 percent of Wyoming production in 1997, thus $\Psi = 8$ percent. Wyoming's mid to late 1990s level of q/R was approximately 7 percent, therefore $\eta = 0.4 + (1 - 0.4)*(0.07/(0.04 + 0.07)) = 0.782$. For Wyoming, simplification of equations (10.A1) – (10.A3) is achieved because the state does not levy a corporate income tax $(\tau_s = 0)$.

New Mexico

The state of New Mexico levies a number of separate production taxes on oil and gas that, in total, yield an effective rate of 8.5 percent. Production taxes are applied to the value of production net of public land royalties, which are set at an effective rate of 9.2 percent. A considerable amount of oil and gas production and exploration takes place on public lands in New Mexico. The state levies a corporate income tax at an effective rate (as applied to operating income) of 5.3 percent. The current nominal percentage depletion rate of 15 percent applied to approximately 63 percent of New Mexico producers in 1997, therefore $\Psi = 9.5$ percent. New Mexico's mid to late 1990s level of q/R was approximately 9 percent, therefore $\eta = 0.4 + (1 - 0.4)*(0.09/(0.04 + 0.09)) = 0.815$.

NOTES

* This research is supported by an appropriation from the Wyoming Legislature (1999 Wyoming Session Laws, Chapter 168, Section 3). However, this chapter may or may not reflect the views of public officials in the State. Gerking also acknowledges the hospitality of CentER, Tilburg University, where portions of this chapter were completed, as well as support from visiting grant B46–386 from the Netherlands Organization for Scientific Research (NWO). We thank Robert W. Noffsinger for research assistance. Michael Greenstone, Laura Marsiliani, John Livernois, and two anonymous reviewers contributed helpful suggestions on earlier versions of this chapter as did seminar participants at the 1999 NWO workshop on Environmental Policy, Competitiveness, and the Location Behaviour of Firms, the UCF/CentER International Conference on Environmental Economics, the University of Colorado, the University of Nevada–Las Vegas, the Tinbergen Institute and the University of York.

1. Effects of environmental regulations pertaining to extraction are not pursued in light of the previous discussion emphasizing the relative importance of regulations that apply to drilling. Moreover, available data on production costs, reported by the Energy Information Administration, US Department of Energy, are of limited value. Production cost estimates are not always disaggregated to the state level and appear not to include expenditure estimates for environmental compliance.

2. At roughly \$0.70 per observation, individual well data would have cost over \$220 000, and precluded disaggregation of the analysis to the firm or field level.

3. We obtain similar results when depth is entered non-linearly (squared and cubed), when well type (oil, gas, dry) is interacted with federal land, and when time-specific effects are omitted.

REFERENCES

American Petroleum Institute (1999), *Basic Petroleum Data Book*, Washington, DC: API.

Becker, Randy and J. Vernon Henderson (2000), 'Effects of air quality regulations on polluting industries', *Journal of Political Economy*, **108**, 379–421.

Bohi, D. and M. Toman (1984), *Analyzing nonrenewable resource supply*, Washington, DC: Resources for the Future.

Bruen, Alexander J., Willard B. Taylor and Erik M. Jensen (1996), *Federal Income Taxation of Oil and Gas Investments*, Boston: Warren, Gorham and Lamont.

Bureau of Land Management (1997), *Estimated Breakdown of Costs from Federal Lease Stipulations*, White River RMP (Northwestern Colorado), July, D6–D7.

Carls, E.G., D.F. Fenn and S. Chaffey (1994), 'Soil contamination by oil and gas drilling and production operations in Padre Island, Texas', *Journal of Environmental Management*, 273–86.

Deacon, Robert T. (1993), 'Taxation, depletion, and welfare: a simulation study of the U.S. petroleum resource', *Journal of Environmental Economics and Management*, **24**, 159–87.

Deacon, Robert, Stephen DeCanio, H.E. Frech III and M. Bruce Johnson (1990), *Taxing Energy: Oil Severance Taxation and the Economy*, New York: Holmes & Meier.

Gerking, S., W. Morgan, M. Kunce and J. Kerkvliet (2000), 'Mineral Tax Incentives, Mineral Production, and the Wyoming Economy', Department of Economics and Finance, University of Wyoming (http://w3.uwyo.edu/~mkunce/StateReport.pdf).

Godec, M.L. and K. Biglarbigbi (1991), 'Economic effects of environmental regulations on finding and developing crude oil in the U.S.', *Journal of Petroleum Technology*, 72–9.

Greene, William H. (1997), *Econometric Analysis*, 3rd edn, Saddle River, NJ: Prentice-Hall.

Greenstone, M. (2000), 'The Impacts of Environmental Regulations on Industrial Activity: Evidence from the 1970 and 1977 Clean Air Act Amendments and the Census of Manufactures', Working Paper 408, Princeton University.

Harder, B., C. John and A. Dupont (1995), 'Impacts of Environmental Regulations on Future Resource Development in Louisiana Wetlands', Society of Petroleum Engineers, Paper Number 009707, March, 167–79.

Henderson, J. Vernon (1996), 'Effects of air quality regulation', *American Economic Review*, **86**, 789–813.

Innes, Robert, Stephen Polasky and John Tschirhart (1998), 'Takings, compensation, and endangered species protection on private lands', *Journal of Economic Perspectives*, **12**, 35–52.

Jaffe, Adam B., Steven R. Peterson, Paul R. Portney and Robert N. Stavins (1995), 'Environmental regulation and competitiveness of U.S. manufacturing: what does the evidence tell us?', *Journal of Economic Literature*, **33**, 132–63.

Krautkraemer, Jeffrey A. (1998), 'Nonrenewable resource scarcity', *Journal of Economic Literature*, **36**, 2065–107.

Kudia, M.S. and B. McDole (1996), 'Managing Drilling Operations in a Sensitive Environment', Society of Petroleum Engineers, Paper Number 35780, June, 203–11.

Kunce, M., S. Gerking and W. Morgan (2000), 'Environmental and Land Use Regulation in the Oil and Gas Industry: Implications from the Wyoming Checkerboard', Mimeo, University of Wyoming.

Levhari, D. and N. Leviatan (1977), 'Notes on Hotelling's economics of exhaustible resources', *Canadian Journal of Economics*, **10**, 177–92.

Levinson, Arik (1996), 'Environmental regulation and manufacturer's location choices: evidence from the census of manufacturers', *Journal of Public Economics*, **62**, 5–30.

Livernois, John L. (1987), 'Empirical evidence on the characteristics of extractive technologies: the case of oil', *Journal of Environmental Economics and Management*, **14**, 72–86.

Livernois, John L. (1988), 'Estimates of marginal discovery costs for oil and gas', *Canadian Journal of Economics*, **21**, 379–93.

McDonald, Stephen L. (1994), 'The Hotelling principle and in-ground values of oil reserves: why the principle over-predicts actual values', *The Energy Journal*, **15**, 1–17.

Moroney, John R. (1997), *Exploration, Development, and Production: Texas Oil and Gas, 1970–95*, Greenwich, Connecticut: JAI Press.

Oates, Wallace E. (1999), 'An essay on fiscal federalism', *Journal of Economic Literature*, **XXXVII**, 1120–49.

Pesaran, M. Hashem (1990), 'An Econometric Analysis of Exploration and Extraction of Oil in the U.K. Continental Shelf', *Economic Journal*, **100**, 367–90.

Pindyck, Robert S. (1978), 'The optimal exploration and production of nonrenewable resources', *Journal of Political Economy*, **86**, 841–61.

Schulz, R.M. (1998), 'Incremental Economic Analysis of Environmental Mitigative Measure on Oil and Gas Operations', Unpublished dissertation, Colorado School of Mines, Golden, CO.

Tannenwald, R. (1997), 'State regulatory policy and economic development', *New England Economic Review*, 37–53.

Turner, John F. and Jason C. Rylander (1998), 'The Private Lands Challenge: Integrating Biodiversity Conservation and Private Property', in Jason F. Shogren (ed.), *Private Property and the Endangered Species Act*, Austin, TX: University of Texas Press.

Uhler, R. (1976), 'Costs and supply in petroleum exploration: the case of Alberta', *Canadian Journal of Economics*, **29**, 72–90.

U.S. Department of Treasury, *Statistics of Income, Corporate Returns*, 1970–97, Washington, DC.

White, H. (1980), 'A heteroskedasticity-Consistent Covariance Matrix Estimator and a direct test for Heteroskedasticity', *Econometrica*, **48**, 817–38.

Wilson, J.D. (1999), 'Theories of tax competition', *National Tax Journal*, **52**, 269–304.

Yücel, M. (1989), 'Severance taxes and market structure in an exhaustible resource industry', *Journal of Environmental Economics and Management*, **16**, 134–48.

11. Using flexible scenarios in benefit estimation: an application to the cluster rule and the pulp and paper industry

Susan Kask, Todd Cherry, Jason Shogren and Peter Frykblom

INTRODUCTION

Cellulose is the fibre found in wood used to produce paper. The cellulose, however, must be separated from the lignin – the substance that holds the wood together. Separating the usable cellulose from the glue-like lignin involves three energy- and chemically-intensive processes. The first stage breaks down the wood into pulp by chemical, semi-chemical and mechanical processes with the resulting pulp containing lignin and the chemicals used in the pulping. The second stage rinses the pulp through a series of screens at high temperatures to remove the lignin and chemicals. This rinsing process generates hazardous gases and liquid effluent as waste byproducts. In the final stage, the pulp is rinsed again and bleached using chlorine, chlorine-dioxide, or totally free chlorine techniques. The final stage may be repeated several times, generating hazardous air emissions and enormous amounts of wastewater. The wastewater resulting from chlorine bleaching processes contains lignin and a host of hazardous chemicals – including dioxin. Even piping the wastewater to municipal treatment facilities does not prevent the eventual deposit of dioxin and other hazardous chemicals in nearby surface waters. The health risks associated with living among dioxins include both (i) the risk of mortality from various types of skin and organ cancer and (ii) the increased risk of many non-life threatening diseases from a reduction in immune response from exposure (Schmidt, 1992). Given the consequences of the waste byproduct, it is amazing that the final stage generating dioxin is solely for aesthetic reasons – to whiten the paper.

The significant levels of air and water pollutants make the pulp and paper industry a target of public concern and regulators. In 1997, the Environmental Protection Agency (EPA) embarked on a new approach to regulate the industry – an integrated rule that coordinates federal efforts under both the Clean Water Act and Clean Air Act. The so-called Cluster Rule sets water and air standards while allowing individual mills to select the best combination of pollution control and prevention technologies to achieve pollution reductions. The Cluster Rule applied to 155 of the 565 pulp and paper mills in the United States and was estimated to require capital expenditures of $1.8 billion and increase annual operating costs by $277 million. The EPA suggests the changes imposed by the Cluster Rule will virtually eliminate dioxins and significantly reduce the other toxic pollutants that pulp and paper mills discharge in the air and waterways during bleaching processes. With the specific benefits, the end result of the Cluster Rule should be a reduction in health risks for the millions of families who live near pulp and paper mills.

What is the value of the risk reduction from the Cluster Rule? And how does it compare to the $1.8 billion regulatory cost? While the estimates of regulatory costs are relatively straightforward, it is often difficult to get a hold on the dollar estimates of the regulatory benefits – especially a complex good such as the low health risks associated with the long-term, low-dosage exposure to hazardous chemicals. Complex goods are particularly concerning when estimating benefits with contingent valuation (CV) methods because the success of a study depends on the definition of the good in that a poorly defined good can bias benefit estimation through so-called scope or embedding problems[1] (Arrow et al., 1993; Hanemann, 1994; Randall and Hoehn, 1996). Evidence further indicates that willingness to pay (WTP) estimates are sensitive to the scenarios presented (for example, Smith and Desvousges, 1987; Shogren, 1990; Loomis and duVair, 1993; Hoevenagel and van der Linden, 1993; Smith et al., 1995).[2] Estimating benefits from complex environmental goods, such as the risk reduction associated with the Cluster Rule, exacerbate these problems due to the difficulties in scenario definition.

This chapter proposes an alternative approach to scenario definition – flexible scenarios – that allows respondents to define the good they value. This flex-scenario approach tries to reduce the problems of embedding and scope by providing more clarity on the sensitivity of WTP estimates to the various components of an environmental good or service.

Studies using a variety of valuation methods have explored how varying degrees of flexibility in the scenario definition affect benefit estimation. Adamowicz et al. (1997) found that their combined revealed and stated preference model based on perceptions of site attributes slightly outperformed the model based on objective data in simulation tests of actual site choices. Alberini et al. (1997) estimate WTP to avoid an illness episode whose attributes are defined by the respondent. Blamey et al. (1999) show that flexibility in the valuation question, which they call a dissonance-minimizing format, reduces the occurrence of yea-saying. Finally, Fries and Gable (1997) present a commodity definition survey for improving the definition of goods given in stated preference studies. But no studies to our knowledge have implemented a fully flexible scenario that allows respondents to define the good based upon their perceptions.

We use a flexible scenario defined by the respondent rather than by a researcher to explore the potential to avoid problems associated with respondent modification of goods in the CV framework. In a flexible scenario respondent perceptions are used for all aspects of the scenario definition. Therefore, respondents state their perceptions about scenario variables which include: the perceived character set of the good, the perceived initial starting level of the good, the preferred policy approach for changing the good, and the perceived level of change of the good. We apply this approach using three of four scenario variables to estimate the benefits of risk reduction from long-term exposure to the hazard posed by the pulp and paper industry. This approach is particularly applicable to the health risks associated with dioxin because of the high potential for respondent modification that arises from the complex nature of the good.

RISK PERCEPTION AND WILLINGNESS TO PAY

Following Ehrlich and Becker (1972), Shogren (1990) and Shogren and Crocker (1991, 1999), consider a simple model of endogenous risk. Assume consumers maximize expected indirect utility over two states of the world. States zero and one represent poor and good health. The probability of poor health depends on the strategies selected to directly reduce the probability of health problems given exposure, R, and those selected to indirectly reduce probability by reducing exposure, Q, to the hazardous chemical, Z, as shown in expression (11.1).

$$p = p(R, Q(Z); p^0) \qquad (11.1)$$

Given this subjective probability, the consumer maximizes indirect utility

$$E(V) = p(R, Q(Z); p^0)V^0(Y - R - Z)$$
$$+ [1 - p(R, Q(Z); p^0)]V^1(Y - R - Z) \qquad (11.2)$$

where Y is consumer income. Let consumer total wealth be written as $W = Y - R - Z$. Selection of R and Z depend on the consumer's perception of the effectiveness of these approaches to reduce risks to health, p_R and $p_Q Q_Z$, and their perceived baseline probability, p^0. Assuming an interior solution, the decision rules for selecting the risk reduction mechanism (hereafter RRM) selection are:

$$R: \quad -p_R(V^1 - V^0) = p V_w^0 + (1 - p) V_w^1 \tag{11.3}$$

$$Z: \quad -p_Q Q_Z(V^1 - V^0) = p V_w^0 + (1 - p) V_w^1 \tag{11.4}$$

Consumers maximize expected indirect utility so the marginal benefit of risk reduction equals the marginal cost, the loss of expected utility from less net wealth. Equations (11.5) and (11.6) show that willingness to pay for self protection and self insurance also depend on consumer perceptions of risk and risk reduction.

$$WTP_R = \frac{dY}{dR} = \frac{p_R(V^1 - V^0) - p V_w^0 - (1 - p) V_w^1}{p V_w^0 + (1 - p) V_w^1} \tag{11.5}$$

$$WTP_z = \frac{dY}{dZ} = \frac{p_Q Q_Z(V^1 - V^0) - p V_w^0 - (1 - p) V_w^1}{p V_w^0 + (1 - p) V_w^1} \tag{11.6}$$

Another version of this story is to frame the valuation problem as the option price, OP, to define the value of an exogenous policy change in risk, $p^0 + \beta$, given optimal investments in self protection and self insurance, R^* and Z^*:

$$
\begin{aligned}
& p(R^*, Q(Z^*); p^0 + \beta) V^0(Y - R^* - Z^* - OP^*) \\
& + [1 - p(R^*, Q(Z^*); p^0 + \beta)] V^1(Y - R^* - Z^* - OP^*) \\
& = p(R^*, Q(Z^*); p^0) V^0(Y - R^* - Z^*) \\
& + [1 - p(R^*, Q(Z^*); p^0)] V^1(Y - R^* - Z^*)
\end{aligned} \tag{11.7}
$$

The incremental option price then is

$$
\begin{aligned}
dOP^*/d\beta = & \{ p_b[V^0(Y - R^* - Z^* - OP^*) \\
& - V^1(Y - R^* - Z^* - OP^*)] \} / \{ p(R^*, Q(Z^*); p^0 \\
& + \beta) V_w^0(Y - R^* - Z^* - OP^*) \\
& + [1 - p(R^*, Q(Z^*); p^0 + \beta)] V_w^1(Y - R^* - Z^* - OP^*) \}
\end{aligned} \tag{11.8}
$$

One can go a step further by using the notions behind Viscusi's (1989) prospective reference theory to modify this marginal option price to include subjective and objective risk perceptions. This would require looking at the probability function as a Bayesian framework. One would redefine the probability function to include both prior beliefs (subjective risk) with new objective information (objective risk), and the weighted scheme between the priors and new information.

Consumers often make decisions in the marketplace regarding uncertain events, such as the purchase of insurance for their home, health, car, or the purchase of goods that they believe will reduce a particular risk such as bottled water, air conditioners, sunscreen, vitamins, and so on. In these cases consumers make choices based on their transformation of the actual risks they face. Their decisions are based on their perception of risk and their perception of the efficiency of different risk reduction mechanisms. Although objective risk information may be given, consumers have their own preferences and values, and their final decisions are based on *their* perceptions of *their* risks and risk reduction. This perception may or may not correspond with objective risk information, including changes in objective risk (Hammitt and Graham, 1999). The potential for significant variation between objective risks and subjective risks has been discussed in the economics and psychological literature (for example Lichtenstein et al., 1978; Viscusi and Magat, 1987; Kunreuther et al., 1978; Smith et al., 1995; Kask and Maani, 1992; Smith and Johnson, 1988; Fischoff, 1975).

When valuing complex environmental goods, as in health risks from long-term low-dosage exposure to hazardous chemicals from pulp and paper production, the potential for respondent modification of the good is exacerbated since people have difficulty transforming low risks accurately. As a result, risk perceptions can over- or underestimate risks (for example Lichtenstein et al., 1978; Kunreuther et al., 1978; Cherry et al., 2001). Plus the human health risks from long-term low-dosage exposure to many hazardous chemicals are not fully understood, thus clarity in good definition becomes a problem. Even though people may be given information on baseline risks (p^0) and risk reduction (p_R and $p_Q Q_Z$) from an environmental hazard and regulatory approach, they may perceive a different level of risk and a different level of potential risk reduction. When values are elicited, people may value their change in subjective risk rather than the objective level defined in a scenario, potentially creating a scope problem in the values derived.

The scope and embedding problems can occur when a person modifies the general characteristics of the good targeted by regulation, or the change in the good that is expected from regulation. For example, people might perceive a risk reduction of, say, 20 percent from a policy rather than the 5 percent defined by the researchers. As a result they provide a value for a 20 percent change rather than the 5 percent that was given in the survey instrument. The embedding problem occurs as a result of the variation between a respondent's perception of, and the researcher's definition of, the good's attribute set. In this case, rather than a person having a different perception of the change in the *quantity* of the good, instead he or she perceives a different *type* of good impacted by the policy change. For example, although a researcher may define the impact of policy as occurring on a single component of the environment, such as a unique stream or lake, a person may consider the impact much broader including the soil, air, flora and fauna. The reverse can also occur. As a result people provide a value for the broader good rather than the more narrowly researcher-defined risk.

If consumer perception of a researcher-defined risk, or risk-reduction strategy, in a CV instrument varies from what the researcher had intended, CV estimates can be biased upward or downward depending on the direction of variation between respondent perception and the researcher-defined good (for example the scope or embedding problems). A recent study by Krupnick et al. (2000) used follow-up questions in a willingness to pay (WTP) study and found that significant scenario modification did occur and that modification did influence respondent WTP in some cases. They found that 20 percent of respondents did not think the baseline risk applied to them, 31 percent had doubts about the risk reduction strategy, 25 percent expected negative side effects while 40 percent expected benefits beyond those stated in the scenario. Of the 31 percent of the sample that doubted the effects of the risk reduction strategy proposed, two-thirds decreased their willingness to pay as a result. Of the 40 percent who believed additional benefits existed, half increased their willingness to pay as a result. Thus in this study modification occurs and resulting impacts on WTP occur in both directions.

If a CV design uses flexible scenarios, for example, respondents define p^0, select R or Z and define p_R, or $p_Q Q_Z$, and people honestly express their perceptions, the estimation of benefits for non-market goods may be improved. Specifically, the problems of the scope and embedding may be mitigated. Furthermore, flexible scenarios can address the potential for policy specific WTP estimates by allowing people to select their preferred policy approach. Finally, to determine if people can define goods in a meaningful way, we look for expected behaviours – explainable and consistent perceptions and choices.

CASE STUDY: THE PULP AND PAPER INDUSTRY

Risk Reduction from the Cluster Rule

Three characteristics of long-term, low-dosage exposure to dioxins discharged by pulp and paper mills increase the potential for respondent modification of the good, reduction in health risks, when estimating benefits. These include the complex package of health problems ranging from mild illness to death from cancer, the low baseline risk level of these health effects causing variation between actual and perceived risks, and the limited scientific knowledge preventing certain definition of the good.

The potential health risks from dioxin exposure are numerous, including both acute and long-term morbidity and mortality effects, which are not easily untangled. However, if we untangle the good, such as looking at mortality, or specific symptoms, as opposed to a package, then results may suffer from an embedding effect (Kahneman and Knetsch, 1992; Randall and Hoehn, 1996; Viscusi et al., 1987). Dickie and Gerking (1991) suggest people might do better valuing bundled health problems when independent risk reduction options do not exist for each health problem.

The potential health effects from dioxin may not occur for many years after a long period of exposure to low dosages, thus the lifetime health risks are expected to be small. Research finds that people often overestimate risks from low risk hazards (see Lichtenstein et al., 1978; Viscusi and Magat, 1987), or underestimate risks when objective risk levels are below some threshold (Kunreuther et al., 1978). Thus benefit estimates for these health risks may be considered upper or lower bounds, depending on the risk behaviour expected or observed (Kask and Maani, 1992). This transformation between actual and perceived risks promotes the scope problem, given that people are likely to have different perceptions regarding the baseline risk level, and thus perceive the significance of a change in risk differently.

The flexible scenario allows us to take several precautions to reduce the potential for embedding and scope in this study. First, we use individual perceptions of the good valued including perceptions of the baseline risk, and their perceptions of the level of risk change. Further, we allow people to choose their preferred policy approach. This flexibility in scenario definition may reduce the potential for respondent modification of a researcher-defined good. This study, however, continues to define the illness character set of the health effects using a split sample. People only define the baseline risk component of this character set. The split sample reduces the potential impact of sequencing on value estimates while allowing the potential for embedding to occur.

Study Site

The sample was taken from an area in western North Carolina and eastern Tennessee that hosts a pulp and paper mill along the Pigeon River. This area provided a unique opportunity to examine the potential for a respondent-defined good given the long history of the mill and the likely awareness and knowledge of the area population. Due to the local pulp and paper production, dioxin is a primary contaminant in the Pigeon River (USEPA, 1989a,b). The mill's 90-year presence and various EPA hearings and activities have informed the region's population about the pollution over time. This provides us with a base information set greater than zero, but certainly less than full information, which implies that priors exist in the population. The survey design elicited both prior and posterior risk perceptions.

Study and Survey Design

We use a block design to elicit the economic values of a reduction in lifetime risk of health problems from dioxin in the environment. Table 11.1 shows the three-block design used for the study.[3] Blocks A and B test for variation between mortality and morbidity bids, and block C and A, and C and B test the variation between these bids and the combined value.

Table 11.1 Survey categories

	Mortality	Morbidity	Combined
Dioxin	A	B	C

The survey contained three parts: the introduction with background questions, the risk reduction mechanism and valuation questions, and the demographic questions.[4] The background questions established the initial pre-information perceptions of a respondent toward risk-related factors including awareness, information levels, exposure, concern, existence of dioxin-related health problems, chances, control, seriousness of health problems, and their prior subjective probabilities. The probability question asked 'What do you think your household's chance is in one million of having health problems from dioxin in any given year?' The question was adjusted for the various design blocks and was tested by four focus groups to ensure clarity and ability to respond.

In part two, people were given information on dioxin. The information was presented in a format that addressed five fundamental questions. What is it? Where does it come from? How can I be exposed? What are the health problems? What is the risk? The information provided in the survey was reviewed by scientists at the Center for Disease Control in Atlanta to ensure accuracy, and reviewed in four focus groups to ensure clarity, readability, and understanding. The information section was adjusted for the different design blocks; for example the mortality survey only provided information on the cancer risks from dioxins. Following the information, respondents were asked if they wanted to change their initial probability and, if so, to give their new estimate. The survey reminded respondents that although actual risks are unknown, policymakers must make decisions regarding risks for the general public.

People were then asked to make a policy choice by selecting a risk reduction mechanism, to estimate their perceived risk reduction from their policy choice and, finally, state their WTP to implement that policy. The selection of the risk reduction mechanism followed a modified decision pathways survey approach (Gregory et al., 1997). Four risk reduction pathways were offered (private protection, private insurance, collective protection and collective insurance),[5] each with a description of what actions may be taken and the possible payment vehicles. Three objectives were provided to frame the choice process: effectiveness, expense and implementation. People ranked the four options using each objective to assist them in their selection of their most preferred choice. Finally, they ranked the four options based on their own and their household's preferences. Given their most preferred choice, they revealed their perceived percentage risk reduction from their preferred option.

The valuation question was presented as a series of three dichotomous choice questions with a subsequent open-ended maximum valuation question. This approach takes advantage of the increased cognitive capacity of the dichotomous choice structure, while the open-ended question was used to distinguish respondents that had a zero bid from those that simply found the first bid too expensive. Zero bidders were asked their reasons for a zero bid.

Demographic questions concluded the survey. In addition to the standard demographic questions, specific questions were included that related to factors that might potentially influence dioxin risk reduction values such as type of employment (for example pulp and paper or chemical industries), veteran status (Vietnam), and outdoor and/or environmental hobbies.

Mail surveys were sent to a randomly selected sample of 2000 households from seven counties in western North Carolina and five counties in eastern Tennessee. A modified Dillman method was used with four sequential mailings: survey–postcard–survey–postcard (Dillman, 1978). A three-week period separated the two survey mailings.

The Sample

We treat this as an exploratory survey given our overall response rate of 17 percent. A comparison of the two respondent groups (first mailing and second mailing) suggests we did broaden the sample with respect to the level of interest (an environmental/outdoor hobby question) and the level of information with the second mailing; thus pooling the two groups provides a sample for exploratory analysis on the potential to use a flexible scenario with the CV approach.

We restricted the sample by removing zero protest bids and inconsistent willingness to pay responses[6] (13.88 percent and 5 percent of the full sample). Item non-responses (15.77 percent) remained in the clean sample as they are automatically dropped during the analysis process. Valid zeros (7.57 percent of the full sample) also remained in the sample. Zero protests comprised 64 percent of all zero responses in the full sample. The final sample included 194 observations.[7]

Table 11.2 gives the demographics for the sample as compared to the region and nation. The sample is slightly older and has slightly higher income levels. Observations in the sample are evenly distributed across the study categories and bid sets.

Table 11.2   Demographics of final sample, region and nation

Demographic characteristic	Sample n = 194	Region sampled	Nation
Median education	13	12	12
Age distribution (% pop > 65)	21	15.7	12.56
Median age	50*	36.7	32.9
Mean household income	34470	30524	29943
Gender distribution %M/%F	55/45	48/52	49/51

Note: *Mean age for sample. Note sample minimum age is 18, as required by law.

RESULTS

Respondent Definition of the 'Good'

Risk perception
An important issue is the ability of people to evaluate the complex package of health problems and define the good they are valuing in a meaningful way. From Table 11.3 we see that people have differentiated between risk types when determining their baseline risk. Evidence from the mean baseline risk estimates for mortality, morbidity and the combined risk shows

Table 11.3   Mean baseline risk by risk types

	Mortality n = 63	Morbidity n = 69	Combined n = 60
Posterior Baseline Risk			
#/1 000 000	10 443	54 800	60 261
%	1.04	5.5	6
% min/max	0/50	0/84	0/100

respondents did evaluate the risks differently, with mortality at 1.04 percent (10 443 persons per 1 000 000) being significantly lower than morbidity at 5.5 percent (54 800 persons per 1 000 000). Interestingly, the combined value of 6 percent is close to the sum of the mortality and morbidity values. These results suggest people in this sample did differentiate between types of complex goods and they were able to define an attribute of the good such as the current level of the good – the baseline risk, p^0, in this case. Findings also suggest people in this sample considered the character set defined by the researcher and not some alternative set defined by themselves when evaluating baseline risk. Embedding does not seem to be an issue.

Table 11.4 shows an OLS regression with baseline risk measured in percentage terms as the dependent variable. We see several variables are significant and have the expected signs. Respondents gave lower baseline risks if they were given a mortality survey (cancer), had higher incomes, believed they had private control over their risk levels, considered themselves informed, or stated they did not believe there was a chance of health risks. Alternatively, if respondents had children, or were aware of dioxins in their area, they stated higher baseline risks. These variables were significant at the 12 percent level or lower. A respondent's age, the amount of time they have lived in the area, and gender did not influence their baseline risks. Interestingly, we find no difference between perceived baseline risks for the morbidity and the combined respondents. This model only explains 7.5 percent of the variation in baseline risk levels and thus there remains much we do not know about respondent risk perceptions.

The results are consistent with expectations of risk behaviour. For example, mortality risks are lower than morbidity risks and factors such as control, awareness and information influence risks as expected. The data suggest that respondents were able to evaluate the risks in a meaningful way, and thus were able to define this component of the complex good for the flexible scenario.

Table 11.4   OLS results for posterior baseline risk model[a]

Variables	Coefficient
Constant	0.19277
	(0.024)
Age	0.00053
	(0.136)
Kids	0.057
	(0.116)
Male	0.026
	(0.333)
Time	−0.0006
	(0.243)
Income	0.0136
	(0.020)
Education (yrs)	−0.0069
	(0.135)
Community Control	0.044
	(0.138)
Private Control	−0.054
	(0.028)
Aware	0.076
	(0.045)
Exposed (No)	−0.025
	(0.175)
Informed	−0.049
	(0.118)
No chance	−0.044
	(0.063)
Don't know chance	−0.043
	(0.188)
Morbidity	−0.0057
	(0.886)
Mortality	−0.065
	(0.014)
Adj-R^2	0.075
P-value	0.04
N	144

Note: a. p-values are in parentheses.

Choice of risk reduction mechanism (RRM)

Table 11.5 shows that people demonstrate clear preferences for the reduction mechanisms. Across all samples, people avoided the collective insurance[8] approach with only 6–9 percent of respondents selecting this option. In contrast, people generally preferred the collective protection approach to all others with 40–43 percent of respondents selecting this option. But in the mortality sample, private approaches were slightly more preferred to collective approaches with only 46 percent selecting collective action.

Table 11.5   Preferred risk reduction option and percent risk reduction by risk types

	Mortality n = 63	Morbidity n = 69	Combined n = 60
Private protection + (% risk reduction*)	27	26	27
	(49)	(52)	(54)
Private insurance + (% risk reduction*)	27	12	17
	(58)	(39)	(53)
Collective protection + (% risk reduction*)	40	53	48
	(57)	(63)	(59)
Collective insurance + (% risk reduction*)	6	9	8
	(38)	(44)	(33)
All collective action+	46	62	56
All insurance action+	33	21	25
Risk reduction*	54.5	55	54.9
(min/max)	0/95	5/100	0/95

Notes:
+ percent selected as most preferred.
* mean values.

Table 11.6 presents the results from multinomial logit and binomial probit analyses of respondent policy choices. Three models are estimated to examine the respondent's choice among the alternative risk reduction mechanism – private-insurance, private-protection, collective-insurance and collective-protection. Model one employs a multinomial logit approach to explain the four policy choices with the characteristics of those policy choices as defined by the respondent. These characteristics include an effectiveness rank, a cost rank and an implementation rank. Aggregating within the categories of risk reduction mechanisms, models two and three use a binomial probit approach to examine the choice

Table 11.6   *Multinomial logit and binomial probit results for risk reduction mechanism choice*

Variable	Model 1[a]	Model 2[b]	Model 3[c]
Constant	n.a.	2.589	0.294
		(0.004)	(0.726)
Effectiveness rank	1.699	n.a	n.a.
	(0.000)		
Cost rank	−0.626	n.a.	n.a.
	(0.001)		
Implementation rank	0.323	n.a.	n.a.
	(0.039)		
A-Private protection	−0.359	n.a.	n.a.
	(0.556)		
A-Private insurance	0.030	n.a.	n.a.
	(0.960)		
A-Collective protection	0.90	n.a.	n.a.
	(0.084)		
% Reduction	n.a.	−0.0312	−0.0177
		(0.140)	(0.388)
% Reduction^2	n.a.	0.0002	0.0003
		(0.210)	(0.185)
Serious	n.a.	−0.0992	0.0174
		(0.008)	(0.634)
Maximum WTP	n.a.	0.0003	−0.0004
		(0.063)	(0.0182)
Age	n.a.	0.0033	−0.0007
		(0.610)	(0.916)
Male	n.a.	0.0696	−0.3806
		(0.734)	(0.079)
Education	n.a.	−0.997	0.0381
		(0.020)	(0.375)
Chi-Square (df)	168.18 (3)	26.76 (8)	14.82(8)
N	126	177	177

Notes:
[a] Four choices: private protection, private insurance, collective protection, or collective insurance.
[b] Two choices: private or collective – private = 1.
[c] Two choices: protection of insurance – protection = 1.
p-values are reported in parentheses.

between private and collective policies and the choice between risk reduction from exposure (protection) or health problems (insurance).

Results from model one illustrate the respondent's ability to make meaningful policy choices. The estimated coefficients are as expected with positive coefficients on the effectiveness and the implementation rankings and a negative coefficient on the cost ranking. Findings therefore suggest people are making rational choices – they are more likely to choose the policy option they consider more effective, more easily implemented, and less costly. The results from models two and three are descriptive models revealing information about who is selecting the different policy options. The results illustrate a preference for collective action by higher educated people and by those who consider the health problems serious. These attributes, however, do not affect the choice for insurance versus protection. If we consider that a respondent's underlying WTP may influence their policy choice, we find persons with a higher maximum WTP are more likely to select private action, but less likely to select insurance.

The results from Tables 11.5 and 11.6 suggest that respondents in this sample did indicate clear preferences among policy options with the choices systematically arising from personal attributes and beliefs.

Perceived risk reduction
The perceived risk reduction from the individual's preferred risk reduction mechanism provides further insight into respondent behaviour. Returning to Table 11.5 we see that the mean values for risk reduction across each risk type are not significantly different, nor are the minimum and maximum values. This finding illustrates that respondents possess substantial variation in their perceptions of potential risk reduction. Although people appear to differentiate between risk types regarding baseline risk and they have clear preferences for a policy approach, their perceptions for risk reduction (ultimately the good they are buying) are similar across the mortality, morbidity and combined samples and are similar across policy options. The mean percent reduction across policy options ranges from 33 percent to 63 percent. However, these values are not significantly different due to the broad range of values given and the high standard deviations. Given the subjective nature of this perception, there is no theoretical basis for determining the consistency, or predictability, of these levels.

The broad range of risk reduction levels and the lack of variation across risk types and policy options suggests that people have widely varying perceptions of the effectiveness of risk reduction mechanisms, and this variation is consistent across reduction mechanisms. For this sample, no policy approach is generally perceived as providing more risk reduction than another approach on average, and respondents do not consider risk reduction more likely to occur for one type of risk over another (for example, mortality, morbidity or the combined risks).

This result suggests this variable has the greatest potential for uncontrolled respondent modification. If respondents' perceptions are so disparate, as these results suggest they may be, the potential that respondents value a different good than the one specified by researchers is not trivial, for example, the scope effect may be significant. As shown in our WTP equation below, stated values depend on their perceived level of risk reduction specified, as expected. The implication is that if a respondent's perception of a specified policy reduction actually can range between 0 and 100 percent and they value their own private perception rather than the objective risk as Krupnick et al. (2000) demonstrated can occur, then analysis of data using alternative researcher-defined scenarios in a block structure could show a scope problem, even when respondent preferences are sensitive to scope. Thus, a solution to the scope problem may be the use of a flexible scenario rather than a block structure.

We conclude from the above analysis that respondents in this sample defined the good in a meaningful way. They revealed consistent and predictable baseline risks while indicating clear and consistent preferences for the policy choice. The analysis also highlighted a potential important source for respondent modification of a good and the scope problem, the wide variation in the perceived risk reduction.

Willingness to Pay for Risk Reduction

Eliciting WTP

The flexibility of the scenario makes it important to consider the choice of welfare measure, compensating versus equivalent surplus. The ability to define the risk reduction and the risk reduction mechanism implies the choice for equivalent surplus (see Johansson, 1993). However, by also allowing respondents to define their baseline risk level, none of the welfare measures is theoretically more correct than the other. Given we set out to measure the WTP for an improvement, the compensating surplus was measured.

People's WTP was elicited using a one-way-up dichotomous choice format followed by an open-ended question. Following Herriges and Shogren (1996), the one-way-up format entails each respondent indicating whether they are willing to pay an initial bid, A_1. If the answer is yes, a higher bid is offered. If the answer to the second bid, A_2, is yes, a final higher bid is offered, A_3.[9]

An open-ended maximum WTP question was asked after the third bid, or as soon as any answer was negative. We extend the literature by using

Kriström's (1997) spike model on the one-way-up design to estimate the WTP probit models.

The WTP models

The probability that an amount A was at least as high as the respondent's WTP is:

$$\Pr(\text{WTP} \leq A) = F_{wtp}(A), \tag{11.9}$$

where $F_{wtp}(A)$ is a continuous nondecreasing function. The functional form of the WTP distribution is assumed to be:

$$F_{wtp}(A) = \begin{cases} 0 & \text{if } A < 0 \\ p & \text{if } A = 0 \\ G_{wtp}(A) & \text{if } A > 0, \end{cases} \tag{11.10}$$

where $p \epsilon (0,1)$ and G_{wtp} is a continuous and increasing function such that $G_{wtp}(0) = p$ and $\lim_{A \to \infty} G_{wtp}(A) = 1$.

An open-ended question was used to determine whether the respondent was willing to pay anything, that is:

$$S_i = 1 \text{ if WTP} > 0 \text{ (0 otherwise)}. \tag{11.11}$$

T_i indicates whether the respondent was willing to pay the ith bid A:

$$T_3 = 1 \text{ if WTP} > A_3 \text{ (0 = otherwise)}$$

$$T_2 = 1 \text{ if WTP} > A_2 \text{ (0 = otherwise)}$$

$$T_1 = 1 \text{ if WTP} > A_1 \text{ (0 = otherwise)} \tag{11.12}$$

$$T_0 = 1 \text{ if WTP} < A_1 \text{ (0 = otherwise)}$$

The log likelihood for the sample is then equal to:

$$l = \Sigma S_i T_3 \ln[1 - F_{wtp}(A_3)] + S_i T_2 \ln[F_{wtp}(A_3) - F_{wtp}(A_2)]$$
$$+ S_i T_1 \ln[F_{wtp}(A_2) - F_{wtp}(A_1)] + S_i T_1 \ln[F_{wtp}(A_1) - F_{wtp}(0)] \quad (11.13)$$
$$+ (1 - S_i) T_0 \ln[F_{wtp}(0)].$$

Following Hanemann (1984), assuming a linear utility function:

$$v(k, y; z) = \alpha_k + \beta y + \gamma s \quad \beta > 0, k = 0,1 \tag{11.14}$$

where α and β are coefficients, y denotes income, γ is a vector of coefficients and s denotes a vector of socioeconomic and demographic characteristics gives:

$$\Delta v = (\alpha_1 - \alpha_0) - \beta A, \qquad (11.15)$$

where Δv denotes an approximation of the utility change. Using a normal distribution G_{wtp}, maximizing the log likelihood function and using Kriström's (1997) expression for the mean WTP:

$$E(wtp) = \int_0^\infty [1 - F_{wtp}(A)]dA = \frac{1}{\beta}\ln[1 + \exp(\alpha_1 - \alpha_0)]. \qquad (11.16)$$

Table 11.7 provides the descriptive statistics and Table 11.8 shows the results using a pooled sample.[10]

Table 11.7 Descriptive statistics for selected variables

Variable	Mean	Median
Maximum WTP ($)	215	100
Baseline risk (%)	4.2	0.00
Risk reduction (%)	55	55
Private insurance = 1	0.18	
Private protection = 1	0.27	
Collective protection = 1	0.47	
Income	34470	35000
Male[a] = 1	0.56	
Child[b]	0.71	
Morbidity = 1	0.36	
Mortality = 1	0.33	

Notes:
[a] Male = 1, (0 otherwise).
[b] Child = 0 if no children, (1 otherwise).

The estimated models provide some intuitively appealing results for risk reduction – people demonstrate a positive and diminishing marginal utility in risk reduction. In further accordance with economic theory, the bid variable is negative and significant in all models.

None of the demographic variables are significant in both models, which may be due to either small sample sizes or simply that the collected demographic variables are not systematically correlated to the WTP.

Table 11.8   Dichotomous choice results using the follow-up DC WTP
            questions[a]

Variables	Model 4[a]	Model 5[a]	Model 6[a]	Model 7[a]
Constant	0.87922	1.0961	0.80483	1.1352
	(0.127)	(0.094)	(0.170)	(0.135)
Bid	−0.00231	−0.00242	−0.00234	−0.00249
	(0.000)	(0.000)	(0.000)	(0.000)
Baseline risk	−0.00004	−0.00005	−0.00001	−0.00002
	(0.661)	(0.450)	(0.919)	(0.796)
Risk reduction	0.06918	0.05230	0.06598	0.04974
	(0.0052)	(0.111)	(0.0140)	(0.302)
Risk reduction^2	−0.00061	−0.000472	−0.00059	−0.00038
	(0.0143)	(0.115)	(0.055)	(0.283)
Income			−0.00002	0.00009
			(0.560)	(0.174)
Male			0.12801	0.10219
			(0.660)	(0.745)
Child			0.07663	−0.03033
			(.030)	(.920)
Morbidity			−0.02643	0.00505
			(0.923)	(0.988)
Mortality			0.10796	0.05041
			(0.759)	(0.902)
Private protection		1.1044		1.2362
		(0.075)		(0.084)
Private insurance		1.2981		1.1339
		(0.043)		(0.135)
Collective protection		0.48581		0.41654
		(0.445)		(0.563)

Note: a. p-values are reported in parentheses.

Although respondents differentiated between risk types in their evaluation of the risk, they did not differentiate by willingness to pay. These
results may be due to respondents failing to differentiate between their perceptions for risk reduction across the risk types, or due to an embedding
effect, or both.

The combined survey results may arise from the presentation of the combined health problems. Throughout the survey respondents are asked about
their knowledge, awareness, preferences and values for health problems
from dioxin. Only the information sheet that discusses health issues presents people with the combination of cancer and health problems. On this

sheet, cancer is presented first in the list of health problems. In the mortality survey, respondents are asked about their awareness, knowledge, preference and values for cancer from dioxin. This result therefore may be exacerbated by survey design. But given the differences found in baseline risk across the samples, it appears respondents did differentiate between the different risk types when evaluating their baseline risk levels despite the survey design. Why not in WTP values? The answer may arise from the lack of difference in respondents' expectations of potential risk reduction across the risk types and that they are focusing on this level of risk reduction instead of risk type.

Table 11.9 shows the WTP estimates to decrease the lifetime risk of health problems by 55 percent, the average expected risk reduction.

Table 11.9   Mean WTP estimates from the spike models

	Model 4	Model 5	Model 6	Model 7
WTP	531	570	502	565
std. dev.	178	202	175	229

Risk reduction mechanism and WTP

A significant benefit of the flexible scenario is to examine the variation in WTP relative to the choice of RRM. Using the pooled sample, we find that the marginal WTP was correlated with the choice of risk reduction mechanism. While collective protection was most preferred, the WTP regressions show greater and more significant coefficients on the variables for private action and private insurance. Allowing respondents to select their RRM may also reduce the potential for protests and ambivalence often found in CV studies (see Blamey et al., 1999; Ready et al., 1995).

SUMMARY AND CONCLUSIONS

We explore the use of flexible scenarios in CV studies by estimating the benefits of regulation on the pulp and paper industry. To illustrate how the estimates from this type of study could be used to determine benefits from the cluster rule, we use the estimated value functions from Table 11.8. Using the average level of risk reduction of 55 percent, we find that the marginal WTP estimate requires the cluster rule to impact at least 85000 households nationwide to achieve a positive net benefit.[11] These numbers, however, are provided purely for illustrative purposes; inferring definitive conclusion from this small sample pilot study is dubious. Our results do provide clear evidence for our primary purpose – exploring the role of flexible scenarios in benefits estimation.

Results indicate that people in our sample were able to define the three dimensions (baseline risk, policy option, and risk reduction) of the flexible scenario for the complex good in question – the reduction of low health risks associated with long-term low-dosage exposure to hazardous chemicals emitted by pulp and paper mills. And further, the definition of the good significantly impacted estimated WTP. In defining the 'good' in a meaningful way, people differentiated between risk types in their determination of perceived baseline risks. They also have clear and predictable preferences for their risk reduction mechanism. We find, however, that people did not distinguish between baseline risks, or risk types, with respect to their perception of risk reduction. This insensitivity to risk result is key, as it may be an underlying cause of the scope problem.

In observing the impact on WTP, we find the perceived level of risk reduction significantly influenced valuation, but respondents failed to distinguish between these risk types (morbidity, mortality, and so on) when determining willingness to pay. This is despite the fact that they do differentiate between risk types when stating risk perceptions. The finding may result from the dominance of their perceptions of risk reduction in the choice process, which was not dependent on risk type or reduction mechanism selected, and/or may be an embedding effect. Our results also show that the choice of the reduction mechanism may be a significant factor when determining the WTP.

The implications of this study on CV survey design are threefold. First, the apparent ability of respondents in this sample to differentiate between risk types when stating baseline risk perceptions, to make policy choices, and to state consistent WTP values based on their scenario definitions is promising for future valuation studies. Our study suggests that respondents can handle the complexity of the flexible scenario CV. Furthermore, a paper by Blamey et al. (1999) suggests respondents may also prefer *more* complexity in the options given in CV studies.

Second, the broad range of perceived risk reduction estimates stated by respondents in this study suggests that the potential for respondent modification of researcher-defined scenarios may be significant and thus may be a cause of the scope problem often cited in CV studies. This result is consistent with the respondent modification found in Krupnick et al. (2000). It is important to note, however, that increased flexibility that allows respondents to define the character set of a good may also be needed to address the embedding problem often observed between a single good and a package. Third, does the policy choice matter? The results suggest that both the risk level and the policy choice may be the critical variables in the scenario definition. Further research to address the robustness of these results is needed. Finally, this study suggests that the gains from flexibility in scenario design may be worth the costs of difficulty for survey respondents and that further research on using flexible survey scenarios is warranted.

ACKNOWLEDGMENTS

Appreciation is extended to the summer grants programme at Western Carolina University for partial funding of this research. Thanks to Joe Kerkvliet and Bengt Kriström for help on the dichotomous choice model, Elizabeth Barnhart at the Center for Disease Control for assistance with the survey information sheet and for general comments on this chapter. The authors accept sole responsibility for all remaining errors in this work.

NOTES

1. The scope problem occurs when there is no observed variation in values between high quantities of the good and low quantities of the good. For example, when respondents appear to value 100 birds the same as 1000 birds. The embedding problem occurs when respondents appear to value a different character set of the good than that presented in the researcher defined scenario. For example they value the environment as a whole instead of a single lake. These two problems are similar, thus in this chapter we are specifically referring to the scope problem when the *quantity* of the good is not clearly defined and we refer to the embedding problem when the *character* of the good is not clearly defined.
2. Evidence also suggests that presentation effects extend beyond hypothetical valuation statements to actual averting behaviour (Smith et al., 1991; Smith et al., 1995).
3. A fourth block was included that used an alternative causal agent, PCB, with mortality risk; however, this data is excluded in this study.
4. The survey and information set were tested using four focus groups with residents of Canton NC, Sylva NC, Cullowhee NC and Newport TN. Focus group participants were self-selected from invitations sent to civic groups in each location. A total of 40 persons participated.
5. 'Insurance' refers to policy options that reduce health risks after exposure and 'protection' refers to policy options that reduce the risk of exposure to the environmental hazard. 'Private' actions are those taken by the respondent and 'collective' actions are those provided by local, state or federal government.
6. Inconsistency was determined by a comparison of the respondent's WTP value for their most preferred policy approach and their least preferred approach.
7. This excludes the PCB sample data.
8. *Insurance* refers to policy options that reduce the severity of the health risks after exposure, and *protection* refers to policy options that reduce the probability of exposure to the environmental hazard.
9. There were five sets of bids: Set 1 – $5, $25, $250; Set 2 – $10, $50, $500; Set 3 – $25, $100, $1000; Set 4 – $50, $250, $2000; Set 5 – $75, $400, $2500.

10.   If we expect respondents to respond in a similar fashion when given a mortality, morbidity, or combined survey, a pooled sample is appropriate. Due to the small sample size
of each of the split samples, we use a pooled model with interactive binary variables to
capture the sample differences.
11.   These calculations use a simple approach to annualizing costs over ten years purely for
illustrative purposes and a simple mean of the model estimates for WTP of $542.00 paid
this year for a reduction in health risks this year of 55 percent.

REFERENCES

Adamowicz W., J. Swait, P. Boxall, J. Louviere and M. Williams (1997), 'Perceptions
versus objective measures of environmental quality in combined revealed and
stated preference models of environmental valuation', *Journal of Environmental
Economics and Management,* **32** (1), 65–84.
Alberini, A., M. Cropper, T. Fu, A. Krupnick, J. Liu, D. Shaw and W. Harrington
(1997), 'Valuing health effects of air pollution in developing countries: the case
of Taiwan', *Journal of Environmental Economics and Management,* **34** (2),
107–26.
Arrow, K., R. Solow, E. Leamer, P. Portney, R. Radner and H. Schuman (1993),
'Report of the NOAA panel on contingent valuation', *Federal Register,* **58** (10),
January 15, 1993.
Blamey, R.K., J.W. Bennett and M.D. Morrison (1999), 'Yea-saying in contingent
valuation surveys', *Land Economics,* **75** (1), 126–41.
Cherry, T.L., T.D. Crocker and J.F. Shogren (2001), 'Rationality spillovers', *Journal
of Environmental Economics and Management,* forthcoming.
Dickie, M. and S. Gerking (1991), 'Valuing reduced morbidity: a household pro-
duction approach', *Southern Economic Journal,* **57** (3), 690–702.
Dillman, D.A. (1978), *Mail and Telephone Surveys: The Total Design Method,* New
York: John Wiley and Sons.
Ehrlich, I. and G. Becker (1972), 'Market insurance, self-protection, and self-insur-
ance', *Journal of Political Economy,* **80**, 623–48.
Fischoff, B. (1975), 'Hindsight ≠ Foresight: the effect of outcome knowledge on
judgment under uncertainty', *Journal of Experimental Psychology: Human
Perception and Performance,* **1** (3), 288–99.
Fries, E.E. and A.R. Gable (1997), 'Defining commodities in stated-preference
experiments: some suggestions', *AERE Newsletter,* **17** (1), 14–18.
Gregory, R., J. Flynn, S.M. Johnson, T.A. Satterfield, P. Slovic and R. Wagner
(1997), 'Decision-pathway surveys: a tool for resource managers', *Land
Economics,* **73** (2), 240–54.
Hammitt, J.K. and J.D. Graham (1999), 'Willingness to pay for health protection:
inadequate sensitivity to probability', *Journal of Risk and Uncertainty,* **18** (1),
33–62.
Hanemann, M. (1984), 'Welfare evaluations in contingent valuation experiments
with discrete responses', *American Journal of Agricultural Economics,* 66, 332–41.
Hanemann, W.M. (1994), 'Valuing the environment through contingent valuation',
The Journal of Economic Perspectives, **8** (4), 19–43.
Herriges, J. and J. Shogren (1996), 'Starting point bias in dichotomous choice questions valuation with follow-up questioning', *Journal of Environmental Economics
and Management,* **30** (1) 112–31.

Hoevenagel, R. and J.W. van der Linden (1993), 'Effects of different descriptions of the ecological good on willingness to pay values', *Ecological Economics*, **7** (3), 223–38.

Johansson, P.O. (1993), *Cost–Benefit Analysis of Environmental Change*, Cambridge: Cambridge University Press.

Kahneman, D. and J.L. Knetsch (1992), 'Valuing public goods: the purchase of moral satisfaction', *Journal of Environmental Economics and Management*, **22** (1), 57–70.

Kask, S.B. and S. Maani (1992), 'Uncertainty, information, and hedonic pricing', *Land Economics*, **68** (2), 170–84.

Kriström, B. (1997), 'Spike models in contingent valuation', *American Journal of Agricultural Economics*, **79**, 1013–23.

Krupnick, A., A. Alberini, M. Cropper, N. Simon, B. O'Brien, R. Goeree and M. Heintzelman (2000), *Age, Health, and the Willingness to Pay for Mortality Risk Reduction: A CV Survey of Ontario Residents*, Resources for the Future Discussion paper 00–37, Washington, DC, September 2000.

Kunreuther, H., R. Ginsberg, L. Miller, S. Phillip, P. Slovic, B. Borkan and N. Katz (1978), *Disaster Insurance Protection: Public Policy Lessons*, New York: John Wiley and Sons.

Lichtenstein, S., P. Slovic, B. Fischoff, M. Laymen and B. Combs (1978), 'Judged frequency of lethal events', *Journal of Experimental Psychology: Human Learning and Memory*, **4** (6), 551–78.

Loomis, J.B. and P.H. duVair (1993), 'Evaluation of the effect of alternative risk communication devices on willingness to pay: results from a dichotomous choice contingent valuation experiment', *Land Economics*, **69** (3), 287–98.

Randall, A. and J.P. Hoehn (1996), 'Embedding in market demand systems', *Journal of Environmental Economics and Management*, **30** (3), 369–80.

Ready, R.C., J.C. Whitehead and G.C. Blomquist (1995), 'Contingent valuation when respondents are ambivalent', *Journal of Environmental Economics and Management*, **29**, 181–96.

Schmidt, K.F. (1992), 'Dioxin's other face: portrait of an environmental "hormone"', *Science News*, **141**, 24–7.

Shogren, J.F. (1990), 'The impact of self-protection and self-insurance on individual response to risk', *Journal of Risk and Uncertainty*, **3** (2), 191–204.

Shogren, J.F. and T.D. Crocker (1991), 'Risk, self-protection, and ex ante economic valuation', *Journal of Environmental Economics and Management*, **21**, 1–15.

Shogren, J.F. and T.D. Crocker (1999), 'Risk and its consequences', *Journal of Environmental Economics and Management*, **37**, 44–51.

Smith, V.K. and W.H. Desvousges (1987), 'An empirical analysis of the economic value of risk changes', *Journal of Political Economy*, **95** (1), 89–114.

Smith, V.K. and F.R. Johnson (1988), 'How do risk perceptions respond to information? The case of Radon', *Review of Economics and Statistics*, **70** (Feb.), 1–8.

Smith, V.K., W.H. Desvousges and J.W. Payne (1991), *Does the Framing of Risk Information Influence Mitigating Behavior*, Resources for the Future, Quality of the Environment Division Discussion Paper: QE92–03.

Smith, V.K., W.H. Desvousges and J.W. Payne (1995), 'Do risk information programs promote mitigating behavior', *Journal of Risk and Uncertainty*, **10** (3), 203–21.

U.S. Environmental Protection agency (USEPA) Region IV (1989a), Fact Sheet: Application for National Pollution Discharge Elimination System permit to discharge treated waste water to U.S. waters, Appl NC0000272, July.

USEPA Region IV (1989b), Fact Sheet amendment based on comments received July 12, 1985–August 25, 1989, September.

Viscusi, W.K. (1989), 'Prospective reference theory: toward an explanation of the paradoxes', *Journal of Risk and Uncertainty*, **2** (3), 235–63.

Viscusi, W.K. and W.A. Magat (1987), *Learning About Risk: Consumer And Worker Responses To Hazard Information*, Cambridge: Harvard University Press.

Viscusi, W.K., W.A. Magat and J. Huber (1987), 'An investigation of the rationality of consumer valuations of multiple health risks', *RAND Journal of Economics*, **18** (4).

12. Trade-off at the trough: TMDLs and the evolving status of US water quality policy

Carol Mansfield and V. Kerry Smith*

1. INTRODUCTION

Few important choices are easy. In the aftermath of hurricanes Dennis and Floyd, many North Carolinians felt policymakers should rethink the role of animal agriculture (especially hogs) in the state's future. As a result, it should not have been surprising in July 2000 when the Attorney General announced he had negotiated a 'surprise' agreement with a consortium of producers led by Smithfield Foods to move toward eliminating waste lagoons.[1] The agreement calls for an evaluation of the technical feasibility, incremental private costs, and impact on industry competitiveness of new waste management technologies.[2] It does not require consideration of whether these changes in industry practices are worth the effort.

A second, equally important, influence on the design and analysis of national water pollution policy took place in July as well. EPA introduced a major change in policies intended to enhance water quality using the TMDL (total maximum daily load) provisions of the Clean Water Act. The EPA strategy takes a watershed perspective and requires states to develop mechanisms to evaluate water bodies. This new approach promises to direct attention to non-point source pollution – agricultural runoff and animal waste, urban stormwater, and even atmospheric deposition.

The programme calls for ambient water quality standards and state-led implementation plans. The TMDL framework poses significant challenges for states to design defensible plans for source reductions that will bring impaired waterbodies into attainment. As point and nonpoint sources face the increasing control costs from these new sets of regulations, many in the impacted industries as well as in local communities are asking, what do these new restrictions yield in beneficial results? Most economists would answer these calls for information by citing measures of the avoided damages to environmental resources. By contrast, policymakers typically would limit their attention to estimates gauging whether the 'costs' of the programmes, in terms of output and employment losses for the affected industries, are held within manageable limits.

In the past, both groups have literally 'talked around' each other. Economists dismiss the policymaker as asking the wrong questions and policymakers conclude economists provide answers irrelevant to their decisions. In this chapter we argue they have actually focused on different aspects of problems that ideally should be treated as giving rise to general equilibrium (GE) effects on a regional economy. This chapter proposes an alternative to efforts to compute GE benefit–cost analysis. In the process we uncover a surprising result. Households seem to have strong preferences for policy elements intended to respond to GE income effects. Thus, even if the analytical machinery were available to reliably compute GE welfare measures, there are other issues that need to be addressed. These issues relate to households' preferences for how compensation to mitigate GE effects is in fact undertaken.

Concern over GE effects is not always warranted, and here is where conventional impact analysis can help. It offers a gauge of how large increases or decreases in a sector's output can impact a regional economy and, in turn, generate GE income effects. It may also generate price effects, but these would not be measured in an impact setting. To develop our argument we selected animal agriculture in North Carolina.

Between 1987 and 1996 the sales of hogs in North Carolina grew by 154 percent. North Carolina's hog production in 1997 was second only to Iowa, surpassing tobacco as the number one agricultural product for the state. The growth in the hog industry is linked to an increase in corporate hog operations. These farms are contract operations with large-sized units that are separated into three stages of production – weaning to feeder, feeder to farrow, and farrow to finishing operations.[3] This has led to higher concentrations of hogs living in smaller areas and corresponding problems of waste treatment and disposal. Environmental problems from these operations received their first widespread public attention in June 1995, with the rupture of a waste lagoon and release of twenty-five million gallons of waste into the New River. Nearly five years later most critics of the industry incorrectly attribute *all* nutrient-related problems of declining water quality, increased algae blooms, and fish kills, to the hog operations.

Our analysis suggests several conclusions. First, hog production is an important source of income and employment in Eastern North Carolina that would be hard to replace. Second, with any impact analysis, the overall effects – positive and negative – have effects in different sectors. In this context, it is important to recognize another important source of income to coastal areas in North Carolina. The state's environmental amenities are complementary inputs (if not essential) to its tourism. Aggregate analysis of this sector's direct and indirect effects suggest changes in spending on tourism per dollar have *larger* effects outside the sector than spending that same dollar on hog production. At some point, negative information may sharply impact recreation spending. This loss is a transfer from one area of the economy to another in just the same way as the direct and indirect spending 'created' by increases in hog production. Overall, then, it is important in counting up the impacts of output transfers that accompany the growth in any one sector to take account of the potential negative external effects on resources that sustain other sectors' demands.

Finally, neither of these evaluations include any of the welfare losses North Carolina households might experience from the diminished environmental quality associated with increases in the hog operations. We measure these losses using estimates of households' willingness to pay to reduce the negative effects of hog operations in the state. In a statewide random sample (conducted before the widespread polarization in public attitudes) we found that North Carolina households are willing to pay to regulate the operation of hog farms. Moreover, what is especially important about these findings is that the willingness to pay differs significantly if the regulations 'cost-share' the capital costs with those being regulated. Attempts to adjust, through the definition of a policy, for GE income effects cannot be accepted as corresponding to a theoretically consistent GE benefit measure. Rather, they are measures of the households' willingness to pay for a plan with some displacement adjustments. Thus, a composite or complementary strategy that uses impact analysis to identify areas likely to have GE income effects, along with CV surveys for 'commodities' (or policies) that build in compensation need to be investigated to learn how these other aspects of a plan would influence household WTP.

Our analysis is reported in the next three sections of the chapter. Section 2 considers the conceptual link between impact analysis and benefit–cost analysis, suggesting one reason why it is appropriate that the former attracts increasing attention as the scale of the project or regulation grows. In Section 3 we describe how the IMPLAN 1994 Input–Output model for North Carolina was used to evaluate the effects of hog production and tourism losses on output and employment in North Carolina. In Section 4 we outline the key features of a survey designed to evaluate regulatory options derived for waste management at hog farms. Section 5 discusses the implications of these two types of analyses for the use of benefit–cost and impact analyses in policy.

2.   INCOME CHANGES AND BENEFIT MEASUREMENT

Conventional practice in benefit–cost analysis holds that the action being evaluated is small in comparison to the economy as a whole. The primary reason for making this assumption is to avoid considering general equilibrium price and income effects. General equilibrium (GE) responses have three important implications for benefit measurement. The first, and most commonly identified issue, involves the price changes that accompany large-scale interventions.[4] To develop the required measures of consumer and producer surplus along general equilibrium demand and supply functions, we must be able to compute the GE prices resulting from any proposed policy measure.[5]

Market distortions, including taxes, are the second consideration in evaluating large policies. If we assume the primary concern for GE welfare analysis arises with measuring changes along the GE demand and supply schedules and measuring any policy-induced income changes, we do not escape the need for some type of model to compute how prices and incomes adjust. Indeed, even the Harberger (1971) approximations for GE welfare gains and losses require that one compute the changes in expenditures on related goods that would be needed to measure the lump sum transfers he assumed would be made to households in order to account, approximately, for the GE income effects in his framework (see Hines, 1999, for a discussion).[6]

The problem becomes even more complex when we consider losses that involve changes in non-market amenities that induce changes in the prices of market goods. While there is little direct experience with these *situations*, what is known suggests that comparison of GE and PE estimates is specific to the model and policy context. For example, in a trade context, Smith and Espinosa (1996) found that omitting environmental effects can change the sign of the general equilibrium measure of the Hicksian compensating variation for a policy change involving a 50 percent reciprocal reduction in the non-tariff barriers to trade in the United Kingdom and each of its European Union trading regions for goods from the durable manufacturing sector. An analysis for the United Kingdom, leaving out the mortality effects of air pollution, would conclude that the change leads to a positive impact, while including them would reverse the conclusion. The same type of change for Germany did not reverse the sign of the net benefit measure but did reduce the measure of net benefits by about 40 percent.

Thus, until we have greater experience with incorporating amenities in GE models, a composite analysis may be warranted. This would first evaluate whether a sector that is proposed for regulation is important to the

Table 12.1   Growth effects on the North Carolina economy: IMPLAN estimates

Source of Growth or Decline	Output Millions of Dollars	Output Multiplier	Employment (Full-time Equivalent Jobs)	Employment Multiplier
I. Direct				
Hogs (+154%)	2704	1.86	34306	2.20
Meat packing (+9.8%)	184	1.79	1573	5.57
Sausage (+47.4%)	1007	2.05	8201	3.47
Total	3895		44080	
II. Indirect				
Coastal tourism, low impact	−23.37	2.56	−432	1.79
Coastal tourism, medium impact	−46.27	2.56	−908	1.79
Coastal tourism, high impact	−344.04	2.56	−6756	1.79

economy via an impact analysis. A second step would estimate household preferences for policies that address income effects of proposed regulations. To the extent an exogenous (from the perspective of the policy being evaluated) distortion in an economy gives rise to income or expense to a household, GE effects require we consider the income changes stemming from the effects of that policy on them.[7] Finally, large interventions, capable of economy-wide effects, are unlikely to be consistent with the assumption of costless adjustment (and, implicitly, full employment of resources before and after the action).

3.   MEASURING THE INCOME AND EMPLOYMENT EFFECTS OF HOG PRODUCTION AND TOURISM

As a practical matter, with a linear impact model we can consider either increases or decreases in hog production to illustrate the issues associated with the income effects of a policy. We selected increases because they were easier to propose and benchmark to existing conditions (in the absence of information on the actual costs of controlling nutrients on large hog farms).

The hog industry in North Carolina has grown dramatically over the last decade. Between 1987 and 1996, hog sales in North Carolina rose by 154 percent, meat packing activity increased 9.8 percent and sausage production increased 47.4 percent (see Table 12.1). The total number of hogs had increased 9.8 million by 1997.[8] In the beginning of the hog debate in North Carolina, few people made the connection between growth in the hog industry and losses in the tourism sector from declining water quality. 'I don't see where [hog farming] affects tourism that much,' said one farmer. 'Have you smelled a hog farm at the beach? I've been to nearly all of our beaches and I never smelled one.'[9] This anecdote misses the interconnections between North Carolina's watersheds and coastal quality. It also overlooks the important role that information, and especially media attention, serves in crystallizing consumer perceptions of deteriorated quality.

Several studies document the impact of information about a real or potential hazard on behaviour including food safety warnings (Foster and Just, 1989, Swartz and Strand, 1981; and Smith et al., 1988). Others have considered the response of property markets to news about natural hazards (see Murdoch et al., 1993) or landfills with potential risks (see McClelland et al., 1990 and Gayer et al., 2000).[10] In each case the announcement of the potential risk triggers a heightened awareness of quality concerns and averting behaviour.

We assume that there is the potential for a similar behavioural response by tourists to media warnings about the consequences of excess nutrients contaminating the quality of coastal waterways. The most serious health threat mentioned in the newspaper stories was from the pfiesteria bacteria, which is suspected of causing fish kills and health problems in humans. News about the hog industry and potential water quality problems in North Carolina appeared in the national presses (for example, *The Washington Post* and *The New York Times*) and even international presses (for example, *The Economist*).

Our analysis uses the IMPLAN input–output model for North Carolina in the base year 1994. Rather than attempt to develop a baseline of the economy without the hog industry (or with a substantially smaller scale), we selected 1994 as our baseline. Approximately 50 percent of the growth in the hog industry between 1987 and 1996 (using cash receipts in 1996 dollars) occurred by 1994. The remaining 50 percent came in the next two years. By assuming 154 percent growth in hog sales in 1994 (along with a 9.8 percent increase in meatpacking and 47.4 percent increase in sausage production) we are effectively calculating the impact of double the increase that was actually realized between 1994 and 1996. Table 12.1 lists the increases in final demand used in our IMPLAN calculations.

To compute the possible effects on tourism, we developed three tourism impact scenarios. Based on the past research and wage trends, we identified a potential range for the impacts of negative information on tourism: high impact (29 percent reduction in coastal tourism), medium impact (3.9 percent reduction) and low impact (1.97 percent reduction). While the articles did not examine tourism, they do suggest a possible range of consumer responses to negative publicity. Smith et al. (1988) examined the decrease in demand for milk in Hawaii after some milk was discovered to be contaminated with heptachlor. The contaminated milk was banned and recalled, but sales of uncontaminated milk dropped 29 percent as a result of the negative publicity. In their analysis, it appears that positive news stories and statements by the government and industry about the safety of the remaining milk for sale had less impact than the negative news stories. Mercury contamination in pheasants led to a drop in hunting in Oregon (Shulstad and Stoevener, 1978). Based on the information reported in this study, the average value of hunting, at the seasonal level, was estimated to have declined by 27 to 29 percent as a result of reductions in hunting activity. The medium impact scenario was derived from an article by Johnson (1988), in which he calculated that negative reports in the media about EDB contamination led to sales losses for grain and packaged mixes of 3.9 percent to 6.2 percent. Finally, the 1.97 percent reduction rate is based on the difference between predicted and actual tourism wages in North Carolina in 1996. Using a simple regression of wages on year dummies from 1987 to 1995, we predicted 1996 total wage payments in the tourism sector and calculated the percentage difference between actual and predicted 1996 wage payments.

Within the IMPLAN model we focused on three tourism-related industries (eating and drinking establishments, hotels and lodging, and amusement). We assumed losses would be confined to 19 coastal counties. These counties account for 14.2 percent of the estimated expenditures on tourism in 1997. To derive the effects of tourism decline on the North Carolina economy for each impact scenario, we multiplied the 1997 tourism expenditures in the 19 coastal counties by the effect implied by each of the three estimated declines (that is, 71 percent, 96.1 percent, and 98.03 percent of baseline tourism expenditures) and estimated the overall effect of each on tourism in the state (that is, 95.9 percent, 99.4 percent, and 99.4 percent of baseline). These percentages were then applied to the three tourism sectors along with the increases in the hog industry related sectors.

From Table 12.1, the growth in the three hog-related sectors resulted in roughly $3.9 billion dollars of increased output and 44 000 jobs. The results for the three tourism impact scenarios are presented in the bottom half of Table 12.1. The impact ranges from $23.4 million to $344 million in lost tourism dollars and between 432 and 6756 fewer jobs. To provide some perspective for these estimates, North Carolina's gross state product in 1997 dollars was $202 billion dollars. Almost 5 percent of this was accounted for by tourism ($9.8 billion). Thus the proposed growth in animal agriculture (about 50 percent beyond what was realized in 1996, using the 1987 base) would equal about 20 percent of *total* tourism spending in the state. Our conservative estimates of the losses, using the largest impact rate (29 percent) are small in comparison to the economic activity generated by animal agriculture. This disparity in the scale of impacts between animal agriculture and tourism helps to explain why state policymakers are concerned about regulations affecting this industry. However, the output and employment figures do not tell the whole story and may not be the most appropriate way to evaluate the input–output results.

To remove the effects of the overall size of each of the sectors involved and the role of scale for our judgements about the importance of these impacts, we can also consider how the output and employment multipliers compare. Table 12.1 presents these results. A $1 increase in demand for hog products resulted in $1.86–$2.05 worth of increased total output for the North Carolina economy. By contrast, the same dollar increase in tourism would increase overall state output by $2.56. Of course, what is at issue is not a comparison of increasing hog production versus tourism. The point of our comparison is that further increases in hog operations could trigger negative perceptions of North Carolina's environmental resources and induce *losses* in tourism spending.

These effects are unlikely to be dollar for dollar. Nonetheless, these multipliers allow us to gauge, in an approximate way, what the size of the loss in tourism needs to be in order to be concerned about how animal agricultural and tourism are connected. If tourism declined by about $0.73 for every dollar spent on hog production then we would have no net gain in overall state output from growth in animal agriculture.[11] As we noted, the available evidence from the literature suggests this decline is unlikely. Tourism effects alone are unlikely to offset the output and employment effects of animal agriculture, especially when we consider that the region in North Carolina (Duplin and Sampson counties) where animal agriculture is contributing the most to local incomes has very little tourist activity.

These findings suggest, based on the employment effects of the growth in the hog sector, that a stringent set of regulations could have important impacts on changes in regional income in areas where the hog operations are most concentrated. Any avoided negative effects on amenity-based sectors because of new regulations are unlikely to be large enough to offset them. As a result, it is prudent to consider how the benefits of protecting coastal amenities (through regulations on effluents from animal agriculture) would be affected by incorporating some strategy for mitigating these indirect effects. These adjustments could include compensation to those experiencing income losses or cost-sharing provisions for the producers adopting the new waste management technologies.

While the regulations could be described as imposing the equivalent of a virtual tax on operations, the effects most relevant to households in the region are likely to be income effects. This finding would suggest we should evaluate the benefits arising from policies that not only regulate sources of environmental externalities from animal agriculture but also attempt to mitigate the income effects on farmers facing these regulations to reduce the direct output and employment impacts of any new waste management regulations.

4. HOUSEHOLDS' WILLINGNESS TO PAY TO REDUCE THE EFFECTS OF ANIMAL AGRICULTURE

To measure the benefits associated with the potential improvements in water quality resulting from stricter regulation of the hog industry and in particular the treatment of hog waste on large farms, we conducted a contingent valuation (CV) survey of North Carolina residents. The survey was conducted between October 1995 and January 1996, using a telephone–mail–telephone format. The first telephone interview collected some demographic and attitude data, as well as the response to one short CV question on an unrelated topic.[12] The respondents were then asked to participate in a second telephone interview. Those who agreed were mailed a booklet describing two separate regulatory proposals. One proposal related to regulating hog farms, and the other proposal related to either wastewater disposal into the ocean or a beach renourishment project.[13]

Our impact analysis suggested the scale of the hog industry and its rapid growth were important to the direct and indirect growth of output and employment in the state. Regulations of the externalities due to hog waste and odour are expected to raise costs substantially and may, as a result, have large negative effects on output and employment. While these are not the full general equilibrium income effects envisioned in Harberger's measures for welfare change, as we indicated in the previous section, they do provide an indication that income effects are likely to be important.

To evaluate whether households have preferences for policy adjustments in response to GE income effects, we have investigated how independent respondents' choices and implied willingness to pay estimates would be altered when the environmental policy explicitly identifies the need to help those impacted by the regulations to avoid negative employment and income impacts. Two potential policies were designed. One focuses exclusively on monitoring to assure regulation on annual waste is enforced. The second considers the same regulation policy combined with an effort to provide financial assistance to farmers to reduce the initial cost impacts of adapting to the regulation.[14]

This was operationalized by preparing two versions of the survey information booklets. The survey booklets described two different regulatory proposals for controlling the wastes generated through the operations of hog farms. Respondents were randomly assigned one of the two – a cost-share plan and an enforcement plan. Both plans closely followed proposals that have been under consideration by the North Carolina legislature during and after the survey, and both plans presented the same hog waste management recommendations. The top half of Table 12.2 contains the text of the management plan contained in the information booklets. Where the two plans differ is in the use of the additional tax revenue to be collected under the plans. Under the enforcement plan, the state would use the extra tax revenue to hire more inspectors for better monitoring and enforcement of the regulations. Under the cost-share proposal, in addition to paying for more inspections, farmers and taxpayers would share the cost of implementing the waste treatment and disposal technologies. The state would collect tax revenue to subsidize one-half of the cost to farmers of the waste treatment technology required under the management plan.

The booklets associated with these plans used the same colour photos of hog operations to describe the water quality problems that have been associated with hog farms. In addition, both booklets described the economic importance of hog farming to Eastern North Carolina. At the close of the booklets, each described in qualitative terms how the regulations would help reduce nutrients from large hog operations in ground and surface water and reduce the probability of future waste spills into the rivers of North Carolina. However, those receiving the cost-share booklet also received more information about the economic benefits of the hog industry and the importance of the industry to Eastern North Carolina, along with a graph of the increases in property tax revenue and employment associated with the hog industry. The enforcement plan booklet contained an extra paragraph describing a very large hog waste spill that occurred in June 1995, along with a diagram of the impact that a hog waste spill has on a river. The lower half of Table 12.2 contains the text that is unique to the booklet for each proposal.

The proposed plans in our study differ in the distribution of costs. Farmers bear the full costs of purchasing the required waste treatment technology under the enforcement plan, while they bear only part of the cost under the cost-share plan. Neither plan fully guarantees that the environmental problems associated with hog farms will be eliminated.

After the participants received the information booklets, they were contacted for the second telephone interview. During this interview, the respondents were asked two CV questions, one for each plan described in their information booklet (the hog management plan and independent plans that described either wastewater disposal into the ocean or beach renourishment).[15] Table 12.3 contains the text of the hog waste management CV questions that were read to the respondents over the phone during the second interview. Both CV questions reiterate that the new regulations would help prevent water quality problems associated with hog waste, but would also cost money for hog farmers and could negatively impact the economy of Eastern North Carolina.

A.   Structure of Survey

Initially, 1002 households in North Carolina were contacted and completed the first stage interview. The first stage interview averaged approximately 14 minutes. Of these, 826 agreed to take part in the second interview and 540 completed the second interview for a second stage response rate of 66 percent.[16] The second interview was conducted with the same individual who had participated in the first. Each respondent was asked if they read the booklet describing a waste management plan.[17] The primary objective of the second survey is to elicit respondents' choices concerning one of the two waste management plans for hog operations. Table 12.3 provides the text of the questions, along with the design points for the proposed payment associated with the plans. The format was designed to conform with what has emerged as the preferred approach for contingent valuation questions – a discrete response – take it or leave it choice.[18] The second interviews lasted approximately 12 minutes.

The overall sample (based on the first interview) was generally familiar with the issue of hog farming in North Carolina. Table 12.4 provides a simple descriptive summary of some of the key variables in the survey. Thirty-two percent thought that regulating hog farms to reduce the chance of future waste spills was somewhat important, while 44 percent thought it was very important (the third alternative offered was a response of not important at all). Of the 540 respondents completing the second interview, 77 percent had read or heard the problems associated with large hog farms. Furthermore, 79 percent of the respondents thought that the nutrients released from hog farms had the same or greater potential for impacts compared to the use of agricultural fertilizer. Of the 1002 people in the full sample, 296 had gone fishing during the past summer in a lake or river anywhere in the US with an average of 13 trips among those who took at least one trip. Also, 196 people took an average of six fishing trips in the ocean anywhere in the US. In North Carolina, 490 respondents had been to a North Carolina beach an average of six times in the past summer.

Table 12.2 Describing programmes for the contingent value questions information booklets

Management Plan

Because the primary source of the problem is large hog farms, further regulations and permits for *large* farms have been proposed. One possible programme would introduce, over the next five years, a new system of waste management with:

(1) waste lagoons required to use mechanical techniques to increase the natural decay of the manure and reduce odour;

(2) lagoons reinforced to reduce the risks of future spills and with plastic liners to prevents seepage of nutrients into groundwater;

(3) annual inspections required along with limits on the spraying of waste within 1000 feet of a wetland or a river.

There would be no change in the regulations facing small farms (250 hogs or less).

Text Differences in Booklets

Enforcement proposal	Cost-share proposal
In June, during a period of heavy rain, a large pond (or lagoon) used to store hog waste collapsed. This caused 25 million gallons of this waste to enter the New River above Richlands. Figure 1 provides a map and description of the effects of the waste on the water quality and the fish in the river. This event focused attention on the location of these hog farms as well as on the storage and disposal of the wastes from their operations.	The growth in the NC hog industry has brought substantial benefits to the state, and especially for the eastern counties where, historically, there has been high unemployment and low income levels. For example, over *$1 billion dollars* worth of hogs from North Carolina were sold in 1994. Moreover, these livestock operations have other effects throughout the economy. The people who work in the industry purchase other goods and services. The industry also uses other materials, feed, fuel, and services. Economists at North Carolina State University have estimated that these other effects add the equivalent of about 15000 full-time jobs in 1993. They have calculated that each dollar in increased sales by hog producers generates another 81 cents in other sales in North Carolina.

Figure 1 illustrates the positive effects of hog farms on employment and support for local government operations. In 1994, for example, $2.84 million in property taxes was paid on NC hog production facilities.

Nutrients from this industry must therefore be seen as part of the overall nutrient management issue faced by the state. The hog industry is only one contributor to existing levels of nutrients in surface waters. Other types of agriculture, municipal wastewater treatment facilities, and air pollution from cars and factories have significant impacts as well.

This proposal, even if introduced over a five-year period, will impose substantially higher operating costs on NC hog producers. Maintaining the economic benefits to the region will require some cost sharing with private farmers. This will allow NC operators to remain competitive with producers in other states and help to assure the viability of these activities in the state while at the same time addressing the nutrient management concerns.

Table 12.3 Contingent value questions: second telephone interview

Enforcement proposal	Cost-share proposal
The booklet described a plan with new regulations for reducing the potential contamination of coastal waters from releases of hog waste in the eastern counties of North Carolina.	The booklet described a plan with new regulations for reducing the potential contamination of coastal waters from releases of hog waste in the eastern counties of North Carolina.
9. Do you remember the plan? 01 yes 02 no (go to 9b)	9. Do you remember the plan? 01 yes 02 no (go to 9b)
9a. As you recall, the plan applies to large hog farms. (go to 9c)	9a. As you recall, the plan applies to large hog farms. (go to 9c)
9b. The plan applies only to large hog farms.	9b. The plan applies only to large hog farms.
9c. It would require three changes in their operations. Their waste lagoons would be required to use mechanical techniques to increase the natural decay of the waste and reduce odor. Reinforced lagoons with plastic liners and annual inspections would be required. This would reduce the chances of accident spills in the leakage of nutrients into groundwater. And finally, spraying of waste would not be allowed within 1000 feet of a wetland or a river. This plan would be in addition to other actions the state is now undertaking.	9c. It would require three changes in their operations. Their waste lagoons would be required to use mechanical techniques to increase the natural decay of the waste and reduce odor. Reinforced lagoons with plastic liners and annual inspections would be required. This would reduce the chances of accident spills in the leakage of nutrients into groundwater. And finally, spraying of waste would not be allowed within 1000 feet of a wetland or a river. This plan would be in addition to other actions the state is now undertaking.
9d. Would you like me to repeat anything about the plan? 01 yes 02 no	9d. Would you like me to repeat anything about the plan? 01 yes 02 no

10. These requirements would raise the costs of operations at hog farms. Because they would be among the most stringent in the nation, it is anticipated that some farms would close and the major firms in the industry would move some operations outside the state. This would increase unemployment in eastern North Carolina.

Here is how the plan for increased regulations and monitoring of the large hog farms would be paid for. Large hog farms would be required to pay for the mechanical processing of the hog waste, the enhanced lagoons, and the controls on spraying. The state would pay for the increased inspections to assure the plan works.

To pay for these annual inspections, there would have to be an increase in North Carolina residents' state income taxes. For your household it would be an additional (randomize: $10, $25, $50, $75, $100, $125, $375, $750) each year. This would be in addition to the amount you now pay in state income taxes. This payment would be required each year to maintain this program. Please keep in mind your current income and the things you now buy.

10. These requirements would raise the costs of operations at hog farms. Because they would be among the most stringent in the nation, it is anticipated that some farms would close and the major firms in the industry would move some operations outside the state. This would increase unemployment in eastern North Carolina. To attempt to reduce these impacts, the plan includes provisions to share the capital costs associated with meeting the new regulations.

Here is how the plan for increased regulations and monitoring of the large hog farms would be paid for. Large hog farms would be required to pay for the mechanical processing of the hog waste, the enhanced lagoons, and the controls on spraying. The state would pay for the increased inspections to assure the plan works. The state would also share the farmers' additional costs by paying one-half the initial capital costs required by these regulations.

To pay for the cost-sharing plan and the annual inspections, there would have to be an increase in North Carolina residents' state income taxes. For your household it would be an additional (randomize: $10, $25, $50, $75, $100, $125, $375, $750) each year. This would be in addition to the amount you now pay in state income taxes. This payment would be required each year to maintain this program. Please keep in mind your current income and the things you now buy.

Table 12.3 – Continued

Enforcement proposal	Cost-share proposal
If this plan to regulate large hog farms were on a statewide referendum with your taxes increased by (repeat amount from above) and you could vote on the plan, would you vote for or against it?	If this plan to regulate large hog farms were on a statewide referendum with your taxes increased by (repeat amount from above) and you could vote on the plan, would you vote for or against it?
01 for the plan (go to 12a)	01 for the plan (go to 12a)
02 against the plan (go to 12)	02 against the plan (go to 12)
03 don't know (don't offer, go to 11a)	03 don't know (don't offer, go to 11a)

Table 12.4   Respondent characteristics for two samples[a]

Variable	Description	Enforcement proposal sample	Cost-share proposal sample
Vote 'Yes' on proposal	% voting 'Yes' on Proposal	0.50 (0.50)	0.43 (0.50)
Tax Amt	Amount taxes would increase under proposal	$10–$750	$10–$750
Spillike	How likely are future spills if regulations and inspections are not increased? 1 = not likely, 10 = very likely	7.51 (2.26)	7.44 (2.22)
Exfarmer	Do you currently live or work on a farm or have you ever lived or worked on a farm? (yes = 1)	0.49 (0.50)	0.46 (0.50)
Married	= 1 if married	0.66 (0.48)	0.70 (0.46)
White	= 1 if Caucasian	0.83 (0.37)	0.88 (0.32)
Hsize	number of people in household	2.72 (1.40)	2.44 (1.09)
Female	= 1 if female	0.52 (0.50)	0.58 (0.50)
Femploy	= 1 if employed full-time	0.62 (0.49)	0.57 (0.50)
Hinc	Household income	40328.57 (28185.69)	39268.65 (25859.35)
Age	Age in years	46.99 (14.56)	47.92 (15.54)
Colgrad	= 1 if graduated from college or graduate school	0.34 (0.47)	0.33 (0.47)
Number of observations		167	160

Note: [a] Standard errors are reported in parentheses.

The framework describing the relationship between an individual's choice to vote for one of the plans to regulate hog operations and his (or her) willingness to pay can be derived from either an indirect utility function (Hanemann, 1984) or a Hurwicz and Uzawa (1971) income compensation function. The latter is an alternative form of the utility comparison envisioned in the definition of Hicksian willingness to pay.

Two aspects of this structure are important to the results derived from discrete response CV questions. First, the estimating equation implicitly restricts the underlying preferences. This point is relevant to any model that is specified to describe outcomes that are assumed to arise from consumer preferences. The ability to recover a different mix of parameters under one organizing framework arises from the restrictions it imposes on preferences.[19] Second, and equally important, these choice models estimate respondents' willingness to pay *for the plans* that are described, *not* for changes in environmental amenities. Of course, the objective of the descriptions of these plans is to provide a convincing method to change amenities. In practice many analysts interpret the results as estimates of the willingness to pay for the resource change.[20] This second point is especially important to our application because the two CV questions have been designed to suggest that the change in amenities is exactly the same. The mechanism used to obtain that change is different and we are using that difference to evaluate whether plans for mitigating the general equilibrium (and adjustment-related) income effects of policies are important to consumers.

B.   Framework for Analysis

To formalize this logic we use an indirect utility function to describe a consumer's choices and add environmental quality (q). It is now rewritten as $V(m, P, q)$. The symbol m designates household income. P is a vector of prices for private goods and q is the specific environmental resource assumed related to the policy. A plan describes some approach for changing these resources, and its cost, t (including a method of payment). Once we allow the attributes of the plan (designated here as 'a') to vary across individuals we could describe the result as a function

$$t = R(\Delta q, a). \tag{12.1}$$

As a rule this is not presented to respondents. Instead the objective in a CV survey is to present a respondent with a single value for t and one set of environmental resource changes, Δq, described as associated with the plan and attributes for the plan, a, to provide those changes.[21] By varying the design across respondents, we test whether the implied relationship between Δq and a would matter to them. Thus a respondent's choice implicitly links Δq and a to that individual's WTP. This relationship is derived from the choice to vote for a plan as described in (12.2).

$$V[m_0 - t, p_0, q_0 + \Delta q(a)] \geq V(m_0, p_0, q_0). \tag{12.2}$$

Table 12.5 *Estimates of willingness to pay for hog waste treatment and support for plans to regulate hog operations*

Initial plan proposal	Median WTP[a] (95% confidence interval)	Follow-up – CV question[b]	
		Enforcement	Cost-share
Enforcement (49%)	$94.90 (46.07–195.50)	–	34%
Cost share (41%)	$36.79 (12.09–111.96)	48%	–

Notes:

[a] These estimates are based on a simple Weibull survival model without additional demographic or independent variables. They are measured in 1995 dollars.

[b] These percentages are based on the full number of respondents (170 for the enforcement plan and 172 for the cost-share plan). If we restrict the sample to respondents reporting sufficient information to estimate the probit choice models in Table 12.7 the percentages for this smaller sample would be given as follows:

Initial plan	Support as Initial proposal	Support as Follow-up proposal
Enforcement	49%	51%
Cost Share	43%	35%

If the two sides of equation (12.2) are equal, we can solve for t and define the willingness to pay (WTP) function with WTP designated as t^* in equation (12.3)

$$t^* = WTP[m_0, p_0, q_0, \Delta q(a)] \qquad (12.3)$$

Notice that for our application Δq and a are listed as functionally related. This expression was selected to emphasize that we do not have independent variation in both Δq and a. Only a varies between the two versions of the questionnaire so we must assume a composite judgement is made about what each plan provides. To implement the model we assume there is unobserved heterogeneity in respondents and characterize it with a distribution for an additive error. Our estimates of WTP for each plan use a Weibull survival model for this error as one convenient approach to constraint t^* to be positive.

Table 12.5 reports our estimates of the median willingness to pay (WTP) based on applying a Weibull survival model separately to each of the samples receiving the different plans.[22] The median WTP for the enforcement plan, $94, is significantly higher than the median WTP for the cost-share programme, $37. A follow-up question was asked of each respondent to consider supporting an alternative plan. The people who received the enforcement plan were asked how they would vote if the extra tax revenue was used to share one-half of the large hog farms' capital costs for the new regulations with the result that there would be fewer state inspectors. The people who had received the cost-share plan were asked how they would vote if the tax revenue was used to increase the number of state inspectors instead of being allocated for the cost-share.[23]

This additional information allows a qualitative appraisal of whether these differences in responses stem from the effort to mitigate the direct impacts of the more stringent regulations. The first column in Table 12.5 reports the percentage who said they would vote 'Yes' on the initial plan offered to them. The third and fourth columns provide the responses to the follow-up question, based on the plan initially offered to them. The level of support for greater enforcement is not significantly different whether the programme was the first or second programme mentioned in the question (the Z-statistics for the difference between two proportions is -0.22 and both the one-sided and two-sided tests are insignificant). The level of support for the cost-share programme diminishes when the plan is presented as an alternative to the enforcement plan (the Z-statistic for a one-sided test that 41 percent is greater than 34 percent is marginally significant at the 10 percent level).

Examining the people who received the enforcement plan first and the cost-share plan as the follow-up, support drops from 49 percent for the enforcement plan to 34 percent for the cost-share plan. This difference is significant at the same level (the p-value for the one-sided test that 49 percent is greater than 34 percent is 0.10). Support moves in the opposite direction when we look at the sample who started with the cost-share programme. Support rises from 41 percent for the cost-share plan to 48 percent for the enforcement plan, and this difference is significant. The percentages in footnote b to Table 12.5 are slightly different from those in the table and refer to comparisons using the sample restricted to those with complete information for estimating the choice model in Table 12.7.

Table 12.6 decomposes responses according to whether or not a respondent is, or ever has been, a farmer. In general, we would expect that farmers would be more supportive of the cost-share plan than the enforcement plan relative to the general public. In the enforcement scenario, a greater percentage of non-farmers supported the plan (summing across dollar amounts, 55 percent of non-farmers voted 'yes' versus 44 percent of farmers). This difference is significant using a one-tailed test. In the cost-share scenario the reverse is true (37 percent of non-farmers voted 'yes' versus 44 percent of farmers), but the one-tailed test is marginally significant with a p-value of 0.13. The level of support from farmers for either plan is not significantly different across the two scenarios, but the level of

Table 12.6   Percentage voting 'yes' for two proposals: farmers versus non-farmers

	Enforcement proposal % voting 'yes'	Cost-share proposal % voting 'yes'	Z-statistic for one-tailed test for column (2)>(3) (p-value)[a]
Non-Farmer	55%	37%	2.31 (0.01)
Farmer	44%	46%	−0.21 (0.58)
Z-statistic for one-tailed test (p-value)[a] LR ch1 2 One-sided Fisher Exact (for farmers different from non-farmers	1.38[b] (0.08) 1.92 (p=0.17) p=0.11	1.11[c] (0.13) 1.22 (p=0.27) p=0.17	

Notes:
[a]   Test for the difference between two proportions.
[b]   One-tailed test of row (2)>(3).
[c]   One-tailed test of row (2)<(3).

support from non-farmers is significantly lower in the cost-share scenario (with a p-value of 0.01 for the one-tailed test). The first of these results is likely due to the small number of farmers in our sample.

Thus, these distinctions generally support our conclusion that independent respondents did recognize the difference in the plans and do have preferences about how the direct costs of controlling hog waste were paid. Overall, the general population does not support efforts to reduce the types of indirect effects identified in the impact analysis. They support a 'polluter pays' principle. Those respondents (that is, farmers) directly affected by the distinction in the two plans react as we would predict based on the implications of the framing of each of the plans.

Table 12.7 expands these simple pairwise comparisons of the choices of different groups to consider the economic, demographic, and attitude based determinants of stated choices, using a simple probit model. The results for each plan are presented separately, along with the joint results from combining the sub-samples with the responses to each of the two plans. Despite some differences between the results for the two plans we found in comparing individual groups' responses to the plans with pairwise comparisons, we do not have a sufficiently large sample to suggest that all the determinants have different effects on these choice models. Thus,

Table 12.7   Probit models for voting 'yes' on the proposal[a]

Variables	Enforcement	Cost-share	Joint
Tax amt	−0.001	−0.002	−0.002
	(−2.94)	(−3.61)	(−4.76)
Spillike	0.21	0.18	0.18
	(3.52)	(2.66)	(4.41)
Exfarmer (= 1)	−0.22	0.43	0.10
	(−0.92)	(1.65)	(0.59)
Married (= 1)	0.83	0.22	0.37
	(2.49)	(0.70)	(1.74)
White (= 1)	0.46	0.73	0.53
	(1.39)	(1.74)	(2.11)
Hsize	−0.22	0.05	−0.06
	(−1.62)	(0.35)	(−0.73)
Female (= 1)	0.64	0.50	0.48
	(2.2)	(1.85)	(2.67)
Femploy (= 1)	−0.32	−0.71	−0.45
	(−1.04)	(−2.41)	(−2.21)
Hinc	6.31e–06	3.92e–06	4.89e–06
	(1.11)	(0.79)	(1.38)
Age	−0.03	−0.03	−0.03
	(−2.09)	(−2.84)	(−3.14)
Colgrad (= 1)	0.38	0.13	0.25
	(1.11)	(0.38)	(1.10)
Mills 1	−0.26	3.12	0.96
	(−0.11)	(1.30)	(0.61)
Mills 2	−2.24	−0.10	−0.84
	(−1.36)	(−0.08)	(−0.89)
Constant	0.86	−2.28	−0.69
	(0.46)	(−1.33)	(−0.59)
Log likelihood	−76.96	−76.07	−162.08
N obs	145	143	288
Pseudo R^2	0.23	0.22	0.19
Likelihood ratio test			18.12
Value[b]			(14)
(degrees of freedom)			

Notes:
[a] The numbers in parentheses below the estimated coefficients are the asymptotic z ratios for the null hypothesis of no association.
[b] Likelihood ratio test for the hypothesis that the coefficients in the Joint model cannot be rejected in favour of separate models for the two proposals. This hypothesis cannot be rejected at the 10 percent confidence level.

comparing each of the two choice models, we can not reject the hypothesis that the coefficients are the same using a likelihood ratio test (reported in Table 12.7).

As expected, the amount of the proposed tax increase, *tax amt*, has a negative and significant effect on the probability of voting 'yes' in all three probit models. People who reported a belief that there was a greater likelihood of future waste spills had a significantly higher probability of supporting both plans.[24] The demographic characteristics with statistically significant effects in all three models include: gender (with females having an increased probability of acceptance), and age with negatively related support for the plans (older people were less likely to support either plan). Some other demographic characteristics, including marital status, employment status and race, are significant in the joint model and have consistent signs across all three models. Income is positive in all three models, but insignificant. The income variable in these models includes predicted values of income for people who did not answer the income question.[25] We also considered the choice model using the subset of respondents who answered the income question. The income variable is positive but insignificant at the conventional levels. Finally the coefficients on the two inverse Mills ratios for two separate selection effects have opposite signs for the two programmes, but are insignificant in all cases.[26]

5. IMPLICATIONS

This chapter uses North Carolina's dilemma with animal agriculture (especially large-scale hog farms) to consider two elements in a policy evaluation of proposed regulations intended to reduce the effects of hog waste on water quality in the state's rivers and estuarine waters. The first involves the positive output and employment impacts (direct and indirect) of the significant growth in the sector over the past decade. The second attempts to measure the damages attributed to the water quality declines from these activities using consumers' willingness to pay to reduce them. The results from the impact analysis are generally the ones sought by political and community leaders while the second type of information is generally what is advocated by economists to address these types of problems. The result has been a 'virtual disconnect' between the two groups.

We have argued that this does not have to be the case. Conventional benefit–cost analyses are based on the premise that general equilibrium price effects and income changes stemming from (as well as costs due to) a policy are small. At a regional level general equilibrium income effects are often large. There has been little explicit consideration of how these practices could be adapted for evaluating environmental regulations. We propose a two-stage effort. In the first step one considers the impact of changes in the sector for output, employment changes, and therefore the potential for appreciable policy related income changes.

The second step is to investigate how consumers' willingness to pay for policies designated to reduce the disamenities would be affected by altering the attributes of these programmes to incorporate some public assistance to mitigate these employment and cost impacts on farms. This approach considers whether it is possible to recover people's preferences for specific changes in policy to mitigate indirect effects.[27] Our example confirms that people do understand and have preferences over attributes of a policy designed to deal with both environmental quality and the indirect impacts of that policy's impacts on a farm's costs. It leads to a very surprising result.

One would expect that significant increases in costs due to the regulation of hog farms would, as a result, reduce income to farmers and local residents. The GE price and income changes counted in assessing the potential efficiency gains from regulations would then reduce net benefits. As a result, we would have expected that offering policies that partially mitigate these effects at the same tax prices and achieve the same environmental quality goals would have led to at least the same levels of support for the policy and very likely equal or greater WTP measures. This is not what we found. Households clearly have preferences for these other elements in a policy structure.[28]

As the introduction to this chapter implied, our benefit estimates are potentially relevant in another context for the changes recently proposed by the EPA for reforming water quality regulations. The new TMDL focus will require policies to consider the overall watershed rather than waterborne emissions of large point sources of water effluents. State implementation plans to address impairment of water bodies will ultimately involve regulations for both point and nonpoint sources and can be expected to have regional impacts. In the face of such large-scale changes it is natural for policymakers to ask how one balances the increased costs, potential for broader economic impacts in the affected regions, and improvement in water quality that is anticipated to result from the new regime. We have suggested a way to begin this process. Our proposal uses the net effects of regulations on output and employment in a region as a gauge of the potential importance of price and income changes that would be relevant to the general equilibrium benefits of policy.[29]

Based on that initial evaluation, one can determine whether benefit analyses need to incorporate policy elements that mitigate indirect effects. Our findings suggest we cannot assume that citizens support such measures. The size of the difference is quite large at an aggregate level. Using the results from Table 12.5 and adjusting from 1995 to 1999 dollars, the two estimates for the aggregate WTP for programmes to control wastes from animal agriculture indicate a marked difference as a result of the effort to mitigate indirect effects. The enforcement plan generates aggregate benefits of almost $225 million dollars, while the cost-share plan results in total benefits less than half this size, about $87 million.[30]

To the extent mitigation plans for employment losses or impacts on small farmers are considered, our findings suggest they may need to be focused on more direct compensation to the affected households, rather than sharing the costs of new waste management technologies with large animal operations. These findings may also suggest that even when the models available to compute GE welfare measures are more completely developed, there will be a continuing need to evaluate how households evaluate policies that seek to improve environmental quality change and to mitigate indirect general equilibrium effects.

NOTES

*   The authors are Senior Economist with the Center for Economic Research, Research Triangle Institute and University Distinguished Professor and Director of CEnREP, Department of Agricultural and Resource Economics, North Carolina State University and University Fellow, Resources for the Future, respectively. Partial support for Smith's research was provided by UNC Sea Grant Project Number R/MD32 and the NC Agricultural Research Service Number NC06572. Thanks are due Dimitrios Dadakas and Randy Walsh for excellent research assistance and to John List and Bill Schulze for very constructive comments on earlier drafts of this chapter presented.
1.   This autumn the second largest pork producer entered into a similar agreement with North Carolina paying $2.5 million in addition to the $15 million provided in the initial Smithfield Foods Agreement. The fund will also be used to help develop what the Smithfield Foods Agreement describes are 'environmentally superior' hog waste treatment technologies. The two firms represent more than 75 percent of hog farms in North Carolina. A hog waste lagoon is a large holding area for waste that permits bacterial decomposition of the waste before it is sprayed on the fields as a source of nitrogen.
2.   The specific elements identified in the agreement as comprising the evaluation of economic feasibility are:

   * The projected 10-year annualized cost of each alternative
   * The projected 10-year annualized cost of a lagoon and sprayfield system that is designed, constructed and operated in accordance with current rules
   * Projected revenues and cost savings from the new technologies
   * Available cost-share monies or other technical and financial assistance from public sources
   * The impact of the alternative technologies on the competitiveness of the NC pork industry compared to other states

   These do not include the benefits from changes in environmental emissions from existing practice to the technologies designated as environmentally superior.
3.   In actual practice several of these stages are sometimes combined at a single farm.

4. Hazilla and Kopp (1990) were the first to identify the importance of price effects in measuring the social costs of environmental regulation.
5. In an intertemporal framework it is also important to consider changes in consumption and saving as a result of the policy. See Hazilla and Kopp (1990) for further discussion within an application of the treatment of these intertemporal effects.
6. This proposal is described in Just et al. (1982, p. 457). It allows the revaluation of individual endowments (of goods and services), changes in earned income (due to modifications in labour/leisure choices) and changes in exogenous income to be taken into account. In a second-best setting, exogenous restrictions to resource allocation can also be a source of income. Thus, these income changes need to be acknowledged as well. For a discussion in the context of GE evaluation of trade distortions see Anderson and Neary (1992).
7. With existing distortions, applied welfare analysis is admittedly analysis of second-best changes. We are not suggesting that these guidelines address the efficiency implications of these pre-existing distortions. They only serve to measure the income changes that arise because a new policy affects the value of the rents due to the existing distortions.
8. North Carolina Agricultural Statistics, 1998.
9. *The News and Observer*, p. A3, 27 March 1997.
10. More generally Farber (1998) reviews a wide array of hedonic studies with different types of spatially delineated effects.
11. This is derived by equating the output gained directly and indirectly from growth in hog production 1.86 to some multiple of output lost due to the associated losses in tourism, that is, $1.86 - \alpha\,2.56 = 0$, solving for $\alpha = (1.86/2.56) = 0.73$.
12. The CV question asked in the initial interview related to a proposal by Virginia to build a pipeline from Lake Gaston to Virginia Beach to provide drinking water for that area. Lake Gaston is on the North Carolina–Virginia border, and North Carolina does not support the plan.
13. In this chapter we only report the results from the hog farm questions. To evaluate the effects of the order of plans described as independent respondents' choices, the survey design allowed for three separate, random subsamples; two in which the hog regulation proposal was described first in the booklet (and the hog CV question was asked first during the second telephone interview), and one in which the hog regulation proposal was the second proposal described in the booklet (and asked in the interview). We report only the data from the two samples in which the hog proposal was the first proposal discussed. This reduces our sample size to 342 of the 540 responding to the second interview. Below we describe the details of the interviewing process.
14. Welsh et al. (1995) is the first study to our knowledge where the indirect effects of a policy (in their case controlling water releases from the Glenn Canyon Dam) were specified in different forms to considered indirect effects.

    Their specific scenario considered whether household preferences and WTP were affected by recognition of the price effects of the policy on electricity available to western ranchers and the sustainability of this rural 'way of life'. They did find variations in this dimension of the policy-impacted choices as the sample was narrowed to the area where these power effects would take place.
15. The results reported here relate to two of three subsamples where the animal waste management plans were asked first. A third treatment asked about the plan after the independent programme. Based on Payne et al.'s (2001) pilot surveys these distinctions in presentation order could have effects on choices, even when respondents know they will be presented in a sequence. Their findings were for plans that would not be independent so they may not be directly relevant here. Nonetheless, we limited our analysis to the subsamples where the management plans were presented first to avoid confounding influences.
16. Out of the 826 who agreed to the second interview, six had disconnected phones and another 146 could not be contacted. The minimum number of attempts to contact people was eight callbacks, and 86 percent were attempted at least 12 times.

17. The interview was rescheduled and a new booklet was mailed if the respondent had not read the booklet. Very few interviews had to be rescheduled.

18. The state of Alaska's Exxon Valdez Survey (see Carson et al., 1992) was the first effort to our knowledge to formalize the use of a plan to provide the proposed resource change. The NOAA Panel subsequently recommended this strategy for CV surveys used in litigation. Nonetheless, there remain some examples where authors continue to question whether an open-ended format might be preferred. See Huang and Smith (1998) for a summary of this literature and Smith (2003) for a general overview of the evolution of contingent valuation methods.

19. See McConnell (1990) for a demonstration of the equivalence of the Hanemann (1984) and Cameron (1988) approaches for measuring WTP with discrete choice models when the underlying preference functions are assumed to be linear.

20. Contingent valuation applications in the context of natural resource damage assessments highlighted this distinction. See Carson et al. (1997) and Smith (2003) for discussion.

21. Smith (1997) provides an example of how the implicit assumption that the plan provides a perfect substitute for a change in the resource can affect willingness to pay for the resource.

22. The Weibull survival function for a random variable, z, is given as:

$$S(z) = e^{-(\lambda z)^{\theta}}$$

with λ, θ parameters.
The median willingness to pay, $W\tilde{T}P$, assuming unobserved heterogeneity induces a Weibull distribution for unobserved WTP, is given as:

$$W\tilde{T}P = \lambda(\ln 2)^{1/\theta}.$$

23. The actual text of the question asked of the enforcement plan sample was: 'If the plan's increased taxes were used to share one-half the large hog farm's initial capital costs for the new regulations and, as a result, there were fewer state inspectors for monitoring large hog farms operations, would you vote for or against this alternative plan?'

    The text of the question read to the cost-share sample was: 'If the plan's increased taxes were not used to help pay the large hog farm's initial capital costs for the new regulations and instead were used only to increase the number of state inspectors for monitoring large hog farm operations, would you vote for or against this alternative plan?'

24. Of course, we should also note that this variable could well be jointly determined with their choices.

25. The equation used to predict income is as follows:

household income $= -20517.54 + 298.63$ age $+ 17618.73$ at least college graduate
$\quad\quad\quad\quad\quad\quad (-2.95) \quad\quad (3.86) \quad\quad\quad (8.72) \quad\quad\quad\quad (=1)$
-8791.68 below high school graduate $+ 19737.89$ trade school graduate
$(-3.19) \quad\quad\quad (=1) \quad\quad\quad\quad\quad (2.26) \quad\quad\quad\quad (=1)$
$+ 8803.03$ fully employed $- 9476.41$ retired $+ 6364.93$ white
$\quad (3.80) \quad\quad\quad (=1) \quad\quad (-2.71) (=1) \quad (2.85) \quad (=1)$
$+ 17135.04$ married $+ 0.89$ median household income census
$\quad (9.13) \quad\quad (=1) \quad\quad (3.95) \quad\quad$ for respondent's county
-6525.76 unable to answer attitude and preference questions in first interview,
(-2.71)

number of observations $= 787$, $R^2 = 0.313$

The numbers in parenthesis below the estimated coefficients are t ratios for the null hypothesis of no association.

26. *Mills 1* is the Mills ratio to adjust for selection effects from people who were contacted but did not participate in the first telephone interview. The ratio is calculated from aggregate county-level data (see Smith and Mansfield (1998) for more information about this variable). *Mills 2* captures the potential selection effects associated with people who participated in the first telephone interview, but not the second.

27. Of course, one could also attempt to compute the income changes due to a policy, but this would require a full general equilibrium model that incorporated the industry's response to regulations, the link between emissions and environmental quality, and consumers' responses to market and non-market goods. This ideal strategy is usually beyond the scope of most policy analyses. Thus, we suggest this choice-based analysis of preferences about mitigation policies as a simpler alternative.
28. In the context of experimental literature and contributions to public goods these other resulting effects have been judged to be potentially important as well.
29. The 'net' effect acknowledges that while regulations convey increased costs to some sectors, enhanced environmental quality can lead to increased activity for other sectors that can have positive income effects.
30. These estimates are derived from the estimates in Table 12.5 by converting to 1999 dollars with the CPI. This scales the median estimates by 1.0932 (for example, $(166.6/1524.4) = 1.0932$). We then divide the 1998 population of North Carolina (7 547 090) by 2.3 to estimate the number of households. We assume that only 66 percent of the estimated number of North Carolina households place a non-zero value on the plans. This percentage corresponds to the response rate for the second telephone survey.

REFERENCES

Anderson, James E. and J.P. Neary (1992), 'A New Approach to Evaluating Trade Policy', Working Paper WPS1022, International Economics Department, The World Bank, Washington, DC.

Cameron, Trudy A. (1988), 'A consistent paradigm for valuing non-market goods using referendum data: maximum likelihood estimator by censored logistic regression', *Journal of Environmental Economics and Management*, **15** (September), 1355–79.

Carson, Richard T., Robert C. Mitchell, W. Michael Hanemann, Raymond J. Kopp, Stanley Presser and Paul A. Ruud (1992), *A Contingent Valuation Study of Lost Passive Use Values Resulting From the Exxon Valdez Spill*, Report to the Attorney General of the State of Alaska, NRDA, Inc., San Diego, California, November 10.

Carson, Richard T., W. Michael Hanemann, Raymond J. Kopp, Jon A. Krosnick, Robert C. Mitchell, Stanley Presser, Paul A. Ruud and V. Kerry Smith with Michael Conaway and Kerry Martin (1997), 'Temporal reliability of estimates from contingent valuation', *Land Economics*, **73** (May), 151–63.

Farber, Stephen (1998), 'Undesirable facilities and property values: a summary of empirical studies', *Ecological Economics*, **24** (1), 1–14.

Foster, William and Richard E. Just (1989), 'Measuring Welfare Effects of Product Contamination and Consumer Uncertainty', *Journal of Environmental Economics and Management*, **17** (November), 266–83.

Gayer Ted, James T. Hamilton and W. Kip Viscusi (2000), 'Private values of risk tradeoffs at superfund sites: housing market evidence on learning about risks', *Review of Economics and Statistics*, **82** (August), 439–51.

Hanemann, W. Michael (1984), 'Welfare evaluation in contingent valuation experiments with discrete responses', *American Journal of Agricultural Economics*, **66** (3), 332–41.

Harberger, Arnold C. (1971), 'Three basic postulates for applied welfare economics: an interpretive essay', *Journal of Economic Literature*, **9** (September), 785–97.

Hazilla, Michael and Raymond J. Kopp (1990), 'The social cost of environmental quality regulations: a general equilibrium analysis', *Journal of Political Economy*, **98** (August), 853–73.

Hines, James R. Jr. (1999), 'Three sides of Harberger triangles', *Journal of Economic Perspectives*, **13** (Spring), 167–88.

Huang, Ju Chin and V. Kerry Smith (1998), 'Monte Carlo benchmarking for discrete response valuation methods', *Land Economics*, **74** (May), 186–202.

Hurwicz, L. and H. Uzawa (1971), 'On the Integrability of Demand Functions', in J.S. Chipman, L. Hurwicz, M.K. Richter and H.F. Sonnenschein (eds), *Preferences, Utility, and Demand*, New York: Harcourt, Brace.

Johnson, F. Reed (1988), 'Economic cost of misinforming about risk: the EDB scare and the media', *Risk Analysis*, **8**, 261–9.

Just, Richard, Darrell Hueth and Andrew Schmitz (1982), *Applied Welfare Economics and Public Policy*, Englewood Cliffs: Prentice Hall.

McClelland, G.H., W.D. Schulze and B. Hurd (1990), 'The effect of risk benefits on property values: a case study of a hazardous waste site', *Risk Analysis*, **10** (4), 485–97.

McConnell, K.E. (1990), 'Models for referendum data: the structure of discrete choice models for contingent valuation', *Journal of Environmental Economics and Management*, **18** (January), 19–35.

Murdoch, James C., Harinder Singh and Mark Thayer (1993), 'The impact of natural hazards on housing values: the Loma Prieta earthquake', *Journal of the American Real Estate and Urban Economics Association*, **21** (2), 167–84.

Payne, John W., David A. Schkade, William H. Desvousges and Chris Aultmann (2001), 'Valuation of multiple environmental programs', *Journal of Risk and Uncertainty*, **21** (July), 95–116.

Shulstad, R.N. and Herbert H. Stoevener (1978), 'The effects of mercury contamination in pheasants on the value of pheasant hunting in Oregon', *Land Economics*, **57** (February), 39–49.

Smith, M.E., Eileen O. van Ravenswaay and S.R. Thompson (1988), 'Sales loss determination in food consumption incidence: an application to milk bans in Hawaii', *American Journal of Agricultural Economics*, **70** (3), 513–20.

Smith, V. Kerry (1997), 'Pricing What is Priceless: A Status Report on Non-Market Valuation of Environmental Resources', in *The International Yearbook of Environmental and Resource Economics 1997/1998*, Cheltenhan, UK and Lyme, US: Edward Elgar.

Smith, V. Kerry (2003), 'Fifty Years of Contingent Valuation', in A. Alberini, D. Bjornstad and J. Kahn (eds), *Handbook of Contingent Valuation*, Cheltenham, UK and Northampton, MA, US: Edward Elgar, in press.

Smith, V. Kerry and J. Andrès Espinosa (1996), 'Environmental and trade policies: some methodological lessons', *Environmental and Resource Economics*, **1** (February), 19–40.

Smith, V. Kerry and Carol Mansfield (1998), 'Buying time: real and hypothetical offers', *Journal of Environmental Economics and Management*, **36** (November), 209–24.

Swartz, D.G. and Ivar Strand Jr. (1981), 'Avoidance costs associated with imperfect information: the case of Kepon', *Land Economics*, **57** (May), 139–50.

Welsh, Michael P., Richard C. Bishop, Marcia L. Phillips and Robert M. Baumgartner (1995), *Glenn Canyon Environmental Studies Non-Use Value Study*, Hagler Bailly Consulting, Madison Wisconsin, Final Report to Glenn Canyon Environmental Studies Non-Use Value Committee.

13. Heterogeneous preferences and complex environmental goods: the case of ecosystem restoration*

J. Walter Milon and David Scrogin

INTRODUCTION

Environmental policy decisions involve diverse groups of citizens and dynamic ecological interactions. In economics, these policy problems are commonly modelled using simple components (for example homogeneous consumers and a single 'public good') in order to highlight the structure of the decision problem. While the assumption of homogeneity in individual preferences is effective for theoretical inquiries into the general properties of environmental problems, propositions based on preference homogeneity offer limited guidance on the distributional consequences of policy decisions involving national and local public goods. Yet with the recognition of heterogeneity across individuals or groups and multiple dimensions in environmental problems, the search for greater relevance may quickly become entangled in intractable complexity.

In this chapter, we investigate two sources of complexity in environmental policy: heterogeneous preferences over individuals and groups and complex environmental goods. Both concerns are receiving increasing attention in the economic literature. Economists (for example Layton, 2000; Breffle and Morey, 2000; Swallow et al., 1994; Train, 1998) have utilized discrete choice techniques to model and measure heterogeneous preferences for public goods in order to: (a) increase the explanatory power of environmental preference models and (b) provide relevant information to policymakers about the distribution of public preferences. Other economists have begun to explore the implications of ecological complexity for economic analysis (for example Commons and Perrings, 1992; Kahn and O'Neill, 1999; Milon et al., 1999a; Turner et al., 1999). This has been a somewhat belated exploration since ecologists have a long-standing interest in alternative explanations for the variety and dynamics of natural systems and the complex relations within these systems (Holling, 1987; Kolasa and Pickett, 1991; May, 1977).

In the following section we provide a discussion of some key issues in modelling heterogeneous preferences and complex environmental goods for public policy analysis. We then relate these issues to the problem of ecosystem restoration in the Florida Everglades. The Everglades/South Florida ecosystem covers more than 69 000 square kilometres and is a mosaic of interrelated terrestrial, freshwater and marine systems. The Everglades restoration, authorized by the US Congress in the Water Resources Development Act of 2000 (Public Law No. 106–541), is an $8 billion project that is one of the most extensive ecosystem restoration efforts undertaken anywhere in the world.[1] And, because of the unique mix of federal and state interests in the Everglades, it provides a classic example of the need for information about economic benefits to guide plan selection and cost-sharing decisions (Milon, 2000). In Section 3 we provide details of a stated choice field experiment with proposed Everglades restoration plans including the survey design, data and econometric modelling issues. Section 4 presents empirical results and a discussion of the information provided from the heterogeneous preference models. We conclude with some observations on the role of heterogeneous preference modelling for policy decisions involving complex environmental goods.

2. MODELLING PREFERENCES FOR COMPLEX ENVIRONMENTAL GOODS

The Random Utility Model and Heterogeneous Preferences

The standard form to represent environmental preferences is in terms of utility, U, for an environmental good. With alternative levels of the environmental good, more of the good is preferred to less if $U(A_2) > U(A_1)$ where A_2 is a higher level of the good than A_1. This framework can be generalized to consider alternatives that include multiple attributes of an environmental good using random utility theory. For a problem with two alternatives, A and B, assume an individual, denoted n, chooses the alternative with a higher level of utility or, in symbolic terms,

$$U_n(X^A) > U_n(X^B)$$

where $U_n(.)$ represents the individual's utility function and X^A, X^B represent sets comprised of I attributes for alternatives A and B. Utility can be decomposed into a systematic component, $v(.)$, determined by the attributes (that is, $v_n (X^A) = v_n (X_1^A, X_2^A, \ldots, X_I^A)$) and a random component, ε_n, such that:

$$U_n = v_n (X) + \varepsilon_n. \qquad (13.1)$$

With either revealed or stated preference choice data from a representative sample of the public, statistical techniques such as multinomial logit (MNL) can be used to estimate the relative weights (marginal utility values) assigned to each attribute in the random utility model (RUM) (McFadden, 1974; Louviere et al., 2000). These weights provide information about public preferences for both environmental and non-environmental attributes of the alternatives. In addition, the attribute weights can be used to estimate utility scores and welfare measures such as compensating variation (Roe et al., 1996; Swallow et al., 1994). These utility metrics can be used to compute rankings and aggregate willingness to pay for alternative bundles of attributes relative to the status quo.

The RUM can be evaluated under the assumption of homogeneous preferences by estimating an additive utility function of the form:

$$U_n = X\beta + \varepsilon_n \qquad (13.2)$$

where β is an $I \times 1$ vector of weights associated with a vector of I attributes of the J alternatives. The marginal utilities (β_is) are independent, so a change in the level of one attribute does not affect the value of another. Homogeneity yields a fixed effects model where β does not vary over individuals, implying that all individuals share a common utility function. Alternatively, the utility function can be specified in polynomial form (for example multiplicative or distributive), but the homogeneity property will be retained.

Heterogeneity can be introduced in the RUM framework by restricting β to be a function of observable socioeconomic characteristics (income, ethnicity, and so on) of the individual:

$$U_n = (S_m X)\beta + \varepsilon_n \qquad (13.3)$$

where S_m represents a vector of m socioeconomic characteristics of the individual and β is an $mI \times 1$ vector. With MNL estimation, this 'classic' form of heterogeneity allows preferences (marginal utilities) for each attribute (or subsets of the attributes) to vary with socioeconomic characteristics and permits group-specific measures of environmental preferences to be estimated (for example Swallow et al., 1994).

An alternative form of heterogeneity can be introduced using random parameters logit (RPL) in which the coefficient vector or a subset of the coefficients varies randomly over individuals (Revelt and Train, 1998, 1999; Train, 1998). Individual preferences may be modelled:

$$U_n = X\alpha + X\alpha_n + \varepsilon_n \qquad (13.4)$$

where α represents a vector of mean population preferences and α_n represents a vector of the nth individual's preferences for the alternative. It is assumed that α_n and ε_n are independent. A variety of alternative assumptions about the distribution of preferences in the population (for example normal, lognormal, and so on) are permitted. This approach introduces heterogeneity into the preference measures but with a lack of specific information about how preferences vary across socioeconomic groups. Although highly flexible, this approach is sensitive to the decision regarding which coefficients are selected to be random and the estimation procedure (McFadden and Train, 2000; Revelt and Train, 1998, 1999).

An additional approach for introducing heterogeneity suggested by Revelt and Train (1999) and Breffle and Morey (2000) combines socioeconomic characteristics restrictions with RPL. The attribute vector is partitioned into j attributes with group-specific effects and i attributes with individual-specific effects. Specifically, preferences can be modelled as:

$$U_n = (S_m X_j)\beta + X_i\alpha + X_i\alpha_n + \varepsilon_n \qquad (13.5)$$

where the symbols are defined as above except now j attributes are modelled as socioeconomic group sources of heterogeneity and i attributes are modelled as individual (random) sources of heterogeneity. While this mixed approach provides a more comprehensive treatment of heterogeneity, there is little theoretical basis for partitioning the attributes into those with parameters that vary within the population and those that do not. Thus, explicit modelling of heterogeneity in environmental preferences with the mixed approach is largely determined by the data set and the estimation decisions of the researcher.

These modelling alternatives offer several choices for public preference research. The homogeneous preferences model (13.2) presents the simplest method to measure preferences, yet important information about differences in preferences across the population cannot be identified. The classic heterogeneity model (13.3) permits differences in preferences to be identified across socioeconomic groups provided that information on individual characteristics exists in the data set. The basic and mixed random parameters models (13.4 and 13.5) can identify both group and individual sources of heterogeneity, but the appropriate choice of fixed and random parameters is primarily an empirical issue. And, because of the estimation procedure for the RPL, consistent parameters may be difficult to estimate with a large number of random parameters.

Attribute Specification for Complex Environmental Goods

While the preferred choice of modelling strategy to measure heterogeneity in environmental preferences is ambiguous, an additional complication is the representation of complex environmental goods in terms of measurable attributes. We define a complex environmental good as any bundle of two or more environmental resources that are related within or across ecological scales. Thus, predator–prey relationships, hierarchical biological communities and ecosystems are all examples of this classification. Single species or locations that have frequently been used in environmental preference studies are not complex environmental goods.

A difficulty with a complex environmental good is that there may be many perspectives on how to characterize the good's multiple attributes, especially in the context of ecosystem restoration (Bratton, 1992; Franklin, 1988; Holling, 1987; Westman, 1991). For example, one way to describe an ecosystem is by *structural* attributes such as population levels of individual and/or keystone species. Wildlife and aquatic species are a common way for the public to think about ecosystems (Wilson, 1984; Kellert, 1996), so representation of restoration alternatives through changes in the levels of species populations is likely to be easily understood. In the context of the Everglades/South Florida ecosystem, one of the primary driving forces for the restoration has been concern about dramatic declines in the number of wading birds over the past 50 years.

An alternative, though not necessarily independent, approach to describe an ecosystem is with *functional* attributes such as the periodicity of wetland flooding or the occurrence of natural successional processes. In an ecosystem such as the Everglades/South Florida system, the spatial and temporal process of wetting and drying determines the diversity of micro and meso habitats within the overall wetland-based ecosystem (Holling et al., 1994). This process is an especially important component of ecosystem restoration in South Florida because water availability for ecosystem functions is limited by urban and agricultural uses of available supplies.

For most complex ecosystems, structural and functional attributes represent different dimensions of the ecosystem, and the exact linkages between these attribute groupings are not well known. Moreover, the attribute groupings could be combined in a number of ways to describe the ecosystem depending on the ecological scale of interest (Noss, 1990). The challenge for economists seeking to measure public preferences for policy alternatives that affect ecosystems is how to specify the attributes of the decision problem. Alternative specifications provide different information to respondents in a stated choice experiment. But, there is no consensus on the quantity or type of information that should be provided (Munro and Hanley, 1999). A large number of interrelated attributes with multiple levels would lead to an intractable choice set. Collapsing the multiple dimensions into a single indicator may lack conceptual validity and fail to provide meaningful policy information.

The approach adopted in this study is to evaluate preferences under alternative specifications of the environmental good (that is functional or structural attributes). Ecosystem restoration based on increasing species levels may lead to different management actions than strategies based on restoring functional properties of the ecosystem (Bratton, 1992; Westman, 1991). In the context of Everglades restoration, more than 50 percent of the original land area of the Everglades has been converted to other uses, so it would be impossible to restore all functional and structural characteristics of the original ecosystem. A functional restoration strategy would emphasize the spatial and temporal dimensions of the hydrological cycle across the landscape of the Everglades. This is essentially the strategy used in the US Army Corps of Engineers' (1999) restoration plan for the Everglades that was approved by the US Congress in the Water Resources Development Act of 2000. Alternatively, a structural restoration strategy would seek to increase species population levels through changes in habitat suitability for specific communities, species groups and/or individual species. This approach to Everglades restoration is described in the US Fish and Wildlife Service's (1999) plan that focuses on recovery and restoration objectives for 68 threatened and endangered species. While neither strategy alone offers a comprehensive blueprint for restoration, it is important to understand how the public perceives an ecosystem in order to inform ecosystem managers about public preferences and willingness to pay for alternative types and degrees of ecosystem restoration.

3. SURVEY DESIGN AND ECONOMETRIC MODELLING

To evaluate the effects of preference heterogeneity with alternative characterizations of ecosystem attributes, two multiattribute stated choice survey instruments were developed based on the RUM framework described above. One instrument was based on structural ecosystem characteristics and included native wildlife species groups classified as:

- *wetland dependent species* such as wading birds and alligators;
- *dryland dependent species* such as deer, hawks and songbirds; and
- *estuarine* (*Florida Bay*) *dependent species* such as pink shrimp, mullet and sea trout.

These species groups have been identified as a principal concern of the restoration effort (US Fish and Wildlife Service, 1999).

Alternatively, the second instrument was based on functional attributes which represented distinct hydrological subregions created through past water management actions. These attributes represented hydrological processes within three subregions:

- water levels and timing in *Lake Okeechobee*;
- water levels and timing in the *Water Conservation Areas*; and
- water levels and timing in *Everglades National Park*.

In addition, the fact that ecosystem restoration objectives in the Everglades/South Florida setting must be considered along with other social objectives, three additional attributes were developed as elements of any restoration plan. These attributes were:

- the *annual cost* of the restoration to households in Florida;
- possible *restrictions on outdoor and indoor water use* in South Florida; and
- changes in *farmland acreage* in South Florida through conversions to wetlands.

These latter three attributes were common to both the structural and functional attribute survey instruments.

Different levels of the structural and functional attributes were selected in consultation with scientists and agency staff knowledgeable about the Everglades ecosystem and the restoration effort. Three attribute levels were selected to represent a baseline (status quo) condition plus intermediate and maximum possible restoration relative to historical conditions (Milon et al., 1999b). In addition, three levels were specified for each of the social attributes to be included in the alternative plans. The combination of three levels for each of the six attributes with either the structural or functional representation of restoration plans results in 3^6, or 729, unique possible attribute combinations. To achieve a more manageable choice set while preserving statistical efficiency, an experimental design was selected based on an additive utility function to evaluate all main effects and first-order interactive effects.[2] Each attribute set for the survey was reduced to 27 combinations using an optimized, orthogonal factorial design (Louviere et al., 2000). The 27 possible combinations in the experimental design for both the structural and functional representations of attributes were further 'blocked' into two groups of seven pairwise choices (two groups times seven pairwise choices equals 28 alternatives with one alternative repeated in each group) so that each respondent only made seven repeated choices. This simplification was based on pretesting and previous studies (for example De Palma et al., 1994) that indicated more than ten pairwise choice tasks were too burdensome for respondents.

A total of 480 household interviews were conducted in five Florida cities in 1998 using randomly selected households from a stratified design based on census tract median income and ethnic composition. The cities were selected to represent the opinions of citizens in South Florida and Floridians in other parts of the state. A split sample design for the survey was used to give an equal proportion of respondents using the functional and structural attribute sets in each city. Examples of the pairwise choice task used in the interviews for the functional and structural attributes are provided in Tables 13.1 and 13.2, respectively. A professional market research firm conducted the interviews; bilingual interviewers were used when necessary. Table 13.3 presents summary statistics for the survey data and respondent socioeconomic characteristics. The statistics show that the attribute means are approximately the midpoint of the upper and lower levels of each attribute. This occurred because the attribute combinations in the orthogonal factorial design were randomly distributed across the sample groups. The reader is referred to Milon et al. (1999b) for complete details regarding the initial focus groups, survey design, interview process and properties of the sample data. The 480 interviews provided 1680 choices for each attribute set (seven choices times 240 respondents) based on the split sample design. Seven alternative RUM models were estimated for each of the structural and functional attribute data sets. The models were:

Model 1: An unrestricted MNL with only structural or functional attributes assuming homogeneous preferences for attributes ($X \beta$) – seven fixed parameters;

Model 2: A restricted MNL with socioeconomic interactions that allows for heterogeneous preferences across socioeconomic groups ($S_m X \beta$) – seven fixed parameters and 48 socioeconomic interaction parameters;

Model 3: An unrestricted RPL that allows heterogeneous preferences to vary randomly across individuals ($X\alpha + X\alpha_n$) – for estimation purposes only the price attribute was treated as a random coefficient;

Model 4: The same as Model 3 except 6 fixed parameter socioeconomic interaction variables are added for Income;

Table 13.1   Example of pairwise choice for the functional attribute model

Plan component	A	B
Lake Okeechobee, Water Levels and Timing	*60%* of the time, lake levels and timing are similar to historic, predrainage conditions	*60%* of the time, lake levels and timing are similar to historic, predrainage conditions
Everglades Water Conservation Areas, Water Levels and Timing	*50%* of areas have water levels and timing similar to historic, predrainage conditions	*50%* of areas have water levels and timing similar to historic, predrainage conditions
Everglades National Park and Florida Bay, Water Levels and Timing	*90%* of the area has water levels and timing similar to historic, predrainage conditions	*50%* of the area has water levels and timing similar to historic, predrainage conditions
Annual cost per household	Utility taxes increased *$25* per year or *$250* over 10 years	*No change* in utility taxes
Restrictions on Household Outdoor and Indoor Water Use	Outdoor use limited to *2 days per week*; indoor use *reduced 25%*	Outdoor use limited to *3 days per week*; indoor use *reduced 10%*
Farm land (acres) in the Everglades Agricultural Area and Western Portions of Palm Beach, Broward and Dade Counties	Reduce farm land acreage by *100000 acres* or 15% of farmed area	*No change* in farm land acreage

Model 5: The same as Model 3 except 12 fixed parameter socioeconomic interaction variables are added for Income and the Number of Years an Individual Lived in Florida;

Model 6: The same as Model 3 except 18 fixed parameter socioeconomic interaction variables are added for Income, the Number of Years an Individual Lived in Florida and the Region where a respondent lived (South Florida or Other);

Model 7: A fully mixed RPL with both socioeconomic group and individual heterogeneity ($(S_m X_j)\beta + X_i\alpha + X_i\alpha_n$) that combines Model 3 with 48 fixed parameter socioeconomic interaction variables.

These alternative specifications allow the full range of heterogeneous preference models to be evaluated with the data sets and determine whether the degree and type of heterogeneity varies with the selection of attribute sets

Table 13.2   Example of pairwise choice for the structural attribute model

Plan Component	A	B
Wetland Dependent Species such as Wading Birds and Alligators	*20% of historic*, predrainage population levels	*20% of historic* predrainage population levels
Dry Land Dependent Species Such as Deer, Hawks and Songbirds	*70% of historic*, predrainage population levels	*50% of historic*, predrainage population levels
Florida Bay Dependent Species Such as Pink Shrimp, Mullet and Sea Trout	*60% of historic*, predrainage population levels	*60% of historic*, predrainage population levels
Annual cost per household	Utility taxes increased *$25 per year or $250 over 10 years*	*No change* in utility taxes
Restrictions on Household Outdoor and Indoor Water Use	Outdoor uses *restricted to 2 days per week*; indoor uses *reduced by 25%*	Outdoor uses *restricted to 3 days per week*; indoor uses *reduced by 10%*
Farm land (acres) in the Everglades Agricultural Area and Western Portions of Palm Beach, Broward and Dade Counties	Reduce farm land acreage by *100 000 acres (15% of farmed area)*	*No change* in farm land acreage

used to represent Everglades ecosystem restoration. For Models 1–7, estimation was performed with Gauss version 3.5 using the random parameter simulator (Train et al., 1999).

4.   EMPIRICAL RESULTS

Selected statistics from the estimation of Models 1–7 using the functional and structural attribute sets for Everglades restoration are presented in Table 13.4. To evaluate the extent of heterogeneity, the null hypothesis that homogeneity correctly characterizes preferences is tested using a log likelihood ratio comparing the unrestricted Model 1 with Models 2–7. Table 13.4 also reports the likelihood ratio test statistics and significance levels for the related chi-square (χ^2) distribution.

Results for the functional attribute models reported in the upper portion

Table 13.3 Variable definitions and summary statistics for the functional and structural attribute models

Attribute/Variable	Definition	Functional attribute models				Structural attribute models			
		Mean	S.D.	Min	Max	Mean	S.D.	Min	Max
Lake Okeechobee	Percent of historic level: 60%, 75%, 90%	0.74	0.12	0.6	0.9	—	—	—	—
Water Conservation Area	Percent of historic level: 50%, 75%, 90%	0.72	0.17	0.5	0.9	—	—	—	—
Everglades National Park	Percent of historic level: 50%, 75%, 90%	0.71	0.17	0.5	0.9	—	—	—	—
Wetland Species	Percent of historic level: 20%, 50%, 80%	—	—	—	—	0.49	0.25	0.2	0.8
Dryland Species	Percent of historic level: 50%, 60%, 70%	—	—	—	—	0.60	0.08	0.5	0.7
Estuarine Species	Percent of historic level: 60%, 75%, 90%	—	—	—	—	0.76	0.12	0.6	0.9
Annual Cost	Annual increase in utilities tax ($)	25	20.02	0	50	25	20.03	0	50
Water Restriction 1	1 if outdoor uses limited to 2 days per week and 25% decrease in indoor use consumption	0.36	0.48	0	1	0.36	0.48	0	1
Water Restriction 2	1 if outdoor uses limited to 1 day per week and 40% reduction in indoor use consumption	0.32	0.47	0	1	0.32	0.46	0	1
Farmland	Decrease in farmland acreage in South Florida ('000 acres)	99.84	80.19	0	200	99.88	80.19	0	200
Political Party	1 if Republican, 0 otherwise	0.25	0.44	0	1	0.27	0.44	0	1
Region	1 if Central Florida, 0 South Florida	0.41	0.49	0	1	0.39	0.49	0	1
Donations	1 if donated to environmental groups, 0 otherwise	0.42	0.49	0	1	0.49	0.50	0	1
Gender	1 if male, 0 female	0.48	0.50	0	1	0.48	0.50	0	1
Years in Florida	Number of years as resident	20.24	14.09	1	73	18.71	12.69	1	71
Income	1 to 9 by $10000 increments (i.e. 1 = less than $10000, 2 = $10000 to $19999, etc.)	4.07	2.06	1	9	4.26	2.08	1	9
Ethnic 1	1 if White-Hispanic or Black-Hispanic, 0 otherwise	0.14	0.35	0	1	0.12	0.33	0	1
Ethnic 2	1 if White-Non-Hispanic, 0 otherwise	0.74	0.44	0	1	0.73	0.45	0	1

Table 13.4 Estimation results for homogeneous and heterogeneous preference models 1–7 with functional and structural attributes

	Model 1	Model 2	Model 3	Model 4	Model 5	Model 6	Model 7
Number of parameters	7	55	8	14	20	26	56
Functional							
Log-likelihood	−1000.36	−950.41	−1000.36	−985.94	−980.81	−975.60	−949.36
Pseudo R^2	0.14	0.18	0.14	0.15	0.16	0.16	0.18
LR Test statistic	–	99.92***	0.00	28.85***	39.10***	49.52***	102.00***
Structural							
Log-likelihood	−1078.96	−1046.72	−1074.91	−1068.33	−1064.21	−1060.41	−1045.65
Pseudo R^2	0.05	0.08	0.05	0.06	0.06	0.07	0.08
LR Test statistic	–	64.48*	8.10***	21.26***	29.50***	37.09***	66.61**

Notes: ***, **, and * denote significance at the 0.01, 0.05, and 0.10 levels, respectively.

of Table 13.4 indicate that heterogeneity attributable to differences in preferences across socioeconomic groups is the dominant form of heterogeneity. In the case of Model 2 with socioeconomic interactions the null hypothesis of homogeneous preferences can be firmly rejected. On the other hand, the first of the random coefficients models, Model 3, provides no statistical improvement over the unrestricted Model 1. Although Models 4–6 show a continual improvement in the likelihood ratio statistic, none of these models performs better than Model 2. The final Model 7 with a random coefficient for price added to Model 2 provides a slight improvement in the likelihood ratio statistic, but the contribution is not significant. Thus, individual heterogeneity has little influence on preferences in this attribute model.

A similar conclusion emerges from the results for the structural attribute model for Everglades restoration in the lower portion of Table 13.4. A comparison of Model 3 with random coefficients to Model 1 using a likelihood ratio test indicates that the null hypothesis of homogeneous preferences would be rejected. The classic heterogeneity Model 2, however, would also reject homogeneity yet it proves superior to Model 3. The combined random coefficients and socioeconomic interactions in Model 7 also reject homogeneity, but the differences between Models 2 and 7 are once again not statistically significant. These results indicate that some individual heterogeneity is present in preferences for structural attributes, but differences in preferences across socioeconomic groups remains the primary source of heterogeneity.

To illustrate the influence of preference heterogeneity on policy options for Everglades restoration, a set of alternative hypothetical restoration plans was constructed based on the attributes in the functional and structural models. Two measures of preferences for each plan were then developed from the estimated utility function: (1) the 'percent in favour' which is constructed by comparing the estimated utility score for a plan to the baseline utility value; and (2) the net willingness to pay (compensating variation) for the plan. The latter measure provides a benefit indicator of potential welfare changes. A comparison of these measures for homogeneous (Model 1) versus heterogeneous (Model 2) preferences reveals the influence of socioeconomic factors. Due to the similarity between the statistical results and preference measures for Models 2 and 7, only Model 2 results are reported here.

For example, Table 13.5 presents four alternative restoration plans and the baseline condition using the functional attribute data. The plans range from full Everglades restoration with none of the costs paid by Floridians (an environmental 'free lunch' courtesy of the US government) to full restoration with significant cost-sharing by Floridians. The last plan in Table 13.5

Table 13.5   Evaluation of selected restoration plans with the functional attribute models by respondent location

Plan description		Percent in favour			Net willingness to pay ($ per year)		
		All	South	Central	All	South	Central
Baseline (no change) hydrology							
Lake Okeechobee: 60%	Costs: 0	NA	NA	NA	NA	NA	NA
Water Conservation: 50%	Farmland Reduction: 0						
Everglades National Park: 50%	Water Restriction: none						
Full restoration without costs							
Lake Okeechobee: 90%	Costs: 0	71.7	87.6	48.9	$58.79	$86.42	$8.24
Water Conservation: 90%	Farmland Reduction: 0						
Everglades National Park: 90%	Water Restriction: none						
Full restoration with minimized costs							
Lake Okeechobee: 90%	Costs: $25	54.3	69.0	33.3	$15.60	$41.43	–$39.41
Water Conservation: 90%	Farmland Reduction: 100,000						
Everglades National Park: 90%	Water Restriction: Level 1						
Full restoration with all costs							
Lake Okeechobee: 90%	Costs: $50	31.1	43.4	13.3	–$61.09	–$22.11	–$131.65
Water Conservation: 90%	Farmland Reduction: 200000						
Everglades National Park: 90%	Water Restriction: Level 2						
Full restoration with all costs/no water restrictions							
Lake Okeechobee: 90%	Costs: $50	41.6	58.9	16.7	–$23.99	$11.90	–$83.01
Water Conservation: 90%	Farmland Reduction: 200000						
Everglades National Park: 90%	Water Restriction: none						

Note: NA – Not applicable.

is included to show the effects of concerns about domestic water use restrictions in the plans. The two preference measures for 'All' respondents in Table 13.5 assume homogeneous preferences while the heterogeneous preferences are displayed according to the sample respondent's location of residence in Florida (South vs Central). The results in Table 13.5 show significant variation in restoration preferences across location. Respondents in South Florida would be more likely to support restoration plans and display a significantly higher willingness to pay (WTP). The homogeneity model indicates almost three-quarters of respondents would support full restoration if it were costless, but the heterogeneity model reveals that less than a majority (48.9 percent) of Central Floridians would favour this plan. Also, the net benefits (net WTP) for South Floridians would be more than ten times greater ($86.42 vs $8.24) than those for Central Floridians. While both South and Central groups would oppose a full restoration plan (and incur net losses) that imposed a significant cost-share burden (that is full restoration with all costs), South Floridians would support and receive positive net benefits ($11.90) from full restoration if the plan imposed no water use restrictions.

Similar results emerge from Table 13.6 which uses the same set of restoration plans based on the functional attribute model except preferences are measured by the respondent's past donations to environmental groups. This variable (see Table 13.3) is a proxy for environmental attitudes that have been shown to be important determinants of preferences for environmental goods (Bateman and Willis, 1999). The results in Table 13.6 again show that heterogeneity is important. Donors to environmental groups are much more likely to favour any restoration plan and have a significantly higher WTP than non-donors. Even donors, however, would incur a net welfare loss from a full restoration plan that included a significant cost-share burden for Floridians. Note also that this disaggregation of preferences reveals that both groups are sensitive to whether water use restrictions are imposed as part of the restoration plan.

A comparable evaluation was conducted with the structural attribute model to determine how preferences were influenced by selection of the attribute set to represent the Everglades ecosystem. Table 13.7 presents four alternative restoration plans and the baseline condition using the structural attribute model. The plans range from full ecosystem restoration with none of the costs paid by Floridians to full restoration and significant cost-sharing by Floridians. In this case the restoration plans focus on wetland and estuarine species restoration because there would be direct substitution between wetland and dryland habitats. The last plan in Table 13.7 is again included to identify the effects of concerns about domestic water use restrictions in the plans. The results in Table 13.7 with preferences

Table 13.6 Evaluation of selected restoration plans with the functional attribute models by past environmental donations

Plan description		Percent in favour			Net willingness to pay ($ per year)		
		All	Donate	No Donations	All	Donate	No Donations
Baseline (no change)							
Lake Okeechobee: 60%	Costs: 0	NA	NA	NA	NA	NA	NA
Water Conservation: 50%	Farmland Reduction: 0						
Everglades National Park: 50%	Water Restriction: none						
Full restoration without costs							
Lake Okeechobee: 90%	Costs: 0	71.7	90.1	58.6	$58.79	$92.26	$27.35
Water Conservation: 90%	Farmland Reduction: 0						
Everglades National Park: 90%	Water Restriction: none						
Full restoration with minimized costs							
Lake Okeechobee: 90%	Costs: $25	54.3	75.8	39.1	$15.60	$41.78	−$30.93
Water Conservation: 90%	Farmland Reduction: 100000						
Everglades National Park: 90%	Water Restriction: Level 1						
Full restoration with all costs							
Lake Okeechobee: 90%	Costs: $50	31.1	52.7	15.6	−$61.09	−$7.68	−$109.35
Water Conservation: 90%	Farmland Reduction: 200000						
Everglades National Park: 90%	Water Restriction: Level 2						
Full restoration with all costs/no water restrictions							
Lake Okeechobee: 90%	Costs: $50	41.6	60.4	28.1	−$23.99	$12.86	−$55.47
Water Conservation: 90%	Farmland Reduction: 200000						
Everglades National Park: 90%	Water Restriction: none						

Note: NA – Not applicable.

Table 13.7 Evaluation of selected restoration plans with the structural attribute models by respondent location

Plan description		Percent in favour			Net willingness to pay ($ per year)		
		All	South	Central	All	South	Central
Baseline (no change)							
Wetland Species: 20%	Costs: 0	NA	NA	NA	NA	NA	NA
Dryland Species: 50%	Farmland Reduction: 0						
Estuarine Species: 60%	Water Restriction: none						
Full (wetland species) restoration without costs							
Wetland Species: 80%	Costs: 0	92.7	88.7	98.9	$69.86	$68.82	$72.42
Dryland Species: 50%	Farmland Reduction: 0						
Estuarine Species: 90%	Water Restriction: none						
Full restoration with minimized costs							
Wetland Species: 80%	Costs: $25	67.9	54.9	88.0	$26.63	$12.02	$50.58
Dryland Species: 50%	Farmland Reduction: 100000 acres						
Estuarine Species: 90%	Water Restriction: Level 1						
Full restoration with all costs							
Wetland Species: 80%	Costs: $50	29.9	26.1	35.9	−$33.64	−$47.85	−$12.63
Dryland Species: 50%	Farmland Reduction: 200000 acres						
Estuarine Species: 90%	Water Restriction: Level 2						
Full restoration with all costs/no water restrictions							
Wetland Species: 80%	Costs: $50	52.1	43.7	65.2	$1.32	−$12.62	$24.50
Dryland Species: 50%	Farmland Reduction: 200000 acres						
Estuarine Species: 90%	Water Restriction: none						

Note: NA – Not applicable.

disaggregated by location indicate that preferences for the structural attributes also differed across individuals. While both groups strongly favoured full restoration with no costs, in this analysis Central Floridians were more likely to favour other restoration plans and to have a higher WTP for these plans than South Floridians. Both groups would oppose full restoration with a high cost-share for Floridians (as in the functional attribute analysis), but the magnitude of the potential welfare loss is smaller for both groups than with the functional attribute model.

Finally, Table 13.8 presents the same set of restoration plans as Table 13.7 except preferences were disaggregated according to whether the respondent had donated to environmental groups. Again both groups strongly favour full restoration with no costs, and those who donated to environmental groups had stronger preferences for restoration than those who had not. But, the differences between group preferences for other plans were much smaller than with the functional attribute model. Also, both groups were very sensitive to the extent of water use restrictions.

5. DISCUSSION AND CONCLUSIONS

In this study we investigated two sources of complexity in environmental policy: heterogeneous preferences over individuals and groups and multi-attribute environmental goods. Our analysis and results were based on a choice experiment using stated preference models for Everglades ecosystem restoration. This project is one of the most extensive and expensive restoration efforts ever undertaken and a classic example of the need for public preference information to guide plan selection and cost-sharing decisions.

Our results suggest that policy analysis based on assumptions about homogeneous preferences may provide incomplete and/or inaccurate information to policymakers. The analysis indicated that disaggregation of preferences by socioeconomic groupings may yield widely differing evaluations of the same restoration plan. For example, if the net willingness to pay estimates from the homogeneous preference model in Table 13.5 were extrapolated to Florida's 2000 population of 5.82 million households,[3] the aggregate annual net benefits for full functional restoration (with no direct costs to Floridians) would be $342.2 million ($58.79 times 5.82 million). By contrast, because 40 percent of all households reside in South Florida, the heterogeneous preference model (Table 13.5) yields annual benefits of $201.2 million for South Floridians and $28.8 million for other Floridians. Total net benefits of $230.0 million are significantly lower with the heterogeneous model. A similar divergence would result for the other policy alternatives in Table 13.5 or if the net benefit results were extrapolated on the

Table 13.8 Evaluation of selected restoration plans with the structural attribute models by past environmental donations

Plan description		Percent in favour			Net willingness to pay ($ per year)		
		All	Donate	No donations	All	Donate	No donations
Baseline (no change)							
Wetland Species: 20%	Costs: 0	NA	NA	NA	NA	NA	NA
Dryland Species: 50%	Farmland Reduction: 0						
Estuarine Species: 60%	Water Restriction: none						
Full (wetland species) restoration without costs							
Wetland Species: 80%	Costs: 0	92.7	93.0	92.4	$69.86	$73.37	$67.23
Dryland Species: 50%	Farmland Reduction: 0						
Estuarine Species: 90%	Water Restriction: none						
Full restoration with minimized costs							
Wetland Species: 80%	Costs: $25	67.9	76.5	59.7	$26.63	$37.81	$15.00
Dryland Species: 50%	Farmland Reduction: 100 000 acres						
Estuarine Species: 90%	Water Restriction: Level 1						
Full restoration with all costs							
Wetland Species: 80%	Costs: $50	29.9	35.7	24.4	-$33.64	-$19.93	-$47.59
Dryland Species: 50%	Farmland Reduction: 200 000 acres						
Estuarine Species: 90%	Water Restriction: Level 2						
Full restoration with all costs/no water restrictions							
Wetland Species: 80%	Costs: $50	52.1	53.9	50.4	$1.32	$8.71	-$4.52
Dryland Species: 50%	Farmland Reduction: 200 000 acres						
Estuarine Species: 90%	Water Restriction: none						

Note: NA – Not applicable.

basis of past environmental donations as presented in Table 13.6. Thus, the homogeneous preference model would overstate annual aggregate benefits for the same policy alternative by a sizable margin.

On the other hand, the structural attributes model did not indicate a wide divergence in preferences between South Floridians and other Florida residents. The results in Table 13.7 for the homogeneous preference model produce an aggregate annual net benefit of $406.6 million ($69.86 times 5.82 million) for full structural (wetland species) restoration with no direct costs to Floridians. With the heterogeneous preference model, annual net benefits from full restoration would be $160.2 million for South Floridians and $252.9 million for other Floridians, a total of $413.1 million. Similarly, there would be a relatively small difference in the aggregate net benefits if the estimates in Table 13.8 were extrapolated on the basis of past environmental donations.

These aggregate benefits for alternative restoration plans can be compared with the estimated $400 million average annual cost (over 20 years) for the US Army Corps of Engineers' (1999) Everglades restoration plan. With both the functional and structural attributes models, the average annual net benefits would not justify the project unless there were no direct costs to Florida residents. This comparison, however, should be used with caution because the restoration alternatives used in this study do not match exactly with the actual Corps' plan. And, possible benefits from Everglades restoration plans to individuals outside Florida have not been measured. Moreover, it should be noted that the US Congress exempted the Everglades restoration project from the standard water resource planning requirement for a benefit–cost analysis (Milon, 2000).

Nevertheless, the empirical evidence from this choice experiment indicates that the type of information provided to respondents about complex environmental goods does matter in the elicitation of environmental preferences. Structural and functional attributes represent two alternative, albeit interrelated, ways to represent a complex environmental good. Both descriptors are consistent with ecological approaches to ecosystem restoration and have policy relevance.

Respondents generally preferred some level of Everglades restoration regardless of the attribute specification. Individuals who lived outside South Florida and those who had not made environmental donations in the past had much weaker preferences for restoration when the restoration plans were specified with functional attributes. Unfortunately, the differences between stated preferences with alternative ecological information are not easy to explain. It is tempting to attribute these differences in preference intensity solely to the socioeconomic characteristics identified in this study. But, as Munro and Hanley (1999) point out, economic theory provides relatively limited guidance on the relationship between environmental information and individual values. The observed socioeconomic characteristics used in this analysis may be proxies for more fundamental attitudes and/or knowledge about ecosystem processes that influence environmental preferences (for example, Kotchen and Reiling, 2000). Nevertheless, these results indicate that further research is warranted into the effects of alternative types of information about complex environmental goods in stated choice surveys.

In summary, empirical public policy analyses such as the choice experiments used in this study are difficult and expensive to conduct. The evaluation of heterogeneity in public preferences and the specification of choice attributes for complex environmental goods raise many difficult issues for survey design and econometric analysis. The search for improved methods to deal with these sources of complexity could significantly enhance the information available for environmental policy decisions.

NOTES

* Paper prepared for the Conference on the Political Economy of Environmental Policy, co-sponsored by the University of Central Florida and the Center for Economic Research, Tilburg, The Netherlands, November 30–December 2, 2000. We are grateful to the editors and an anonymous reviewer for helpful comments and suggestions on the paper. All errors and interpretations are the responsibility of the authors.
1. Complete information about the Everglades restoration project is available through the website: http://www.evergladesplan.org.
2. For completeness other utility functions with multiple interaction effects could have been evaluated, but this would have significantly increased the scope and extent of the experiment. Louviere et al. (2000) succinctly summarize this research dilemma in their observation that additivity of utility should be regarded from the outset as very naïve and simplistic. Yet, with more complex problems, it may not be practical (or even possible) to use designs that provide efficient estimates of main effects and multiple interactions. 'Hence, in many cases, one must use main effects designs or do nothing' (Louviere et al., 2000, p. 88).
3. The willingness to pay estimates were extrapolated on the basis of household units because this was the sampling unit in the survey design. Also, the cost attribute used in the multiattribute models was expressed in terms of annual household costs.

REFERENCES

Bateman, I. and K. Willis (1999), *Valuing Environmental Preferences*, New York: Oxford University Press.
Bratton, S. (1992), 'Alternative Models of Ecosystem Restoration', in R. Costanza, B. Norton and B. Haskell (eds), *Ecosystem Health: New Goals for Environmental Management*, Washington, DC: Island Press, pp. 170–89.

Breffle, W. and E. Morey (2000), 'Investigating preference heterogeneity in a repeated discrete-choice recreation demand model of atlantic salmon fishing', *Marine Resource Economics*, **15** (1), 1–20.

Commons, M. and C. Perrings (1992), 'Towards an ecological economics of sustainability', *Ecological Economics*, **6** (1), 7–34.

De Palma, A., G. Myers and Y. Papageorgiou (1994), 'Rational choice under an imperfect ability to choose', *American Economic Review*, **84** (3), 419–40.

Franklin, J. (1988), 'Structural and Functional Diversity in Temperate Forests', in E.O. Wilson (ed.), *Biodiversity*, Washington, DC: National Academy Press, pp. 166–175.

Holling, C. (1987), 'Simplifying the complex: the paradigms of ecological function and structure', *European Journal of Operational Research*, **30**, 139–46.

Holling, C.S., L.H. Gunderson and C.J. Walters (1994), 'The Structure and Dynamics of the Everglades System: Guidelines for Ecosystem Restoration', in S. Davis and J. Ogden (eds), *Everglades – the Ecosystem and Its Restoration*, Delray Beach, FL: St. Lucie Press.

Kahn, J. and R. O'Neill (1999), 'Ecological interaction as a source of economic irreversibility', *Southern Economic Journal*, **66** (2), 391–402.

Kellert, S.R. (1996), *The Value of Life: Biological Diversity and Human Society*, Washington, DC: Island Press.

Kolasa, J. and S. Pickett (1991), *Ecological Heterogeneity*, New York: Springer-Verlag.

Kotchen, M. and S. Reiling (2000), 'Environmental attitudes, motivations, and contingent valuation of nonuse values: a case study involving endangered species,' *Ecological Economics*, **32** (1), 93–107.

Layton, D. (2000), 'Random coefficient models for stated preference surveys', *Journal of Environmental Economics and Management*, **40** (1), 21–36.

Louviere, J.J., D.A. Henscher and J.D. Swait (2000), *Stated Choice Methods: Analysis and Applications*, Cambridge, UK: Cambridge University Press.

May, R. (1977), 'Thresholds and breakpoints in ecosystems with a multiplicity of stable states', *Nature*, **269** (5628), 471–7.

McFadden, D. (1974), 'Conditional Logit Analysis of Qualitative Choice Behaviour', in P. Zarembka (ed.), *Frontiers in Econometrics*, New York: Academic Press, pp. 105–42.

McFadden, D. and K. Train (2000), 'Mixed MNL models for discrete response', *Journal of Applied Econometrics*, **15** (5), 447–70.

Milon, J. (2000), 'Who wants to pay for Everglades restoration', *Choices*, 2nd Quarter, 12–16.

Milon, J.W., C. Kiker and D. Lee (1999a), 'Ecosystems and Social Conflict: Lessons from the Florida Everglades', in R. Just and S. Netanyahu (eds), *Conflict and Cooperation on Trans-Boundary Water Resources*, Boston: Kluwer Academic Publishers.

Milon, J.W., A.W. Hodges, A. Rimal, C.F. Kiker and F. Casey (1999b), 'Public Preferences and Economic Values for Restoration of the Everglades/South Florida Ecosystem', Economics Report 99–1, Food and Resource Economics Department, University of Florida, Gainesville, FL.

Munro, A. and N. Hanley (1999), 'Information, Uncertainty, and Contingent Valuation', in I. Bateman and K. Willis (eds), *Valuing Environmental Preferences*, New York: Oxford University Press, pp. 258–79.

Noss, R.F. (1990), 'Indicators for monitoring biodiversity: a hierarchical approach', *Conservation Biology*, **4** (4), 355–64.

Revelt, D. and K. Train (1998), 'Mixed logit with repeated choices: households' choices of appliance efficiency level', *Review of Economics and Statistics*, **80** (4), 647–57.

Revelt, D. and K. Train (1999), 'Consumer-Specific Taste Parameters and Mixed Logit', (mimeo), Department of Economics, University of California, Berkeley.

Roe, B., K. Boyle and M. Teisl (1996), 'Using conjoint analysis to derive estimates of compensating variation', *Journal of Environmental Economics and Management*, **31** (2), 145–59.

Swallow, S., T. Weaver, J. Opaluch and T. Michelman (1994), 'Heterogeneous preferences and aggregation in environmental policy analysis: a landfill siting case', *American Journal of Agricultural Economics*, **76** (3), 431–43.

Train, K. (1998), 'Recreation demand models with taste differences over people', *Land Economics*, **74** (2), 230–39.

Train, K., D. Revelt and P. Ruud (1999), 'Mixed Logit Estimation Routine for Cross-Sectional Data', Department of Economics, University of California, Berkeley, [http://elsa.berkeley.edu/Software/abstracts/train0196.html].

Turner K., K. Button and P. Nijkamp (1999), *Ecosystems and Nature: Economics, Science and Policy*, Cheltenham, UK and Northampton, MA, US: Edward Elgar.

U.S. Army Corps of Engineers and the South Florida Water Management District (1999), *Final Integrated Feasibility Report and Programmatic Environmental Impact Statement*, Jacksonville, FL.

U.S. Fish and Wildlife Service (1999), *South Florida Multi-Species Recovery Plan*, Atlanta, GA.

Westman, W. (1991), 'Ecological restoration projects: measuring their performance', *The Environmental Professional*, **13** (3), 207–15.

Wilson, E.O. (1984), *Biophilia*, Cambridge, MA: Harvard University Press.

14. Incentives in public goods experiments: implications for the environment

Jacob Goeree, Charles Holt and Susan Laury*

INTRODUCTION

Although the costs associated with pollution abatement are primarily borne by those who invest in such reduction efforts, a major share of the benefits may accrue to others external to this decision (for example, communities down-river or downwind from the one making the investment). If people consider only their own private benefits from such reductions in pollution, then economic theory would predict inefficiently low levels of pollution abatement. Obviously the market failure will not be as severe if those incurring the costs of the abatement decision also consider the benefit to others.

In the case of point-source pollution, the polluting source is known and one can force it to internalize this externality, for example, by imposing taxes or fines on the polluting entity. However in recent years increased attention has been paid to non-point source pollution. In this environment the source of pollution is not known and therefore it is not obvious who should be taxed for the pollution. Therefore voluntary investment in pollution abatement becomes an interesting alternative.

Experiments have been widely used to investigate the effects of financial incentives on the choices that individuals make. A laboratory experiment in a controlled setting allows one to assess the extent to which individuals are affected by their own payoffs and the extent to which they are willing to make sacrifices to help others. This permits an empirical approach to issues that cannot be resolved on the basis of theoretical arguments alone. For example, experiments are an ideal setting in which to investigate choices where an externality (either positive or negative) is involved. This chapter reports on an experiment designed to evaluate the effects of such externalities by systematically altering the costs and benefits of the investment that corresponds to pollution abatement.

In this experiment subjects must choose a level of (costly) investment that benefits not only the person investing but also another person. Even when the cost of the investment is relatively low and the benefit to others high, suboptimal investment is observed. However, the degree of under-investment (relative to the social optimum) is sensitive to both the internal cost and external benefit of this investment. Moreover, in all sessions more investment is observed than would be the case with individuals who are solely maximizing own earnings.

We use a modified public goods experimental design (see Ledyard, 1995, for details of the standard public goods design). Subjects begin with an endowment of 'tokens' that can either be kept or invested. Each token that a subject keeps yields a constant monetary return for the subject, and each token that is invested also yields a return, both for that subject and for all others in the group. The value of a token kept is the opportunity cost of investment. The earnings structure in this experiment is designed to simulate the incentive structure of the pollution abatement decision. The sum of both group members' returns from the investment typically exceeds the individual's return from keeping the token, so group earnings are maximized by full investment. From a selfish point of view, however, the net monetary loss from making an investment is the difference between the value of a token that is kept and what the subject earns from a token invested. A net loss ensures that the Nash equilibrium is to invest nothing, at least in a one-shot game with no altruistic feelings about others' payoffs. Of course, if one cares about others' earnings, this may induce some to invest even in this setup.

Following Carter et al. (1992), we decompose the return from a token invested so that the one investing may earn a different return than the other who also benefits. For example, a token, worth 5 cents if it is kept, may yield a return of 4 cents to the subject who makes the investment and a poten-tially different amount, say 2 cents, to the other person in the group. The net loss from making an investment, therefore, is simply the difference between the private value of the token and the return to the one investing, or 5 cents minus 4 cents = 1 cent in this example. By independently varying the internal and external benefits we can analyse how the net cost of invest-ing versus the benefit to others affects investment decisions.[1]

The next section describes the laboratory procedures and experimental design, and the third section describes the data from our experiments. The final section discusses the implications of this and other public goods experiments for environmental decisions.

EXPERIMENTAL DESIGN AND PROCEDURES

A total of 130 subjects participated in 13 sessions at the University of Virginia and the University of South Carolina. Participants were recruited from undergraduate economics and business classes, and none had participated in a previous public goods experiment. All subjects in a session were in the same room, but were visually isolated from other participants by the use of blinders. Subjects were provided with a written copy of the instructions (see Appendix A), which were read aloud by the experiment monitor.

Table 14.1   Experimental design

Session numbers	Earnings from a token kept	Own earnings from a token invested (internal return)	Other's earnings from a token invested (external return)	Number of participants
1, 2, 3	5 cents	4 cents (0.8)	2 cents (0.4)	30
4, 5, 6	5 cents	4 cents (0.8)	4 cents (0.8)	30
7, 8, 9	5 cents	4 cents (0.8)	6 cents (1.2)	30
10	5 cents	4 cents (0.8)	12 cents (2.4)	10
11, 12, 13	5 cents	2 cents (0.4)	6 cents (1.2)	30

The procedures implemented in these experiments are based on those used by Isaac and Walker (1988). At the start of each round an individual was endowed with 25 tokens, which could be kept or voluntarily invested in an account that benefited all in the group. A token kept earned a constant return of 5 cents, and a token invested earned a return both to the individual and to another participant, with whom this person was matched. Table 14.1 shows the value of a token invested, both to the investor and the other participant, in each of our five treatments. The *internal return* is the value of the token invested (2 cents or 4 cents) to the person investing the token, relative to the cost of the investment (5 cents in each of our treatments). For example, when a token invested earns 2 cents to the person investing, this corresponds to an internal return of 0.4, which is calculated as the 2 cent 'internal' payoff divided by the 5 cent opportunity cost of investing the token. The *external return* is the relative value of the investment to the other person (2 cents, 4 cents, 6 cents or 12 cents). Therefore, the external returns are 0.4, 0.8, 1.2 and 2.4, respectively. For each of the five treatments shown in Table 14.1, one session was conducted at the University of South Carolina (with the exception of the fourth row, in which only one session was conducted at the University of Virginia), and all remaining sessions were conducted at the University of Virginia. Individual data for all sessions are reported in Appendix C.

Notice that the value of a token kept (5 cents) is greater than the individual's return from a token invested (2 cents or 4 cents) in all treatments. Thus the single-round dominant strategy is for each subject to invest nothing. However it is also the case that the sum of the own and other's earnings from a token invested is greater than the 5 cent value of a token kept. Thus investing fully would maximize group earnings in all treatments.

At the beginning of each decision period, each person wrote their own investment decision (which was any number of tokens from 0 to 25) on a record sheet. Then all record sheets were collected and subjects were paired according to a predetermined schedule of matchings. The other participant's investment was written on the individual's record sheet, earnings were calculated, and record sheets were returned. Each person then made a decision for the next round, and a new pairing was implemented. This process was repeated for nine rounds. There were 10 subjects in each session, and pairings were determined so that no one was ever matched with the same person more than once. Participants were told that the other person's identification number would be written on their record sheet so they could observe that there were no repeated matchings. This was done to reduce incentives for signalling with high investments in order to encourage the same person to reciprocate in a later round and therefore to isolate the treatment effect of interest.

Each person knew the number of rounds, their own and the other's token endowments in each round and how all payoffs were calculated, that is, their own and others' earnings from tokens kept or invested. Prior to the start of each round subjects could see on their record sheet the number of tokens invested by the other participants with whom they were matched in the previous rounds, and their own earnings in previous rounds.

After record sheets were collected for round 9, subjects were asked to forecast the investment decision of the person with whom they would be matched in the current round.[2] Instructions for this are presented in Appendix B. Subjects were paid a small reward based on the accuracy of this forecast, calculated as 200 cents less the squared deviation of their forecast from the other's actual investment. While we expected there to be a relationship between one's investment decision and one's expectation of what the other person would choose to invest, we elicited this forecast only after all subjects had entered their last investment decision, to ensure that their decisions were not biased by the act of asking the forecasting question.[3]

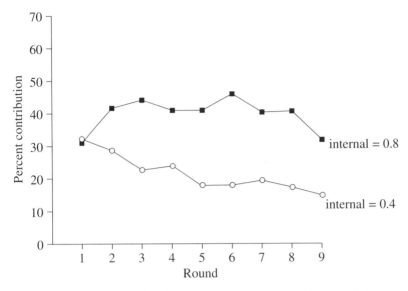

*Figure 14.1   The effect of a change in internal return (0.4 versus 0.8),
holding external return constant at 1.2*

Participants were paid, in cash, the sum of their earnings from the nine decision-making rounds, their forecasting reward and a $6 participation fee. Earnings ranged from about $14 to $26. Sessions lasted no more than 90 minutes, including subject payment.

BEHAVIOUR

Overall, the percentage of tokens invested follows a similar pattern to that typically observed in public goods experiments. Initial investments are between 30 and 60 percent of the aggregate endowment, and substantial levels of investment are observed in the last round. Moreover, investments generally decline over time in most of our treatments. See Ledyard (1995) and Isaac et al. (1994) for an overview of the most common treatment effects. These similarities with previous public goods experiments are interesting to note given two differences in our design relative to other studies: we restrict our attention to groups of size two, and subjects are never paired with the same person more than once.[4]

Figure 14.1 shows the effect of a change in internal return (from 0.4 to 0.8) holding the external return constant at 1.2. This figure shows a time-series of investment decisions (averaged across all three groups in each treatment) in each round of the experiment. Clearly, increasing the internal return (which results in a decrease in the net cost of investing) has a substantial effect on investment decisions. This effect is noticeable after the first round of the experiment, and becomes accentuated in the late rounds after investment choices in the 0.4 treatment declined by about 30 percent from their initial level. In the last half of the experiment (rounds six to nine), about twice as many tokens are invested in the high internal return treatment as in the low internal return treatment. This is shown in Table 14.2, which presents summary statistics for individual investments in the last four rounds of each of our treatments.[5]

Table 14.2   Summary of individual investment choices (number of tokens invested out of an endowment of 25, last 4 rounds)

	Mean	Median	Std. dev	Observations
internal = 0.8 external = 0.4	5.00	2	6.77	120
internal = 0.8 external = 0.8	7.83	5	8.68	120
internal = 0.8 external = 1.2	9.99	5	10.96	120
internal = 0.8 external = 2.4	11.23	5	10.97	40
internal = 0.4 external = 1.2	4.43	0	6.69	120

Our hypothesis that a decrease in the net cost of giving will increase the level of investment predicts that investment by the three groups with an internal return of 0.8 will exceed that by those facing a 0.4 internal return. Because each subject in a session is matched with every other subject one time, observations within a session are not independent. Therefore, the investment decisions by all subjects within a session must be averaged, resulting in one independent observation in each session. Using the average investment in the last four rounds as our unit of observation, the session averages are 0.5, 5.8 and 7.0 tokens for the low internal return treatment, and are 6.6, 11.2 and 12.1 for the high internal return treatment. Therefore there is one reversal relative to the predicted order: the lowest observation in the 0.8 internal return treatment (6.6 tokens) is less than the highest observation in the 0.4 treatment (7.0 tokens). Using a Mann–Whitney rank sum test (and three observations per treatment), this difference is significant at the 10 percent level.[6]

We next consider the effect of an increase in the external return (0.4, 0.8,

1.2 and 2.4), holding constant the net cost of investing (as measured by the internal return). Figure 14.2 shows the investment averages in these four treatments, in the nine rounds of the experiment. These results provide some evidence of altruism in subjects' investment decisions. With the internal return from investing held constant at 0.8, investment choices increase with an increase in external return. Although early-round investments for the middle two treatments (external returns of 0.8 and 1.2) intersect, and are at times reversed, by the final rounds of the experiment the treatment averages are lined up in the predicted order (at about 20, 30, 40 and 50 percent). This effect is significant at the 5 percent level, using the Jonckheere test for ordered alternatives on the treatments with external returns of 0.4, 0.8 and 1.2. (To test for significance we again average investment decisions across subjects in a session, so that we have three independent observations in each treatment.)

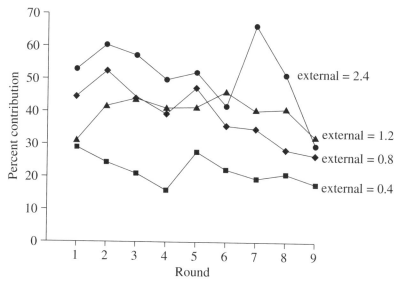

Figure 14.2   *The effect of a change in external return (0.4 to 2.4), holding internal return constant at 0.8*

We can examine the effect of each of our treatments on individual investment decisions using regression analysis. Because each individual makes nine investment decisions, a panel regression is appropriate. Using a random effects model, we estimated the effect of the decision round (*round*), internal return (m_I) and external return (m_E) on the individual's investment.[7] This obtained:

$$invest = -1.30 - 0.35^* Round + 10.59^* m_I + 3.58^* m_E$$
$$\qquad\;\; (2.99)\quad (0.07)\qquad\quad (3.47)\qquad (1.15)$$

The coefficients on all of our treatment variables are the predicted sign, and significant at any standard level of confidence. Individual investment decreases, on average about 0.4 tokens per round. An increase in internal return by 0.4 (2 cents) results in an increase in investment by 4.2 tokens, while the effect of an increase in external return is about one third as large: an increase by 0.4 in external return causes a 1.4 token increase in investment.

If this behaviour is due to altruism, it is not of the warm-glow variety (defined as increased utility from the act of giving, rather than from what the other receives) because it is responsive to the external return (see Palfrey and Prisbrey, 1997). But neither are subjects acting as pure altruists, that is, they do not behave in a way to maximize the other's earnings. Other-regarding behaviour is more common in our data when the benefit to the other of investing increases, holding constant the private cost of the investment. Thus we see a type of price-sensitive or *economic* altruism.

We can define the 'price' of investing a token as the benefit relative to the cost of investing. In this context, this is calculated as the benefit the other receives divided by the net cost to the person investing. For example, consider the treatment (internal = 0.8, external = 0.4). In this treatment one earns 5 cents for a token kept; a token invested earns 4 cents to the one investing and 2 cents to the other person. Therefore the benefit the other receives is 2 cents; the net cost of investing is the 1 cent the subject gives up in order to invest the token (5 cents minus the 4 cent internal return).

Two of our treatments have an identical price of investing. In the first line of Table 14.2 (internal = 0.8, external = 0.4), the other person receives 2 cents at a net cost to the investor of 1 cent, as explained above. Therefore, the price of investing a token in this treatment is 2, which is the ratio of the benefit to the other person (2 cents) to the net cost of investing (1 cent). Similarly, the last treatment in Table 14.2 (internal = 0.4, external = 1.2) also has a price of 2, since the benefit to the other person is 6 cents, and the net cost of investing is 3 cents. Notice in the second column of Table 14.2, the mean investments in these two treatments are quite close (5.0 versus 4.43). The similarity in investment decisions is even more dramatic when you compare the distribution of *individual* investment decisions over all rounds of the experiment. Figure 14.3 shows histograms of individual investment decisions in both of these treatments. Not only are the mean investment decisions quite close, the distribution of individual decisions is virtually identical.

As these histograms suggest, the average investment choices reported

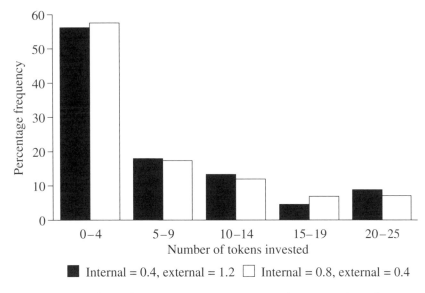

Figure 14.3 Choice frequency: two treatments with constant 'price'

above mask a notable feature of the data from these experiments: many individual investments are at or near the extremes of the distribution, and not in the middle as the mean would indicate. However it is also the case that the treatment affects at which extreme the individual investment decisions are located. This is supported by Figure 14.4, which presents histograms of individual investments in each of the first four treatments in Table 14.2. As the external return increases, the percentage of decisions that are at or near full investment (in the 20–25 token range) increases dramatically. Just 7.5 percent of observations are in this interval when the external return is 0.4, compared with 42.5 percent when the external return is 2.4.

Although more than half of all investment decisions fall in the extreme intervals containing either zero or full investment, many choices involve splitting (keeping only a portion of the endowment and investing the rest). Very few individuals always invest fully or nothing. Overall, only 22 of 130 subjects fall into one of these categories (17 invest nothing in all rounds and 5 always invest fully).[8]

The final aspect of individual behaviour to consider is how the investment choice depends on what the other person is expected to do. If a person invests only because the other is expected to invest a similar number of tokens (perfect reciprocity), then there would be a high correlation between investment decisions and forecasts. Recall such forecasts were elicited (without prior warning) *after* everyone had made a round nine investment

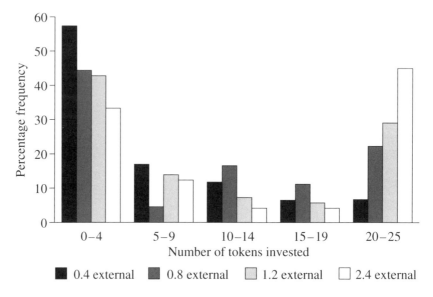

Figure 14.4   Choice frequency: change in external return

decision (the final choice in the experiment). Although they had seen eight other decisions at this point, they had never before been matched with the person whose investment choice they were forecasting. Figure 14.5 shows the frequency distribution of the round nine investments and forecasts, which are remarkably similar. However, these aggregate frequencies do not address the issue of a correlation between each person's investment and that person's forecast of what the person with whom they were matched would do.

Figure 14.6 shows individual forecasts and investments, where the individuals are sorted from left to right in order of their investment level. Each person's investment decision and forecast are shown together in a single column. This figure shows the correlation between one's decision and one's expectation, but does not reflect the accuracy of these forecasts. First consider those who invested nothing, that is, those on the left half of the graph. Of these, about 40 percent were conscious free-riders, anticipating that the other person would make a positive investment. You can see these people as dots at zero tokens invested; the triangles representing their forecast of the other's investment choices are above their zero-investment decisions for nearly half of this group of subjects. Of those who invested five or more tokens, on the right half of the graph, about two-thirds were expecting the other person to make a *lower* investment (the triangles for these subjects are below the dot-investment marker). This pattern is universal among those

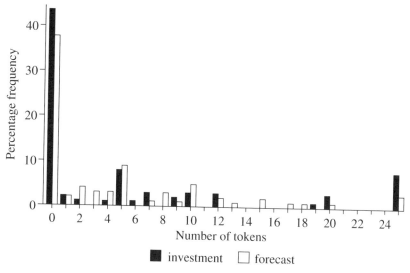

Figure 14.5   Frequency distribution of round 9 investment choices and forecast of other's choice

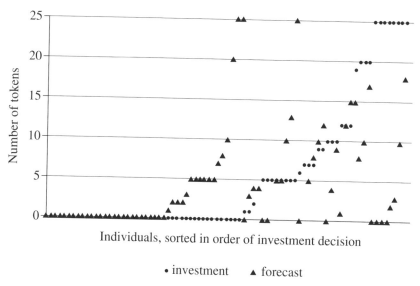

Figure 14.6   Individual investments matched with forecasts

who invested all 25 tokens. Therefore the majority of those investing did so with no expectation that this investment would be reciprocated.

Given the correlation observed in this figure (and also looking at individual investment decisions in Appendix C), we estimate a model that includes the other subject's investment decision. Specifically we look at whether behaviour changes due to previous experience. If subjects update their beliefs based on past experience, the lagged investment by the person with whom the subject was matched may serve as a proxy for the subject's expectation of the other's investment choice. This yields:

$$invest = -1.37 - 0.37^*Round + 9.71^*m_I + 3.16^*m_E + 0.16^*others_{t-1}$$
$$\quad\ (3.12)\ (0.08) \qquad\qquad (3.63) \quad\ (1.20) \qquad (0.02)$$

The coefficients on all of our treatment variables change very little when the other person's lagged investment is included in the random effects regression. The other's lagged investment is of small magnitude (one's investment increases by 0.2 given a one-token increase in the other's investment in the previous period), but is positive and significant.

CONCLUSIONS AND IMPLICATIONS

This chapter reports the results of an experiment in which individuals are given the opportunity to invest in a good that provides both a private benefit to the person investing and also an external benefit to another person. This setup simulates one of the key features of many environmental cleanup problems: the costs of the cleanup are borne by those investing in technologies designed to reduce pollution or by those undertaking efforts to clean up existing pollution. Meanwhile, some external to this decision also enjoy the benefits of this investment (those who are downstream or downwind of the cleanup efforts, for example). This is particularly applicable to nonpoint source pollution problems where the source of the pollution cannot be identified and therefore traditional economic remedies may not be applied. Although economic theory predicts an inefficiently low level of investment in these cleanup efforts will result, if those investing consider not only their own private costs and benefits, but also the benefits enjoyed by others, the degree of market failure may be mitigated.

The data provide evidence that investment is correlated with changes in the external return, holding the internal return constant, and are correlated with the internal return, holding the external return constant. These effects support the notion of *economic altruism*, that is that people are more likely to take actions that raise others' payoffs when the ratio of the benefit to others to the private net cost of investment is relatively high. Moreover the frequency distributions of investments are virtually identical for two treatments with internal and external returns that are configured to hold constant this price ratio (of external benefit to net cost). The response to treatment effects is variable across subjects and over time for the same subject, suggesting that subjects experiment with their investment decisions, and respond to others' investment decisions.

Taken together these results provide support for the standard view that individuals (or communities) will not fully consider the benefits to others when choosing the level of resources to devote to cleanup efforts. However their choices may be sensitive to the cost of undertaking this investment or the amount others stand to benefit. This suggests that programmes emphasizing (or advertising) external benefits of pollution abatement, may increase investment in such technologies. More effective (though more costly to government or private agencies) might be programmes that subsidize or otherwise reduce the net cost of cleanup activities.

These conclusions should be interpreted with a degree of caution, however. This experiment was conducted in a very stylized setting in order to cleanly address the relative importance of net personal gain and external benefit. Certainly further experiments in a setting that more closely resembles environmental cleanup decisions are in order. For example, future experiments might incorporate groups making decisions (perhaps in an electoral or referendum-based process). Moreover it would be instructive to implement heterogeneity into the payoff structure, both in terms of the potential costs and benefits of investment choices. The advantage to this is that it adds realistic context, although at the cost of some laboratory control. This is a fruitful area of research that can nicely supplement the more controlled parallel laboratory studies.

APPENDIX A: INSTRUCTIONS

You are going to take part in an experimental study of decision making. At this time, you will be given $6 for coming on time. All the money that you earn after this will be yours to keep, and your earnings will be paid to you in cash at the end of today's experiment. We will start by reading the instructions, and then you will have the opportunity to ask questions about the procedures.

Your Decision

The experiment consists of 9 rounds. In each round you will make a decision. For each decision, you will be paired with *one* other participant.

Your earnings will depend upon the decisions that you make and the decisions that the other participant makes. You will be paired with a *different* person in each round. You will never be paired with the same person twice.

In every round you will each have 25 tokens. You must choose how many of these tokens you wish to keep and how many tokens you wish to invest. The amount of money you earn in a round depends on how many tokens you keep, how many tokens you invest, and how many tokens are invested by the other participant who is matched with you. You can invest any number of your tokens, from 0 tokens to 25 tokens, and the balance is what you keep.

You will earn 5 cents for each token that you keep. For each token that you invest, you will earn 4 cents and the other participant will earn 2 cents. Likewise, you will earn 2 cents for each token the other person invests.

To summarize, your earnings in each round are determined as follows:
your earnings = 5 cents times the number of tokens you keep
+ 4 cents times the number of tokens that you invest
+ 2 cents times the number of tokens the other participant invests.

Recording Your Decision

Each of you should examine your record sheet, which is the last page attached to these instructions. Your identification number is written on the top-right part of this sheet. At the beginning of each round, you will decide how many tokens you wish to invest and how many you wish to keep. You will begin by writing down in Column 2 how many tokens you wish to invest in round 1 (any number of tokens from 0 to 25). The remaining tokens, 25 minus the number you invest, is the number of tokens you keep. We will enter this number for you in Column 3.

After you make your decision for round 1, we will collect all record sheets. Then we will match you with another person. After this, we will write the other's investment decision on your record sheet (and your investment decision on the other participant's record sheet), record your earnings, and return the record sheet to you. Then you will make and record your decision for round 2, we will collect all record sheets, match you with a *different* participant, write the other's decision on your record sheet, and return it to you. This same process will be repeated for a total of 9 rounds. Remember, you will be matched with a different person in *every* round. We will write the other participant's identification number in Column 6 of your record sheet so you can see that you are never matched with the same person more than once.

Summary

To begin, participants make and record their decisions by writing the number of tokens they wish to invest in Column 2 of their record sheet. Then the record sheets are collected and participants are matched. Once the matching is done, we will enter the number of tokens you keep (25 minus the number you invest) in Column 3, and then record the other's investment decision in Column 7. These decisions determine each person's earnings as described above (you will earn 5 cents for each token you keep, you will earn 4 cents for each token that you invest, and 2 cents for each token that the other person invests). We will write earnings information on the record sheets and return them. Then participants make and record their decisions for the next round. Note that a new matching is conducted for each round.

Final Remarks

At the end of today's session, we will pay to you, privately in cash, the amount that you have earned. You have already received the $6 participation payment. Therefore, if you earn an amount $X during the exercise that follows, you will receive a total amount of $6.00 + $X. Your earnings are your own business and you do not have to discuss them with anyone.

During the experiment, you are not permitted to speak or communicate with the other participants. If you have a question while the experiment is going on, please raise your hand and one of us will come to your desk to answer it. At this time, do you have any questions about the instructions or procedures? If you have a question, please raise your hand and one of us will come to your seat to answer it.

APPENDIX B: ROUND 9 FORECAST INSTRUCTIONS

Part B

Please answer the following question while we calculate your earnings.

How many tokens do you think the person you were matched with in this round (round 9) invested?

Your earnings from this question will be based on how close you are to the other person's actual investment. Your earnings will be calculated as:

$$\text{your earnings} = \$2 - (\text{your answer} - \text{the other's investment})^2$$

If this is a negative number, your earnings from this part of the experiment will be zero.
If this is a positive number, we will add this amount to your experiment earnings.

Your earnings (in cents) =
$$200 \quad -[\qquad\qquad\qquad\qquad\qquad]^2$$
your answer − other's investment
$$= 200 -$$

Your earnings from Part B are:
We will add this amount to your earnings from part A (your earnings in rounds 1 through 9) to determine your total earnings for this experiment.
   1. Your Earnings from Part A:
   2. Your Earnings from Part B:
   Your Total Earnings (line 1 + line 2):

APPENDIX C: INDIVIDUAL DECISIONS

Key: number of tokens the subject invested (number of tokens other subject invested)

Session 1:   Internal Return = 0.8, External Return = 0.4, University of Virginia

	subject 1	subject 2	subject 3	subject 4	subject 5	subject 6	subject 7	subject 8	subject 9	subject 10
Round 1	0 (0)	0 (0)	10 (17)	17 (10)	0 (8)	8 (0)	25 (17)	17 (25)	5 (0)	0 (5)
Round 2	0 (10)	0 (0)	10 (0)	12 (19)	0 (0)	8 (0)	19 (12)	14 (0)	0 (8)	0 (14)
Round 3	0 (0)	0 (2)	5 (0)	17 (0)	0 (5)	0 (0)	0 (0)	0 (2)	2 (0)	0 (17)
Round 4	0 (0)	0 (2)	0 (2)	2 (0)	0 (0)	0 (2)	0 (0)	2 (0)	2 (0)	0 (0)
Round 5	0 (0)	0 (0)	0 (0)	0 (0)	0 (0)	0 (25)	25 (0)	20 (0)	0 (0)	0 (0)
Round 6	0 (0)	0 (2)	0 (0)	10 (15)	0 (0)	2 (0)	0 (8)	15 (10)	8 (20)	0 (0)
Round 7	0 (10)	0 (2)	0 (2)	10 (15)	0 (0)	2 (0)	9 (8)	10 (10)	3 (0)	0 (0)
Round 8	0 (0)	0 (9)	0 (13)	0 (0)	0 (3)	1 (0)	9 (0)	13 (0)	0 (0)	0 (9)
Round 9	0 (1)	0 (0)	0 (0)	0 (0)	0 (12)	1 (0)	0 (0)	12 (0)	0 (0)	0 (1)
Round 9 Forecast	3	5	0	0	0	0	0	0	1	0

Session 2: Internal Return = 0.8, External Return = 0.4, University of South Carolina

	subject 1	subject 2	subject 3	subject 4	subject 5	subject 6	subject 7	subject 8	subject 9	subject 10
Round 1	13 (10)	10 (13)	5 (5)	5 (5)	4 (8)	8 (4)	7 (0)	0 (7)	0 (15)	15 (0)
Round 2	10 (3)	12 (3)	3 (10)	0 (2)	3 (12)	7 (0)	2 (0)	5 (13)	0 (7)	13 (5)
Round 3	12 (0)	5 (0)	6 (10)	4 (10)	10 (6)	16 (10)	0 (12)	10 (16)	0 (5)	10 (4)
Round 4	6 (5)	3 (10)	5 (0)	15 (15)	3 (5)	15 (15)	5 (3)	10 (3)	0 (5)	5 (6)
Round 5	8 (25)	4 (4)	4 (4)	25 (8)	20 (11)	11 (3)	3 (11)	7 (0)	0 (7)	11 (20)
Round 6	15 (2)	2 (18)	0 (9)	20 (7)	2 (15)	18 (2)	4 (0)	7 (20)	0 (4)	9 (0)
Round 7	8 (7)	9 (15)	2 (4)	15 (9)	15 (0)	4 (2)	1 (6)	7 (8)	0 (15)	6 (1)
Round 8	7 (0)	10 (3)	10 (15)	20 (10)	10 (20)	15 (4)	3 (10)	15 (10)	0 (7)	4 (15)
Round 9	12 (10)	0 (5)	2 (6)	20 (0)	25 (0)	10 (12)	6 (2)	0 (25)	0 (20)	5 (0)
Round 9 Forecast	12	5	4	8	0	4	0	2	7	5

Session 3:   Internal Return = 0.8, External Return = 0.4, University of Virginia

	subject 1	subject 2	subject 3	subject 4	subject 5	subject 6	subject 7	subject 8	subject 9	subject 10
Round 1	5	4	5	10	20	10	9	0	0	5
	(4)	(5)	(10)	(5)	(10)	(20)	(0)	(9)	(5)	(0)
Round 2	4	8	0	18	20	5	3	0	0	5
	(0)	(20)	(4)	(3)	(8)	(0)	(18)	(5)	(5)	(0)
Round 3	0	12	3	13	15	0	2	0	0	15
	(2)	(0)	(15)	(15)	(3)	(0)	(0)	(0)	(12)	(0)
Round 4	2	0	2	7	10	0	0	0	0	25
	(25)	(0)	(0)	(0)	(0)	(7)	(10)	(0)	(2)	(13)
Round 5	3	25	1	8	0	5	12	0	0	20
	(8)	(1)	(25)	(3)	(20)	(12)	(0)	(0)	(0)	(2)
Round 6	1	1	1	4	0	5	21	0	0	20
	(0)	(5)	(20)	(0)	(1)	(1)	(0)	(0)	(21)	(0)
Round 7	6	3	0	1	5	0	4	0	0	25
	(0)	(1)	(0)	(3)	(0)	(0)	(25)	(4)	(5)	(1)
Round 8	2	5	1	2	0	0	5	0	0	25
	(0)	(5)	(0)	(0)	(2)	(0)	(5)	(6)	(2)	(4)
Round 9	0	7	0	1	0	0	7	0	0	25
	(0)	(25)	(7)	(0)	(0)	(0)	(0)	(0)	(1)	(7)
Round 9 Forecast	0	5	0	3	0	0	0	0	0	3

Session 4:   Internal Return =0.8, External Return =0.8, University of Virginia

	subject 1	subject 2	subject 3	subject 4	subject 5	subject 6	subject 7	subject 8	subject 9	subject 10
Round 1	10 (10)	10 (10)	0 (10)	10 (0)	20 (25)	25 (20)	20 (25)	25 (20)	25 (2)	2 (25)
Round 2	12 (0)	15 (25)	0 (12)	10 (18)	25 (15)	25 (25)	18 (10)	25 (5)	25 (25)	5 (25)
Round 3	10 (20)	20 (25)	0 (0)	10 (0)	0 (0)	25 (25)	20 (10)	25 (25)	25 (20)	0 (10)
Round 4	20 (3)	25 (25)	0 (25)	10 (25)	20 (17)	25 (10)	17 (0)	25 (25)	25 (0)	3 (20)
Round 5	20 (10)	25 (0)	0 (25)	10 (20)	20 (2)	25 (15)	15 (25)	25 (25)	25 (25)	2 (20)
Round 6	20 (0)	0 (25)	0 (0)	10 (25)	0 (20)	25 (0)	15 (25)	25 (10)	25 (0)	0 (0)
Round 7	15 (25)	15 (10)	0 (0)	10 (15)	5 (25)	0 (0)	15 (3)	25 (15)	25 (5)	3 (15)
Round 8	25 (25)	20 (15)	0 (0)	10 (5)	5 (10)	0 (2)	15 (20)	0 (0)	25 (25)	2 (0)
Round 9	0 (1)	15 (0)	0 (15)	10 (25)	25 (0)	1 (0)	15 (0)	0 (25)	25 (10)	0 (15)

Session 5: Internal Return =0.8, External Return =0.8, University of South Carolina

	subject 1	subject 2	subject 3	subject 4	subject 5	subject 6	subject 7	subject 8	subject 9	subject 10
Round 1	10 (15)	15 (10)	4 (15)	15 (4)	5 (5)	5 (5)	10 (5)	5 (10)	10 (5)	5 (10)
Round 2	15 (3)	15 (0)	3 (15)	20 (25)	0 (15)	25 (10)	25 (20)	5 (7)	10 (25)	7 (5)
Round 3	5 (15)	10 (20)	2 (0)	25 (0)	0 (2)	15 (7)	15 (5)	7 (15)	20 (10)	0 (25)
Round 4	0 (2)	25 (8)	5 (0)	25 (10)	0 (5)	10 (25)	5 (5)	8 (25)	15 (10)	2 (0)
Round 5	5 (23)	15 (6)	6 (15)	23 (5)	0 (8)	12 (2)	2 (0)	10 (15)	15 (5)	8 (0)
Round 6	5 (5)	5 (8)	7 (0)	20 (15)	5 (5)	8 (8)	2 (12)	15 (15)	15 (10)	0 (0)
Round 7	20 (17)	10 (0)	8 (5)	0 (10)	25 (5)	5 (5)	2 (15)	17 (20)	10 (2)	1 (7)
Round 8	25 (10)	0 (0)	1 (5)	15 (10)	0 (10)	4 (8)	5 (1)	20 (20)	10 (25)	0 (2)
Round 9	9 (4)	5 (5)	9 (20)	0 (0)	25 (15)	4 (0)	5 (0)	20 (1)	12 (25)	0 (4)
Round 9 Forecast	10	10	12	10	2	4	0	17	15	0

329

Session 6: *Internal Return =0.8, External Return =0.8, University of Virginia*

	subject 1	subject 2	subject 3	subject 4	subject 5	subject 6	subject 7	subject 8	subject 9	subject 10
Round 1	15 (5)	5 (15)	0 (0)	0 (0)	10 (12)	12 (10)	10 (15)	15 (10)	24 (10)	10 (24)
Round 2	20 (0)	3 (8)	0 (20)	10 (10)	8 (3)	18 (0)	10 (10)	25 (10)	0 (18)	15 (25)
Round 3	15 (10)	3 (0)	5 (12)	15 (10)	12 (5)	0 (25)	10 (15)	25 (15)	0 (3)	10 (15)
Round 4	0 (10)	0 (0)	10 (4)	5 (0)	10 (10)	0 (5)	10 (10)	0 (0)	4 (10)	10 (0)
Round 5	20 (10)	0 (14)	14 (0)	10 (20)	25 (7)	0 (10)	10 (0)	0 (5)	5 (0)	7 (25)
Round 6	10 (0)	0 (0)	20 (10)	15 (0)	0 (10)	0 (0)	5 (5)	0 (15)	5 (5)	10 (20)
Round 7	0 (0)	0 (10)	20 (0)	10 (0)	5 (5)	0 (20)	0 (10)	0 (0)	5 (5)	10 (0)
Round 8	0 (10)	0 (0)	20 (0)	0 (0)	0 (0)	0 (0)	0 (0)	0 (20)	10 (0)	0 (0)
Round 9	0 (0)	0 (0)	0 (0)	0 (0)	20 (0)	0 (0)	0 (0)	0 (20)	0 (0)	0 (0)
Round 9 Forecast	5	5	0	0	10	2	0	25	0	0

Session 7: Internal Return = 0.8, External Return = 1.2, University of Virginia

	subject 1	subject 2	subject 3	subject 4	subject 5	subject 6	subject 7	subject 8	subject 9	subject 10
Round 1	13	0	25	0	15	0	0	0	0	5
	(0)	(13)	(0)	(25)	(0)	(15)	(0)	(0)	(5)	(0)
Round 2	0	25	25	0	20	10	4	10	0	0
	(25)	(20)	(0)	(4)	(25)	(0)	(0)	(0)	(10)	(10)
Round 3	10	25	25	0	20	5	6	10	0	5
	(6)	(0)	(20)	(5)	(25)	(10)	(10)	(5)	(25)	(5)
Round 4	3	25	25	0	25	5	8	15	0	0
	(0)	(15)	(0)	(5)	(8)	(0)	(25)	(25)	(25)	(3)
Round 5	0	25	25	0	25	0	4	25	0	0
	(0)	(25)	(25)	(0)	(0)	(4)	(0)	(0)	(25)	(0)
Round 6	25	25	25	5	25	5	9	20	0	0
	(25)	(5)	(0)	(20)	(25)	(25)	(0)	(5)	(9)	(25)
Round 7	0	25	25	5	25	10	0	25	0	0
	(25)	(5)	(10)	(25)	(0)	(25)	(0)	(0)	(25)	(0)
Round 8	20	25	25	5	25	15	0	15	0	0
	(0)	(0)	(15)	(25)	(5)	(0)	(25)	(25)	(20)	(15)
Round 9	0	0	25	5	5	5	0	25	0	0
	(5)	(0)	(0)	(0)	(25)	(0)	(25)	(5)	(5)	(0)
Round 9 Forecast	0	5	0	25	0	0	0	10	20	5

Session 8: Internal Return $=0.8$, External Return $=1.2$, University of South Carolina

	subject 1	subject 2	subject 3	subject 4	subject 5	subject 6	subject 7	subject 8	subject 9	subject 10
Round 1	10	2	7	12	5	7	3	2	12	0
	(2)	(10)	(12)	(7)	(7)	(5)	(2)	(3)	(0)	(12)
Round 2	15	4	7	5	15	9	5	0	0	0
	(7)	(15)	(15)	(5)	(4)	(0)	(5)	(0)	(9)	(0)
Round 3	5	5	2	6	15	8	6	25	0	0
	(6)	(0)	(15)	(0)	(2)	(25)	(5)	(8)	(5)	(6)
Round 4	8	0	1	0	15	10	1	25	0	0
	(0)	(1)	(0)	(8)	(0)	(1)	(10)	(0)	(0)	(15)
Round 5	2	2	0	2	15	9	25	25	0	0
	(0)	(25)	(0)	(9)	(25)	(2)	(15)	(2)	(0)	(2)
Round 6	0	2	0	0	15	10	25	25	0	0
	(15)	(10)	(0)	(25)	(0)	(2)	(0)	(0)	(25)	(0)
Round 7	0	4	0	5	0	10	25	25	0	0
	(25)	(5)	(10)	(4)	(0)	(0)	(0)	(0)	(0)	(25)
Round 8	0	0	0	0	25	12	0	25	0	0
	(0)	(0)	(25)	(25)	(0)	(0)	(0)	(0)	(0)	(12)
Round 9	5	0	0	7	0	10	10	25	0	0
	(10)	(0)	(10)	(0)	(25)	(5)	(0)	(0)	(7)	(0)
Round 9 Forecast	5	8	0	8	0	9	0	0	0	1

Session 9: Internal Return = 0.8, External Return = 1.2, University of Virginia

	subject 1	subject 2	subject 3	subject 4	subject 5	subject 6	subject 7	subject 8	subject 9	subject 10
Round 1	25	0	12	25	3	5	15	5	25	0
	(0)	(25)	(25)	(12)	(5)	(3)	(5)	(15)	(0)	(25)
Round 2	25	25	20	20	4	25	10	5	25	0
	(20)	(4)	(25)	(10)	(25)	(25)	(20)	(0)	(25)	(0)
Round 3	25	15	25	25	3	25	10	0	25	0
	(10)	(25)	(3)	(0)	(25)	(25)	(25)	(25)	(15)	(5)
Round 4	25	25	25	25	2	0	15	0	25	0
	(0)	(0)	(25)	(0)	(15)	(25)	(2)	(25)	(25)	(25)
Round 5	25	15	25	25	0	0	10	0	25	0
	(25)	(25)	(15)	(25)	(0)	(10)	(0)	(25)	(0)	(0)
Round 6	25	25	25	25	0	0	5	0	25	0
	(0)	(0)	(0)	(0)	(25)	(25)	(25)	(25)	(5)	(25)
Round 7	25	15	25	25	0	0	5	0	25	0
	(0)	(25)	(0)	(15)	(25)	(25)	(0)	(25)	(5)	(25)
Round 8	25	25	0	25	10	0	5	0	25	0
	(25)	(5)	(0)	(10)	(25)	(25)	(25)	(0)	(0)	(5)
Round 9	25	15	0	25	25	0	5	0	25	0
	(0)	(0)	(5)	(25)	(0)	(25)	(0)	(25)	(25)	(15)

Session 10: Internal Return =0.8, External Return =2.4, University of Virginia

	subject 1	subject 2	subject 3	subject 4	subject 5	subject 6	subject 7	subject 8	subject 9	subject 10
Round 1	0 (15)	15 (0)	20 (25)	25 (20)	12 (5)	5 (12)	15 (25)	25 (15)	10 (5)	5 (10)
Round 2	0 (25)	13 (6)	25 (0)	25 (25)	6 (13)	5 (8)	25 (25)	24 (20)	8 (5)	20 (24)
Round 3	0 (25)	20 (2)	20 (1)	25 (20)	1 (20)	5 (25)	25 (0)	25 (5)	2 (20)	20 (25)
Round 4	0 (20)	2 (25)	20 (2)	25 (5)	0 (25)	5 (25)	25 (0)	25 (2)	2 (20)	20 (0)
Round 5	0 (24)	6 (5)	5 (6)	24 (0)	0 (20)	25 (25)	25 (25)	25 (0)	0 (25)	20 (0)
Round 6	0 (3)	0 (25)	5 (20)	0 (25)	3 (0)	25 (0)	25 (1)	25 (0)	1 (25)	20 (5)
Round 7	0 (25)	25 (25)	15 (25)	25 (25)	1 (25)	25 (15)	25 (0)	25 (0)	25 (1)	0 (25)
Round 8	0 (0)	12 (25)	21 (25)	20 (0)	0 (20)	25 (0)	25 (12)	25 (21)	0 (0)	0 (25)
Round 9	0 (0)	19 (0)	0 (0)	25 (0)	5 (25)	0 (0)	0 (0)	25 (5)	0 (25)	0 (19)
Round 9										
Forecast	25	15	0	0	13	0	0	18	2	0

334

Session 11: Internal Return = 0.4, External Return = 1.2, University of Virginia

	subject 1	subject 2	subject 3	subject 4	subject 5	subject 6	subject 7	subject 8	subject 9	subject 10
Round 1	10 (20)	20 (10)	12 (25)	25 (12)	5 (0)	0 (5)	0 (0)	0 (0)	7 (25)	25 (7)
Round 2	20 (0)	5 (10)	0 (20)	10 (0)	10 (5)	0 (25)	0 (10)	0 (25)	25 (0)	25 (0)
Round 3	25 (0)	0 (7)	0 (15)	0 (25)	15 (5)	0 (5)	0 (25)	5 (0)	7 (0)	25 (0)
Round 4	10 (25)	5 (0)	0 (0)	15 (0)	20 (0)	0 (15)	0 (20)	0 (5)	0 (0)	25 (10)
Round 5	15 (18)	0 (0)	0 (0)	18 (15)	0 (25)	0 (0)	0 (0)	0 (0)	0 (0)	25 (0)
Round 6	5 (20)	0 (0)	0 (25)	17 (0)	20 (5)	0 (0)	0 (0)	0 (17)	0 (0)	25 (0)
Round 7	25 (0)	0 (10)	0 (0)	10 (0)	12 (0)	0 (0)	0 (25)	0 (25)	0 (12)	25 (0)
Round 8	19 (0)	0 (0)	0 (0)	0 (10)	10 (0)	0 (25)	0 (0)	0 (0)	0 (19)	25 (0)
Round 9	3 (0)	0 (25)	0 (0)	0 (0)	10 (1)	0 (3)	0 (0)	1 (10)	0 (0)	25 (0)
Round 9 Forecast	21	0	0	0	0	0	25	0	0	0

335

Session 12:   Internal Return = 0.4, External Return = 1.2, University of South Carolina

	subject 1	subject 2	subject 3	subject 4	subject 5	subject 6	subject 7	subject 8	subject 9	subject 10
Round 1	4 (15)	15 (4)	5 (10)	10 (5)	10 (5)	5 (10)	8 (2)	2 (8)	12 (13)	13 (12)
Round 2	8 (2)	20 (15)	2 (8)	5 (3)	15 (20)	10 (3)	3 (5)	4 (20)	3 (10)	20 (4)
Round 3	3 (5)	20 (13)	0 (20)	2 (0)	20 (0)	2 (7)	5 (3)	7 (2)	13 (20)	0 (2)
Round 4	4 (15)	13 (3)	10 (0)	8 (25)	5 (6)	25 (8)	6 (5)	3 (13)	0 (10)	15 (4)
Round 5	5 (9)	2 (5)	5 (2)	9 (5)	5 (5)	6 (8)	5 (5)	8 (23)	23 (8)	5 (5)
Round 6	4 (10)	15 (0)	2 (3)	0 (11)	10 (4)	0 (15)	7 (10)	11 (0)	10 (7)	3 (2)
Round 7	5 (5)	5 (12)	0 (5)	12 (5)	12 (13)	5 (0)	9 (5)	5 (5)	13 (12)	5 (9)
Round 8	4 (12)	15 (8)	2 (10)	6 (5)	5 (6)	0 (8)	8 (15)	10 (2)	12 (4)	8 (0)
Round 9	3 (5)	20 (2)	2 (15)	5 (12)	12 (0)	5 (3)	15 (2)	0 (12)	12 (5)	2 (20)
Round 9 Forecast	4	9	6	5	10	7	10	7	12	7

Session 13: Internal Return = 0.4, External Return = 1.2, University of Virginia

	subject 1	subject 2	subject 3	subject 4	subject 5	subject 6	subject 7	subject 8	subject 9	subject 10
Round 1	5 (10)	10 (5)	0 (13)	13 (0)	0 (0)	0 (0)	12 (5)	5 (12)	10 (0)	0 (10)
Round 2	2 (0)	13 (0)	0 (2)	1 (5)	0 (13)	0 (0)	5 (1)	10 (0)	0 (0)	0 (10)
Round 3	0 (0)	12 (0)	0 (0)	5 (0)	0 (0)	0 (0)	0 (0)	5 (0)	0 (0)	0 (10)
Round 4	0 (0)	5 (0)	0 (0)	0 (0)	12 (0)	0 (5)	0 (12)	0 (5)	0 (12)	0 (5)
Round 5	0 (5)	0 (0)	0 (0)	5 (0)	0 (0)	0 (0)	0 (0)	0 (0)	0 (0)	0 (0)
Round 6	3 (0)	5 (0)	0 (0)	0 (0)	0 (3)	0 (5)	0 (0)	0 (0)	0 (0)	0 (0)
Round 7	0 (0)	5 (0)	0 (0)	0 (5)	0 (0)	0 (0)	0 (0)	0 (0)	0 (0)	0 (0)
Round 8	0 (0)	3 (0)	0 (0)	5 (0)	0 (5)	0 (0)	0 (3)	0 (0)	0 (0)	0 (0)
Round 9	0 (0)	0 (0)	0 (0)	0 (0)	0 (0)	0 (0)	0 (0)	0 (0)	0 (0)	0 (0)

NOTES

*   Corresponding author: Susan Laury, Department of Economics, Andrew Young School of Policy Studies, Georgia State University, Atlanta, GA 30303–3083, slaury@gsu.edu, http://www.gsu.edu/~ecoskl. This work was funded in part by the National Science Foundation (SBR-9753125 and SBR-9818683). The research assistance of Cara Carter is gratefully acknowledged. The comments of Dave Bjornstad, participants at the UCF/CentER International Conference on Environmental Economics and an anonymous referee are gratefully acknowledged.
1. In the standard public goods experiment, the internal and external returns are identical. The marginal per capita return or MPCR, is calculated as the (common) benefit of an investment divided by the value of a token kept. Thus the standard treatment change in the MPCR will alter both the internal and external returns together.
2. No forecast was elicited in three sessions held at the University of Virginia (those labelled sessions 4, 9 and 13).
3. Laury (2001) shows no systematic effect on contributions to the public good when forecasts are elicited at the same time that the investment decision is made.
4. Andreoni (1988) and others, including Carter et al. (1992), conducted experiments in which subjects never participated in the same *group* more than once. However the group composition was determined by a new random matching in each round and there was a high probability that one would play against some group members more than one time. In Andreoni's study, for example, 20 subjects in a session played in groups of five for ten repetitions. Therefore it was certain that they would meet at least some participants more than one time.
5. In early rounds of experimental sessions, investment choices display a lot of noise and there is some indication that subjects experiment with their decisions. This change in behaviour over time may be the result of learning and adjustment to the typical level of investment by others. Regardless of the reason, we restrict our attention to the final rounds of a session.
6. Regression results are presented below.
7. It is quite possible that demographic factors (gender, race, major and income, for example) may also affect investment choices. However we did not elicit such information from our subjects. Andreoni and Miller (2002) and Goeree et al. (2002) both report that there is little difference in average altruism estimates between men and women but that the estimates for men tend to be more extreme than for women.
8. Goeree et al. (2002) present a formal model of investment behaviour that incorporates altruism and logit errors into the decision-making process. In this model, altruism is measured by incorporating the external benefit that the other person receives from an investment into the individual's utility function. Incorporating noisy decision-making accounts for the 'U-shaped' distribution of investment decisions, with the majority of decisions located at the upper or lower bounds (depending on the treatment), which represent 'optimal' decisions from a theoretic point of view.

REFERENCES

Andreoni, J. (1988), 'Why free ride? Strategies and learning in public goods experiments', *Journal of Public Economics*, **37**, 291–304.
Andreoni, J. and J.H. Miller (2002), 'Giving according to GARP: an experimental test of the consistency of preferences for altruism', *Econometrica*, **70**, 737–53.
Carter, J., B. Drainville and R. Poulin (1992), 'A Test for Rational Altruism in a Public-Goods Experiment', working paper, College of Holy Cross.

Goeree, J., C. Holt and S. Laury (2002), 'Private costs and public benefits: unraveling the effects of altruism and noisy behaviour,' *Journal of Public Economics*, **83**, 255–76.

Isaac, M. and J. Walker (1988), 'Group size effects in public goods provision: The voluntary contribution mechanism', *Quarterly Journal of Economics*, **103**, 79–200.

Isaac, R., J. Walker and A. Williams (1994), 'Group size and the voluntary provision of public goods: experimental evidence utilizing large groups,' *Journal of Public Economics*, **54**, 1–36.

Laury, S. (2001), 'Individual Motives for Giving Under Real and Hypothetical Incentives', Georgia State University Working Paper.

Ledyard, J. (1995), 'Public Goods: A Survey of Experimental Research', in J. Kagel and A. Roth (eds), *The Handbook of Experimental Economics*, Princeton, NJ: Princeton University Press, 111–94.

Palfrey, T. and J. Prisbrey (1997), 'Anomalous Behaviour in Linear Public Goods Experiments: How Much and Why?', *American Economic Review*, **87**, 829–46.

15. An experimental test for options value: relevance for contingent value elicitation*

David Bjornstad, Paul Brewer, Ronald Cummings and Michael McKee

1. INTRODUCTION

This chapter deals with the behavioural foundations of option value and its relationship to value elicitation responses to questions posed using the contingent valuation method (CV). More specifically, it is suggested that if people evaluate CV queries applying criteria consistent with the model of irreversible investment theory (Dixit, 1992; Dixit and Pindyck, 1994), they should systematically offer responses that embed a use and/or non-use value *plus* an option value. It has long been recognized that responses to CV questionnaires sometimes appear to overstate 'rational' values, and in extreme cases appear to be 'protests' (see, for example, Bjornstad and Kahn, 1996: Part IV). To the extent that irreversible investment theory provides a logical foundation for addressing (at least) a subset of these concerns it affords the opportunity for improving the accuracy of the CV method.

More specifically, we provide a formal experimental test of the foundational investment theory that arguably would form an individual's basis for responding to CV queries, if the queries were framed so as to correspond to the theory's assumptions. We examine the following circumstances. An income-maximizing individual is contemplating undertaking an investment under the following set of conditions: (a) the investment is largely irreversible (for example, salvage values are zero or very small); (b) returns from the investment are uncertain but this uncertainty dissipates over time with new information; and (c) the opportunity to invest is not foregone if the investment decision is postponed to a later time when information will become available which will resolve the uncertainty. That is, this individual faces the option of investing now or later, and it is the availability of this option that is the focus of a recent development in the theory of investment under uncertainty – the options model (OM).[1] If under these circumstances and given appropriate parametric specification, individuals systematically choose waiting, it follows that they systematically evaluate positive returns and negative returns differently, a principal result of the option model that is called the 'bad news principle'. The potential for this asymmetry, which gives rise to the option premium, to carry over into responses to CV queries is the principal result of interest.

The parallel between the options model found in the investment literature and that found in the environmental literature is much closer than many environmental economists realize. We describe the evolution of this literature in Section 2 below. This is followed by a formal statement of the model we wish to test in Section 3 and by a description of our experimental design in Section 4. Section 5 presents our results and Section 6 describes the implications of our results.

In sum, our results fail to reject the Bad News Principle. The subjects are found to focus on the downside risk when making their investment choice and to be insensitive to potential upside gains. Such behaviour is also, of course, consistent with loss aversion, though we do not test separately for this effect.

The question then becomes, do CV respondents apply this model? To do so they would have to interpret the CV question in the following manner. Consider a programme to protect the environment from an irreversible loss that is uncertain, for example, loss of an endangered species from a local habitat. The scenario states that we are uncertain whether or not the species may be found in other habitats but that research will identify the facts over time. Developing the habitat would yield substantial, relatively certain benefits, and the results from the CV will be used in a benefit–cost study to evaluate the development. The CV questionnaire requires a current response in the form of a dollar value for the habitat. If the respondent wishes to wait, an option not offered but implicitly logical given the scenario, he or she can simply add a premium to the dollar value which, in the limit, represents a large option premium approximating a protest bid. This response, however, may be lost if the researcher 'trims' the response set to eliminate extreme values.

2. BACKGROUND

Weisbrod (1964) first introduced the concept of option value to the study of natural resources by observing that many goods exhibit both individual and collective consumption attributes. Reasoning from the example of a park that cannot fully support itself through user fees he argued that the 'existence of people who anticipate purchasing the commodity (visiting the park) but who in fact will never purchase (visit) it . . . gives rise to a willingness-to-pay to preserve the option to visit the park'. This willingness-to-pay or option value should be considered by government, he argued, in assessing the total social benefits accruing to the park. At the time Weisbrod was writing, establishing this value was of considerable importance, because it provided a qualitative justification for adding a premium to estimates of direct use values when considering appropriate provision of environmental services by governments.

Weisbrod sparked a debate that proceeded in two directions. The first, a 'timeless analysis' applied what might be termed a contingent state (expected utility) approach to estimate consumer values across a probabilistic frontier in which consumers are assumed to allocate incomes, given prices and preferences, against the uncertainties that alternative states obtain. Within the natural resource literature, this has been termed the 'options' value literature.

The second strand is termed the 'quasi-option' value literature. This approach added the dimension of time explicitly by assuming consumers make choices across some time horizon, minimally in two periods – today and the future. The approaches differ in their treatment of the source and resolution of uncertainty and hold considerably different implications for government policy toward environmental resources.

Following a considerable debate, the notion of option value that emerged from this literature was less than satisfactory.[2] The problem was that because option value was defined as the difference between willingness to pay and expected consumer surplus its value hinged on subtle specifications of risk preferences and on the marginal utility of money. Whereas it was hoped that an unequivocal positive sign for this value would establish econometric estimates of expected consumer surplus as a lower bound for natural resource values, the emergence of the contingent value of natural resources provided a natural means to estimate willingness to pay directly. Finally, there was some question as to the appropriateness of incorporating risk aversion as an explicit means to derive willingness to pay for public goods decisions, following work by Arrow and Lind (1970), which argued that for public goods shared by large numbers of consumers risk premiums should go to zero, implying that the expected value of consumer surplus was the proper value for policy.

It was left to Arrow and Fisher (1974) to remedy this situation by introducing their concept of 'quasi-option' value. Their argument was stated in terms of a choice between the alternatives of preservation and development of a natural environment. By assumption development is irreversible or at least very costly/lengthy. The question is whether to develop in period 1, period 2, or not at all. Differences between period 1 and 2, known costs and benefits in period 1 and expected benefits in period 2 (evaluated in period 1) and realized costs and benefits in period 2 are driven by choices made in period 1 plus the reduced uncertainty that occurs with the passage of time (between periods 1 and 2). In general, they find that expected net benefits are less under certainty than under uncertainty with the difference being what they term a quasi-option value. This value is always positive, implying that uncertainty raises a bias against development under uncertainty and irreversibility. Arrow and Fisher (1974) suggest that the model encourages small developments to gain information rather than all or nothing development.[3]

The next notable contribution came from Bernanke (1983) who reinterpreted the notion of quasi-option value within the more general context of investment theory. One insight of particular importance was his statement of the 'bad news principle' – the observation that under uncertainty and with sunk cost (irreversibility) investors look to the 'downside' rather than the 'upside' in evaluating investments. In other words, the 'option' value becomes a cost of new information that is traded off against the benefit of avoiding expected losses (due to sunk investment costs). When expected losses are small new information has little value and vice versa. Of note is the asymmetry in that increases in expected gains do not impact the decision to invest, because there is no corresponding element to offset sunk costs. Hence, by waiting, the investor gives up only gains that would have occurred had investment taken place in period 1 rather than in period 2. Several other papers have extended these results and made them more accessible, notably Pindyck (1991), Dixit (1992), Dixit and Pindyck (1994) and Hubbard (1994). Finally, in a recent paper Fisher (no date) has 'closed the loop' between the option concept embedded in irreversible investment theory and in quasi-option value theory by demonstrating their equivalence.

Despite the potential importance of the options-based model for policy, and in the case of CV questionnaire design, there have been limited efforts to empirically test the efficacy of this model of investment behaviour. As one example, Caballero and Pindyck (1992) analyse the determinants of the rate of return required for investment in US manufacturing industries and find that such returns depend positively on the volatility of the marginal profitability of capital – a finding that is *consistent* with predictions of the options-based model. Pindyck and Solimano (1993), using investment data for a set of 38 countries, find that the ratio of investment to GDP varies positively with the mean of the log change in the marginal returns to capital, and negatively with the standard deviation, a finding that again is consistent with the options-based model. But on the other hand, there are studies of the relationship between 'adjustment costs' and observed investment responses to changes in the user cost of capital that suggest consistency between observed investment behaviour and behaviour that would be implied by a 'neoclassical' model that involves only the current NPV of returns and ignores the value of the option to wait (for example, see Cummins et al., 1994).[4]

None of the empirical tests conducted to date of the OM – by either investment or CV researchers – examine the behavioural aspect that is (arguably) most interesting for policy design: the extent to which the Bad News Principle in fact describes individual investment-making decisions. Thus, as noted by Hubbard (1994, p. 1829), 'empirical research has not quite caught up with the rapidly changing theoretical developments in this literature' and there is an obvious need for a great deal more in the way of empirical efforts to explore the *behavioural* implications and policy relevance of options models.

This chapter reports on the results of a series of experiments designed to empirically test behavioural hypotheses concerning investment behaviour that derive from options theory. Specifically, the goal is to address the following questions. In a simplified decision-making setting where individual agents face investment opportunities characterized by irreversibility, uncertainty, and the ability to wait, is the options model effective in predicting observed investment behaviour? Of particular interest, does observed behaviour comport with the Bad News Principle? Answers to these questions may be particularly important for the way that CV questionnaires might be designed but also for structuring of public policies to stimulate certain types of private investments that satisfy these conditions. The laboratory offers considerable control over the decision setting and is an excellent environment for the investigation of behavioural issues (Roth, 1987).[5] The power of the lab is that it facilitates explicit tests for the presence of a Bad New Principle as a behavioural phenomenon. This is important since, despite the conceptual equivalence of the two views (hurdle rate versus Bad News Principle), the policy implications are vastly different.

3. OPTIONS-BASED INVESTMENT RULES: A TWO-PERIOD EXAMPLE

Assume that agents are offered a contract that allows them to make an investment now or to delay until the future state of nature is revealed.[6] There is a fixed cost of the investment, C, an initial period payoff of X, and two possible payoffs in the future period, L and H (for Low and High respectively). The payoff in the bad state of nature is L and the probability that the bad state occurs is $1 - p$. The values of the parameters are such that $L < C < H$.

An investment represented by the purchase of a contract with these characteristics satisfies the assumptions underlying the options model of investment. The investment is irreversible, returns are uncertain, and the uncertainty dissipates over time as new information is automatically forthcoming. Finally, the opportunity to invest is not foregone if the investment decision is postponed.

Let the option of investing in the current period be labelled O_1 and in the future be O_2. The information settings are I_1 and I_2. Thus, $(O_i|I_i)$ denotes choosing option i given information level i. The options theory of investment (OM) predicts that the risk-neutral agent will invest in period 1 only when the *ex ante* expected value of investing in period 1 ($EV(O_1|I_1)$) exceeds the expected value of investing in period 2 ($EV(O_2|I_1)$). The expected value of investing in period 1 is given by:

$$EV(O_1|I_1) = X + pH + (1-p)L - C \qquad (15.1)$$

To calculate $EV(O_2|I_1)$ consider that if the agent postpones the investment decision to period 2 he forgoes the period 1 yield X. However, he does not forego the opportunity to invest in period 2 after observing the (then) certain period 2 yields. The agent, relying only on I_1, can determine how he would use the information I_2 in the following way. With probability p, the yield in period 2 will be H. Since $H > C$, it is clear that the profit maximizing agent would then invest in period 2. With probability $1 - p$, the yield will be L. Since $L < C$, it is equally clear that the agent would *not* invest in period 2 – he would not wish to incur the known loss $L - C$. It then follows that the expected value in period 1 of postponing the investment decision to period 2 is given by:

$$EV(O_2|I_1) = p(H - C) + (1 - p)(0) = pH - pC. \qquad (15.2)$$

The condition for investment in period 1 predicted by the OM then becomes:

$$X + pH + (1 - p)L - C > pH - pC, \qquad (15.3a)$$

or equivalently, since the pH terms cancel,

$$X + (1 - p)(L - C) > 0. \qquad (15.3b)$$

The two features of the OM mentioned in the introduction are represented in (15.3b). First, Dixit's value of waiting, the value that 'must be set against the sacrifice of current profits' (Dixit, 1992, p. 109), is clearly identified: it is the value of the expected loss $(1 - p)(L - C)$. Current profit X is rationally sacrificed under the OM if it is insufficient to offset this expected loss.

Second, (15.3b) makes manifest what is the most distinguishing feature of the OM, the *Bad News Principle*. The investment decision is determined solely by investment costs and the potential for low yield outcomes. The high yield, H, does not appear in (14.3b) thus the implied investment rule is one where the investment decision is independent of H.

This situation is exacerbated should the decision makers be subject to risk avoidance associated with various forms of non-expected utility behaviour such as loss aversion or rank dependent expected utility (Machina, 1987; Kahneman and Tversky, 1979). Loss aversion is represented by utility functions of the form:

$$V(x) = p_1 u(x_1) + p_2 u(x_2) \qquad (15.4)$$

where p_i is the probability of state i and the reference level of payoff is normalized to 0. Then $u(x) = x$ if $x \geq 0$ and $u(x) = \lambda x$ if $x < 0$ where $\lambda < 1$. Potential losses are weighted more heavily than equivalent gains. The implication for the OM predictions is clear – delay to await new information is desirable and will be an increasing function of C and L, and will be weakly related to or independent of H and will be decreasing in p.

The primary interest is with tests of hypotheses concerning the extent to which investment behaviour by agents involving the purchase of contracts described above are effectively predicted by the OM rule (15.3b) and the extent to which agents are observed to obey the Bad News Principle. The data for these tests are obtained through a series of laboratory market experiments and the design of these experiments is discussed in the next section.

4.   EXPERIMENTAL DESIGN

In an experimental laboratory market the individual subjects are asked to choose between two investment contracts. Under one contract the investment is undertaken in the current period while under the alternative contract, the investment decision is delayed until the second period. Each subject faces a series of such decisions with each decision being independent. This section begins with a description of the experimental procedures and elicitation of agents' decisions. The parameter values used in all contracts are described, as are expected values $EV(O_1|I_1)$ and $EV(O_2|I_1)$ implied by each contract's set of parameters, and the associated OM prediction for each contract. Absent knowledge of the subjects' weighting parameter, λ (in equation (15.4)), it is impossible to compute utility equivalents but the prediction is that loss aversion will bias decisions toward delaying investment by selecting Option 2. Finally, the various series of experiments conducted are described.

4.1 Experimental Procedures

An example (Contract Z) of the investment contracts used in our experiments is provided in Figure 15.1. This example contract is shown to participants as a part of the instructions.[7] Contract Z provides for either a high return $H = \$19.00$ or a low return $L = \$4.00$. Whether the contract will pay H or L depends on the colour of a ball that is drawn from a bingo cage. The probability of H is determined by the distribution of the balls in the cage. Participants are informed that there are 100 balls in the cage, and are told how many of the balls are red and how many are white. For example, for $p = 0.5$, participants are told that there are 50 red balls and 50 white balls in the cage. Participants are invited to inspect the cage and, if they wish, to count the balls. They are routinely shown several of the balls taken at random from the cage so that they can ascertain that the only difference between the balls is their colour. After all the participants have made their contract decision, the bingo cage is spun. The colour of the ball that falls out of the cage determines the payoff: a red ball will mean that the contract will pay the H ($19.00) return; a white ball will mean that the contract will pay the L ($4.00) return.

Returning to Contract Z, participants are told that they must choose between two options in each contract and only one of the options may be selected for each contract. Option 1 is to buy the contract *before* the cage is spun, that is, before it is determined whether the ball is red or white. Option 2 is to postpone the decision as to whether or not they wish to buy the contract until *after* the cage is spun. If they choose Option 1, they pay the contract cost C and receive an immediate payment of X ($3.00). After the cage is spun, they will receive an additional amount: $19.00 if a red ball drops out of the cage; $4.00 if a white ball drops out. If they choose Option 2, they make no decision as to whether or not they want to buy the contract until after the cage is spun and they know whether the ball is red or white; they forgo, however, the immediate payment of X. In presenting Contract Z the Option 1 and Option 2 yields, and how they are determined, are made explicit. For example, the Option 1 gross yield is described as $3.00 + $19.00 = $22.00 with a red ball; $3.00 + $4.00 = $7.00 with a white ball. The Option 2 gross yield is described as either $19.00 with a red ball or $4.00 with a white ball. This detail is provided to enhance participant comprehension and to reduce maths errors.

COST: $10.00

PUT A CHECK IN THE BOX [ ] FOR THE OPTION THAT YOU
CHOOSE:

OPTION 1:

I will buy this contract for $10.00 *before* the bingo cage is spun.

I will immediately receive $3.00,

AND, after the cage is spun

• if a red ball is drawn, I will get an additional $19.00
 (total earnings in this case: $3.00 + $19.00 = $22.00)

• if a white ball is drawn, I will get an additional $4.00
 (total earnings in this case: $3.00 + $4.00 = $7.00)

I choose OPTION 1: I will purchase this contract *before* the cage is spun:
A red ball earns $22.00 total.
A white ball earns $7.00 total.

OPTION 2:

I will wait until *after the bingo cage is spun* to see whether the ball
is red or white before I decide whether or not I want to buy this
contract for $10.00.

I will then decide if I want to pay $10.00 for this contract to
receive:

$19.00 if the ball is red (total earnings = $19.00)

OR

$4.00 if the ball is white (total earnings = $4.00)

I choose OPTION 2: If I buy this contract *after* the cage is spun:
A red ball earns $19.00 total.
A white ball earns $4.00 total.
If I don't buy this contract after the cage is spun, I spend nothing.

Figure 15.1   Example contract, as seen by participants, CONTRACT Z

This description of a contract is repeated with a second example contract that has different values for X, H, L and C; participants' questions are invited to ensure that they understand the substance of a contract and their options. Participants are then told that they will be given a packet that includes 16 contracts (17 contracts are used in one experiment series for reasons that are discussed below). Each of the 16 (17) contracts are formatted exactly like the example Contract Z and differ only in the values for X, H, L or C. Subjects make their Option 1 or Option 2 decision for all of the 16 (17) contracts.[8] However, only *one* of the 16 (17) contracts – a 'binding contract' – will involve actual cash payments. The binding contract is determined by a draw by one of the subjects. Subjects are shown (and can inspect) an empty paper bag and 16 (17) slips of paper. Written on each slip of paper is one of 16 (17) letters, A to P (Q), corresponding to the letters that identify each of the contracts (for example, Contract F). One subject shakes the bag to mix up the slips of paper and places the bag on a desk in full view of all subjects. *After* subjects have made their decisions for all 16 (17) contracts, one subject is asked to reach into the bag and pull out one of the slips of paper. The letter on this slip of paper identifies the binding contract. The terms of the binding contract are then carried out. Thus, subjects who had chosen Option 1 for the binding contract pay the required C and receive the immediate payment of X while those who had chosen Option 2 wait until the ball is drawn from the bingo cage before making their investment decision. These procedures imply that our experiments effectively involve a compound lottery to the subjects, the potential implications of which are taken up later.

4.2 Contract Parameters and Behavioural Predictions

The contracts used in the experiment, A to Q, all have the same structure as Z and differ only in their values for X, H, L and C. These values are reported in Table 15.1 as are the values for $EV(O_1|I_1)$ and $EV(O_2|I_1)$ associated with each contract for a given value of p (the probability of a high return, H). Three different values of p are used: $p=0.35$, $p=0.5$ and $p=0.65$.

The predictions of the OM, assuming risk neutrality, are readily determined from the information given in Table 15.1. The OM predicts that the risk-neutral agent will choose Option 1 when $EV(O_1|I_1)>EV(O_2|I_1)$. From Table 15.2, one can verify that this condition is satisfied in very few contracts when $p=0.35$ (Contracts G, N, P and Q). Contracts that satisfy the OM condition for choosing Option 1 when $p=0.5$ and $p=0.65$ are also summarized in Table 15.2.

Table 15.1   Contracts, parameters and expected values for options

Contract	Parameter Value X	H	L	C	$EV(O_1\|I_1)$ $p=0.35$	$p=0.5$	$p=0.65$	$EV(O_2\|I_1)$ $p=0.35$	$p=0.5$	$p=0.65$
A	2	16	1	10	−1.75	0.50	2.75	2.10	3.00	3.90
B	2	20	1	10	−0.35	2.50	5.35	3.50	5.00	6.50
C	2	16	1	5	3.25	5.50	7.75	3.85	5.50	7.15
D	3	16	4	10	1.20	3.00	4.80	2.10	3.00	3.90
E	2	22	1	10	0.35	3.50	6.65	4.20	6.00	7.80
F	3	16	3	10	0.55	2.50	4.45	2.10	3.00	3.90
G	2	16	1	4	4.25	6.50	8.75	4.20	6.00	7.80
H	3	16	1	10	−0.75	1.50	3.75	2.10	3.00	3.90
I	3	16	5	10	1.85	3.50	5.15	2.10	3.00	3.90
J	2	16	1	8	0.25	2.50	4.75	2.80	4.00	5.20
K	5	16	1	10	1.25	3.50	5.75	2.10	3.00	3.90
L	2	24	1	10	1.05	4.50	7.95	4.90	7.00	9.10
M	2	16	1	6	2.25	4.50	6.75	3.50	5.00	6.50
N	8	11	3	10	3.80	5.00	6.20	0.35	0.50	0.65
O	2	18	1	10	−1.05	1.50	4.05	2.80	4.00	5.20
P	3	16	6	10	2.50	4.00	5.50	2.10	3.00	3.90
Q	6	16	1	10	2.25	n.a.	n.a.	2.10	n.a.	n.a.

Table 15.2   Predictions of the option model

	Contracts for which OM Predicts the Choice of Option 1:	
$p=0.35$	$p=0.50$	$p=0.65$
only contracts G, N, and P and Q	contracts G, N, P, and I and K	contracts G, N, P, I, K, and C, D, F and P

4.3   The Experimental Design

Three sets of experiments were planned for the purpose of testing the behavioural responses to changes in the value of *p*. Student subjects were recruited for the experiments, and they were paid a $10.00 participation fee as well as their earnings from the session.[9] Three values of *p* were used and for a given value of *p*, each experiment was repeated until at least 100 persons had participated.

Table 15.3 summarizes the series of experiments. Referring to the first three series, the value of *p* (0.35, 0.5 or 0.65) used in each series is given in column 2. Contracts used in the series are specified in column 3. The 16

Table 15.3   Experimental design

Series	Probability of high return	Contracts	Design	Number of subjects	Subject Pool
1	$p=0.5$	{A,...,P}	Compound lottery	39	GSU
				29	GSU
				55	GSU
				(total 123)	
2	$p=0.35$	{A,...,Q}	Compound lottery	38	GSU
				23	GSU
				49	GSU
				(total 110)	
3	$p=0.65$	{A,...,P}	Compound lottery	23	GSU
				30	GSU
				49	DeVry
				(total 102)	
4	$p=0.5$	A	Single contract	61	GSU
		L		59	GSU
		H		58	GSU

contracts A to P are used in series 1 and 3. Series 2, which uses $p=0.35$, uses contracts A–P and a 17th contract, Contract Q. This latter contract is added in order to provide, in the set of contracts with $H=\$16$, $L=\$1$ and $C=\$10$ one contract for which the OM predicts the choice of Option 1.[10]

Column 5 describes the number of subjects in each session, and column 6 identifies the subject pool. For all but one session the subjects are drawn from the pool at Georgia State University (GSU). One session used students recruited at neighbouring DeVry University. Each subject participated in only one session with a given probability level, p.

In the primary series of experiments subjects make the decision – whether or not to buy a contract – for either 16 or 17 different contracts and one of these contracts is selected to be binding. As noted earlier, this design avoids possible income effects, and it ensures that each decision is independent, but it implements a compound lottery from the perspective of the subjects. A fourth experiment set was introduced to test for the presence of an effect due to the compound lottery design. Column 4, the 'Design' column in Table 15.3, designates whether the experiment involves a compound or a simple, single contract, lottery.

Subjects in experiments 1, 2 and 3 make decisions between Option 1 vs Option 2 for 16 (or 17) contracts but only one contract is selected (randomly) for actual payment. This design allows the collection of up to 16 observations per subject, and it avoids possible income effects which may affect behaviour in later rounds of an experiment. However, the design requires subjects in the series 1–3 experiments to play a compound lottery. A question then arises as to whether or not a mechanism involving a compound lottery is incentive compatible, a question that Hey and Orme (1994) see as depending 'on how subjects reduce multi-stage gambles to single stage gambles' (Hey and Orme, 1994, p. 1295, fn. 5).

Holt (1986) argues that, if subjects are not expected utility maximizers, a compound lottery design may not induce honest reporting of preferences. The issue has not been fully resolved and recent empirical studies have concluded that Holt's concerns may not be a problem in practice (Starmer and Sugden, 1991). Since it remains an open question as to whether the introduction of a compound lottery will lead the subjects to misstate preferences, a fourth series of experiments is conducted that *do not* involve a compound lottery. In this series, subjects choose only one contract (A, L or H) with p set at 0.5. The results from this series and series 1–3 allow a test of the hypothesis that the observed Option 1 vs Option 2 choices are independent of the lottery context in which they are observed. The results of this test will be discussed below, but they were consistent with the conclusions of Starmer and Sugden (1991).

5.   EXPERIMENTAL RESULTS

5.1   Descriptive Statistics and Evaluation

Results from the experiments can be described by the number (percent) of participants choosing Option 1 for each contract under conditions where $p = 0.35$, 0.5 and 0.65. These results for the 17 contracts are given in Table 15.4, where the 17 contracts are grouped into four sets of contracts in which the value of a single parameter is varying.[11] Inspection of the experimental parameters in Table 15.1 reveals that there are some contracts for which the payoff to Option 1 is negative (contracts A, B, H and O when $p = 0.35$). Rational subjects that understand the decision task will not select Option 1 for these contracts. A total of 12 of our subjects did select Option 1 for these contracts (Table 15.4). That is, approximately 10 percent of the subjects either do not understand the decision setting or are not rational.

On the other hand, the majority of the subjects do seem to understand the instructions and to make rational decisions. Waiting to invest is particularly attractive to individuals who are risk-averse or subject to loss aversion. Consider the graphical representation of the data for each of the probability levels, shown in Figures 15.2, 15.3 and 15.4. In these figures, the contracts are arranged such that those for which the payoff to Option 1 is

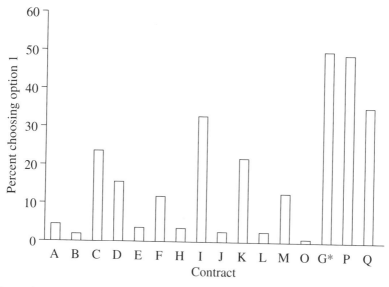

Figure 15.2   Probability = 0.35

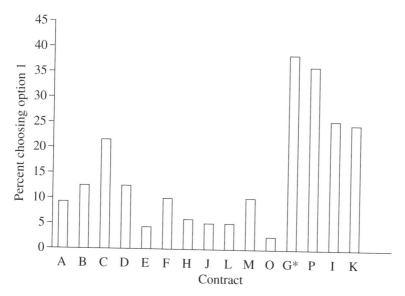

Figure 15.3   Probability = 0.50

Table 15.4 *Observed choices of Option 1*

A Contracts with varying X (H = 16, L = 1, C = 10)

| | | Participants choosing Option 1 when: | | | | | |
| | | p = 0.35 | | p = 0.50 | | p = 0.65 | |
Contract	Value of X	Number (n = 110)	Percent	Number (n = 123)	Percent	Number (n = 102)	Percent
A	$2	5	5	14	11	18	18
H	3	4	4	8	7	15	15
K	5	26	24	37	30	36	36
Q	6	43	39	–	–	–	–

B Contracts with varying L (X = 3, H = 16, C = 10)

| | | Participants choosing Option 1 when: | | | | | |
| | | p = 0.35 | | p = 0.50 | | p = 0.65 | |
Contract	Value of L	Number (n = 110)	Percent	Number (n = 123)	Percent	Number (n = 102)	Percent
F	3	14	13	15	12	22	22
D	4	19	17	19	15	27	27
I	5	40	36	38	31	40	40
P	6	60	54	54	44	53	52

C Contracts with varying C ($X=2, H=16, L=1$)

Participants choosing Option 1 when:

Contract	Value of C	p = 0.35		p = 0.50		p = 0.65	
		Number (n = 110)	Percent	Number (n = 123)	Percent	Number (n = 102)	Percent
A	$10	5	5	14	11	18	18
J	8	3	3	7	6	23	23
M	6	16	14	15	12	29	29
C	5	29	26	32	26	43	42
G	4	61	55	58	47	51	50

D Contracts with varying H ($X=2, L=1, C=10$)

Participants choosing Option 1 when:

Contract	Value of H	p = 0.35		p = 0.50		p = 0.65	
		Number (n = 110)	Percent	Number (n = 123)	Percent	Number (n = 102)	Percent
A	$16	5	5	14	11	18	18
O	18	1	1	3	3	13	13
B	20	2	2	18	15	21	21
E	22	4	4	6	5	19	19
L	24	3	3	7	6	17	17

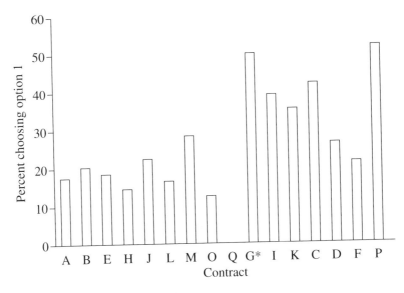

Figure 15.4   Probability = 0.65

greater than Option 2 are all grouped together at the right-hand side of the figure. In each figure, the contract G is the first of the set for which this condition holds. For all probabilities, the modal response of the subjects is to pick Option 1 in those contracts. Further, the subjects are responsive to changes in the probability of the H payoff. That is, as p increases, the set of contracts for which Option 1 yields a higher expected payoff increases and the subjects respond by selecting Option 1 more frequently in those cases. However, with few exceptions, Option 1 is still selected by less than half of the subjects.

This is an interesting observation. The general preference is to delay until the new information becomes available. This suggests that the subjects are very sensitive to the downside risk associated with the period 2 payoff. Such emphasis on the downside risk is also consistent with non-expected utility behaviour such as loss aversion.

The prevalence of the OM's Bad News Principle is apparent in the data in Table 15.4D and Figure 15.5. For a given value of p, changes in H do not appear to systematically affect the choice of Option 1. Either the percent selecting Option 1 is relatively constant (as for $p = 0.65$) or we find that it is not correlated with the value of H (as for $p = 0.50$). As seen in Table 15.4D, any correlation between the percent of Option 1 choices and the value of H is clearly absent. Individuals are not sensitive to changes in the magnitude of the high payoff. However, increases in p, the probability of the H

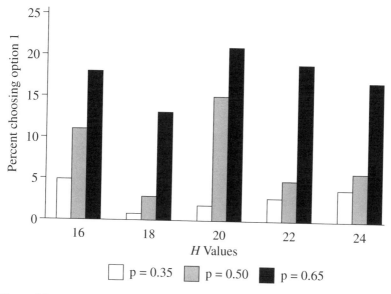

Figure 15.5   Varying values of H

yield, would likely be expected to result in an increase in the percent of sub-jects choosing Option 1.[12] This prediction is confirmed in the set of con-tracts where *H* varies (Table 15.4D and Figure 15.5). Here it shows that for each value of *H*, as *p* increases, the percent choosing Option 1 increases. There is an apparent tradeoff. That is, there is less desire to delay when the probability of the high payoff in period 2 is higher.

The subjects do react to changes in the value of *L* in a manner that is con-sistent with the OM. Specifically (Figure 15.6) for higher values of *L*, the subjects are *more* likely to select Option 1. Since delay is a means of reduc-ing the exposure to risk, it is expected that the subjects delay when the potential low payoff is small. The higher the value of *L, ceteris paribus,* the smaller the downside risk and the less desirable is delay.

The results for different values of *C* are interesting. For high values of *C,* the subjects are quite sensitive to changes in *p*. When *C* is 10, the fraction of the subjects opting for Option 1 increases from 5 to 18 percent as *p* increases from 0.35 to 0.65 (Figure 15.7). On the other hand, when *C* is 4, there is very little difference as *p* varies. Individuals are more likely to be concerned about potential bad outcomes when the cost of the irreversible investment is high. In equation (15.3b), the coefficient on *C* is negative and our subjects' behaviour is consistent with that prediction.

It is interesting to study the interaction between the fraction of the sub-jects choosing Option 1 (invest now) and the difference in the payoffs

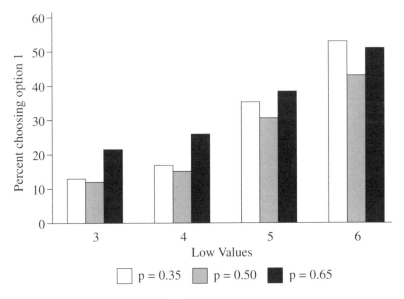

Figure 15.6   Varying values of L

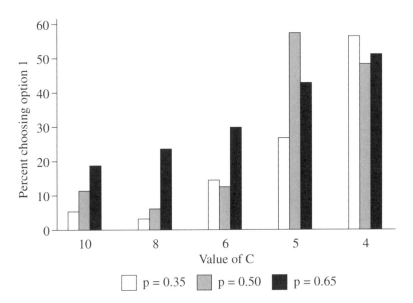

Figure 15.7   Varying values of C

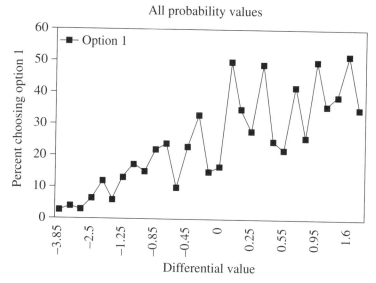

Figure 15.8   The relationship between the payoff to waiting (differential value) and the decision to invest now (Option 1)

between investing now and waiting until the next period. The data are plotted in Figure 15.8. The options model would predict that the behaviour would produce a logistic relationship. The individuals would prefer to wait (Option 2) in all instances where the differential is negative (fraction choosing Option 1 is zero) and prefer Option 1 in all cases where the difference is positive. In fact, there is a relationship that is close to this but obviously not an exact fit. A model of the behaviour would be written as:

$$\% \text{ Opt1} = \beta_0 + \beta_1 \text{ Diff}^\gamma$$

where % Opt1 is the percent choosing Option 1 and Diff is the payoff from investing now minus the payoff from waiting. The model was estimated using a Box–Cox transformation with the following results:

$$\% \text{ Opt1} = 4.997 + 1.065 \text{ Diff}^{0.267}$$
$$(4.86) \quad (3.59)$$

where parameter t-statistics are shown in the parentheses and the t-statistic on the exponent term is 2.48. The overall goodness of fit is quite high. The F-statistic is significant at the 0.01 level.

Clearly, individual behaviour is consistent with a preference for waiting when the payoff to waiting warrants. This is true even when the payoff to option 1 is positive. Thus, while the behaviour is broadly consistent with risk aversion, there is an overemphasis on waiting that is the hallmark of the OM.[13]

5.2 Testing for Compound Lottery Effects

To evaluate the potential compound lottery effect, compare the number of participants choosing Option 1 for Contracts A, L, and H (with $p = 0.5$) in the Series 1 experiment which uses a compound lottery with Option 1 choices for these contracts observed in the Series 4 experiment which did *not* use a compound lottery (Table 15.5). Subjects in the Series 4 experiment were offered only one contract: either Contract A, L or H. Using these data, the hypothesis that Option 1 responses observed for any of these contracts are independent of treatment – with or without the compound lottery is tested. Using a Pearson chi-square test, this hypothesis is rejected at any conventional level of significance for all three contracts – there is no strong evidence that would suggest that the use of a compound lottery design changes the choices given in the experiments.[14]

Table 15.5   Simple vs. compound lottery

Contract	Number (%) of participants choosing Option 1 with: Compound lottery (Series 1) (n = 123)	Number (%) of participants choosing Option 1 with: Simple lottery (Series 4)
A	14 (11%)	7 (n = 61; 12%)
L	7 (6%)	6 (n = 58; 10%)
H	8 (7%)	6 (n = 58; 10%)

Finally, the only difference between Contract A and Contract L is the value of *H*; values of $X = \$2$, $L = \$1$, and $C = \$10$ are the same in both Contracts A and L. $H = \$16$ in Contract A and $24 in Contract L. The finding of no significant difference between Option 1 choices for these contracts across the two designs – with and without the compound lottery – may then be viewed as reinforcing our findings of the prevalence of a bad news effect.

6.   CONCLUSIONS

There is a class of investment decisions for which uncertainty decreases over time, waiting is an option, and sunk costs may not be recoverable. In these settings, the OM predicts that agents will ignore variations in the high payoff when making investment decisions and focus on the magnitude of the low payoff. This has been described as the Bad News Principle. To investigate individual behaviour, a series of laboratory market experiments was conducted with results that appear to support the predictions of the OM. The subjects are insensitive to changes in the size of the high payoff. The fraction of the subjects choosing to delay the investment is unchanged as the potential high payoff varies. On the other hand, the subjects do seem to look at the low payoff but in a manner that could be argued is consistent with the predictions of the OM. The frequency of the choice of immediate investment (Option 1) increases as the size of the low payoff increases. That is, as the downside risk falls, the individuals are more willing to invest now. Finally, the potential of a loss is increasing in the size of the investment cost. Individuals are more likely to defer the investment to the second period (Option 2) when the initial cost is high.

The implications of these results for the CV practitioner are straightforward. Many, if not most, environmental resources are potentially subject to irreversible damages. Often the nature or extent of these damages are uncertain and there is no immediate return (x). Waiting is not allowed. If the CV scenario frames a resource valuation question in a manner in which the respondent can reasonably conclude that additional information, pertinent to the resource decision, will become available in the foreseeable future, he or she may consider an option premium to the CV query (would you be willing to pay $C) that appears to understate a 'rational value', essentially imposing an ability to wait by decreasing the probability that the loss will be incurred. Such responses may or may not pass scope tests and other tests of internal consistency. Yet they can logically be argued to recover the parameters of the individual's preference function.

Field data are generally inappropriate to test such behavioural phenomena owing to the presence of confounding effects and aggregation. The laboratory offers the level of control that is essential to investigation of behavioural phenomena such as the effects of changes in investment behaviour in response to parameter changes. In particular, it is possible to separate behaviour associated with non-symmetrical responses to expected gains and losses. Previous studies using secondary data have been unable to draw this distinction.

Based on these findings, we anticipate undertaking a systematic enquiry of CV response conditioned by alternative specifications of uncertainty, irreversible losses and waiting periods, employing experimental methods developed for tests of hypothetical bias.

NOTES

*   The authors gratefully acknowledge financial support for this research provided by the US Department of Energy's Global Climate Change Integrated Assessment Program directed by Dr John Houghton. We also wish to express our appreciation for research assistance provided by Harold Ball, Kelly Brown, Kate Gardner, James Murphy and Tom Stevens, graduate students at Georgia State University. Particularly helpful comments on earlier drafts of this paper were provided by Chris Bollinger, Charles Holt, Charles Plott, Rubin Saposnik, Mary Beth Walker and Melanie Williams.

1.   Bernanke (1983) examines investment decisions when the option to delay exists within a macroeconomic framework (see, also, Cukierman, 1980). More recently, Dixit (1989, 1992) and Pindyck (1991) apply the options-based model to investment decisions of the firm, and provide a number of extensions that are reviewed by Hubbard (1994).

2.   Schmalensee (1972) takes sharp issue with arguments that option value was simply the expected value of consumer surplus associated with the good in question across alternative states of the world and therefore equal to zero, as well as Fisher et al.'s (1972) argument that option value should be positive. His vehicle was a formal model which defined option value as the difference between option price, essentially the willingness to pay to have the resource available, and expected consumer surplus, the value that attaches to all goods in a contingent state model. Focusing on preference uncertainties, the demand side, he demonstrated that the sign of option value was uncertain, *a priori*. This in turn sparked a series of papers that expanded and refined the concept of option value within the contingent state model. Freeman corrected an error in an earlier paper with Cicchetti (Cicchetti and Freeman, 1971) and argued that for plausible representations of natural resources and risk-averse consumers option values would be positive, but small, relative to expected consumer surplus. Smith (1974) further clarified these analytical results and suggested that the source of the uncertainty, its resolution, and the role of information in its resolution provide natural criteria for evaluating the options concepts.

3.   At about the same time Henry (1974) published a similar paper that reached roughly the same conclusion. This work was subsequently extended by Conrad (1980), who interpreted the quasi-option value as a conditional value of information, and by Fisher and Hanemann (1987) who clarified the robustness of the positive quasi-option value and by Hanemann (1989) who explored that role of information and uncertainty in determining quasi-option values.

4.   The neoclassical model is simply that agents apply, naively, the NPV rule and invest when the present value of returns exceeds cost. The term 'neoclassical' here is subject to some controversy, because it suggests there is something profoundly different about the options model that deviates from classical economic thought. This is not so. The options model is completely consistent with the use of NPV, and can be seen as simply showing the correct way to calculate the opportunity cost of giving up the option to wait, so that it can be included in the NPV of an agent's investment decision.

5.   Camerer (1995) reviews several experiments that use what are now standard techniques for creating uncertain investments in laboratory experiments. Our laboratory procedures are comparable to those described by Camerer.

6.   The following discussion is based heavily on Dixit and Pindyck (1994).

7.   The instructions are available upon request.

8.   Subjects consider the contracts one at a time, and move from one contract to another when instructed that they may do so by the experimenter. Subjects are instructed to place their pencils on the table when they have completed their decision for the contract under consideration. When all subjects had placed pencils on the table, the experimenter instructs them to turn to the next contract.

9.   Subjects were instructed that there was no requirement or expectation that they would or would not buy a contract.

10.   Referring to Table 15.1, the set of contracts {A,H,K} involve three different values of X ($2.00, $3.00 and $5.00, respectively) with *H, L,* and *C* fixed at $16.00, $1.00 and $10.00,

respectively; similar sets of contracts can be constructed for cases where H, L or C is the parameter being varied. For $p = 0.5$ and $p = 0.65$, the set $\{A,H,K\}$ includes contracts that do (Contract K) and do not (Contracts A and H) satisfy the OM condition for choosing Option 1. However, when $p = 0.35$, the OM condition for choosing Option 1 ($EV(O_1 I_1) > EV(O_2 I_1)$) does not hold in Contracts A, H or K. Contract Q, wherein the value of X ($6.00, holding $H = 16.00$, $L = 1.00$ and $C = 10.00$) is such that the OM condition for choosing Option 1 *is* satisfied, is then used in the series of experiments where $p = 0.35$.

11. For these purposes, Contract N which does not fit in any of these sets, is excluded. Contract N was a special contract in which the dominant strategy would be to choose Option 1. Thus, referring to Table 15.1, the Option 1 return, *even with a white ball*, exceeds the contract cost ($8 + $3 = $11 > $10). The rational choice is then always to choose Option 1. This contract was included to provide, necessarily, limited insight as to the performance of the experimental design. In many sessions, almost all subjects chose Option 1 for Contract N. In other sessions, this was not the case. Across all sessions in series 1–3, 17 percent of the subjects failed to choose Option 1 for this contract. This finding is not surprising, however. It parallels findings reported in other experiments of this type, all of which point to inconsistencies in individual decision making and the added difficulty of designing mistake-proof experimental methodologies. For related discussions, see Hey and Orme (1994).

12. Recall the OM condition for choosing Option 1 (equation (15.3b), increases in p reduce $(1 - p)$ and, with $L < C$, reduce the expected value of losses associated with the choice of Option 1. Rewriting (15.3b) as $X - (1 - p)(C - L) > 0$, the OM rule is $X > (1 - p)(C - L)$, and $(C - L)$ is the expected loss from an Option 1 choice.

13. We present additional information on individual behaviour that further supports this conclusion in Bjornstad et al. (1996).

14. P-values were 0.985, 0.258, and 0.367 for contracts A, L and H, respectively.

REFERENCES

Arrow, K.J. and A.C. Fisher (1974), 'Environmental Preservation, Uncertainty, and Irreversibility', *Quarterly Journal of Economics*, **88**, 312–19.

Arrow, K.J. and R.C. Lind (1970), 'Uncertainty and the evaluation of public investment decisions', *American Economic Review*, **60**, 364–78.

Bernanke, Ben (1983), 'Irreversibility, uncertainty, and cyclical investment', *Quarterly Journal of Economics*, **98**, 85–106.

Bjornstad, David J. and James R. Kahn (1996), *The Contingent Valuation of Environmental Resources*, Cheltenham, UK and Brookfield, US: Edward Elgar.

Bjornstad, David J., Paul Brewer and Ronald Cummings (1996), 'Investment Behavior in the Case of Irreversibility and Decreasing Uncertainty: An Experimental Laboratory Investigation', Final Report for the Global Climate Research Program, Office of Energy Research, US Department of Energy, Georgia State University, December 9, 1996.

Caballero, Ricardo J. and Robert S. Pindyck (1992), 'Uncertainty, Investment, and Industry Evolution', Working Paper No. 4160, National Bureau of Economic Research, Washington, DC.

Camerer, Colin (1995), 'Individual Decision Making' in John H. Kagel and Alvin E. Roth (eds), *The Handbook of Experimental Economics*, Princeton, NJ: Princeton University Press.

Cicchetti, C.J. and A.M. Freeman, III (1971), 'Option demand and consumer surplus: further comment', *Quarterly Journal of Economics*, **85**, 528–39.

Conrad, Jon M. (1980), 'Quasi-option value and the expected value of information, *Quarterly Journal of Economics*, **85**, 813–20.

Cukierman, Alex (1980), 'The effects of uncertainty on investment under risk neutrality with endogenous information', *Journal of Political Economy*, **88** (3), 462–75.

Cummins, Jason G., Kevin A. Hassett and R. Glenn Hubbard (1994), 'A reconsideration of investment behavior using tax reforms as a natural experiment', *Brookings Papers on Economic Activity*, **2**, 1–59.

Dixit, Avinash (1989), 'Entry and exit decisions under uncertainty', *Journal of Political Economy*, **97**, June, 620–38.

Dixit, Avinash (1992), 'Investment and hysteresis', *Journal of Economic Perspectives*, **6** (1), 107–32.

Dixit, Avinash K. and Robert S. Pindyck (1994), *Investment Under Uncertainty*, Princeton, NJ: Princeton University Press.

Fisher, Anthony C. (no date), 'Investment Under Uncertainty and Option Value in Environmental Economics', unpublished ms., Department of Agricultural and Resource Economics, University of California (Berkeley).

Fisher, A.C. and W. Michael Hanemann (1987), 'Quasi-option value: some misconceptions dispelled', *Journal of Environmental Economics and Management*, **14**, 183–90.

Fisher, A.C., J.V. Krutilla and C.J. Cicchetti (1972), 'The economics of environmental preservation', *American Economic Review*, **62**, 605–19.

Hanemann, W. Michael (1989), 'Information and the concept of option value', *Journal of Environmental Economics and Management*, **16** (1), 23–37.

Henry, C. (1974), 'Option values in the economics of irreplaceable assets', *Review of Economic Studies, Symposium on the Economics of Exhaustible Resources*, 89–104.

Hey, John D. and Chris Orme (1994), 'Investigating generalizations of expected utility theory using experimental data', *Econometrica*, **62** (6), 1291–326.

Holt, Charles (1986), 'Preference reversals and the independence axiom', *American Economic Review*, **76**, 508–14.

Hubbard, R. Glenn (1994), 'Investment under uncertainty: keeping one's options open', *Journal of Economic Literature*, **32**, 1816–31.

Kahneman, Daniel and Amos Tversky (1979), 'Prospect theory: an analysis of decisions under risk', *Econometrica*, **47**, 263–91.

Machina, Mark J. (1987), 'Choice under uncertainty: problems solved and unsolved', *Journal of Economic Perspectives*, **1**, 121–54.

Pindyck, Robert S. (1991), 'Irreversibility, uncertainty and investment', *Journal of Economic Literature*, **29**, 1110–48.

Pindyck, Robert S. and Andres Solimano (1993), 'Economic Instability and Aggregate Investment', in *Macroeconomics Annual*, Cambridge, MA: MIT Press, pp. 259–303.

Roth, Alvin (1987), *Laboratory Experiments in Economics: Six Points of View*, New York, NY: Cambridge University Press.

Schmalensee, R. (1972), 'Option demand and consumer surplus: valuing price changes under uncertainty', *American Economic Review*, **62**, 813–24.

Smith, V.K. (1974), *Technical Change, Relative Prices, and Environmental Resource Evaluation*, Baltimore, MA: Johns Hopkins Press.

Starmer, C. and R. Sugden (1991). 'Does the random-lottery incentive system elicit true preferences?' *American Economic Review*, **81**, 971–8.

Weisbrod, Burton A. (1964), 'Collective-consumption services of individual-consumption goods', *Quarterly Journal of Economics*, **78**, 471–7.

16. Is the scope test meaningful in the presence of other-regarding behaviour?

William Schulze, Gregory Poe, Ian Bateman and Daniel Rondeau

1. INTRODUCTION

This chapter begins by reviewing the literature on scope testing and possible problems with warm glow and altruistic values in contingent valuation. Evidence from experimental economics is also presented that suggests that these problems are not only present in hypothetical situations, but also affect actual contributions in public good experiments. A theoretical model that attempts to integrate various hypotheses is then developed. This model shows that the scope test may be inadequate since contingent values for public goods are potentially made up of a combination of: (1) individual private values for the good; (2) warm glow from the act of contributing; (3) non-paternalistic altruism and (4) paternalistic altruism. From the perspective of efficiency, warm glow and non-paternalistic altruism are invalid sources of value. Warm glow is derived strictly from the monetary contribution rather than from the provision of a commodity, and non-paternalistic altruism double counts benefits under some circumstances. A scope test may not demonstrate validity in and of itself because it cannot rule out the possibility that benefit estimates remain contaminated by warm glow and non-paternalistic altruism. It is argued that laboratory economic experiments and eventually field experiments are a way to develop methods to isolate the various components of value necessary to sort out these issues.

2.　OTHER-REGARDING BEHAVIOUR, EMBEDDING AND SCOPE IN THE CONTINGENT VALUATION LITERATURE

Contingent valuation research has long been burdened by the notion that 'all contingent valuation studies provided estimates which approximate some fixed amount, say \$30' (Boyle et al., 1993, p. 65). It has often been said that reported values are invariant to the magnitude or scope of the good being valued. While such a criticism has been longstanding, issues of sensitivity to scope gained prominence in the debate over the validity of contingent valuation with the publication of the NOAA panel report (Arrow et al., 1993). The panel concluded that a scope test should be required to assess whether a contingent valuation study is consistent with neoclassical theoretical predictions (Arrow et al., 1993).

In the years since the NOAA panel report, a heated debate over scope has permeated the environmental economics literature. A number of studies have provided data suggesting that contingent values do not demonstrate adequate scope sensitivity (for example, Desvousges et al., 1993; Schkade and Payne, 1994; Diamond et al., 1993; Hammitt and Graham, 1999), although the findings of some of these studies have been challenged on the basis of design flaws or statistical analyses (for example, Smith, 1992; Carson, 1997). On the other hand, a body of research has emerged suggesting that contingent valuation responses are responsive to scope (for example, Carson and Mitchell, 1993; Smith and Osborne, 1996). Still other research argues that, due to diminishing marginal utility, it is possible to observe scope and scope insensitivity in the same study (Rollins and Lyke, 1998; Loomis et al., 1986).

In a more troubling study, Schulze et al. (1998) find that some respondents do respond to scope, but others do not. Further, scope-insensitive respondents are able to self identify. However, these respondents remained unresponsive to scope in a between-respondent statistical test even after they were given an opportunity to revise their values. This suggests that the same survey may have respondents who only have a warm glow motive as well as respondents who have a traditional economic-commodity value.

The purpose of this section is to highlight factors that can affect responses to contingent valuation questions in ways that potentially undermine the validity of scope tests. We briefly discuss warm glow, paternalistic and non-paternalistic altruism, quantitative and qualitative nesting, as well as ordering and sequencing effects.

2.1. Warm Glow

At about the same time the NOAA Report was released, Kahneman and Knetsch (1992) published an influential paper on embedding that concluded that the contingent value for the 'same good is assigned a lower value if WTP (willingness to pay) for it is inferred from WTP for a more inclusive good than if the particular good is valued on its own' (p. 58). They also argue that 'the inevitable consequence of the insensitivity of WTP to inclusiveness is that estimates of the same particular good differ – by a factor of 16 for medians or 8 for means – depending on the scope of the initial question'. (p. 62). Their explanation for these results is that respondents are not purchasing the environmental good described in the survey, but rather moral satisfaction from the 'contribution' itself. A related phenomenon, warm glow, has been extensively explored in both the general and experimental economics literature as an explanation for charitable contributions (see for example, Andreoni, 1989).

Warm glow is typically understood to be invariant with scope since it is not related to the commodity under study. Its presence in hypothetical CV (contingent valuation) responses causes two practical concerns. From the perspective of efficiency, the warm glow component of value must be subtracted from CV responses since they do not reflect the individual's benefits from the provision of the public good. With respect to scope testing, the presence of a subset of individuals whose only motive for contributing is warm glow can make it more difficult for the results of CV studies to pass the statistical implementation of a scope test.

2.2. Quantitative and Categorical Nesting

The debate over scope sensitivity has been hampered, to some extent, by confusion in the terminology relating scope and embedding, sequencing and order effects (Carson and Mitchell, 1995; Georgiou et al., 2000). Here we adopt Carson and Mitchell's (1995) terminology that distinguishes between quantitative and categorical nesting.

Let A and B denote two different goods. *Quantitative nesting* indicates that A and B are measured on a common scale (for example, A could be 20 days of improved visibility and B could be 6 of those 20 days, and so on) (Carson and Mitchell, 1995 p. 157). Thus, A and B enter as a single argument in the utility function. As shown in Carson et al. (1998) and elsewhere, standard utility theoretic assumptions of non-satiation lead to unambiguous results when goods are quantitatively nested. That is, for three quantitatively nested goods, where A is preferred to B and B is preferred to C, then $WTP(A) \geq WTP(B) \geq WTP(C)$.

In contrast, *categorical nesting* is taken to mean that A is composed of, for example, two goods (20 days of improved visibility and raising the water quality in a river basin from fishable to swimmable) while B is composed of only one good (20 days of improved visibility) (Carson and Mitchell, 1995, p. 157). In this latter form of embedding, the component goods or characteristics of A and B enter as separate arguments of the utility function. Thus, if A, B and C are categorically nested, tests of scope sensitivity are much more difficult to devise as information on the economic interaction (that is, substitutability and complementarity) in the more inclusive good will generally be lacking. Whilst Carson and Mitchell (1993) suggest that bundles of goods will be substitutes, there is little *a priori* evidence to suggest that these results can be generalized. Thus the strong substitute arguments leading to super additivity in values remains a possibility but not a certainty when dealing with qualitatively embedded goods.

2.3.   Sequencing and Order Effects

It is also important to distinguish between sequencing effects and ordering effects. Sequencing effects arise when respondents are presented with a list of goods, which are mutually inclusive. For example, if we have three goods; A, B and C, then sequencing effects are liable to occur when the respondent is asked to value good A then told that in addition to good A they can also obtain good B and are asked for a valuation of this addition; and then respondents are told that in addition to goods A + B they can also obtain good C and are asked to value this addition. In such circumstances, income and substitution effects could easily explain an observed decline in WTP for a good as it appears lower in an inclusive list (Randall and Hoehn, 1996; Carson and Mitchell, 1995; Carson, 1997; Carson et al. 1998). This may occur[1] whether that particular question is hypothetical or real[2] (if the good is nested within the prior good, or vice versa, then we have an embedding effect). Expanding upon this line of reasoning, Carson et al. (1998) argue that valuations of a good obtained from a sequence can only be expected to be 'context independent' (that is, invariant to the position of that good within the sequence) if it can be established that changes in the provision of all the other goods within the sequence will leave the expected value of the good in question unchanged. Carson et al. argue that this is unlikely to hold in many circumstances where the other goods in the sequence are in some way substitutes for the good in question.

These sequencing effects are expected where goods presented lower down a list are to be provided in addition to those described earlier in that list. However, economic theory provides no such expectation where goods in a list are mutually exclusive. So, for example, if respondents are asked their

WTP for good A but then told that instead of good A they can have good B and are asked to value the latter, then (provided that the scenario is fully understood and the respondents do not think that this is indeed a sequence as defined above) economic theory provides no grounds for expecting that the value of good B presented second in the list should be different to its value when presented as the first good valued by respondents. Similarly if respondents are subsequently asked to value the provision of good C instead of good B economic theory again provides no expectation that this stated value should be different from that obtained from valuing good C on its own or at the start of a mutually exclusive list. We can term any such difference in the stated value of a good derived from such a mutually exclusive list as indicating an 'ordering effect'.

The theoretical and empirical evidence suggests that sequencing effects do exist and that context matters. (Hoehn and Randall, 1982; Hoehn, 1983; Randall et al., 1981; Tolley et al. 1985; Carson et al. 1998; Brookshire et al. 1990). If we define a top-down question format as one eliciting $WTP(C_I^T)$ then $WTP(B_{II}^T)$ then $WTP(A_{III}^T)$ and a bottom-up format as measuring $WTP(C_I^B)$ then $WTP(B_{II}^B)$ then $WTP(A_{III})$, the evidence shows that $WTP(C_I^T) < WTP(C_{III}^B)$, and $WTP(A_{III}^T) < WTP(A_I^B)$.

The evidence on ordering effects, however, has been mixed. For example, in investigating qualitatively embedded goods Boyle et al. (1993) find that order effects do occur in some cases (that is commercial boaters on the Grand Canyon) but not in others (for example private boaters on the Grand Canyon). In the case of the health and visibility benefits of improved air quality, Schulze et al. (1998) find a strong evidence of super additivity among some respondents and additivity for others. For quantitatively embedded goods, although economic theory suggest no effects, the psychological construct arguments presented in Kahneman and Knetcsh would suggest that top-down and bottom-up valuation ordering of goods would provide divergent values. Indeed, preliminary evidence from Bateman et al. (2001) suggests that such divergence occurs between top-down and bottom-up ordered questions when the respondent is not aware that the second and third questions are going to be asked. However, when the respondent is informed about the entire series of questions in advance, field results in Carson and Mitchell (2000) and Georgiou et al. (2000) suggest that there are no sequencing or ordering effects, respectively.

2.4. Non-paternalistic and Paternalistic Altruism

Individuals have altruistic motives if their utility level is positively linked to the consumption or welfare of other people. Madariaga and McConnell (1987) and McConnell (1997) explore the consequences of altruism for contingent values. An individual A consuming a generic good Y_A has a non-paternalistic altruism component if his or her own utility from providing a good R to a person B can be written as $U^A(Y_A, U^B(Y_B, R))$. Individual A cares about the level of utility attained by B, whether B's utility is obtained through the consumption of R or through his consumption of other goods (Y_B). In contrast, paternalistic altruism takes the form $U^A(Y_A, R)$, with A's utility depending specifically on B's consumption of R.

The distinction between the two motives for altruism is quite important. Because the welfare of a paternalistic altruist depends directly on the services provided (to other individuals) by the public good R, these benefits are a legitimate measure of R's value to society. On the contrary, the welfare of a non-paternalistic altruist depends on other individuals' total utility and must therefore account for the payments that other individuals must make in order to access the good R in question. If the B individuals do not find it worthwhile for themselves to fund the public good, then A's should not include an altruistic component in calculating their WTP for the good. Without due considerations by non-paternalistic altruists for the cost of public good provision borne by others, CVM (contingent valuation method) runs the risk of inappropriately inflating the value of public goods.

2.5. To Sum Up

With several possible causes for the observed lack of sensitivity of CV to changes in the scope commodities, the debate over the validity of the contingent valuation method remains unsettled. Other-regarding behaviour, in particular, warm glow, has been used to discredit contingent valuation, while supporters have argued that embedding-like effects can be explained by neoclassical theory (and should apply to private as well as public goods).

Since the experimental laboratory may help sort out alternative hypotheses, we now turn to a review of the experimental economics literature on the funding of public goods, where other-regarding behaviour has also emerged as an important issue and suggest how that research might be extended.

3. OTHER-REGARDING BEHAVIOUR IN PUBLIC GOODS EXPERIMENTS

Concerns in the literature about altruism, embedding and warm glow have largely centred on the role of such factors in contingent values for public goods. Yet, it is important to recognize that embedding has also been shown to exist in actual and experimental private good markets (Randall and

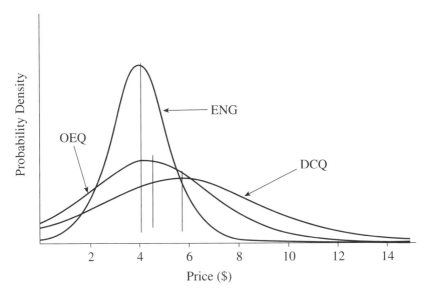

Figure 16.1   Corresponding estimated probability density functions

Hoehn, 1996; Bateman et al., 1997). For its part, altruism is recognized as a motivating factor in actual participation to environmental programmes (Clark et al., 1999; Messer, 1999). As importantly, warm glow and altruistic behaviour have been observed in controlled laboratory experiments of contributions to public goods (Ferraro et al., 2002; Palfrey and Prisbrey, 1997).

The attraction of laboratory experiments is that they allow the economist to control the economic environment by defining the agents' preferences through induced values, as well as the institutions through which agents interact (Smith, 1976; Friedman and Sunder, 1994). By controlling these factors and using real money, the experimental laboratory offers a more efficient method of testing economic hypotheses and behaviour. For example, Figure 16.1, taken from Balistreri et al. (2001) demonstrates a number of important features of the laboratory environment. First, the authors wanted to examine hypothetical and real values for a commodity that had an uncertain value. Thus, they chose an insurance policy that would prevent the loss of $10 to subjects if a red chip was drawn out of a bag containing 40 red chips and 60 white chips. From a theoretical perspective this insurance policy should have a value close to $4 for all respondents. To measure the actual value, an English auction was employed which has been shown to have excellent demand-revealing properties. Other groups of subjects were asked for either their open-ended willingness to pay or their willingness to purchase the policy at one of seven posted prices (dichotomous choice). Fitted distributions are shown for actual bids in the English auction, as well as for the open-ended hypothetical values to allow comparison to the fitted distribution of the dichotomous choice treatment. Four results are apparent. First, actual bids in the English auction fall very close to expected values. Second, both the open-ended and dichotomous choice hypothetical values overstate willingness to pay. Third, this problem is more serious for dichotomous choice, consistent with other evidence of yea-saying bias. Fourth, hypothetical values show much greater variance than the actual values. Note that these results were obtained for a direct data collection cost on the order of $10000. To obtain similar results in a CV field study would easily cost $100000 or more and it is likely that no actual values would be available to provide a basis for comparison. In addition to reduced data collection costs, the reduced variance of actual as opposed to hypothetical behaviour allows statistical testing with much smaller sample sizes.

Turning to public goods, most experimental work has utilized the Voluntary Contributions Mechanism (VCM). In a typical VCM experiment, subjects are given an endowment, and must determine how to divide this endowment between a private account and investing it in a public account (Isaac et al., 1984). Allocations to the public account yield a return to each of the N individuals in the group. If the marginal return to the contributor is less than one, but the sum of marginal returns to group members is greater than one, the Nash equilibrium is zero while the social optimum is for everyone to contribute their entire endowment.

In one-shot public good games with a dominant strategy to contribute nothing to the collective cause, subjects contribute at levels far above the theoretically predicted value, typically in the range of 40–60 percent of endowments (see Davis and Holt, 1993 and Ledyard, 1995 for a survey of this literature). Although the observation of higher than predicted rates is indisputable, the causes of this phenomenon are controversial (Ledyard, 1995, p. 148). Notably, individuals may contribute at higher than expected levels because of confusion or if their utility function includes social and cultural influences that are beyond the control of the experimenter. In this case, they may gain utility from increases in the utility of others (pure or non-paternalistic altruism, Milgrom, 1993), or they may gain utility from the act of consumption of others of a merit good (McConnell, 1997), or they may gain utility from the act of giving itself (impure altruism or warm glow, Andreoni, 1989, 1990). In addition, it has been argued that they may have concerns about fairness (Rabin, 1993), group ethics (Margolis, 1982) or reciprocity (Sugden, 1984). Here we selectively review experiments that have attempted to isolate these hypothesized motives in public goods games.

In an attempt to assess the relative importance of confusion (that is, decision error) and kindness (that is, fairness, altruism, and warm glow) in public goods games, Andreoni compared contributions to a standard multiple-round VCM game with contributions to a game in which payoffs are determined by the relative ranks of players in terms of their experimental earnings. That is, in the Rank payoff version subjects with the highest experimental earning received the highest payoffs. The ranking structure reinforces the dominant strategy to free-ride, but creates a zero-sum game out of the standard public-goods game. As noted by Andreoni, 'Not only are their no monetary gains from cooperation, the potential for kindness or altruism would also appear to be largely eliminated. The incentives for reciprocal altruism have been removed.' In order to isolate the magnitude of kindness and confusion, he created an intermediate experimental variant in which participants were informed of their rank but paid according to their experimental earnings. This research suggests that about half of observed cooperative behaviour can be attributed to confusion about incentives and about half can be attributed to some form of kindness. Importantly, Andreoni concludes that the focus on 'learning' in multiple round experimental economic research 'should shift to include studies of preferences for cooperation'.

Palfrey and Prisbey (1997) adapt the standard multiple-round VCM to allow for both positive and negative subject errors, rather than simply relegating errors to be positive deviations from the dominant Nash strategy of zero contributions. As in the standard VCM, the individual payoffs of the public good varied linearly with the total contributions by the group and all subjects had the same commonly known value for the public good. However, subjects were randomly assigned different rates of return from their private accounts, and these rates were changed from round to round. In such a design 'subjects whose value for the private good is less than their value for the public good have a dominant strategy to contribute all of their endowment; subjects whose value for the private good have a dominant strategy to keep all of their endowment or to free ride' (p. 829). The authors then used econometric techniques to discriminate among decision errors, repeated game effects, warm glow and altruism. Palfrey and Prisbey conclude that warm glow giving and random error played important and significant roles in individual decisions. On the other hand, altruism played little or no role in probit models of contributions. They further found that experience is a significant explanatory variable, and a leading factor in declining contribution rates.

Recognizing that multiple-round experiments allow for positive (reciprocity) and negative (free-riding) learning and the possibility of strategic play, Goeree et al. (2000) analyse contribution decisions in ten 'one-shot' public goods games in which no feedback is provided to the subjects. In an additional departure from the standard VCM experiment they allow contributions to have two effects, an 'internal return' to oneself and an 'external' return to others in the group. By creatively varying these across subjects and across games, and by varying the group size, they provide evidence to suggest that altruism is not simply the 'warm glow variety, i.e. giving for the sake of giving' (p. 15).

The above approaches have involved clever manipulations of the VCM, and in the case of Palfrey and Prisbey and Goeree et al., are highly dependent upon econometric specifications. Also, as recognized by each of the authors, there is the possibility that warm glow and other-regarding behaviour might change across rounds. In an effort to draw a parallel to real world and contingent valuation single-shot giving and to directly control the strategy set of individuals, Ferraro et al. (2002) attempted to explicitly isolate 'other-regarding' behaviour by comparing contribution patterns in all human groups with contribution patterns when humans were grouped with automata. Those groups with virtual agents contributed significantly less to public goods in a voluntary contributions setting, providing evidence that other-regarding behaviour is both significant and substantial. Additional exploration by the authors suggests that motivations associated with fairness are a non-trivial factor in determining individual contributions.

In ongoing research examining whether the provision point mechanism (PPM) or the voluntary contribution mechanism (VCM) is likely to perform better in a single-shot environment, Poe et al. (not yet available) find that both the contributions to the VCM and PPM increase linearly in induced values. Thus, if a subject's induced value is increased by one dollar the contribution increases by ten cents in the VCM, but by about fifty cents in the PPM. Remarkably, they also find that the relationship for both the VCM and PPM has a statistically significant and identical positive intercept which is plausibly attributed to other-regarding behaviour. Initially, it was hoped that the single-shot PPM was approximately demand-revealing (Rondeau et al., 1999). However, with a positive intercept of about $1.50 and a mean induced value of about $3.00 (about half of which is reflected in the contribution) it is easy to understand why the investigators thought that the mean contribution of about $3.00 in the Rondeau et al. experiments might reflect demand revelation in their original PPM experiments. This research leads to the question of whether or not incentive-compatible public good mechanisms have shown evidence of other-regarding behaviour, since future research for contingent valuation would necessarily be aimed at identifying actual values which requires use of an incentive-compatible or at least a demand-revealing mechanism.

Limited evidence does exist in this regard. In two laboratory studies of a bitter tasting liquid, sucrose octa acetate, private values were first obtained for avoiding a taste experience using a competitive auction (Coursey et al., 1987). In the second experiment, public good values were obtained for the experimental group as a whole to avoid the same taste experience using an incentive-compatible Smith public good auction (Brookshire et al., 1990). While the bids across repeated non-binding 'practice' rounds in the private good market remained constant, in the public good market bids declined sharply across the analogous non-binding 'practice' rounds. In the final round of both auctions, the average values were statistically similar, about $1.00 per subject. If one assumes that the first round results would predict a single-shot experiment, a factor of about 2.5 separates the values. Although speculative, it is interesting to note that the initial public good values exceeded the private good value by about $1.50 – very similar to the intercept in the VCM/PPM experiments described above. However, the Smith public good auction used in these experiments is fairly complicated in that it rebates any excess contributions above costs to each subject in proportion to their bid's share of total bids, and requires a unanimous vote for implementation. This probably contributes to a lack of transparency in the mechanism that typically requires multiple rounds of experience to overcome. What is needed to facilitate research on contingent valuation and other-regarding behaviour is a public good mechanism that reveals demand in a single-shot environment. Ideally, the mechanism would also be consistent with the procedures in a demand-revealing private good market since, as shown in the two studies above, an ideal experiment would obtain both private and public good values for the same commodity. For example, since experiments that examine nesting require sequences of bids for the same or different goods, transparency and demand revelation are essential. In what follows we suggest just such a set of experimental mechanisms.

A new experimental design would ideally satisfy the following criteria: (1) Demand-revealing mechanisms must be used that are sufficiently transparent that they work in a single-shot setting, comparable to contingent valuation. (2) Since altruistic and warm glow values must be separated from private values as components of public good value, we require commodities that can be presented both in private and public good contexts so that the value difference can be identified either for individuals or groups. In the case of induced values, this objective can be trivially accommodated. However, commodities like sucrose octa acetate can also be employed that may allow for richer possibilities such as merit goods to be introduced. As noted above, the problem with the two studies that employed sucrose octa acetate is that both the competitive auction employed for the private good and the Smith public good auction utilized for the public good are not very transparent and require multiple rounds to be demand-revealing. Further, because they require several rounds to be demand-revealing, they prevent realistic use of within-subject designs where both mechanisms are utilized with the same subjects.

As an alternative pair of mechanisms, in future research we intend to use the Becker, DeGroot, Marschak mechanism (BDM) for private value treatments and a new public good/BDM mechanism for the public good. It has been shown that the BDM is a very transparent mechanism (Irwin et al., 1998; Boyce et al., 1992) with excellent demand-revealing properties. In the BDM, a subject submits a bid for a private good. The good is purchased only if the individual's bid equals or exceeds a randomly drawn price. Often the price is drawn from a bingo cage to assure subjects that the price is truly random, with a known distribution of prices marked on the balls. This mechanism can be extended to the case of a public good by having subjects indicate if they would vote yes or no on the provision of the public good to the group (for example, all individuals in the group avoid tasting sucrose octa acetate) for each price in the bingo cage. A single price is then drawn for the group and the number of positive votes for that particular price are tallied. If a majority vote yes, then all subjects must pay that price and the public good is provided. Note that subjects must, in reality, just indicate the highest price of the prices placed on balls in the bingo cage at which they would still vote yes. Laboratory experiments have demonstrated the incentive compatibility and transparency of voting in numerous experiments (see, for example, Plott and Levine, 1978). However, the mechanism we propose which combines voting and the BDM is not only likely to be transparent, but also provides a discrete estimate of maximum willingness to pay for each subject. In addition, the mechanism avoids the problem of yea saying that has plagued dichotomous choice contingent valuation because respondents are presented with an array of prices. It also is consistent with the private good BDM and easily allows within-subject treatments. Prior to suggesting an experimental approach for addressing other-regarding behaviour in the contingent valuation of public goods, we attempt to summarize the issues in a simple theoretical model appropriate for structuring future experiments.

4.   A SIMPLE THEORETICAL MODEL OF SCOPE AND OTHER-REGARDING BEHAVIOUR

The notation used to explore the relationship between scope testing, warm glow, and paternalistic and non-paternalistic altruism, as well as to motivate future experiments, is defined as follows:

Let

X_i = consumption of the single purely private good (composite commodity) by individual i ($i = 1,...,n$),

G_{ih} = consumption of good h ($h = 1,...,m$) by individual i which can be publicly or privately provided,

$G_{ih} = G_h$ ∀ i if good h is publicly provided,

$V^i(G_{i1},...,G_{im})$ = utility derived from consumption of potential public goods by individual i,

M = multiple public goods

$M^{ij}(G_{j1},...,G_{jm})$ = utility derived by i from the consumption of merit potential public goods by individual j (paternalistic altruism),

$W_i(\Sigma_h \omega_{ih} p_{ih})$ = warm glow from payments, p_{ih}, for publicly provided goods ($h = 1,...,m$),

$A^i = \Sigma_{j \neq i} \beta_{ij} U^j$ = the pure altruistic utility derived by individual i from the direct utility of others, where,

$U^i = X_i + V^i + \Sigma_{j \neq i} M^{ij} + W_i$ = direct utility of individual i, and

$U^i + A^i$ = total utility of individual i.

The additive separability used in the theoretical model is employed both for notational simplicity and because, for the relatively small monetary amounts that can be employed in the laboratory, main effects are likely to dominate second-order effects with respect to income. It should be noted that close substitute commodities have been shown to exhibit super-additivity in the laboratory. However, it is likely that the laboratory cannot rule out the possibility of order effects on WTP that derive from diminishing marginal utility of income. This might occur, for example, outside the laboratory if a respondent were first to pay to eliminate hazardous wastes from a landfill adjacent to their home (property value studies suggest that WTP is on the order of $20000). If the respondent is then asked to pay for another environmental cleanup of air pollution, WTP for air pollution control would likely be diminished (Carson and Mitchell, 1995). In a laboratory situation, it is, however, reasonable to assume that direct utility, U^i, is linear in money expenditures on the composite commodity, X_i, so the marginal utility of money is assumed constant and equal to unity. Since utility is then defined in dollars, the separable utility of public goods, V^i, is equal to the value of those goods and is assumed to be a strictly concave function of the vector of public goods.

The value of warm glow, $W_i(\Sigma_h \omega_{ih} p_{ih})$, is also a strictly concave function of payments made for public goods, following Andreoni (1990) and Kahnemann and Knetsch (1992). However, recognizing that not all people may derive warm glow from all public goods, these contributions are weighted by $\omega_{ih} \geq 0$. Thus, an individual may derive warm glow from a contribution to health research h ($\omega_{ih} > 0$), but none from a contribution to an environmental good, g ($\omega_{ig} = 0$). All such contributions or payments are perfect substitutes in this formulation.

Similarly, the dollar merit value (paternalistic altruism) to individual i from the public goods consumption of another individual $j \neq i$, M^{ij}, is also assumed to be a strictly concave function of the other individual's consumption of public goods. Note that, in this formulation, merit value will increase with the number of other individuals and is independent of other individuals' expenditures on those public goods. Finally, non-paternalistic altruism is captured by each individual weighting the direct utilities of others by $\beta_{ij} \geq 0$. This is a common formulation in the economics of the family, where altruism is a clear motive.[3]

Since the incentive mechanism that we propose involves voting, an individual described above will vote for an increase in the provision of G_h from G_h^0 to G_h' at a price p_h' (where $p_h^0 = 0$) if

$$[U_i(G_h', p_h') + A_i(G_h', p_h')] \geq [U_i(G_h^0, p_h^0) + A_i(G_h^0, p_h^0)] \qquad (16.1)$$

where, implicitly, $X_j = X_j^0 - p_h$ $\forall j$ since, if the good is provided, everyone must pay p_h. The maximum willingness to pay, p_h^{max}, is the maximum p_h' at which the individual will still vote to fund the good, so, is defined by equality in (16.1) above.

The scope test can be applied in its most simple form by testing to see if $\partial p_h^{max} / \partial G_h' > 0$. Assuming equality in (16.1) and differentiating yields

$$\partial p_h^{max} / \partial G_h' = [\Sigma_j \beta_{ij} (V_h^i + \Sigma_{j \neq i} M_h^{ij})] / [\Sigma_j \beta_{ij} (1 - \omega_{ih} W_j')] \qquad (16.2)$$

where, for notational convenience, $\beta_{ii} = 1$.

Note that, from an efficiency standpoint, both pure altruism and warm glow should be excluded, and (16.2) should ideally take the form:

$$\partial p_h^{max} / \partial G_h' = V_h^i + \Sigma_{j \neq i} M_h^{ij}. \qquad (16.3)$$

It is obvious from inspection that the scope test can be biased by non-paternalistic altruism and warm glow.

First, consider the impact of non-paternalistic or pure altruism. As has been noted before, voting provides a mixed impact compared to the arguments of Milgrom that contingent values are upward biased by pure altruism. To show this, consider the case of identical preferences. In this case, the term $\Sigma_j \beta_{ij}$ can be factored out of the numerator and the denominator and cancels out. In other words, non-paternalistic altruism will have no effect in a laboratory experiment with homogeneous subjects – not an entirely unreasonable proposition. Further, a similar result can be obtained if the voter/subject believes him/herself to be the median voter with a symmetrical distribution of values for others. Psychologists argue that most voters tend to think that they are the median voter and are surprised when the outcomes of elections do not conform to their beliefs. Again, such beliefs may lead people to eliminate non-paternalistic altruism from their values revealed through voting behaviour. In Milgrom's analysis, the term $\Sigma_j \beta_{ij}$ is missing from the denominator of (16.2) increasing both the marginal and total willingness to pay because he assumes that survey respondents do not consider the costs that providing a public good imposes on others (Andreoni coined the term 'cold-prickle' to describe the negative feelings that can be associated with contributing to a good with negative returns to other subjects). Again, the laboratory is the perfect place to test this problem in both actual and hypothetical environments.

Perhaps, surprisingly, warm glow may cause an upward bias in the response to scope as shown in (16.2) because the monetary cost of paying for the public good is reduced in the denominator by the warm glow associated with making the contribution. In the case where the numerator of (16.2) is zero (no one has either private or merit value for the good), bids will not respond to scope. However, a positive bid will still result since the subject or respondent will choose p_h^{max} to set $V_h^i = 1$ so as to maximize the utility of a contribution from warm glow alone.

The case in which (16.3) is equal to zero but (16.2) is positive is of particular interest. This can occur if an individual has no private or merit good value of their own for the commodity, but has pure altruism for others who the individual believes have private or merit values. Depending on the distribution of private values (where some may even have negative environmental values, for example hot rodders who despised the early emissions regulations on cars) and warm glow (which may tend to amplify responsiveness to scope), a scope test may be very misleading in that a responsiveness to scope in no way rules out the presence of warm glow or pure altruism.

5. FUTURE RESEARCH

It is our view that laboratory experiments are possibly the most fruitful approach for attempting to untangle the nature of other-regarding preferences. Although field experiments using contingent valuation studies could certainly be employed, their cost would be prohibitive by comparison to laboratory experiments. In this regard, note that the increased variance as shown in Figure 16.1, of hypothetical as opposed to actual values, implies that sample sizes can be much smaller to obtain the same level of confidence in the laboratory. Although the goods that can be used in the laboratory are not environmental commodities, which is a disadvantage, goods can be employed such as risk of financial loss or the bitter tasting liquid, sucrose octa acetate, that have a number of similar attributes. In future work using such commodities, we hope to be able to not only detect if other-regarding behaviour is present by comparing public to private good values, but also to separate out warm glow (which should not be responsive to group size) from altruistic values (which should be responsive to group size). Further, paternalistic and non-paternalistic altruism may well be differentiated by the way values respond to differences in costs imposed on others.

Experiments could then proceed to use commodities such as insurance policies which can be structured as either public or private goods that may be viewed as merit goods when contrasted with, for example, lottery tickets. As noted above, there is a ready list of commodities that lend themselves to laboratory experimentation that can be provided either as private or public goods. The purpose of these experiments would be to develop methods for disentangling the various sources of value before proceeding to field tests of CV methods developed in the laboratory.

NOTES

1. As Carson and Mitchell (1995, p.160) state, the difference in the value of a given good presented at different points in two sequences (that is an external validity test) arises 'because of differences that respondents perceive in the available choice set . . . and because of differences in whether the respondent believes he or she already possesses the complement of the good being valued (the top-down case) or has just purchased it (the bottom-up case)'.
2. As Schuman (1996, p. 79) notes, 'if CV responses are expected to be unaffected by question order, it would be of value to show that ordinary purchases are normally unaffected by the order in which they are presented to a set of prospective buyers'. The available evidence suggests that, at least in experimental investigations, embedding also occurs in real money transactions (Bateman et al., 1997).
3. For example, Bergstrom (1996) argues that β_{ij} may be taken to be the coefficient of relation between i and j (the fraction of shared genes – 0.5 for a parent and biological child or 0.5 for two biological sisters). Thus, in this biological theory of altruism, non-paternalistic altruism is argued to exist between father and son because the son carries half of the father's genes. Since evolution has insured that the son's preferences will maximize the probability of reproduction and survival of his own genes, evolution will in turn insure that the father behaves as if he loves his son half as much as himself, that is, put a weight of 0.5 on his child's utility. Following this biological argument, the coefficient of relation may be larger than is typically supposed for the general population because, for example, recent genetic evidence suggests that all Europeans may have descended from approximately 10 males. Note that, in contrast to the case of merit goods, weight is placed on both the costs to others as well as the benefits to others of providing a public good. Also, the formulation employed here excludes reflection effects – utility derived from the utility that

others get from others. Milgrom (1993) has argued that such values will bias contingent valuation responses since the efficiency condition for public goods is unaffected by pure altruism. For a detailed discussion of paternalistic and non-paternalistic altruism, see Lazo et al. (1997) and McConnell (1997).

REFERENCES

Andreoni, J. (1989), 'Giving with impure altruism: applications to charity and Ricardian equivalence', *Journal of Political Economy*, **97** (6), 1447–558.

Andreoni, J. (1990), 'Impure altruism and donations to public goods', *Economic Journal*, **100**, 464–77.

Arrow, K., R. Solow, E. Leamer, R. Radner and H. Schuman (1993), 'Report of the NOAA Panel on contingent valuation', *Federal Register*, **58** (10), 4602–37.

Balistreri, E., G. McClelland, G.L. Poe and W.D. Schulze (2001), 'Can hypothetical questions reveal true values? A laboratory comparison of dichotomous choice and open ended contingent values with auction values', *Environmental and Resource Economics*, **18** (3), March, 275–92.

Bateman, I., P. Cooper, S. Georgiou and G.L. Poe (2001), 'Scope Sensitivity: Can Ordering Effects be Eliminated?', Draft Manuscript, CSERGE, University of East Anglia, Norwich, UK.

Bateman, I., A. Munro, B. Rhodes, C. Starmer and R. Sugden (1997), 'Does part–whole bias exist: an experimental investigation', *The Economic Journal,* **107** (441), 322–32.

Bergstrom, T. (1996), 'Economics in a family way', *Journal of Economic Literature*, **34**, 1903–34.

Boyce, R.R., T.C. Brown, G.H. McClelland, W.D. Schulze and G.L. Peterson (1992), 'An experimental examination of intrinsic environmental values', *American Economic Review*, **82** (5), 1366–72, December.

Boyle, K.J., M.P. Welsh and R.C. Bishop (1993), 'The role of question order and respondent experience in contingent-valuation studies', *Journal of Environmental Economics and Management*, **25**, S80–S99.

Brookshire, D.S., D.L. Coursey and W.D. Schulze (1990), 'Experiments in the Solicitation of Private and Public Values: An Overview', in L. Green and J.H. Kagel (eds), *Advances in Behavioral Economics*, Vol. II, Westport, CT: Ablex Publishing.

Carson, R.T. (1997), 'Contingent valuation surveys and tests of insensitivity to scope', in R.J. Kopp, W.W. Pommerehne and N. Schwarz (eds), *Determining the Value of Non-Marketed Goods: Economic, Psychological, and Policy Relevant Aspects of Contingent Valuation Methods*, Boston, MA: Kluwer Academic Publishers.

Carson, R.T. and R.C. Mitchell (1993), 'The issue of scope in contingent valuation surveys', *American Journal of Agricultural Economics*, **75** (5), 1263–67.

Carson, R.T. and R.C. Mitchell (1995), 'Sequencing and nesting in contingent valuation surveys', *Journal of Environmental Economics and Management*, **28** (2), 155–73.

Carson, R.T. and R.C. Mitchell (2000), 'Public Preferences Toward Environmental Risks: The Case of Trihalomethanes', in A. Alberini, D. Bjornstad and J. Kahn (eds), *The Handbook of Contingent Valuation*, Cheltenham, UK and Brookfield, US: Edward Elgar.

Carson, R.T., N.E. Flores and W.M. Hanemann (1998), 'Sequencing and Valuing Public Goods', *Journal of Environmental Economics and Management*, **36**, 314–23.

Clark, C.F., M.J. Kotchen and M.R. Moore (1999), 'Internal and External Influences on Behavior: An Analysis of Participation in a Green Electricity Program', Unpublished Manuscript, School of Natural Resources and the Environment, University of Michigan.

Coursey, D.L., W.D. Schulze and J. Hovis (1987), 'On the supposed disparity between willingness to accept and willingness to pay measures of value', *Quarterly Journal of Economics*, August, 679–90. Also reprinted in J.D. Hey and G. Loomes (eds), *Recent Developments in Experimental Economics*, Aldershot, UK and Brookfield, US: Edward Elgar (1992).

Davis, D.D. and C.A. Holt (1993), *Experimental Economics*, Princeton, NJ: Princeton University Press.

Desvousges, W.H., F.R. Johnson, R.W. Dunford, K.J. Boyce, S.P. Hudson and K.N. Wilson (1993), 'Measuring Natural Resource Damages With Contingent Valuation: Tests of Validity and Reliability', in J.A. Hausman (ed.), *Contingent Valaution, A Critical Appraisal*, North Holland, pp. 91–164.

Diamond, P.A., J.A. Hausman, G.K. Leonard and M.A. Denning (1993), 'Does Contingent Valuation Measure Preferences? Experimental Evidence', in J.A. Hausman (ed.), *Contingent Valuation: A Critical Appraisal*, North Holland.

Ferarro, P.F., D. Rondeau and G.L. Poe (2002), 'Detecting other-regarding behavior with virtual players', forthcoming in *Journal of Economic Behavior and Organization*.

Friedman, D. and S. Sunder (1994), *Experimental Economics: A Primer for Economists*, Cambridge UK: Cambridge University Press.

Georgiou, S., I. Bateman, M. Cole and D. Hadley (2000), 'Contingent Ranking and Valuation of River Water Quality Improvements: Testing for Scope Sensitivity, Ordering and Distance Decay Effects', CSERGE Working Paper GEC.

Goeree, J.K., C.A. Holt and S.K. Laury (2000), 'Private Costs and Public Benefits: Unraveling the Effects of Altruism and Noisy Behavior', Unpublished Manuscript, Dept. of Economics, University of Virginia, Charlottesville.

Hammitt, James K. and John D. Graham (1999), 'Willingness to pay for health protection: inadequate sensitivity to probability?', *Journal of Risk and Uncertainty*, **8**, 33–62.

Hoehn, J.P. (1983), 'The benefits–costs evaluation of multi-part public policy: A theoretical framework and critique of estimation methods', Ph.D. Dissertation, University of Kentucky.

Hoehn, J.P. and A. Randall (1982), 'Aggregation and Disaggregation of Program Benefits in a Complex Policy Environment: A Theoretical Framework and Critique of Estimation Methods', paper presented at the annual meetings of the American Agricultural Economics Association, Logan, Utah.

Irwin, J.R., G.H. McClelland, M. McKee, W.D. Schulze and N.E. Norden (1998), 'Payoff dominance vs. cognitive transparency in decision making', *Economic Inquiry*, **36** (2), 272–85, April.

Isaac, R.M., J. Walker and S. Thomas (1984), 'Divergent evidence on free riding: an experimental examination of possible explanations', *Public Choice*, **43**, 113–19.

Kahneman, D. and J.L. Knetsch (1992), 'Valuing public goods: the purchase of moral satisfaction', *Journal of Environmental Economics and Management*, **22** (1), 57–70.

Lazo, J.K., G. McClelland and W.D. Schulze (1997), 'Economic theory and psychology of non-use values', *Land Economics*, **73** (3), 358–71.

Ledyard, J.O. (1995), 'Public Goods: a Survey of Experimental Research', in J.H. Kagel and A.E. Roth (eds), *The Handbook of Experimental Economics*, Princeton, NJ: Princeton University Press.

Loomis, J.B., M. Lockwood and T. DeLacy (1986), 'Some empirical evidence on embedding effects in contingent valuation of forest protection', *Journal of Environmental Economics and Management*, **24**, 45–55.

Madariaga, B. and K.E. McConnell (1987), 'Exploring existence value', *Water Resources Research*, **23** (5), 936–42.

Margolis, H. (1982), *Selfishness, Altruism, and Rationality*, Cambridge, UK: Cambridge University Press.

McConnell, K.E. (1997), 'Does altruism undermine existence value?', *Journal of Environmental Economics and Management*, **32** (1), 22–37.

Messer, K.D. (1999), 'Implicit Markets for Environmental Conservation: The Case of Shade Grown Coffee', Unpublished M.S. Thesis, University of Michigan.

Milgrom, P. (1993), 'Is Sympathy an Economic Value? Philosophy, Economics and the Contingent Valuation Method', in Jerry Hausman (ed.), *Contingent Valuation: A Critical Asssessment*, Amsterdam: Elsevier–North Holland, pp. 417–41.

Palfrey, T.R. and J.E. Prisbey (1997), 'Anomalous behavior in public goods games: how much and why?', *American Economic Review*, **85** (5), 829–46.

Plott, C.R. and M. Levine (1978), 'A model of agenda influence on committee decisions', *American Economic Review*, **68**, 147–60.

Rabin, M. (1993), 'Incorporating Fairness into Game Theory and Econometrics', *American Economic Review*, **83** (5), 1281–303.

Randall, A. and J.P. Hoehn (1996), 'Embedding in Market Demand Systems', *Journal of Environmental Economics and Management*, **30**, 369–80.

Randall A., J.P. Hoehn and G.S. Tolley (1981), 'The Structure of Contingent Markets: Some Empirical Results', paper presented at the Annual Meeting of the American Economic Association, Washington, DC.

Rollins, K.S. and A.J. Lyke (1998), 'The case for diminishing marginal existence values', *Journal of Environmental Economics and Management*, **36**, 324–44.

Rondeau, D., W.D. Schulze and G.L. Poe (1999), 'Voluntary revelation of the demand for public goods using a provision point mechanism', *Journal of Public Economics*, **72** (3), 455–70.

Schkade, David A. and John W. Payne (1994), 'How people respond to contingent valuation questions: a verbal protocol analysis of willingness to pay for an environmental regulation', *Journal of Environmental Economics and Management*, **26** (1).

Schulze, W.D., G.H. McClelland, J.K. Lazo and R.D. Rowe (1998), 'Embedding and calibration in measuring non-use values', *Resource and Energy Economics*, **20** (2), June, 163–78.

Schuman, H. (1996), 'Chapter 5: The Sensitivity of CV Outcomes to CV Survey Methods', in D.J. Bornstad and J.R. Kahn (eds), *Contingent Valuation of Environmental Resources; Methodological Issues and Research Needs*, Cheltenham, UK and Northampton, MA: Edward Elgar.

Smith, V.K. (1992), 'Arbitrary values, good causes and premature verdicts', *Journal of Environmental and Economic Management*, **22** (1), 71–89.

Smith V.K. and L. Osborne (1996), 'Do contingent valuation estimates pass a scope test? Meta-Analysis', *Journal of Environmental Economics and Management*, **31** (3), 287–301.

Smith, V.L. (1976), 'Experimental economics: induced value theory', *American Economic Review*, **66** (2), 274–9.

Sugden, R. (1984), 'Reciprocity: The Supply of Goods Through Voluntary Contributions', *Economic Journal*, **94**, 772–87.

Tolley, G.A., A. Randall, et al. (1985), 'Establishing and Valuing the Effects of Improved Visibility in the Eastern United States', U.S. Environmental Protection Agency, Office of Research and Development.

Index